INSECTS HARMFUL TO FOREST TREES

R. Martineau

Published by Multiscience Publications Limited in co-operation with the Canadian Forestry Service, Environment Canada and the Canadian Government Publishing Centre, Supply and Services Canada.

ISBN 0-919868-21-5
©Minister of Supply and Services Canada — 1984
Catalogue Number: Fo 64-32/1984E

The Canadian Forestry Service
is now part of Agriculture Canada
instead of Environment Canada.

ACKNOWLEDGMENTS

The author would like to mention the great interest shown by the management of Laurentian Forest Research Centre of Environment Canada and the encouragement received, in carrying out this work. He also wishes to thank officials of the Quebec Department of Energy and Resources for permission to use a number of very useful files. He is most grateful to Lionel Daviault, Paul Benoit, and R. Blais for their critical review of the text. He extends thanks to the forest technicians of FIDS (Quebec Region) who participated in the observation and collection of entomological material, the photographing of insects and tree damage, and the reading of manuscripts. Particular thanks go to T. Arcand, technician at FIDS (Quebec Region) for her valuable assistance in the rearing of insects and the photography of live specimens in the laboratory, as well as in the preparation and layout of plates.

II

CONTENTS

FOREWORD

Forests constitute one of Canada's most important natural resources, supplying raw materials to a highly developed and diversified industry. They play an important role in soil protection, wildlife conservation, regulation of climate, and the flow of water, and also serve as rest and recreation areas for an increasing number of Canadians.

Such a valuable asset deserves to be carefully maintained and conserved for the benefit of future generations. In particular, it must be protected against the many enemies that attack it from all sides, notably insects. Because of the vastness of our forests, long felt to be inexhaustible, we could, in the past, ignore the devastation caused by these pests. This situation has changed considerably with the gradual reduction of timber stocks resulting from constant harvesting carried out to satisfy the growing demand for wood on domestic and world markets. Thus, insect control has now become a priority issue. Over the past 50 years we have made enormous progress in our knowledge of the systematics and biology of most of the insect pests that attack the forests, and this knowledge has led to the development of a variety of methods of control. Unfortunately, many of these new developments have only been published in specialized journals, which are often inaccessible to practising foresters. This volume is intended to provide, simply and precisely, all the information they require to identify and fight against the important enemies of forest trees in eastern Canada.

A book of this type could only be written by someone having a vast experience in forest entomology and complete familiarity with the literature on this subject. René Martineau is eminently qualified to succeed in this enormous task. After obtaining his degree in forestry engineering at Laval University, Quebec, in 1939, he spent 4 years doing further study at Illinois and Yale universities in the United States. During the next 35 years, until his retirement in 1980, he did a great deal of original research on the biology of a number of the more harmful insects in our forests and wrote extensively on the subject. He was also an active participant in the annual Forest Insect and Disease Survey (FIDS) in Quebec. In preparing this book, he was fortunate in having the use of the very well-stocked library of Environment Canada's Laurentian Forest Research Centre, as well as having daily contact with the Centre's team of highly qualified and experienced scientists and technicians.

Because of its vast documentation and rich illustrations, including several hundred color photographs, many types of readers will appreciate the book he has prepared, but especially those who, in their professions, devote themselves to the protection of our trees.

Lionel Daviault
Former Director
Laurentian Forest Research Centre

INTRODUCTION

Insects depend mainly on plants in their environment for food and shelter. The hundreds of insect species living in Eastern Canada's forests are no exception and, consequently, they exert a strong influence on all parts of the tree, from the seedling stage to maturity. Fortunately, some species are useful, such as those that feed on dead trees, forest debris, or other insects and most of them cause only negligible damage to their hosts, so that they generally go unnoticed and may be ignored.

A certain number of insects, however, are considered as pests when they multiply in an extraordinary manner and cause considerable damage to vast stretches of woodland. An illustration of this is the devastation caused by the European spruce sawfly, the hemlock looper, and the famous spruce budworm, three species that, over the past few decades, have forced governments to spend enormous amounts of money in an effort to reduce and to limit their damage.

Until fairly recently, our forest managers were totally powerless to stop such catastrophes, and infestations followed their course unimpeded. During the last 50 years, however, foresters have been better equipped to prevent epidemics and to organize the fight against most of the known forest pests, due mainly to the astonishingly rapid increase in knowledge of the systematics, biology, and ethology of the various species and the consequent development of practical methods for checking, or even preventing, their proliferation. This progress has been accomplished through research by many entomologists, working in a vast network of well-organized, well-equipped laboratories, located over the entire wooded area of Canada, and, more specifically, through the organization by the federal government, in 1936, of a highly efficient survey and detection service for forest insects, known as the Forest Insect Survey (FIS). This service was developed gradually in the various regions of Canada, except in Quebec where, from 1938 on, that province organized its own detection service, known as the Reconnaissance des insectes forestiers (RIF). From 1953 on, however, the federal government has supplemented the survey in Quebec and continues to do so, under the name of the Forest Insect and Disease Survey (FIDS). The annual reports of FIDS have provided most of the information on history of outbreaks that is found in the text.

It was impossible to cover in this book all the species of insects that might threaten each tree species of eastern Canada. Those chosen are among the most common and the most destructive found on what are considered to be the most important tree species; namely, among the softwoods, spruce, larch, pine, fir, and arbor-vitae; and, among the hardwoods, birch, oak, maple, elm, and poplar.

Intended for use both by scientists and by practising foresters, in the control of forest insect pests, this book will also be particularly valuable to forest managers, teachers, and students in forestry schools, nursery gardeners, horticulturists, and agriculturists. Young naturalists, amateur entomologists, and nature photographers will also use it to recognize the insects they find in the forests.

To make the information contained in this volume more easily accessible, insects are grouped according to the tree species that they attack rather than by their entomological classification, and, for this reason, insects found on a given tree species are presented in the same chapter. Information on the host tree itself introduces each chapter, followed by data on the insects, which are grouped in the following order: defoliators, miners, suckers, gall makers, and borers. Within each group, the insects are listed according to decreasing economic importance. Polyphagous insects are presented under their primary host, but are also mentioned under their secondary hosts.

Because it was impossible to include extensive detail on each insect, only the most important information on the history of past outbreaks, the description of known life cycles, biology, the appearance of damage, and the main elements that can be used in diagnosis have been included. The text also includes brief summaries of natural regulating factors and of artificial methods of control, and a list of references consulted. To aid in the identification, the descriptions are generally accompanied by color photographs, most of them original, that illustrate the main stages in the life cycle of each insect

as well as the damage caused. The photographs were taken either in the field or using live insects in the laboratory. Some of them have been enlarged to bring out particular morphological characteristics and thus, to obtain a fair idea of actual dimensions, the reader should refer to the text or to the explanatory legend accompanying each plate.

The other insect pests that deserve mention for each group of tree species are presented in tabular form at the end of each chapter. Some information on their biology is illustrated by photographs incorporated in one of the plates. These tables also include insect species that may be treated elsewhere in the book, given their greater importance on a different species of tree; in these cases, reference is made to the primary host.

The nomenclature used for insects and trees follows the practice normally adopted for scientific names. The common names of insects are taken from the fourth edition of *Common names of insects and related organisms* (Werner 1982). The names and details of host trees given at the beginning of each chapter are drawn from *Native trees of Canada* (Hosie 1979), *Native trees of Newfoundland and Labrador* (Bearns 1968), and *Forest trees of Maine* (Labonté et al. 1968). Data on the various tree species merchantable timber were taken from *Canada's forest inventory 1981* (Bonnor 1982).

The information on procedures to be followed in controlling the various species of insect pests is the most recent. However, because of the many changes made every year in information on insecticides, the author has indicated only the mode of action of the recommended insecticide.

CHAPTER I
Insects harmful to spruce

The genus *Picea* includes five species of spruce native to Canada, of which only three are found in the eastern provinces: white spruce (*P. glauca* (Moench) Voss), black spruce (*P. mariana* (Mill.) B.S.P.), and red spruce (*P. rubens* Sarg.). A certain number of hybrid and exotic spruces are also found, the most common being Norway spruce (*P. abies* (L.) Karst.) and blue spruce (*P. pungens* Engelm.).

White spruce and black spruce are found all over Canada, whereas red spruce is found only in southeastern Quebec, New Brunswick, and Nova Scotia. These three species are the conifers most sought after by industry and the most abundant throughout eastern Canada. The gross merchantable volume of spruce known in the six eastern provinces amounts to about 3 361 million m^3 (Bonnor 1982); Quebec contains the greatest proportion of this volume at 52.9 percent, and Ontario comes next with 38.4 percent.

Spruce trees grow in well-defined habitats and are often associated with other species. White spruce flourishes on shallow soil, rocky sites, and old pastureland, both in pure stands and stands mixed with other softwoods and even hardwoods. Black spruce grows on high ground, along streams, and in swampy areas; it is generally found in pure stands, but also in mixtures with other conifers. Red spruce grows best on well-drained soils, at moderate elevations, in pure and in mixed stands similar to white spruce.

Among the native spruces, white spruce and red spruce are trees of medium size and attractive appearance. In general, spruce wood is valued because it is soft, light, and moderately strong; the trade makes little difference between wood from the three species, because their mechanical properties are about the same.

All three species are used for pulpwood and sawtimber and in light and medium construction. White spruce and red spruce are also used for ornamental purposes and as Christmas trees.

Spruces have many natural enemies and insects are rated among the most important. Throughout its development, that is from the seedling stage to maturity, all parts of the tree are exposed to harmful insects. Enormous quantities of spruce wood have been destroyed since the beginning of this century as a result of damage caused by only a few species. The most important insects, from the point of view of their abundance and damage, belong to the phyllophagous group, and include defoliators, miners, and gall makers. Certain species are harmful only to spruce, but the majority attack several conifer species. All insect species that attack spruce are important, however, because they contribute to the depreciation of trees both useful and valued from an economic as well as an esthetic viewpoint.

European spruce sawfly
Plate 1

The European spruce sawfly, *Gilpinia hercyniae* (Htg.), was first found in 1922 in Canada and in 1929 in the United States, but attracted the attention of foresters only in 1930 because of serious damage inflicted on spruce stands in the interior of Quebec's Gaspé Peninsula. The outbreak extended rapidly to the entire northeastern part of the North American continent, where the insect posed a threat to all spruce forests, but, since 1945, populations have fallen to extremely low levels and no major damage has been reported. This sawfly attacks all spruce species. Its present range in Canada is from the Atlantic Ocean to the center of Manitoba, where it has been reported only since 1972, whereas in the United States, its range includes the New England states, New York, New Jersey, and Minnesota.

This sawfly is now only of a minor commercial concern, but its history is worth telling.

History of outbreaks

The first outbreak of the European spruce sawfly began in a small area of spruce forest in the Gaspé Peninsula in 1930. By the following year, it had made enormous territorial gains and, in succeeding years, it extended to almost all forests of eastern North America. New Brunswick and Nova Scotia were infested shortly after eastern Quebec. The insect was reported in Newfoundland in 1942, and although local outbreaks occurred until 1948, defoliation at that time never exceeded 10 percent. The insect continued to gain ground, however, and, by 1966, its range had extended throughout the island. In Ontario, the presence of this insect was reported in 1936, both near the Quebec border and along the New York and Minnesota borders. The insect's range continued to increase until 1964, by which time it had covered the entire province. Populations were nevertheless always at low levels, and no appreciable damage was reported.

In all regions, populations of this sawfly began to decline in 1938, with the appearance in the forest of a viral disease that affected the larva, and, by 1945, populations had fallen to an endemic level at which they have remained ever since.

Description and biology

Adult. Resembles a wasp, with four membranous wings; brown. Length: male, 6-7 mm; female, 8-9 mm (Plate 1, A and D).
Egg. Oval in shape; white (Plate 1, B).
Larva. Elongated; head black and body yellow green initially, then head brown and body green; during the fourth and fifth instars, body striped with five longitudinal white lines (Plate 1, E). Length when full grown: 20 mm (Plate 1, F).
Pupa. Cocoon cylindrical with rounded ends; smooth; golden yellow to brown. Length: 10 mm (Plate 1, C).

The European spruce sawfly has one generation each year in the northern part of its range, but two in southern Quebec, one in the spring and one in the summer (Fig. 1), whereas in certain parts of United States there is a third, partial generation when climatic conditions are particularly favorable to its growth.

The adult emerges from the cocoon buried in the ground in the spring and at once climbs the tree or flies to the top to lay its eggs. Males are extremely rare, about five per thousand, and the species must consequently increase by parthenogenesis. Each female lays an average of 35 eggs, deposited singly in slits cut with its ovipositor in the previous year's needles (Plate 1, A and B). Incubation lasts about 10 days, and, once hatched, the young larva feeds itself by devouring almost exclusively the old foliage, the current year's growth being attacked only in cases of food shortage. Larvae molt five times during their existence; they are solitary and are generally well distributed throughout the crown of trees. Once fully grown, the larvae drop to the ground where each spins a silken cocoon that may be found near the surface in humus or moss at the base of damaged trees. Cocoons are occasionally found in a mass in the tunnels of small mammals

who feed on them. In regions where only one generation occurs each year, the larvae remain dormant until the following spring, whereas in regions having two generations, some of the spring generation individuals transform to pupae and then to adults in the same season to produce the summer generation. The rest of the population goes immediately into diapause until the following spring. Larvae of the summer generation go into diapause in the fall and transform to adults in the spring. Thus, the adult population found on or near trees at the beginning of the season is made up of individuals from the previous year's two generations and occasionally from earlier years, because a small portion of the population may prolong its diapause and reach the adult stage only 1 or 2 years later.

Damage and diagnosis

The only damage of the European spruce sawfly is caused by the larvae, which feed on old foliage and, exceptionally, on new needles. Total defoliation generally kills the tree. Severe defoliation does not always cause tree mortality, but decreases the tree's growth and vitality, with disastrous consequences if repeated for several years in succession. Spruce trees thus defoliated and weakened then become an easy prey for secondary insects and pathogens.

The damage caused by this insect was catastrophic in many areas. It has been estimated that, between 1930 and 1939, in the Gaspé region alone, losses reached 11 million m^3 of spruce, and that losses for the entire 20 000 km^3 of affected territory totalled 36 million m^3.

Infestation by the European spruce sawfly is easily recognized by the missing old foliage and the presence of green larvae with white stripes in the crowns of spruce trees during two periods, June to July and August to September. Examination of cocoons in the soil under contaminated crowns yields interesting conclusions concerning current or past outbreaks as well as forecasts on the probable size of the insect population during the coming year.

A

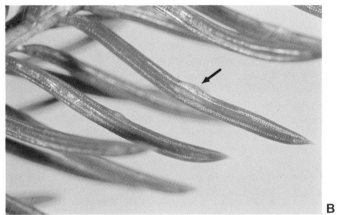

B

C

D

E

F

G

I

H

PLATE 1

European spruce sawfly, *Gilpinia hercyniae* (Htg.)

A. Female laying eggs on a white spruce needle.
B. Position of eggs on needles.
C. Cocoon (length: 10 mm).
D. Dorsal view of female (length: 8-9 mm).
E. Young larvae on white spruce needles, showing white stripes on body.
F. Mature larva (length: 20 mm).
G. Diseased larva.
H. Old spruce forest infested.
I. Young white spruce growing in the open and severely defoliated.

3

Natural control

When the European spruce sawfly was introduced onto the American continent, it had no indigenous natural enemies and, for this reason, it spread across the continent very rapidly. Certain native predators gradually adapted to this new prey and have become important factors of control. These are insect predators, both small insect-eating mammals living in the ground and birds. Oddly enough, no native parasite has been discovered. To bridge this gap, many species of parasites have been imported from Europe since 1935, and several of them have become acclimatized. Unfortunately, few have been effective, and the sawfly continued its depredations and would have extended them, had it not been for the timely appearance, in 1938, of a microorganism called *Borrelinavirus hercyniae*, accidentally introduced from Europe, which caused a virus disease in the larval population (Plate 1, G). This disease brought about a decline in the infestation and continues to be a key factor in maintaining populations at endemic levels in many regions. The life cycle (Fig. 2) was prepared from data collected in Quebec and shows the relative importance of mortality factors at each stage of development over two generations.

Artificial control

Under present circumstances, artificial methods of control are not justified, given the normally low population levels of the European spruce sawfly. If abnormal increases in population should occur, control could be effected by spraying a polyhedrosis virus on larval populations to encourage the development of the disease.

Small isolated trees are easily relieved of their larval population by shaking the trunk vigorously, which causes the larvae to fall. Crowns may also be sprayed with stomach insecticides when the larvae are feeding.

References

Gobeil 1938a; Martineau 1943, 1963; McGugan and Coppel 1962; and Neilson et al. 1971.

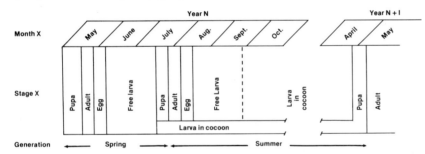
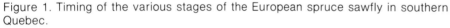

Figure 1. Timing of the various stages of the European spruce sawfly in southern Quebec.

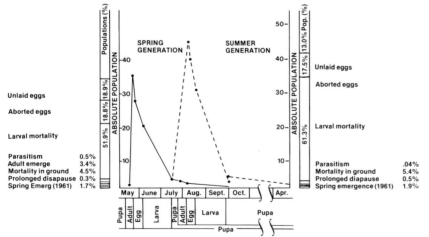

Figure 2. Development of spring and summer generations of the European spruce sawfly in southern Quebec, during 1960.

Other spruce sawflies

Two other fairly common spruce defoliators are so similar in their morphology and their biology that they are presented together: the yellowheaded spruce sawfly, *Pikonema alaskensis* (Roh.), and the greenheaded spruce sawfly, *P. dimmockii* (Cress.).

Yellowheaded spruce sawfly
Plate 2

The yellowheaded spruce sawfly, *Pikonema alaskensis* (Roh.), was described in 1911 from adult specimens collected in Alaska, thus its specific name *alaskensis*. However, the first larvae of this insect were observed only in 1916, in Massachusetts in the United States; since that time, it has been reported throughout most of the range of spruce in North America. In Canada and the United States, it is fairly common and its present range extends from coast to coast and to Alaska. In Canada, the insect was observed for the first time in Manitoba in 1926. This defoliator is always associated with spruce and presents a special threat to young trees in predominently sunny exposures. It is found on ornamentals, in hedges, windbreaks, nurseries, young plantations (Plate 2, A), cutover areas, or on young natural regeneration. To date, it has been most harmful in the Prairie provinces, especially in Manitoba and Saskatchewan, where great quantities of spruce have been planted around farms as shelterbelts. It rarely attacks mature spruce stands in the forest; however, two exceptions have been reported in the eastern part of the continent.

History of outbreaks

In the East, the yellowheaded spruce sawfly has long been recognized as a common insect that makes its presence felt by sudden local outbreaks of varying intensity and duration. In Newfoundland, the insect has been most harmful to black spruce, whereas in the other provinces, damage has been reported on the three native spruces. This sawfly has normally concentrated its attacks on young spruce stands in the open leading to mortality of a few stems, but it is rarely found in the forest.

One exception did, however, occur during 1933 and 1934 (Forbes 1949; Twinn 1934) in spruce forests located around Lac Sainte-Anne in the Gaspé region of Quebec. That area was already infested by the European spruce sawfly, *Gilpinia hercyniae* (Htg.), which had already destroyed the previous years' foliage. The current year's foliage was then eaten by swarms of the yellowheaded spruce sawfly on black spruce about 7 m high. The trees, thus stripped of all their foliage, died very quickly. Fortunately this outbreak did not spread and the infestation quickly disappeared.

A similar situation occurred in a 6-km² forest in Maine in 1947 (Peirson 1947).

Description and biology

Adult. Similar to a wasp, with four membranous wings; straw yellow to reddish yellow, brown, and even black. Length: 8-10 mm (Plate 2, F and G).

Egg. Oval; pearl white. Diameter: 1.3 mm (Plate 2, B).

Larva. Elongated; head brown; body olive green, striped with dull grey green longitudinal dorsal lines. Length full grown: 16-20 mm (Plate 2, C and D).

Pupa. Cocoon elliptical, narrower at one end, papery but rough coated, encrusted with soil particles. Length: 10-14 mm (Plate 2, H).

In spite of the frequency in annual sampling of the yellowhead spruce sawfly, many details of its biology remain unexplained.

This sawfly has only one generation each year. The adult emerges from the cocoon from the end of May to mid-June and immediately flies to spruce crowns to lay its eggs. The eggs are inserted singly in slits cut by the females' ovipositor at the base of new needles and occasionally between needles in the soft skin of twigs. The incubation of the egg lasts 5 to 10 days. The first larvae appear in June and some may be found in tree crowns as late as October. The young larvae feed on new foliage, first stripping the edges of the needles. When half grown, they eat the new needle completely before moving into older foliage. The crown of a severely infested tree is some-

times totally defoliated and, in such cases, it is easy to recognize larval excrements accumulated under the crown. Larvae normally hold themselves securely on the needles with their legs, but, when disturbed, they raise the two extremities of their bodies and eject a viscous liquid through the mouth. The feeding period lasts from 30 to 40 days. The larva then drops to the ground and spins a cocoon in which it overwinters. The first cocoons appear at the beginning of July and the last in October. When spring arrives, the larva transforms to a pupa and, a short time later, the adult insect emerges.

Damage and diagnosis

All damage by the yellowheaded spruce sawfly is caused by the larvae that feed first on the current year's needles and then on those of previous years. Most spruce trees die after complete defoliation. Some trees survive serious defoliation, but in this case part of the stripped branches may die and a considerable decrease in radial growth is recorded. Fortunately, infestations of this insect affect only a part of plantations and last only a short time in any one place.

In July, the presence of the sawfly larvae is easily detected by observation of patches of severely defoliated young spruce trees, whereas older ones in the vicinity remain generally intact. At that time of year, examination of spruce crowns should reveal the presence of olive green feeding larvae, and the ground literally covered with larval excrements. Later in the season, excrements are still present and the cocoons found on the ground or in the litter serve to identify the insect concerned. During the winter, examination of damage to crowns may also be useful in establishing the probable causal agent.

Natural control

Natural enemies of the yellowheaded spruce sawfly in Canada are numerous and varied. Many species of parasites were obtained through laboratory rearings: 13 in Ontario (Raizenne 1957); 12 in Saskatchewan, 6 of which were already obtained in Ontario; and 9 in Quebec, 2 of which had previously been recorded. The most detailed study on natural enemies of this sawfly was carried out by Houseweart and Kulman (1976) in Min-

nesota. These authors obtained 17 species of parasites and observed the predatory action of various species of insects, birds, and small insectivorous mammals. They were even able to note the action of an unidentified disease.

Moreover, these authors worked out life tables showing that, in 1973 and 1974, parasites destroyed about 20 percent of the mature larvae and insect predators and small mammals devoured 65 percent of the overwintering population: in addition, part of the population of the last three larval instars was killed by a disease.

The beneficial action of microorganisms had previously been observed in Maine in a severely infested area (Peirson 1947). In Quebec, Smirnoff and Juneau (1973) reported three species of entomopathogenic fungi and one microsporidia.

Artificial control

Artificial methods of control against the yellowheaded spruce sawfly are sometimes justified to preserve ornamental trees or plants in nurseries and plantations. On a small number of fairly young trees it is easy to collect or dislodge larvae, or to cut and burn the affected branches. In large stands or on tall trees, foliage may be protected by spraying the crowns with a stomach insecticide before defoliation is too far advanced.

6

Greenheaded spruce sawfly
Plate 2

The greenheaded spruce sawfly, *Pikonema dimmockii* (Cress.), has only attracted attention through occasional high populations in samplings made for other insect species harmful to spruce. This sawfly was first reported in Canada in 1937; nevertheless it was mentioned a short time later, that its presence had been recorded from Labrador to British Columbia.

History of outbreaks

Although it is known to be common in eastern Canada, populations of the greenheaded spruce sawfly have never developed excessively except on the following two occasions: the first at Bay d'Espoir, Newfoundland where high population levels were reported in 1962, and the second in Quebec in 1969, when severe local infestations were recorded. No major damage was reported in either of these cases.

Description and biology

Because of its relative harmlessness, no major studies have as yet been done on the biology of the greenheaded spruce sawfly, and, consequently, documentation is scarce.

The morphology of this sawfly strongly resembles that of the yellowheaded spruce sawfly at all its stages. Larvae of the two species can, however, be distinguished easily by the color of their heads (Plate 2, J).

Only one generation of this insect is produced each year, at least in Quebec. Adults emerge at the beginning of May, larvae are present from the end of May until the end of September, and cocoons may be found from mid-June on. The insect overwinters in the larval or prepupal stages in a cocoon in the ground where it continues to develop in the spring, transforming to pupa and then to adult.

Damage and diagnosis

Damage is caused by the larvae of the greenheaded spruce sawfly, which prefer to feed on the current year's growth of spruce, although populations are rarely large enough to cause any spectacular defoliation.

Spruce crowns infested by this sawfly may be identified by the presence, from June to September, of totally green larvae. Defoliation is rarely apparent unless this sawfly is associated with another species that would be the main defoliator.

Natural control

To date, ten species of entomophagous parasites have been obtained through laboratory rearings, five for Canada as a whole (Brown 1941), three in Ontario (Raizenne 1957), and two in Quebec.

With respect to microorganisms, one virus and one fungus have been isolated from specimens collected in Quebec, but their role in regulating populations of the greenheaded spruce sawfly has not yet been assessed (Smirnoff and Juneau 1973).

Artificial control

The greenheaded spruce sawfly has never been present in numbers large enough to necessitate the use of direct methods of control. If control were ever necessary, good results might be obtained, as in the case of the yellowheaded spruce sawfly, by spraying the foliage of infested crowns with a stomach insecticide when the larvae are active.

References

Bracken 1961; Brown 1938, 1941; Forbes 1949; Gobeil 1938b; Hopping 1938; Houseweart and Kulman 1976; Nash 1939; Pierson 1947; Peterson 1945; Raizenne 1957; Smirnoff and Juneau 1973; Twinn 1934; and Wilson 1962a.

PLATE 2

Yellowheaded spruce sawfly, *Pikonema alaskensis* (Roh.), and greenheaded spruce sawfly, *P. dimmockii* (Cress.)

A. Spruce plantation severely defoliated by *P. alaskensis*.
B. Spruce needles showing eggs of *P. alaskensis*.
C. Colony of young *P. alaskensis* larvae on black spruce twig.
D. Colony of mature *P. alaskensis* larvae on white spruce twig.
E. Close-up of mature *P. alaskensis* larva (length: 16 to 20 mm).
F. *P. alaskensis*, adult female (length: 8 to 10 mm.).
G. *P. alaskensis*, adult male.
H. *P. alaskensis*, open cocoon.
I. Dorsal view of mature *P. dimmockii* larva.
J. Lateral view of mature *P. dimmockii* larva.
K. Front part of body of *P. dimmockii* larva showing parasite egg on side of head.

7

A

B

C

D

E

G

F

H

PLATE 3

Spruce bud moth, *Zeiraphera canadensis* Mut. and Free., lesser yellow spruce shootworm, *Z. fortunana* Kft., and purplestriped shootworm, *Z. destitutana* (Wlk.)

A. New shoots on healthy white spruce.
B. New shoot on white spruce infested by *Zeiraphera*.
C. *Z. canadensis* larva, showing damage inside a spruce shoot, and silk envelope.
D. *Z. destitutana* larva on spruce shoot.
E. *Z. destitutana* pupa in natural surroundings.
F. Pinned *Z. canadensis* moth (wingspan: 13 mm).
G. Pinned *Z. fortunana* moth (wingspan: 13 mm).
H. Pinned *Z. destitutana* moth.

Spruce bud moths

In North America, many species of microlepidoptera belonging to the bud moth group may be found at any one time on spruce foliage, and two of these deserve closer attention: the spruce bud moth, *Zeiraphera canadensis* Mut. and Free., formerly known by the scientific name *Z. ratzeburgiana* Ratz., and the lesser yellow spruce shootworm, *Z. fortunana* Kft. The first species was introduced from Europe at the end of the 19th century, and the second appears to be native. The damage they cause is often confused with that of the notorious spruce budworm, *Choristoneura fumiferana* (Clem.), but they differ from the latter in that they are more active on open-grown spruce rather than in the forest.

A third species, the purplestriped shootworm, *Z. destitutana* (Wlk.), also attacks spruce at the same time of the year and behaves in practically the same way as the other two bud moths (Plate 3, D, E and H).

In Canada, the range of the first two species is transcontinental and practically identical, covering a good part of the spruce range. In British Columbia, however, the lesser yellow spruce shootworm ranges farther north and not so far west. In the United States, the spruce bud moth is found over the entire spruce range, but information on the distribution of the lesser yellow spruce shootworm is still sketchy, except for the State of Maine (Baker 1972).

White spruce is the preferred host of all three insects. The first two may be found occasionally on 12 other conifers. The spruce bud moth and the lesser yellow spruce shootworm are presented together because of their close systematic affinity and the similarity of their life cycle and part of their biology. A major study was made of the biology of the spruce bud moth by Pilon (1965), but little is known about the second species.

History of outbreaks

These two bud moths were first reported in eastern Canada in 1938 in the Maritime Provinces, in 1941 in Quebec and Ontario, and in 1943 in Newfoundland. In eastern Canada, the spruce bud moth has always been more common than the lesser yellow spruce shootworm. Both attracted the attention of foresters between 1939 and 1958, during the spectacular outbreak of the spruce budworm, because larvae of all three species participated in the damage. Once the spruce budworm outbreak had faded, the other two species remained common on open-grown white spruce in Quebec. According to a study carried out in 1959 on a total of 13 defoliators collected on spruce in Chaleur Bay, these two species were the most common; they were also very abundant in 8 of the 12 areas sampled in the southern part of the province (McLeod and Blais 1961). At the same time, reports from Ontario mentioned that these two bud moths were included in a group of six species attacking developing shoots on open-grown white spruce. In recent years, local outbreaks have been occasionally reported in other provinces.

Description and biology

Spruce bud moth, *Z. canadensis*

Adult. Pale brown moth, forewings with clear pattern, especially when folded on back. Wingspan: 13 mm (Plate 3, F).
Egg. Oval; yellow orange to orange.
Larva. Elongated but corpulent; creamy yellow. Length: 10 mm (Plate 3, C).
Pupa. Glabrous; brown. Length: 3 mm.

The spruce bud moth produces only one generation each year. Moths may be found on trees from the end of July to the end of August. They are not particularly active and are rarely seen flying; however, when disturbed, they will fly to another branch a short distance away. They prefer small spruce trees about 2 m in height. Eggs are deposited singly or in groups of two to seven at the base of new shoots, and may be found from the end of July on. The insect normally overwinters in the egg stage or occasionally in the larval stage, and the eggs normally hatch the following June. The larva, generally visible from June to the end of July, is a solitary webworm that lives mainly under the bud cap and is held in place by silk strands. Thus sheltered, it feeds safely, eating the edges of the needles or cutting them at the base; it may even attack the bark. The larva goes through four larval instars and when fully grown, moves about freely. Between the end of July and mid-August, it drops to the ground, either freely or using a strand of silk, and transforms to a pupa without spinning a cocoon, either on the ground or in the litter.

Description and biology

Lesser yellow spruce shootworm, *Z. fortunana*

Adult. Moth similar to the spruce bud moth; forewings brown with a less pronounced pattern because of white scales. Wingspan: 13 mm (Plate 3, G).
Larva. Elongated; creamy yellow; presence of an anal comb that distinguishes it from the spruce bud moth.
Pupa. Yellow to brown.

The biology of the lesser yellow spruce shootworm differs little from that of the spruce bud moth. It too has only one generation a year, but the various stages of its life cycle appear a week to 10 days earlier. The moth prefers slightly higher trees, about 7 m tall; it is very active and continually flutters about the crown or flies from one crown to another regardless of the weather. Apart from the fact that the larva feeds singly by grazing on the foliage, little else is known about the other stages.

Damage and diagnosis

Most of the damage by spruce bud moth and lesser yellow spruce shootworm is caused by the larvae of either species feeding on foliage. The needles are partially stripped or cut at the base and, in all cases, the foliage eventually takes on a reddish color (Plate 3, B). Damage is usually greater on apical shoots and particularly the terminal growth, but such damage is not serious and does not even cause a reduction in annual increment. More serious is the damage that occurs when larvae attack the tender bark of twigs, because this activity causes deformation of the growing shoot. This shoot tends to bend towards the chewed side and in some cases breaks off. Crowns damaged repeatedly in this way take on an abnormal shape and become unattractive. Signs of the presence of these bud moths are the prolonged presence of the bud caps on spruce apical shoots (Plate 3, C), particularly on open-grown white spruce; the presence of deformed apical shoots in the upper part of the crown; and the presence and behavior of moths around crowns.

Natural control

During his research carried out on the spruce bud moth in Chaleur Bay, Que., Pilon (1965) obtained one egg parasite and eight species of larval parasites. His report also mentioned three other species of parasites collected by Daviault in the southern part of the province between 1949 and 1951. However, their importance is minimal, because population reduction was estimated at about 12 percent by Pilon and 4 percent by Daviault. Bradley (1974) mentioned four species of parasites, two of which had already been listed by Pilon.

Two of the parasitic species found on the spruce bud moth also attack the lesser yellow spruce shootworm (Bradley 1974).

Artificial control

From studying the biology of the spruce bud moth and the lesser yellow spruce shootworm, it appears that their control presents difficulties due to the protection provided by the bud cap under which the larva stays throughout most of the feeding stage. Satisfactory results may, however, be obtained by applying a contact insecticide on the foliage as soon as the first needles appear and by repeating the treatment 2 weeks later.

References

Baker 1972; Bradley 1951, 1974; Linquist 1964; MacAndrews 1927; McLeod and Blais 1961b; Miller 1950; Pilon 1965; and Prentice 1965.

Coneworms
Plate 4

Two species of coneworms frequently attack conifer cones in eastern North America: the spruce coneworm, *Dioryctria reniculelloides* Mut. and Mun., and the fir coneworm *D. abietivorella* (Grote). These two species are presented together because they are closely related in the entomological classification and their biology is also similar. In Canada, the range of the former species is transcontinental but in the northeastern United States, it extends only from the Atlantic Ocean to the Great Lakes, whereas that of the latter species is holarctic.

The spruce coneworm is found on many conifer species, but it prefers white spruce and balsam fir. It is mainly harmful to cones, feeding on the foliage only when cones are lacking. The fir coneworm is found mainly on two species, black spruce and jack pine, and occasionally on other conifers. It attacks both the foliage and the cones. Commercial damage by these two species occurs because they are often associated with other phyllophagous insects, such as the spruce budworm, and thus contribute to accelerated deterioration of the crowns.

History of outbreaks

The spruce coneworm is more common and better known than the fir coneworm in eastern Canada. It was first reported in 1937 and has been collected almost every year since. It is particularly abundant in the Maritime provinces, where outbreaks have been reported since 1969. It has been reported in Newfoundland since 1959, but damage has been negligible. In Quebec, outbreaks were reported from 1945 to 1956, and again from 1969 on; in Ontario a series of outbreaks occurred between 1937 and 1946, and another began in 1968. The years of greater insect abundance coincided with outbreaks of the spruce budworm, *Choristoneura fumiferana* (Clem.). Populations of the spruce coneworm appear to be largest during years of high production of cones (McLeod and Daviault 1963).

The fir coneworm was first noticed in this country in 1939 and has occasionally been reported since that time. Its apparent rarity is perhaps due to the sampling methods used to date, which were aimed mainly at collecting foliage insects, whereas this species feeds inside cones and cannot easily be dislodged. Local outbreaks have nevertheless been reported occasionally in Quebec and Ontario.

Description and biology

Spruce coneworm, *D. reniculelloides*

Adult. Medium-sized moth; forewings bronze, gray marked crosswise with white zigzag lines bordered with black. Wingspan: 25 mm (Plate 4, G).

Egg. Flat, more or less circular in shape with irregular edges; white initially, then turning to pink and to brown during its development.

Larva. Elongated; head brown, body dirty yellow with pale brown and longitudinal lines on back and another dark-colored line on each side of body. Length: 19 mm (Plate 4, B).

Pupa. Spindle-shaped; brown. Length: 10 mm (Plate 4, C).

The spruce coneworm produces one generation each year, and its life cycle necessarily varies with environmental conditions. In Quebec, the adults appear by mid-June and are visible until the end of August. Shortly after emerging, the females lay their eggs singly or in groups of two or three in various parts of the crown, including the bark, foliage and cones. The eggs take about 10 days to develop and, once hatched, the young larvae move into the cones to complete part of their development before hibernating. In the spring, the larvae (Plate 4, A) leave the cones and feed on needles until they are full grown. Larvae from eggs laid late in the year may spin hibernacula in which to pass the winter and attack cones only the following year (Plate 4, E). If cones are unavailable, the newly hatched larva mines one or two old needles, penetrating by the base, before attacking buds and, later new needles. The period of greatest larval abundance is in July, but larvae may be seen throughout the year. The larva goes through five instars. It then spins a silken cocoon in the foliage in which it transforms through pupa to adult.

A

B

C

D

F

E

G

PLATE 4

Spruce coneworm, *Dioryctria reni-culelloides* Mut. & Mun., and fir coneworm, *D. abietivorella* (Grote)

A. Young *D. reniculelloides* larva in a spruce shoot.
B. Mature *D. reniculelloides* larva on spruce twig (length: 19 mm).
C. *D. reniculelloides* pupa (length: 10 mm).
D. White spruce trees defoliated partly by the spruce budworm and partly by *D. reniculelloides*.
E. White spruce cones and shoots attacked by *D. reniculelloides*.
F. *D. reniculelloides* adult at rest.
G. Pinned *D. reniculelloides* adult (wingspan: 25 mm).
H. Pinned *D. abietivorella* adult (wingspan: 25 mm).
I. Mature *D. abietivorella* larva.

H

I

The larvae occasionally prey upon other phyllophagous larvae, particularly those of the spruce budworm.

Description and biology

Fir coneworm, *D. abietivorella*

Adult. Moth similar to the spruce coneworm but with darker forewings and less pronounced markings. Wingspan: 25 mm (Plate 4, H).

Egg. Oval.

Larva. Differs from the spruce coneworm in color, which ranges from flesh-color to reddish brown, and has very dark, almost black, longitudinal lines (Plate 4, I).

Pupa. Almost identical to that of the spruce coneworm.

The fir coneworm, like the spruce coneworm, produces one generation a year and its life cycle is similar, although less well known. According to Brown (1941) and Daviault (1951c), a second flight may occur at the end of the season. Adults appear about 2 weeks before those of the spruce coneworm. Egg laying has not been observed in the field, but, in the laboratory, eggs have been deposited singly in crevices near cone scales on red pine. The larva goes through five instars, as does that of the spruce coneworm, and feeds not only inside cones but also on the needles of terminal shoots and on the bark of trunks and of large branches. Its growth is completed towards the end of September, and the larva drops to the ground where it spins a silken cocoon in which it pupates and transforms to a moth.

Damage and diagnosis

These two coneworms cause some similar damage by mining the host's cones to form galleries. The spruce coneworm also mines or chews needles, whereas the fir coneworm attacks foliage and may occasionally dig galleries in the bark of stems or branches.

The presence of galleries in conifer cones is often an indication of damage by one of these two species. Identification of these coneworms and of their damage is always difficult and for greater certainty, it is best to have larva and moth specimens examined by an entomologist who specializes in this field.

Natural control

A number of species of insect parasites have been obtained in the rearings of spruce coneworm larvae carried out in Canada; 24 species have been recovered in Quebec, 8 by FIDS and 16 others from material collected in southern Quebec between 1943 and 1951 (McLeod and Daviault 1963). Three species of parasites reported in southern Ontario had already been observed in Quebec (Raizenne 1952) and, of a total of nine species reported from various parts of Canada, four appear in the Quebec list (Bradley 1974).

Symptoms of an unidentified disease have also been observed on last instar larvae in southern Quebec and the Gaspé peninsula. Considerably fewer species were recovered for the fir coneworm; only five species of parasites were reported, two by Lyons (1957) and three by Bradley (1974), probably because the fir coneworm has been reared much less intensively than the spruce coneworm.

Artificial control

Control of these two coneworms by artificial means cannot be justified under forest conditions. However, ornamental trees or small stands may be protected by collecting cones and burning them while the insects are still inside. For the spruce coneworm this burning may be done in fall and winter, whereas for the fir coneworm, it should be completed before the beginning of September.

Spruce coneworm larvae may also be poisoned by spraying foliage with a stomach insecticide dissolved in oil when larvae are feeding on the foliage.

References

Bradley 1974; Brown 1941; Daviault 1951c; Lyons 1957; MacKay 1943; McLeod and Daviault 1963; Prentice 1965; and Raizenne 1952.

Two insect miners are occasionally found on spruce in eastern Canada: the orange spruce needleminer, *Pulicalvaria piceaella* (Kft.), and the European spruce needleminer, *Epinotia nanana* Treit.

Orange spruce needleminer
Plate 5

The orange spruce needleminer, *Pulicalvaria piceaella* (Kft.), formerly grouped successively in the genera *Recurvaria*, *Evagora*, and *Eucordylea*, is mainly a needleminer, but also attacks spruce buds and cones. In Canada, it occurs from Newfoundland to Alberta and, in the United States, from Maine to Colorado. The known hosts are white spruce, black spruce, red spruce, Norway spruce, and blue spruce. This microlepidoptera was first observed in Canada in 1930, and its presence has been reported at various times since then. However, this insect generally goes unnoticed, because its damage is not apparent and is of little consequence.

History of outbreaks

Four epidemics of the orange spruce needleminer have been reported to date, three in Ontario in 1940 and 1941 and one in Quebec in 1941. Its relative abundance in Quebec was established in 1959 when a survey was carried out both in the Gaspé and in the southern part of the province. It ranked fourth among the 13 defoliators collected on white spruce in the Gaspé whereas in southern Québec, it ranked as one of the two principal species in 6 of the 12 areas sampled (McLeod and Blais 1961a). In 1961, and on subsequent occasions, this species was probably part of a group of six defoliators sometimes under the name of *Eucordylea* sp., causing severe damage to spruce in several localities in Ontario.

PLATE 5

Orange spruce needleminer, *Pulicalvaria piceaella* (Kft.), European spruce needleminer, *Epinotia nanana* Treit.

A. Pinned adult of *P. piceaella* (wingspan: 10-13 mm).
B. Pinned adult of *E. nanana*.
C. Adult of *E. nanana* at rest.
D. Young spruce needles damaged by *E. nanana*.
E. and F. Larval damage of *E. nanana*, in the spring and in the fall.
G. and H. Young larva of *E. nanana* out of its tunnel, life size and enlarged.
I. *E. nanana* larva in its tunnel.
J. Mature larva of *E. nanana* out of the pupa silk.
K. *E. nanana* pupa out of its silk.

13

Description and biology

Adult. Small moth, mainly gray. Wingspan: 10-13 mm (Plate 5, A).

Egg. More or less cylindrical. Diameter: about 0.5 mm.

Larva. Elongated; brown orange before hibernation, becoming pink to brick red in winter. Length: 8 mm.

Pupa. Brown orange; enclosed in a silken cocoon. Length: 4 mm.

The biology of the orange spruce needleminer was practically unknown before the publication of studies carried out in Quebec (McLeod 1962, 1966; McLeod and Blais 1961a).

This miner has one generation a year. The insect overwinters in the form of a more or less developed larva. In the spring, the larvae complete their development and form chrysalids between May and the end of August. The pupal stage lasts about 12 days. Adults lay their eggs either singly or in groups of two or three near bud scales, or in needles, cones, or flowers damaged by poor weather conditions or other pests. The egg stage lasts 7-10 days.

Environmental conditions have a great influence on larval growth. On hatching, the young larva penetrates inside either old or new needles through a circular hole burrowed through the base. It then mines a tunnel in the needle, and at the same time builds a silken passage to a second needle or to the stem. When the first needle has been hollowed out, it attacks and destroys the second, and can in this way damage up to five needles. Larval behavior is often complicated by the fact that they may attack dead or damaged foliage, cones, frozen buds, flowers, and foliar galls, or any other damaged plant material, that they like to feed on. In September, the larvae have more or less completed their development, depending on the time of their birth, and, whatever their age, they go into hibernation.

Damage and diagnosis

The tunnels mined by larvae of the orange spruce needleminer in feeding cause the needles to dry out and when a good part of the foliage is affected, the crowns become unattractive and lose most of their aesthetic value.

Spruce trees bearing needles that are hollowed-out, dry, or inhabited by brown orange to brick red larvae, in summer or fall, indicate damage by the orange spruce needleminer. For positive identification, however, it is preferable to submit a specimen of the insect or the damage caused to a specialist.

Natural control

Studies by McLeod (1966) in Quebec yielded 35 species of entomophagous parasites attacking the orange spruce needleminer, but it was impossible to estimate their relative importance in reducing populations. No other studies have been published from other parts of the country. Nevertheless, Bradley (1974) mentions two parasitic species, one of which had already been reported in Quebec, and Raizenne (1952) gives one species for Ontario that is not listed elsewhere.

Artificial control

Control of the orange spruce needleminer with ordinary insecticides presents great difficulties, because the larvae are hidden almost constantly in needles or in silken shelters. They are vulnerable only during one period of their existence, that is from the time they leave the egg until they penetrate into needles; this period occurs about 10 days after the adults swarm. It would then be a good time to spray with a stomach or contact insecticide. It might also be possible to reach larvae in their tunnels by using a systemic insecticide sprayed on foliage when larvae are active.

European spruce needleminer
Plate 5

The European spruce needleminer, *Epinotia nanana* Treit., is of European origin and attacks more particularly Norway spruce and blue spruce, but is also found on ornamental white spruce and on red spruce. This species is mainly a miner of needles, feeding only on old needles. It is smaller than the orange spruce needleminer. The egg is pale yellow at the beginning but it bears a red or orange band as it develops. The larva is brown yellow at first and, although keeping its basic brown color, it gradually turns to creamy gray. The pupa is light brown.

The biology and behavior of the European spruce needleminer correspond to those of the orange spruce needleminer. Rearing of this miner produced several parasite species in Quebec (Daviault and Ducharme 1966) and artificial methods of control were not developed.

References

Bradley 1951; Daviault and Ducharme 1966; Lindquist and Harnden 1966; McLeod 1962, 1966; McLeod and Blais 1961a; Prentice 1965; and Raizenne 1952.

Eastern spruce gall adelgid
Plate 6

Several species of aphids cause gall formations on spruce shoots. The most widely spread species in eastern North America, known as the eastern spruce gall adelgid, *Adelges abietis* (L.), produces a small pineapple-shaped gall at the base of current-year shoots. This adelgid was introduced from Europe where it has been considered harmful to ornamental spruces since the 16th century. In North America, this adelgid is found throughout Canada and across the northern United States mainly on Norway spruce and white spruce, but other spruce species are also occasionally attacked.

History of outbreaks

The eastern spruce gall adelgid is very common in eastern Canada, where it was observed at least as early as 1929. It is of lesser importance in the Maritime provinces, and in Newfoundland, where its presence was first reported in 1943. It is considered a serious spruce pest in Quebec and Ontario, where it has caused major damage, notably in 1941 in the southern part of these two provinces and in 1945 in young spruce plantations across southern Ontario.

Description and biology

Several studies were made on the biology of the eastern spruce gall adelgid, both in Europe and in North America.

The adult is a sucking insect about 4 mm long, which resembles a tiny wasp. It is difficult to see the insect itself, but its presence may easily be detected by the gall it produces. The gall originates in the cortical cell of the twig and begins to form in the spring when the first adults appear and attach themselves to the base of new needles to lay their eggs. The young nymphs that emerge from these eggs settle near the area damaged by the mother and continue the attack.

This adelgid's entire life cycle takes place on one host, and all individuals are female. There are two generations each year, one in the spring and one in the summer. It overwinters as a mature nymph at the base of buds, and in May, becomes active again, transforms to an adult (Plate 6, D), and attaches itself to a twig where it immediately lays its eggs in a mass of filamentous wax resembling white cotton, and then dies. About 2 weeks later, these eggs hatch and the young nymphs crawl to the base of new needles inside recently opened buds; their bites cause the needles to hypertrophy, resulting in the formation of conical galls (Plate 6, A), pale green at the beginning and later developing red markings; each gall contains a number of cells (Plate 6, B). Towards the end of the summer, from August to October, the gall cells open and release mature nymphs (Plate 6, C), which immediately transform to adults having black heads and yellowish bodies with transparent wings. Then the adult settles itself on the bark near new buds and lives just long enough to lay its eggs. Egg development lasts about 3 weeks. From these eggs, the nymphs of the second generation emerge and crawl to the base of needles where they spend the winter.

Although this insect is winged, it is dispersed mainly by the action of wind and of birds; it also spreads through the transfer of plants from one nursery to another where it is very active especially on young trees.

Damage and diagnosis

Damage by the eastern spruce gall adelgid results from adults and young nymphs feeding on sap at the base of needles, which causes galls to form. This damage consists mainly in the decreased aesthetic value of ornamental spruce trees or of those intended for sale as Christmas trees. In heavily infested plantations, nearly all shoots may be affected on some trees; thus Patch (1909) counted up to 995 galls on a spruce 1 m tall. Over the years, in addition to the presence of old galls, mortality of the distal part of affected branches and subsequent crown deformity can be seen on heavily infested trees.

An outbreak of the eastern spruce gall adelgid can easily be recognized during the summer by the presence of green galls shaped like miniature pineapples at the base of new shoots on Norway spruce and white spruce. These indicate that an outbreak is under way, and the proportion of shoots affected is an indication of the intensity of the attack. The presence of old brown or black galls indicates a previous outbreak.

Natural control

Some authors mention the presence of parasites, predators and birds among factors controlling the eastern spruce gall adelgid; however, their importance appears to be negligible.

Artificial control

Various artificial methods have been developed to control the eastern spruce gall adelgid, aimed either at preventing infestations or improving the condition of affected trees. These may be summarized as follows:

- Cut and incinerate the green galls at mid-summer when adelgids are still inside;
- Spray the buds of Norway spruce and white spruce with an emulsion of superior oil before buds open in April; or
- Spray the buds of the same tree species with a residual-action insecticide in May, when nymphs migrate, and repeat the operation in October.

References

Cumming 1959; Patch 1909; Philip 1978; Plumb 1953; Turner et al. 1975; and Wilford 1937.

Cooley spruce gall adelgid
Plate 6

A second species of gall adelgid, known as the Cooley spruce gall adelgid, *Adelges cooleyi* (Gill.), is occasionally found in eastern North America. Its range is practically the same as that of the eastern spruce gall adelgid, *A. abietis*, but it is mainly abundant in the West. In the East, it is a fairly rare species, found mainly on ornamental spruces. It has been reported in all eastern provinces of Canada, except the Maritimes. Its preferred hosts are Engelmann spruce and white spruce; in the West, it has an alternate host, Douglas-fir. Other species sometimes mentioned as hosts are blue spruce, Norway spruce, black spruce, red spruce, and Sitka spruce.

Description and biology

The biology of the Cooley spruce gall adelgid has mainly been studied in the West. It is similar to that of the eastern spruce gall adelgid with the important difference that, in the West, the first adelgid passes part of its life cycle on spruce and completes it on a different host, Douglas-fir. In the West, its life cycle includes six different forms, starting with the stem-mother responsible for the formation of the galls on spruce; the complete cycle takes 2 years. In the East, the complete cycle is known to take place on spruce, but little is known as yet about the development.

As in the case of the eastern spruce gall adelgid, gall formation on spruce is the result of the insect feeding at the base of needles. Young galls are green or purple, whereas old galls are reddish brown.

Damage and diagnosis

Damage to spruce by the Cooley spruce gall adelgid is generally the same as that described for the eastern spruce gall adelgid and consists mainly of the production of galls that affect the aesthetic value of infested trees. The gall is elongated and may cover either the whole length of the shoot or only the distal part (Plate 6, G); the shoot gradually bends. On Douglas-fir, no gall is formed but the needles turn yellow and drop.

Natural control

Nothing is known as yet about the factors providing natural control of the Cooley spruce gall adelgid in the East, but in the West, there have been reports of activity by predators such as insects and spiders, as well as adverse climatic conditions.

Artificial control

Artificial methods of control for the Cooley spruce gall adelgid are the same as those suggested for the eastern spruce gall adelgid.

References

Cumming 1959; Daviault 1950b; Friend 1936; Friend and Wilford 1933; Patch 1909; Philip 1978; Plumb 1953; Turner et al. 1975; and Wilford 1937.

Spruce spider mite

A lthough it belongs to the class of arachnids, the spruce spider mite, *Oligonychus ununguis* (Jac.), is treated here because its damage is similar to that caused by insects. Acarids are small pests, barely visible to the naked eye, but, under a magnifying glass, they appear as small creatures with four pairs of legs and a body partly covered with sparse long hairs. This mite is the most important acarian found on spruce. It is harmful to ornamental and plantation trees, especially when trees have been treated abundantly with insecticides to control insect defoliators, as this also destroys insect predators. The tree species most subject to attack are white spruce and blue spruce, eastern white cedar, and eastern hemlock, but this mite is also found on juniper, larch, and some species of pine. Its range in Canada is transcontinental, but it has generally been more harmful in the western provinces. In the East, its presence has been reported occasionally on spruce planted as ornamentals.

PLATE 6

Eastern spruce gall adelgid, *Adelges abietis (L.)*, Cooley spruce gall adelgid, *Adelges cooleyi* (Gill.), and spruce gall adelgid, *Adelges lariciatus* (Patch)

A. New spruce shoots bearing galls of *A. abietis*.
B. Cross-section of young *A. abietis* galls showing the interior of cells and contents.
C. Cells of *A. abietis* galls which have opened naturally to release adults, still near the gall.
D. and E. Close-up of *A. abietis* adults, wings folded and wings spread.
F. Old *A. abietis* gall still with its normal shape.
G. Spruce shoots with *A. cooleyi* galls.
H. Black spruce shoots bearing *A. lariciatus* galls.
I. *A. lariciatus* adult.

Description and biology

Adult. Small spider with four pairs of legs, dark green to dark brown. Length: 0.5 mm.

Egg. Spherical; pale yellow, later turning reddish brown. Diameter: about 0.1 mm.

Larva. Resembles a small spider with only three pairs of legs; pink initially, then turning green once feeding begins.

Nymph. Similar to larva, but having four pairs of legs; green.

The biology of the spruce spider mite is as yet relatively unknown.

This acarid overwinters in the egg stage under the loose scales of buds or at the base of needles. Four or more generations are produced each year, depending on the region, the first in the spring and the last in September. In the Maritime provinces, eggs hatch early in June, and the first generation lasts about a month, so that the second generation appears at the beginning of July. In Ontario, larvae leave the eggs in late April and in the summer a generation appears every 15 days (Turner et al. 1975). Mites of the first generation attack old foliage, whereas subsequent generations feed on new foliage. All active stages of this acarian feed by inserting their mouth parts into foliar tissue to suck sap and while feeding, they spin great amounts of silk webbing around needles and twigs. Damage begins on the inside section of the branches of the lower crown, then spreads to the higher and outermost branches.

Damage and diagnosis

The numerous punctures made by the spruce spider mite cause needles to dry gradually, turning pale green and then reddish brown, and finally to fall to the ground. The interior of the crown begins to darken and then takes on a brown color. During a severe outbreak, a few trees may die, but most trees survive.

An outbreak of this mite may be recognized first by the dusty appearance of needles, which then turn brown and fall. The presence of silk webbing between needles is an indication of high populations of mites.

Natural control

A ladybug, *Stethorus punctillum* Weise, was observed to prey actively on the spruce spider mite on conifers in Pennsylvania and also in Ontario, but no estimate has been made of its importance in reducing populations. Climate, more specifically, heavy precipitation and high humidity, constitute the most important factor of control of populations of this acarid.

Artificial control

The proliferation of the spruce spider mite may be delayed temporarily by treating tree crowns with a strong spray of water at relatively short intervals. This destroys webs, dislodges part of the population, and raises the humidity level in the foliage so as to check the development of the mite.

A more costly method is to spray affected trees with an acaricide as soon as the mites enter their active phase. Because of the many generations produced each year, the treatment must be repeated as required; final treatment is recommended in September to eliminate the last generation.

Another method is to apply a dormant oil in April in order to destroy eggs before they hatch; however, in this instance, it is important that the tree species requiring treatment is not sensitive to oil.

References

Canadian Forestry Service 1974e; Connecticut Agricultural Experiment Station 1956; Cornell University 1976; Johnson and Lyon 1976; Philip 1978; Turner et al. 1975; Wheeler et al. 1973; and Wilson 1977.

Spruce beetle
Plate 7

The spruce beetle, *Dendroctonus rufipennis* (Kby.), is a bark borer. Studies by Wood (1969) showed that this species now comprises three pests of spruce known previously as *Dendroctonus piceaperda* Hopk., *D. obesus* Mann., and *D. engelmannii* Hopk. Reported for the first time in Canada in 1923 under the name of *D. piceaperda*, it was present in this country before that time because it is indigenous to North America. Its range is transcontinental. It was known for the damage caused to white spruce in the northeastern United States and in British Columbia, and on Engelmann spruce in Colorado. Hosts include all species of spruces as well as shore pine when it grows with one of the spruces, and mature stands are generally the most seriously affected. The insect is not abundant at present in the East, but is a constant threat in the western part of the continent.

PLATE 7

Spruce beetle, *Dendroctonus rufipennis* (Kby.)

A. Close-up of base of an infested spruce trunk, showing flow of resin and exit holes made by adults.

B. Adult (length: 5-6 mm).

C. Cross-section showing adult gallery through bark.

D. Bark dust at adult entrance hole shortly after attack.

E. Adult on resin at entrance hole of a gallery.

F. Resin agglutinated at entrance hole of a gallery.

G. Mature white spruce heavily damaged by spruce budworm, *Choristoneura fumiferana*, and attacked by the spruce beetle.

History of outbreaks

In the East, the spruce beetle took on considerable importance on three occasions. The first epidemic lasted from 1897 to 1901 over a vast area including Maine, New Brunswick, and eastern Quebec, particularly in the Dartmouth and York river basins. A second outbreak originated in 1915 in windthrown stands in the same area, and this time the York, Saint John, and Dartmouth river basins were under attack until 1921. A third, more virulent epidemic between 1928 and 1934 swept all the river basins east of the Matapedia valley, as well as part of the North Shore and Anticosti Island; the heaviest damage was recorded in the Marsoui, York, and Cascapedia river valleys. According to Gobeil (1938a), some 18 million m^3 of spruce wood were destroyed in the last outbreak alone.

Since then, the beetle has been collected only occasionally in all provinces of eastern Canada, but these were only local attacks in old spruce stands.

Description and biology

Adult. Small beetle cylindrical, dark brown to black. Length: 5-6 mm (Plate 7, B).

Egg. Oblong; pearl white. Length: about 1-2 mm.

Larva. Cylindrical and legless; body creamy white with brown head. Length at maturity: about 6 mm.

Pupa. Resembles adult but creamy white. Length: about 5 mm.

The life cycle of the spruce beetle lasts 1-3 years depending on climatic conditions, which vary across its range.

In the case of the shortest cycle, the adult appears from mid-June to mid-July and, shortly after emerging the female bores an entry hole in the trunk bark and constructs an egg gallery (Plate 7, C) that measures about 13 cm long and runs in a straight line along the grain at the surface of the wood. As boring progresses, the male assists the female by carrying off the boring dust (Plate 7, D) that may, however, remain attached to resin exuding from the orifice. One couple may construct more than one gallery during a single season. The female lays up to 200 eggs in slits she bores in the sides of the main gallery. On emerging, the larvae remain in groups throughout the first third of their development; the rest is completed during the summer, each larva boring a horizontal gallery more or less perpendicular to the main gallery and having an average length of 13 cm. This gallery ends in a pupation cell where, in about mid-October, the insect pupates. Adult emergence takes place the following spring.

In the case of the 2 year cycle, the adult appears in July and development of immature stages is slower than in the short cycle. By mid-October, the larva has completed only half its development and overwinters in that stage. The adult stage is reached in June and July of the following year and emergence takes place in August and September. At this time, adults seek a shelter in which to overwinter for a second time, normally in bark crevices at the base of damaged trunks. The following spring, they leave their shelter and attack new stems, and the cycle begins again.

Damage and diagnosis

Damage by spruce beetle consists of a network of parental and larval galleries at the wood surface. On living trees, the effect of this damage is to loosen the bark from the wood and gradually to cut off sap circulation. Foliage then wilts and takes on a brownish color (Plate 7, G): finally the leaves fall and the tree eventually dies. In severe epidemics, entire stands may be destroyed. It is noteworthy that the insect prefers large-diameter trees in blowdowns, cull logs, and waste left at felling sites.

The first indications of attack by this beetle are entry holes and rounded masses of resin about the size of a thumb known as pitch tubes on the lower part of the trunk (Plate 7, A, E and F). As the outbreak progresses, the foliage takes on an abnormal color, needles fall, bark loosens from trunks, and the parental and larval galleries may be seen easily on the surface of the wood.

Natural control

Most of the data on factors in the natural control of the spruce beetle was obtained from studies carried out in the West. Massey and Wygant (1954) noted that 75 percent of the original population of spruce beetles was eliminated, between the second half of larval development and the emergence of the adult due to the combined action of parasites, predators, and low temperatures. Schmid and Beckwith (1975) report that natural factors usually maintain populations at low levels, but are insufficient during outbreaks. Parasite and predator liberations were carried out in Quebec by the federal government in 1933 and 1934, but without success (McGugan and Coppel 1962).

Artificial control

A number of artificial methods of control are available to the forest manager seeking to prevent damage by the spruce beetle, but few of them were developed for use during an epidemic. Thus damage may be prevented or limited by:
- harvesting spruce stands before trees are too large;
- cutting old spruces in middle-aged stands;
- eliminating cull logs and large waste on felling sites;
- rapid salvage of spruce logs after a windthrow;
- use and subsequent destruction of trap trees intended for egg laying; and
- use of sun heat or of insecticides to kill populations in infested logs.

References

Canada Department of Agriculture 1923; Daviault 1949b; Gobeil 1938a; Massey and Wygant 1954; McGugan and Coppel 1962; Schmid and Beckwith 1975; Swaine 1924; and Wood 1969.

Large spruce weevil
Plate 8

The large spruce weevil, *Hylobius piceus* (DeG.), a boring insect once included in the genus *Hypomolyx*, is now classified in the genus *Hylobius*, but its true systematic position is still in doubt. This species is apparently native to the northern forests of North America. It was recorded in Canadian forests from the very beginning of the FIDS, and has been collected almost every year since. Its range is transcontinental, and its preferred hosts are Scots pine, jack pine, shore pine, and white spruce, but red pine, white pine, and limber pine, red spruce, black spruce, and Norway spruce, balsam fir and larch are also affected. It is one of the insects most commonly found in the adult stage on conifer foliage.

History of outbreaks

The presence of the large spruce weevil has been noted in all the eastern provinces of Canada, but only Quebec has reported major damage. In that province two outbreaks were reported, the first lasting from 1936 to 1940 in a plantation of Scots pine and red pine at Grand'Mère, the second was detected in 1954, and is still going on in a plantation of Scots pine, eastern white pine, and Norway spruce at Valcartier. A large number of trees succumbed during these two epidemics.

Description and biology

Adult. Shaped like a miniature elephant with snout (rostrum) slightly curved in; basic color brown black, with thin, straw-colored hairs. Length: about 12 mm (Plate 8, B).

Larva. Legless, plump, and curved; body uniformly white, head varying from brown orange to dark brown. Dimensions: 6 by 12 mm (Plate 8, E).

Pupa. Resembles adult with appendages folded under body; completely white in color.

The biology of the large spruce weevil is not well known, no doubt due to the difficulty in observing immature stages. The main studies on this insect were carried out in Quebec and Manitoba.

The life cycle varies with environmental conditions and may occasionally extend over more than 2 years, causing some stages to overlap. Two stages are normally present in the spring, adult and larva. In Quebec, adults were collected on foliage from the beginning of June until October 15; the lifespan of the adult may last 2 years. They feed on the foliage of the host, on the bark of twigs, and on small roots. The females lay their eggs in small pockets chewed with their snout in the bark near the larval tunnels or around the tree collar (Plate 8, A and B). Larval development takes about 12 months, and is spent inside a gallery constructed in the bark near the cambium, at the root or collar level. Small trees may be completely girdled by a gallery, although this is fairly rare in large trees. Similarly, 2.5-7.5-cm roots are more subject to attack than those of more than 10 cm. Larval feeding provokes a flow of resin that is used to form a tube that protects the larva (Plate 8, F). The full-grown larva constructs a shelter made of an accumulation of coagulated resin, about 20 mm long and 10 mm wide, in which it pupates. The pupal stage lasts 20 to 22 days and takes place from mid-June to mid-August.

Damage and diagnosis

Punctures made by adult large spruce weevils in the bark of twigs (Plate 8, A) or in roots seldom pose a threat to the tree; at most, some twigs or small roots will die. The most serious damage is caused by the larvae which, when numerous, may girdle the trunk or its roots and kill them (Plate 8, C and D). Heavily infested trees normally die after 3 or 4 years of attack, but large-diameter trees generally survive.

Moreover punctures caused by adults and larvae allow pathogenic fungi to enter.

The presence of adults in crowns and of damage resulting from punctures, especially on the upper surface of young twigs, are signs of an on-going infestation. Contaminated trees are easily detected by the accumulation of coagulated resin found at the base of the trunk, which once hardened looks like granulated sugar.

Natural control

No information is available on natural factors regulating the large spruce weevils.

Artificial control

It has been clearly established that the large spruce weevil prefers damp places where a thick layer of humus or plant waste covers the ground. This being the case, it is possible to prevent or limit damage by taking the following precautions:

- Remove humus around collar and large roots;
- Avoid planting susceptible tree species on humid sites, and remove all plant debris from ground before planting; and
- Prune branches up to 1 m from the ground on Scots pines and red pines measuring 2 cm in diameter at the base and clear away the forest litter.

If populations become too large in spite of these precautions, threatened trees may be protected by spraying their roots and the lower part of the trunk with an emulsion of residual-action insecticide.

References

Daviault 1949a; Simmons and Wilson 1977; Warren 1953, 1956a, 1956b; Warren and Whitney 1951; and Wood 1957.

A

B

C

D

E

F

PLATE 8

Large spruce weevil, *Hylobius piceus* (DeG.)

A. Bark of fir twig chewed by adult.
B. Adult on spruce stem.
C. Base of infested Scots pine still surrounded by forest litter.
D. Base of infested Scots pine with forest litter removed.
E. Dorsal view of mature larva (length: 12 mm).
F. Tunnel made of agglutinated resin allowing the larva to move about.

Table 1. Other insects harmful to spruce — Other insects that are regarded as pests of spruce are listed in this table. For some insects, their characteristics are described in the chapter that applies to their primary hosts, and in such cases, that chapter (in Roman numerals) and the appropriate plate numbers are given. For other insects, a plate number alone is shown; and for the remaining insects, this table provides the only information.

Common and scientific names	Hosts (chap.)	Plate no.	Type of insect	Destructive stages	Period of activity	Importance*
Balsam fir sawfly *Neodiprion abietis* (Harr.)	Balsam fir (IV)	38	—	—	—	A
Balsam twig aphid *Mindarus abietinus* Koch	Balsam fir (IV)	41	—	—	—	C
Eastern blackheaded budworm *Acleris variana* (Fern.)	Balsam fir (IV)	39	—	—	—	B
Fir harlequin *Elaphria versicolor* (Grote)	Conifers	—	Defoliator	Larva	June to Sept.	C
Gray spruce looper *Caripeta divisata* Wlk.	Conifers	—	Defoliator	Larva	May to Oct.	C
Gypsy moth *Lymantria dispar* (L.)	Birch (VI)	46	—	—	—	A
Hemlock looper *Lambdina fiscellaria fiscellaria* (Guen.)	Balsam fir (IV)	37	—	—	—	A
Pine leaf adelgid *Pineus pinifoliae* (Fitch)	Pine (III)	22	—	—	—	C
Ragged spruce gall adelgid *Pineus similis* (Gill.)	Spruce, pine, larch	22	Sucker	Adult and nymph	May to Oct.	C
Red spruce adelgid *Pineus floccus* (Patch)	Spruce, pine	22	Sucker	Adult and nymph	June and Aug.	C
Red striped needleworm *Griselda radicana* Wlshm.	Spruce, conifers	—	Defoliator	Larva	May to Sept.	C
Small conifer looper *Eupithecia transcanadata* MacK.	Conifers	—	Defoliator	Larva	April to Oct.	C
Smoky moth *Lexis bicolor* (Grote)	Conifers	—	Defoliator	Larva	May to Sept.	C
Spruce budworm *Choristoneura fumiferana* (Clem.)	Balsam fir (IV)	36	—	—	—	A
Spruce false looper *Syngrapha alias* (Ottol.)	White spruce, conifers	9	Defoliator	Larva	May to Oct.	C
Spruce gall midge *Mayetiola piceae* (Felt)	Spruce	—	Gall-maker	Larva	June to Oct.	C
White pine weevil *Pissodes strobi* (Peck)	Pine (III)	24	—	—	—	A
Whitespotted sawyer *Monochamus scutellatus* (Say)	Balsam fir (IV)	43	—	—	—	B

*A: Of major importance, capable of killing or severely damaging trees.
B: Of moderate importance, capable of sporadic and localized injury to trees.
C: Of minor importance, not known to present a threat to trees.

PLATE 9

**Spruce false looper, *Syngrapha alias*
(Ottol.)**

A. White spruce twig showing nor-
   mal buds and young cones.
B. White spruce bud bored by the
   larva for food.
C. Pupa in normal position.
D. Adult at rest on a spruce twig.
E. Larva feeding in a bud.
F. Side view of the larva feeding on
   a needle.

CHAPTER II
Insects harmful to larch

The genus *Larix* is represented in Canada by three species: western larch (*L. occidentalis* Nutt.), alpine larch (*L. lyallii* Parl.), and tamarack (*L. laricina* (Du Roi) K. Koch), also known as American larch, or hackmatack.

Tamarack is the most common and is found in all provinces. It is the only native species in eastern Canada, and is generally found throughout the area. Its commercial range in the eastern provinces includes the southern half of Ontario and Quebec, New Brunswick, Nova Scotia, and Newfoundland. This species is commonly found in cool, damp places, where it is often mixed with black spruce; it also grows on better-drained ground mixed with trembling aspen and birch. Other larch species found are exotic and are used in plantations and as ornamentals in gardens and parks; of these the most common are European larch, Siberian larch, and Japanese larch.

In the forest inventory of Canada, the gross merchantable volume of larch is included in that for unspecified conifers, which is estimated to be about 363 million m^3 (Bonnor 1982). It is these other conifers besides larch that account for Newfoundland having 92.2 percent of this volume.

Tamarack is a slender tree reaching 15-18 m in height and 0.5 m in diameter. It has an attractive form; its deciduous foliage is light green, silky, delicate, and deciduous; its wood is hard, strong, and heavy; and its heartwood is very durable.

Tamarack is used widely as an ornamental tree because of its attractive appearance. The trunk is used in making pit-props, pilings, fence-posts, and poles, and for various purposes on farms. It was traditionally used as sawtimber and in making railway ties, but stands that supplied wood for these purposes were destroyed by larch sawfly attacks at the end of the 19th century. Thus, the species has lost much of its importance in the lumber industry.

Tamarack has relatively few enemies in the insect kingdom, but the most harmful of them may cause appreciable losses or even kill the tree. Defoliators take first place, and, in the past, some species caused tremendous damage to vast stretches of forest during outbreaks lasting several years.

Larch sawfly
Plate 10

The larch sawfly, *Pristiphora erichsonii* (Htg.), is rightly considered the worst pest of larch in North America. This insect is found in many countries in the northern hemisphere. It was described by Hartig in Europe in 1837, whereas in North America its presence was first mentioned in the United States in the state of Massachusetts in 1880 and in Canada, in the province of Quebec in 1882. It is still uncertain whether or not the insect is native to North America. Except for an irregular strip at the northern edge the larch sawfly now occurs over the whole tamarack range, from Quebec to the Northwest Territories and extending through the Yukon and the greater part of Alaska. It is also found throughout the entire range of western larch in Canada and a small part of its range in the United States.

This sawfly is specific to larch, and in Canada, its preferred host is tamarack.

History of outbreaks

Little information is available on early outbreaks of the larch sawfly; however, examination of growth rings of overmature larches, has shown a first reduction in growth rings between 1829 and 1845 (Daviault 1948b). The first recorded outbreak in Canada began about 1878 and was observed in Bury in the Eastern Townships of Quebec; it spread to Ontario, New Brunswick, and Nova Scotia during the next few years, and declined after having destroyed all stands of commercial-sized larch in eastern North America. A second outbreak occurred in eastern Canada from 1906 to 1916. Between 1924 and 1940, this sawfly drew attention every year by outbreaks in many eastern provinces.

The most prolonged and most serious wave of outbreaks began in 1938 in Manitoba and extended in two directions, reaching as far as the Atlantic Ocean in the east. These outbreaks raged in northwestern Ontario from 1948 to 1952 and in the central and eastern parts of that province from 1953 to 1958, and then gradually declined from that time on with a few pockets of severe infestation until 1965. Population increases were recorded in 1966 and 1967, followed by slight fluctuations until 1973, when populations again fell to low levels throughout the province. This series of outbreaks reached western Quebec in 1957 and spread throughout that province during the next ten years. In 1968, populations collapsed in all areas, reaching endemic levels the following year, at which they remained until 1974. The wave of outbreaks from the west reached the Maritimes in 1963 and caused damage in New Brunswick until 1968 and in Nova Scotia from 1968 to 1974.

In Newfoundland, outbreaks developed independently of those in other provinces. In 1942, dramatic population increases were recorded in two large areas, and populations remained high until 1949, when a general decline was reported. A new series of outbreaks began in 1953 in two main centres, with population fluctuations lasting until 1968, when they disappeared due to unfavourable weather conditions. A slight increase in populations was recorded in 1970 and 1971, but insect numbers returned to endemic levels the following year.

Description and biology

Adult. Female resembles a slender wasp with four transparent wings; antennae and body generally black in color with a very characteristic orange band crossing the abdomen. Length: 10 mm (Plate 10, B). Male identical to female except for its smaller size and its yellow antennae.

Egg. Translucid. Length: 1.5 mm (Plate 10, D and E).

Larva. Cream with brown head, becoming gray green with whitish ventral section and black head. Length at maturity: about 25 mm (Plate 10, G).

Pupa. Cocoon resembles large golden yellow bean, gradually turning black. Dimensions 2 by 10 mm (Plate 10, A).

The larch sawfly produces only one generation a year. Adults emerge over a period of about 3 months that is from June to the end of August. Males form only 2 percent of the population, and fertilization is unnecessary, because reproduction is parthenogenic. Females are thus ready to lay their eggs upon leaving the cocoon. They lay them singly but in rows in slits cut in the stems of new shoots (Plate 10, C). Each shoot may have 15-30 slits, depending on its length, and a female lays all of her 75-80 eggs in five or six shoots. Incubation lasts about 10 days.

Larvae from one set of eggs remain in colonies (Plate 10, F) for the first two-thirds of their life cycle, that is about 20-30 days, and they then scatter throughout the crown. There are five larval instars. In light outbreaks, defoliation is concentrated in certain parts of the crown (Plate 10, H), but the entire crown may be stripped in periods of severe infestation. Once the larvae finish feeding, they drop to the ground to spin individual cocoons either in the litter or in the ground. In the spring, they pupate and then emerge as adults. However, a small percentage of individuals remain in diapause and complete their development a year or more later.

PLATE 10

Larch sawfly, *Pristiphora erichsonii* (Htg.)

A. Appearance of healthy cocoon (length: 10 mm).
B. Adult on larch foliage (length: 10 mm).
C. New larch shoot curled into a question mark following wounds inflicted by adult during egg-laying.
D. Position and appearance of freshly laid eggs on a twig.
E. Appearance of twig after larval emergence.
F. Colony of young larvae on larch twig.
G. Mature larva (length: 25 mm).
H. Partially defoliated larch stand.
I. Old shoots curled and killed following egg-laying in previous years, and normal new shoots.

A

B

D

E

C

G

F

I

H

27

Damage and diagnosis

Initial damage by the larch sawfly is caused by the series of slits cut in new shoots by the female larch sawfly laying eggs. Shoots thus damaged dry and curl (Plate 10, C), causing interruption in the growth of twigs, reduction in bud formation, and, eventually, deformity of the crown.

The greatest damage, however, is done by the larvae feeding on needles. Light to moderate defoliation is of little consequence, but severe defoliation repeated over several consecutive years kills the tree. Studying experimental defoliation on young larch over a period of 4 consecutive years, Graham (1931) found that total defoliation inevitably caused tree mortality, but that trees experiencing only 75 percent defoliation showed little visible damage. However, larch being a deciduous tree, seems to tolerate defoliation more easily than other conifers that do not shed their foliage. In the Maritime provinces, Reeks (1954a) observed that larch may survive defoliation varying from moderate to severe over a period of 9 years.

One important consequence of defoliation is a decline in radial growth. The only information gathered on outbreaks in the early 19th century was based on decreases in radial increment. In studies carried out in Minnesota, Drooz (1960) observed reductions of up to 83 percent in annual radial growth.

Damage can be anticipated when adult larch sawflies resembling black wasps with an orange band are observed on foliage during the summer and especially in June and July. During the months of June, July, and August, the presence of egg scars on the current year's growth (Plate 10, E), or larval colonies on larch twigs, indicate that an outbreak is in progress. The number of new shoots that are curved in the shape of a question mark, serve to establish the intensity of the attack.

A past infestation is recognized by shoots that are curled, dried, and blackened. They can be seen all year round, even persisting for several years following an attack. The best information on the time, length, and intensity of a past outbreak can be obtained by examining the growth rings of living larch.

Examination and counting of cocoons of the larch sawfly in the ground under larch crowns also provides information on past or ongoing attacks.

Natural control

When the larch sawfly was discovered in North America, no natural enemies were known, but the presence of two species of native parasites, *Bessa harveyi* (Tns.) and *Tritneptis klugii* (Ratz.), was reported later (Turnock and Muldrew 1971). The paucity of native parasites led to the development of control programs involving the relocation of these two parasites and the introduction of parasites from outside. This was attempted first in 1910, resumed again in 1927, and has continued ever since without any major interruptions. An evaluation of these programs for the period up to 1959 can be summarized as follows: of the many parasites introduced from other continents, only *Mesoleius tenthredinis* Morley has been successful in areas of new introduction; the transfer of native or imported parasites, in areas where they already existed, was unsuccessful, as were attempts at importing parasite species from other hosts. At the present time in eastern Canada, besides the two native species, two imported insects, *Drino bohemica* Mesn. and *M. tenthredinis*, appear to be well established.

Besides entomophagous parasites, several pathogenic microorganisms were found to attack larch sawfly, but none of these deserves special mention. The rare attempts to use these microorganisms for controlling larch sawfly were unsuccessful. However, predators play a very important role in reducing populations, particularly shrews and voles that eat the insect in the cocoon. According to Buckner (1953), small insect-eating mammals, reduce populations at certain times, by as much as 90 percent, and they thus constitute a key factor in population dynamics when the numerical levels of these insects are relatively low. The introduction of a shrew, *Sorex cinereus cinereus* (Kerr.), to Newfoundland in an attempt to control the larch sawfly was a complete success, not only against the target species, but also against other insect species.

Many bird species feed on the larvae of the larch sawfly, but their role in reducing populations has not yet been clearly established (Buckner 1953).

Various climatic factors may, at times, also play an important role in reducing sawfly populations, but as yet, little is known about their action. Some interesting research on natural control factors has been carried out in Manitoba, and the results are contained in a number of publications by Muldrew and his associates.

Artificial control

Larvae of larch sawfly may easily be dislodged from small and medium-sized ornamental trees by shaking branches vigorously or by using a strong stream of water. Once on the ground, the larvae cannot easily return to the tree.

When ornamentals are too numerous or too large, adequate protection of foliage may be obtained by spraying the crowns with a water suspension of a stomach insecticide while the larvae are feeding in colonies; this treatment may have to be repeated several times, because of the extended egg-laying period. In areas where the use of chemical insecticides constitutes a danger to humans or domestic animals, a biological insecticide is recommended.

Treatment of forest trees does not appear justifiable, because larch is, at present, of negligible commercial importance.

References

Buckner 1953; Coppel and Leins 1955; Daviault 1948b, 1949b; Drooz 1956, 1960; Fletcher 1885; Graham 1931; Lejeune 1955; McGugan and Coppel 1962; Provancher 1886; Raizenne 1957; Reeks 1954a; Turnock and Muldrew 1971; and Webb and Drooz 1973.

Larch casebearer
Plate 11

The larch casebearer, *Coleophora laricella* (Hbn.), was probably introduced into North America on plants imported from Europe. It was first observed in the United States in Massachusetts in 1886, and in Canada in the province of Ontario in 1905. Its present distribution in eastern North America covers almost all the territory from latitudes 40° to 50° north and from the Atlantic Ocean to the province of Manitoba and the state of Minnesota. In the far western part of the continent, it is less evenly distributed and is confined to the northeastern part of Washington state, northern Idaho, northwestern Montana, and southern British Columbia.

This insect feeds exclusively on larch, either native or exotic, and in Canada is now considered the worst enemy of larch after the larch sawfly.

History of outbreaks

Through analysis of data collected annually by FIDS, Webb (1952) determined that outbreaks of the larch casebearer occur with a certain regularity and at intervals of about 8 years. The first recorded outbreaks were generally longer lasting and more severe than is the case now, no doubt because larch was more abundant and the insect had fewer natural enemies. Outbreaks normally begin in small areas and spread gradually over vast stretches of territory. Between outbreaks, the insect is easy to find, but causes only minor damage.

Description and biology

Adult. Tiny silver gray moth, with wings fringed with hairs of the same color. Wingspan: about 8 mm (Plate 11, G).
Egg. Brownish red, with 12 ridges extending from the base to the tip.
Larva. Elongated; head black, body brown red; normally hidden inside a cigar-shaped case. Length at maturity: about 5 mm.
Pupa. Enclosed in larval case.

Thorough studies have been conducted on the biology of the larch casebearer, both in Europe and in North America. Only one generation of larch casebearer occurs per year. The adult ordinarily appears during the last two weeks in June and lays its eggs on the underside of larch needles. Incubation takes about 10 days, and as soon as the newborn larva emerges, it bores a hole through the epidermis of a needle and hollows it out. The larva lives as a miner until September, by which time the first needle is often completely mined (Plate 11, B). After lining the inside of the hollowed part of the needle with silk, the larva cuts the needle off to make a sheath that it carries about during the rest of its development period; hence the name casebearer (Plate 11, C, D and E). It subsequently ties the fore-end of the case to another needle, into which it mines as far as it can reach. With the advent of cold weather in the fall, the larva fastens its case securely to a twig near the base of new buds, where it overwinters (Plate 11, F).

In the spring, once the needles have reached 3-6 mm in length, the larva begins feeding again by mining them. The hind part of its body is kept constantly hidden in the case, and only the head and legs can be seen. When the case becomes too small, the larva enlarges it or abandons it and makes another one. In May, the larva has completed its development and transforms to a pupa inside its case, which had been fastened to a needle or twig. The pupal stage lasts 2-3 weeks.

Damage and diagnosis

The most serious damage by the larch casebearer appears in the spring when mature larvae attack new needles and cause them to dry out. When most of the foliage is affected, the stand takes on a light brown color like that seen after a late frost (Plate 11, A). Light defoliation, on the other hand, often goes unnoticed and can only be detected by an experienced person. Following severe defoliation, most larch trees refoliate during the pupal period; thus, healthy trees manage to survive, even when outbreaks occur for several consecutive years. Radial growth is, however, reduced. When defoliation occurs repeatedly, foliage becomes less abundant, needles and terminal shoots are shorter, and some twigs may die.

Infested larch are easily recognized in the spring by partially discolored foliage and the presence on green needles of small cigar-shaped cases.

At the end of June or beginning of July, tiny silver grey moths fluttering around larch crowns are a warning of attacks in the fall and the following spring. This forecast is confirmed by September when, following leaf fall, small light brown, cigar-shaped cases 5 mm in height, can be seen moving slowly on needles or securely attached to twigs. When the narrow end of the case is squeezed between two fingers, a small yellow caterpillar emerges. In the fall, the ratio of cases to buds is a good indication of the intensity of the following summer's outbreak.

Natural control

The larch casebearer was introduced to North America without the natural enemies found in its country of origin. Many native parasites and predators have, however, become progressively adapted to this new prey. More than 50 species of native parasites were recovered from rearings carried out from many localities in eastern North America, but none of these appear able to maintain populations of the microlepidoptera at an endemic level (Webb and Denton 1973). Almost half of the species were found in Quebec; 10 in the Berthierville area (Daviault 1949c), 9 in the south-central part of the province (Bracken 1959), and 5 in other regions.

The rate of parasitism varies considerably between regions and between years, but it is never high enough. In an attempt to supplement the action of native parasites, a number of species were imported from Europe in the early 1930s and 1940s, and two of these, *Chrysocharis laricinellae* (Ratz.) and *Agathis pumila* (Ratz.) are now well established. Nevertheless parasitism is still insufficient to control this casebearer and efforts continue to introduce a new species, *Diadegma laricinellum* (Strobl).

Among predators, particular mention is made of a species of miridae usually responsible for destroying about 20 percent of the eggs. Predation by birds has been observed in winter and spring and may occasionally be quite extensive. Birds are said to have destroyed up to 75 percent of overwintering larvae in moderately infested areas of Michigan (Webb 1952).

A

C

D

B

E

F

G

PAGE
B/W

Other factors play an important role in fluctuations of casebearer populations. Observations carried out in Europe showed that these fluctuations are partly dependent on weather, site and foliage conditions at the time of adult emergence, mating, and egg-laying (Webb and Quednau 1971).In New Brunswick, a close relation has been established between epidemics and successive periods of below normal rainfall in May (Webb and Denton 1973). Repeated defoliation causes trees to gradually weaken, resulting in thinner and smaller needles, and the insect eventually starves.

Artificial control

Use of chemical insecticides to control the larch casebearer has never been found necessary in forests because of the low commercial value of larch, but it may be justified to protect valuable ornamental larch or those in plantations. A treatment can be made between the first warm weather in the spring and the time buds open, when larvae become active and move around freely while waiting for new foliage to appear. Affected trees should then be sprayed with a stomach insecticide.

Some degree of success may also be obtained by spraying foliage with a contact insecticide during the two feeding periods; in May to destroy the larvae of the generation completing its cycle, and in September to prevent newborn larvae of the next generation from becoming established.

References

Bracken 1959; Clark and Raske 1974; Daviault 1949c; Johnson and Lyon 1976; Quednau 1970; Webb 1952, 1957; Webb and Denton 1973; and Webb and Quednau 1971.

PLATE 11

Larch casebearer, *Coleophora laricella* (Hbn.)

A. Severely defoliated larch stand in early spring.
B. Cluster of mined needles showing entry holes.
C. First case as it appears in June.
D. Young larva moving about a larch twig with its case.
E. Larva moving with its case among larch needles (length; about 5 mm).
F. Cases fastened to twig after needle drop in the fall.
G. Adult at rest on needles (wingspan: 8 mm).

Larch needleworm
Plate 12

The larch needleworm, *Zeiraphera improbana* (Wlk.), that is found on larch in North America, was initially confused with the European species, *Zeiraphera diniana* Guen., but Mutuura and Freeman (1966) determined that it was a different species and called it *Z. improbana*. This insect occurs all across Canada and northern United States, and was first recorded in Canada in 1937. It has been found on three species of larch, four spruces, four firs, two pines, and one hemlock, but it is most harmful to tamarack and occasionally to black spruce.

History of outbreaks

The larch needleworm sometimes causes severe epidemics, but these are of short duration and are limited in area. A first outbreak of this type was reported on western larch in British Columbia in 1965; subsequently, outbreaks of this insect have been observed mainly on tamarack in eastern Canada. In 1970, an outbreak was reported in Ontario, and populations rose considerably in Newfoundland, covering the entire province the following year. In the same year, heavy defoliation of larch was reported on Anticosti Island in Quebec, and pockets of moderate to severe defoliation occurred throughout that 225-km long island during the following year. In 1975, infestations began to wane, and two years later they had disappeared. In 1975, small pockets of severe defoliation were discovered in two districts of Ontario and, in 1976 and 1977, four isolated pockets were detected in eastern Quebec.

Description and biology

Adult. Small brown moth. Wingspan: about 17 mm (Plate 12, B).
Egg. Chorion silver gray, transparent through which can be seen grayish green to orange yellow embryo. Length: 0.6 mm (Plate 12, C).
Larva. Yellow at first, then cream, finally turning to black and gray with dark head. Length: 10-12 mm (Plate 12, D and F).
Pupa. Conical, light brown. Length: 8 mm (Plate 12, G).

No major study has as yet been made of the larch needleworm. Only one generation of this microlepidoptera occurs per year. In eastern Canada, the moths appear from mid-June to mid-August, and may even be seen as late as September. Eggs are laid in clusters under the scales of cones where they overwinter. The larvae emerge very early in the spring and move about singly. The larva first attacks a cluster of young larch needles, on which it feeds for a short period. Later, it leaves this first feeding site to attack a cluster of longer needles, which it ties together with silk. Feeding is usually at its peak in June and the larva is full-grown by mid-July. Once the larva has completed five instars, it drops to the ground where it spins a cocoon in the litter and pupates.

Damage and diagnosis

The only damage by the larch needleworm results from defoliation by the feeding larvae. This has little effect except to reduce radial growth, because it occurs early enough in the season that even severely defoliated trees (Plate 12, A) can refoliate during the same season. During the outbreak on Anticosti Island, severely defoliated trees grew a second complement of foliage by August.

The presence of small larch needleworm larvae on larch foliage in May and June, indicates that an outbreak of this insect is underway.

In July, severe defoliation of larch and occasionally black spruce is a clear indication of an outbreak, and collection of moths can confirm this.

In August and September, the appearance on larch of lighter foliage and shorter needles than normal leads a trained observer to suspect the presence of the insect.

Natural control

Laboratory rearings of larvae collected in the field yielded some parasites of the larch needleworm; Raizenne (1952) obtained two ichneumonids from material collected in southern Ontario and Lindquist (1973) recovered a braconid, an ichneumonid, and three chalcids in the central part of that province.

According to Lindquist, the infestation in central Ontario had regressed by 1972 due to the action of parasites combined with a reduction in the quality of food resulting from the activity of two other major defoliators, the larch casebearer and the spruce budworm. Similar observations were made during the Anticosti Island outbreak, where larch sawfly was responsible for reducing the foliage.

Artificial control

Attempts to control the larch needleworm in forests have not been made due to the small size of larch stands and the relatively low commercial value of the wood. Control of this insect on valuable ornamentals is warranted, however. Good protection is afforded by spraying infested crowns with a stomach or contact insecticide when buds are bursting.

References

Bradley 1974; Lindquist 1973; Mutuura and Freeman 1966; Prentice 1965; and Raizenne 1952.

PLATE 12

Larch needleworm, *Zeiraphera improbana* **(Wlk.)**

A. Severely defoliated larch stand.
B. Adult at rest (wingspan: 17 mm).
C. Egg cluster under scales of a larch cone.
D. Larva surrounded by debris on foliage (length: 10-12 mm).
E. Aerial view of a severely defoliated stand.
F. Larva in the prepupal stage on the foliage.
G. Newly formed pupa on foliage (length: 8 mm).

33

A

B

C

D

E

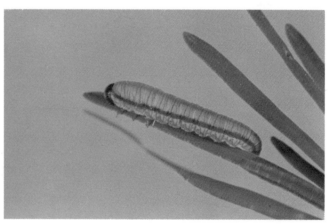

F

G

Other larch sawflies
Plate 13

Two other species of sawflies specific to larch are mentioned here because they are often found along with the most important insect pest of this tree, the notorious larch sawfly, *Pristiphora erichsonii* (Htg.). Their presence on other conifers is always accidental. These two species were formerly known as *Anoplonyx laricis* Merl. Studies by Wong (1955) established that there are five species of this genus in Canada and that only two of them are found in the East, the threelined larch sawfly, *A. luteipes* (Cress.), and the onelined larch sawfly, *A. canadensis* Hgtn. In Canada, the threelined larch sawfly occurs from the Atlantic to Alberta, whereas the onelined larch sawfly is found no farther west than Saskatchewan. Of the two species, the threelined larch sawfly is by far the most common, but populations normally remain at a relatively low level and thus no serious damage occurs. Occasionally, however, its population reaches levels high enough to cause light to moderate defoliation generally for a short duration.

PLATE 13

Threelined larch sawfly, *Anoplonyx luteipes* Cress., and onelined larch sawfly, *A. canadensis* Hgtn.

A. *A. luteipes* adult (length: about 5 mm).
B. *A. luteipes*, male and female cocoons (lengths: 6.0 and 8.0 mm).
C. *A. canadensis*, adult (length: about 5 mm).
D. Young *A. luteipes* larva, showing the three body lateral lines and brown color of head.
E. Older *A. luteipes* larva.
F. *A. canadensis* on larch foliage, showing single body lateral line and darker head color.
G. Older *A. canadensis* larva.

History of outbreaks

Damage of this type, was observed in Quebec in 1939 and 1940, in 1949 and 1950, and in 1975. Similar occurrences were reported in Ontario in 1940 and 1941, and in Newfoundland in 1971 and 1972.

Description and biology

Adult. Resembles a black, four-winged wasp. Length: about 5 mm (Plate 13 A and C).
Egg. Oval in shape; yellowish white. Length: about 0.9 mm.
Larva. Light green with lines running along each side of the body; three in the case of the threelined larch sawfly (Plate 13 D and E), and only one in the case of the onelined larch sawfly (Plate 13 F and G). Length: 8-15 mm.
Pupa. Cocoon oval in shape; doubledwalled, with the outer wall being covered with particles of soil, leaf debris, or dead litter. Length: 6-8 mm (Plate 13, B).

Little is known about the biology of the larch sawflies and the only published data are those collected by Wong (1955) in Manitoba. In that province, adults of the threelined larch sawfly can be seen on trees in May and larvae are visible from the end of June to the end of August. Adults of the onelined larch sawfly appear slightly later, that is at the end of May, with larvae visible from the end of August to the end of September. In Quebec, in 1959, larvae of both species were present simultaneously for at least 2 months.

The eggs are laid in larch needles, usually one and occasionally up to three per needle. The larvae are solitary. They feed at first on the sides of needles leaving a central spine, but, as they grow, they devour the needles completely. Larvae at rest have a very characteristic appearance, completely stretched out and flattened right against the needle. Pupation occurs in cocoons on the ground.

Damage and diagnosis

The only damage caused by these larch sawflies is defoliation generally ranging from trace to light, and, in exceptional cases, to moderate. The maximum damage observed in Quebec was the complete stripping of a few crowns.

During the summer months, infested trees can be recognized by the presence of solitary, light green larvae up to 15 mm long on larches that normally show little defoliation. In the fall, small cocoons may be found in the litter at the base of defoliated trees.

Natural control

To date, eight species of entomophagous parasites of the larch sawflies have been reported from rearings carried out in Ontario (Raizenne 1957), and five microorganisms have been observed in Quebec (Smirnoff and Juneau 1973). The role played by these organisms has not yet been determined.

Artificial control

Control by artificial methods is not necessary for forest trees, because damage caused by these larch sawflies is limited. Special treatment may be required for seriously defoliated ornamentals. In such cases, any stomach insecticide applied in suspension in water to infested trees while the larvae are active will give satisfactory results.

References

Bracken 1960, 1961; Raizenne 1957; Smirnoff and Juneau 1973; and Wong 1951, 1955.

Chainspotted geometer
Plate 14

The chainspotted geometer, *Cingilia catenaria* (Drury), is an insect native to Canada, and was identified as far back as 1770. This polyphagous insect is quite common in eastern North America, where it has been collected on 45 species of plants, both herbaceous and woody. However, it is mainly active in swampy areas where it attacks blackberries, blueberries, and cranberries. From time to time, it becomes excessively abundant and when foliage on these small fruit-bearing plants becomes scarce, it attacks any tree species in the vicinity, and particularly larch. The trees listed as hosts in Canada are white spruce, black spruce, fir, larch, jack pine, alder, trembling aspen, and willow.

This looper occurs mainly in northern regions. Outbreaks have however been reported in several New England states and as far west as Minnesota. In Canada, its range extends from the Atlantic provinces to Manitoba, where the insect is considered rare, although it occasionally becomes abundant on low plants.

History of outbreaks

The first infestation of chainspotted geometer in eastern Canada was reported in Nova Scotia in 1939. In that year, all the trees and blueberry bushes at Joran Falls were severely defoliated and larches at Clyde River, as well as various tree species in Annapolis County, were attacked. The second outbreak took place in Quebec from 1973 to 1975 in a peat bog covering 50 km² at Rivière Ouelle in Kamouraska County, where many woody species were completely defoliated. The insect was observed during the same period in swamps in neighbouring counties and as far as Lotbinière.

Description and biology

Adult. Medium-sized pale gray moth; with fore and hind wings crossed by three characteristic irregular lines made up of black dots.
Maximum wingspan: 35 mm (Plate 14, E and F).

Egg. Elliptical; greenish yellow initially, turning lilac-colored at an early stage and becoming darker as it develops. Diameters: 0.7 and 1.8 mm.

Larva. Slender, cylindrical; yellow, bearing two black spots above spiracles. Length: 45 mm (Plate 14, A and D).

Pupa. White with black spots. Length: 20 mm (Plate 14, B and C).

The biology of the chainspotted geometer was studied in Maine by Phipps (1928) and in Quebec by Daviault (1937). Only one generation occurs per year. Adults are diurnal and may be seen from the end of July until late fall, sometimes in numbers large enough to give the impression of a snowstorm (Webster 1892). Eggs are laid on twigs and fall easily to the ground where they overwinter. The first larvae appear in early summer and are visible until fall. When a larva is disturbed, it stands up on its two abdominal prolegs, and holds itself stiffly at an angle to the plant stem, and appears to look like a twig. The larva feeds on foliage and goes through five instars; when fully grown, it builds a pupal cocoon woven in a loose net of yellow silk and attached to leaves. Pupation lasts 3-4 weeks, at the end of which time the moth appears.

Damage and diagnosis

All damage is caused by the feeding larvae, which consume the foliage. Outbreaks of the chainspotted geometer begin on low plants in swamps and on low ground (Plate 14, G) and, when food becomes scarce, the larvae migrate in close ranks, advancing like armyworms toward higher ground and devouring everything in their path (Plate 14, H). Fortunately, damage to forest trees is usually light, because infestations are generally of short duration.

During the growing season, severe defoliation of all plant species in a swampy area indicates of the presence of this looper, and this may be confirmed by looking for yellow larvae. In the fall, the presence of numbers of pale grey moths with three dotted lines crossing their wings is a sign of an on-going, or imminent, outbreak. In such cases, it is recommended that emergence of adults be monitored and that the ground surface be examined to see if eggs are present.

Natural control

Several species of insect parasites and entomophagous predators are mentioned in the literature, but no details are given about their role in reducing populations of the chainspotted geometer. Birds are also of some importance as predators. Phipps (1928) observed the sudden disappearance of populations of the chainspotted geometer during an outbreak in Maine and he attributed this phenomenom to the action of parasites and of a disease of undetermined origin. During the 1973 outbreak in Quebec, the presence of a nuclear polyhedrosis caused by *Baculovirus catenaria* (Smirnoff 1973) was reported in the two main centers of infestation, and this organism was most likely responsible for the sudden drop in populations.

Artificial control

Constant vigilance is probably the best measure to adopt against the chainspotted geometer, and prompt action should be taken at the first sign of an outbreak. Experience in Maine showed that an infestation can be stopped by spraying with a stomach insecticide at the proper time. When it comes to protecting a crop of small edible fruits, a biological insecticide such as *Bacillus thuringiensis* Berl. would probably produce equally satisfactory results with no danger to the consumer.

The most effective method, however, would be to spray larvae with a suspension of the virus at the first signs of an outbreak, thus allowing the development of the polyhedrosis. Besides destroying the active population, this treatment would ensure the spread of the disease to later populations, because the virus can survive for a certain length of time in the environment.

References

Britton 1924; Daviault 1937; Phipps 1928, 1930; Smirnoff 1973; and Webster 1892.

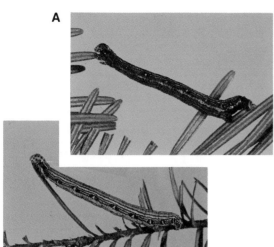

A

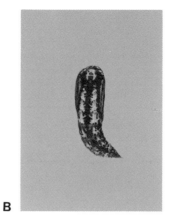

B

C

D

E

G

F

H

PLATE 14

Chainspotted geometer, *Cingilia catenaria* (Drury)

A. Dark larva on fir needles (length: 45 mm).
B. Dorsal view of a dark pupa (length: 20 mm).
C. Ventral and dorsal views of a pale pupa.
D. Pale larva on fir needles.
E. Adult male (wingspan: 35 mm).
F. Adult female.
G. Larval damage to lower plants in swampy area.
H. Typical defoliation on alder branch.

Table 2. Other insects harmful to larch — Other insects that are regarded as pests of larch are listed in this table. For some insects, their characteristics are described in the chapter that applies to their primary host, and in such cases, that chapter (in Roman numerals) and the appropriate plate numbers are given. For other insects, a plate number alone is shown; and for the remaining insects, this table provides the only information.

Common and scientific names	Hosts (chap.)	Plate no.	Type of insect	Destructive stages	Period of activity	Importance*
Black larch aphid *Cinara laricifex* (Fitch)	Larch	—	Sucker	Adult and nymph	May to Sept.	C
Eastern larch beetle *Dendroctonus simplex* Lec.	Larch	15	Borer	Adult and larva	May to Oct.	C
Hairskirted caterpillar *Tolype laricis* (Fitch)	White spruce, balsam fir, larch	—	Defoliator	Larva	June to Sept.	C
Larch looper *Semiothisa sexmaculata* (Pack.)	Larch	—	Defoliator	Larva	June to Oct.	C
Larch shoot moth *Argyresthia laricella* Kft.	Larch	—	Borer	Larva	May, June, Sept. and Oct.	B
Large spruce weevil *Hylobius piceus* (DeG.)	Spruce (I)	8	—	—	—	B
Pale spruce gall adelgid *Adelges laricis* Vallot	Black spruce, larch	—	Sucker	Adult and nymph	May to Sept.	C
Ragged spruce gall adelgid *Pineus similis* (Gill.)	Spruce, pine, larch	22	Sucker	Adult and nymph	May to Oct.	C
Redheaded pine sawfly *Neodiprion lecontei* (Fitch)	Pine (III)	17	—	—	—	A
Spruce budworm *Choristoneura fumiferana* (Clem.)	Balsam fir (IV)	36	—	—	—	A
Spruce gall adelgid *Adelges lariciatus* (Patch)	Larch, spruce	6	Sucker	Adult and nymph	May to Aug.	C
Spruce spider mite *Oligonychus ununguis* (Jac.)	Spruce (I)	—	—	—	—	B
Whitespotted sawyer *Monochamus scutellatus* (Say)	Balsam fir (IV)	43	—	—	—	A

*A: Of major importance, capable of killing or severely damaging trees.
 B: Of moderate importance, capable of sporadic and localized injury to trees.
 C: Of minor importance, not known to present a threat to trees.

B

A

C

D

E

G

F

H

PLATE 15

Eastern larch beetle, *Dendroctonus simplex* **Lec.**

A. Stand of larch severely damaged.
B. Larch trunks partially barked after a severe attack.
C. Adults in their tunnel.
D. Eggs in the adult tunnel.
E. Larval tunnels at the wood surface.
F. Mature larva in its tunnel.
G. Nymph in its case.
H. Adult exit hole at the wood surface.

CHAPTER III
Insects harmful to pine

Of the 35 species of the genus *Pinus* native to North America, only 9 are part of the Canadian flora. Of this number, four occur naturally in eastern Canada: eastern white pine (*P. strobus* L.), red pine (*P. resinosa* Ait.), jack pine (*P. banksiana* Lamb.), and pitch pine (*P. rigida* Mill.). The first three species are fairly common, except in Newfoundland, where red pine is not abundant and jack pine is absent. The fourth species, pitch pine, is not familiar to Canadians in general because it grows only in two limited areas, in southern Ontario and in southern Quebec.

Other pines found in eastern Canada are exotics, the most common being Scots pine (*P. sylvestris* L.), which is used mainly in reforestation, and Austrian pine (*P. nigra* Arnold) and Mugho pine (*P. mugo* Turra var. *mughus* Zenari), both of which are ornamentals.

When the first settlers came to Canada, vast areas of the eastern provinces were covered with forests of eastern white pine and red pine of great commercial value. Such forests are now rare because of over-cutting to satisfy market demands and of the difficulty of promoting natural regeneration in spite of many attempts at reforestation. Nowadays, extensive stands of jack pine exist, but this species is not much in demand by the forest industry. The gross merchantable volume of pine in the eastern provinces has been estimated at 811 million m^3 (Bonnor 1982). The province of Ontario ranks first with 68.1 percent of the total volume and it is followed by Quebec with 27.8 percent. The economic importance of eastern white pine, red pine, and jack pine is considerable.

Pines in general are not very exacting and grow in soils that are relatively poor, dry, and not particularly fertile; but they do not reproduce easily. The order of tolerance to competition of the four species is as follows: eastern white pine, red pine, jack pine, and pitch pine, whereas the order with respect to their adaptability to soil dryness is reversed.

The eastern white pine is the most beautiful and most majestic of the eastern pines; it grows to an average height of 25 m and diameter of 80 cm, and may be found in pure stands or mixed with red pine, spruce, or fir. Its wood is light, soft, and resistant except when in contact with the ground; it is particularly valued for finish lumber, for frames and sashes, and in pattern-making.

Red pine is another very beautiful conifer, second to the eastern white pine with respect to size; it grows to an average height of 21 m and diameter of 50 cm. It is found in pure stands or mixed with other species of pines or other conifers. The wood is heavier and harder than that of eastern white pine and it is quite strong; it is often used for the same purposes as eastern white pine as well as for structural timber, pulp wood, and for reforestation.

Jack pine is less elegant and does not grow to the same size as eastern white or red pine; its average height is 15 m and its diameter, 25 cm. It is mainly found in pure stands. The wood is heavy and fairly hard, but is not very strong; it is used in light to medium construction, as pulp wood, and for poles and railway ties.

Pitch pine is the smallest of the pines in eastern Canada, averaging 9 m in height and 25 cm in diameter. It normally grows in the open in pure stands or mixed with various hardwoods. The wood is heavy and relatively hard, but is of little value except in construction and as pulp.

Pines have many natural enemies, the most numerous of which are insects. Insects may attack all parts of the tree, from the tip to the root. Of the many types of insects that attack pines, the great majority are phyllophagous. In view of the high commercial value of the tree species they attack, with the exception of pitch pine, all these insects have a certain importance.

Swaine jack pine sawfly
Plate 16

The Swaine jack pine sawfly, *Neodiprion swainei* Midd., is a gregarious defoliator native to Canada. It is recognized as one of the major pests of jack pine, but until 20 years ago, it received little attention because jack pine was not at that time considered valuable to the pulpwood industry. This sawfly occurs throughout the entire range of jack pine except in its northern extension, where the insect is limited by low temperatures. Jack pine is practically its only host; however, it occasionally attacks other pines such as red pine and Scots pine where they grow mixed with jack pine.

History of outbreaks

The Swaine jack pine sawfly has been collected regularly every year in Canada since 1936 and has acquired a bad reputation following the destruction of vast stands of jack pine, mainly in Quebec and some in Ontario. As early as 1938, Atwood reported that, during the preceding 10 years, various sawflies, particularly the Swaine jack pine sawfly, had destroyed great stretches of jack pine in eastern Canada. In 1941, Lambert reported that this sawfly occurred in Quebec from the Ontario border as far east as Saguenay County, and, in 1946, that part of the jack pine stands in the upper St. Maurice valley had succumbed. Serious outbreaks have been reported every year since then, and more specifically in nine main centers of western and central Quebec (McLeod 1970). Between 1960 and 1970, this pest constituted a major problem to forestry in Quebec. In Ontario, outbreaks were concentrated in two main areas, Gogama and Temagami. Elsewhere in Canada and United States, no serious outbreaks have been reported to date.

Description and biology

Adult. Resembles a medium-sized wasp; body more or less dark brown. Length: 6-8 mm (Plate 16, A).

Egg. Oval in shape; whitish (Plate 16, C and D).

Larva. Elongated, cylindrical; head color varying from reddish brown to brownish black; body yellowish green with two longitudinal dark stripes on the back ending with a black spot. Length at maturity: 25 mm (Plate 16, B).

Pupa. Cocoon cylindrical in shape, with rounded ends; golden brown. Length: about 6 mm.

Several studies on the biology of the Swaine jack pine sawfly, begun in 1955 in Quebec by Tripp and his colleagues, have been published (Tripp 1962, 1965; Price and Tripp 1972).

This insect usually produces one generation a year. Adults emerge in June or July and, shortly after, the females lay their eggs close to the sheaths of new jack pine needles, one to each needle. This is done while the two needles are still attached together, so that each pair of needles involved contains one pair of eggs face to face; this explains why some authors have called this insect the twin-egg sawfly. A female normally lays all her eggs on one shoot. The egg is fully developed within 3 to 4 weeks. On hatching, the larvae head for old needles, where they gather into colonies of 10 to 60 (Plate 16, F) and immediately begin eating the foliage, with two or three larvae per needle (Plate 16, E). Initially, the young larvae feed only on the edge of the needle and leave a central spine, but once they reach a certain size, they devour the needles completely. New foliage is attacked only after the old needles have been entirely consumed. The development of the larva includes from four to seven instars and ends in August or September depending on weather conditions. When fully grown, the larva drops to the ground where, in the litter, it spins a cocoon in which it overwinters (Plate 16, G). Pupation takes place the following spring, except for a small proportion of individuals who remain dormant for a longer period.

Damage and diagnosis

Damage by the Swaine jack pine sawfly is caused only by larvae during their feeding period (Plate 16, I and J). When old foliage only is attacked, there is little reduction in tree growth and no tree mortality is observed. On the other hand, when old foliage is totally stripped and new foliage is also destroyed, the trees will inevitably die (Plate 16, H). Within a stand, trees usually begin to die in the year following their total defoliation, and may continue for 5 years.

An outbreak of the Swaine jack pine sawfly can be recognized by various signs that become more numerous in the foliage as the season advances:

- June until the following year: the main signs of an infestation are twin egg slits on new needles that contain sound or hatched eggs; the number of egg colonies determines the intensity of the outbreak;
- June and July: needles with serrated edges indicate that young larvae are feeding;
- August until spring: the presence of sheaths with needles missing is a sign that older larvae are present; and
- September until spring: the absence of old foliage on part or all of the crown is a sign that a severe attack has lasted for 1 year or more. The presence of sound cocoons at the base of infested trees indicates that an outbreak is in progress, whereas empty cocoons indicate a past outbreak.

Natural control

The Swaine jack pine sawfly has many natural enemies. Twenty-three parasitic species, attacking eggs, larvae, and cocoons have been recovered in Quebec; four of these were introduced in Canada about 1940 for the control of other forest pests. The most important parasite, *Spathimeigenia spinigera* (Tns.), is a native diptera that attacks the larva. In 1962, the rate of parasitism by this species and others from the ichneumonid group was estimated at 27.9 percent (Tripp 1962). Ten years later Price and Tripp (1972) determined that cocoon parasites reduced the host population by 66 percent, whereas insect predators destroyed only 10 percent.

C

D

H

I

J

A

B

E

F

G

PLATE 16

Swaine jack pine sawfly, *Neodiprion swainei* Midd.

A. Lateral view of adult female (length: 6-8 mm).
B. Lateral view of mature larva (length: 25 mm).
C. and D. Egg scars on jack pine needles; close-up of scar.
E. Three larvae feeding on one jack pine needle.
F. Colony of young larvae on jack pine shoot.
G. New cocoons (length: 6 mm).
H. Mature jack pine forest destroyed after a severe attack.
I. Section of a young jack pine severely defoliated.
J. Aerial view of a severely damaged jack pine forest.

43

Tostowaryk (1972) found that 30 species of Elateridae feed on this sawfly, but play only a minor role because of the abundance of other food. This author did, however, determine that five species of ground beetles can significantly affect the populations of this sawfly. In a study on the underground activity of small mammals, results of which have not yet been published, McLeod determined the relative importance of eight entomophagous species in destroying the contents of cocoons.

A weak virus, observed for the first time in Ontario in 1953, appeared again 3 years later at Lake Gagnon in the St. Maurice valley of Quebec. A more virulent strain was subsequently developed through experiments carried out in the laboratory and in the field, and was used with some success in Quebec (Smirnoff 1961).

Climate also plays an important role in regulating populations of this pest. Low temperatures prevent it from surviving in the northern part of the jack pine range. It has been observed repeatedly that, under natural conditions, a significant reduction in population occurs when larval development is delayed by cool summer temperatures. In such cases, development is completed at low temperatures in the fall.

Unfortunately, the combined action of all these factors is not always sufficient to check outbreaks of this species, and direct methods of control must then be used.

Artificial control

In seeking long-term results against the Swaine jack pine sawfly, foreign parasites and predators could be introduced to reinforce the action of existing natural enemies.

To protect young, isolated trees, it is recommended that shoots bearing eggs be cut off before the larvae hatch, or else that larvae be dislodged by shaking the tree vigorously.

In the case of local infestations, one remedy might be to use the virulent strain of virus developed in Quebec, but, because this virus gradually loses its strength once applied to trees, the operation would have to be repeated. The application of chemical, stomach, and contact insecticides is also a practical, fast, and effective way to end outbreaks, even when they are fairly widespread. In fact in 1965 and 1967, aerial sprayings with a chemical insecticide were carried out in Quebec, and populations of this insect were almost totally destroyed, mortality reaching 99 percent.

References

Daviault 1946b; Lambert 1941b; McLeod 1970; Price and Tripp 1972; Smirnoff 1961; Tostowaryk 1972; and Tripp 1962, 1965.

Redheaded pine sawfly
Plate 17

The redheaded pine sawfly, *Neodiprion lecontei* (Fitch), is one of the most serious pests of young pines in eastern Canada and United States. This native North American species has been known since 1858, although it only began to attract the attention of foresters around 1920. It is found in the provinces of Quebec and Ontario and in the eastern half of the United States; reports of its presence in the Maritime provinces have not been confirmed. All native and exotic hard pines are attacked. If food is scarce, this sawfly may also feed on the foliage of soft pines, Norway spruce, and larch, but the last two tree species are never used for egg-laying. Preferred hosts in Canada are red pine, jack pine, and Scots pine. The insect prefers trees lower than 3 m high in plantations or natural stands, but it occasionally infests mature stands.

PLATE 17

Redheaded pine sawfly, *Neodiprion lecontei* (Fitch)
A. Plantation of young red pines killed by the insect.
B. Dorsal view of female.
C. Adults mating (lengths: male, 5-6.5 mm; female, 6-9.5 mm).
D. Arrangement of eggs on pine needles.
E. Young larva feeding on red pine needle.
F. Larval colony on Scots pine shoot.
G. Mature larva (length: 20 mm).
H. Female and male cocoons (lengths: 10.3 and 7.5 mm).

A

B

F

C

E

D

G

H

History of outbreaks

The redheaded pine sawfly is collected every year in Canada and its populations reach epidemic proportions at fairly short intervals, and for a 3- or 4-year duration. In Ontario, it was considered a serious pest in pine plantations in 1937, and was very abundant from 1958 to 1960, from 1964 to 1967, and from 1974 on. In Quebec, outbreaks were recorded in 1940 and 1941, in 1949 and 1950, from 1962 to 1967, and from 1974 to 1978.

Description and biology

Adult. Wasp-like; male completely black with feathery antennae, female with head and first two thoracic segments brownish red. Lengths: male 5-6 mm, female 6-9.5 mm (Plate 17, B and C).

Egg. Oval in shape; translucid white. Dimensions: 0.25 by 0.5 mm.

Larva. Elongated and cylindrical in shape; newly hatched larva with dark brown head and basically white body; older larva with dark orange head and light yellow body with six rows of black spots. Length when full grown: 20 mm (Plate 17, E and G).

Pupa. Cocoon cylindrical and rounded at both ends; red brown; papery. Dimensions: male, 3.6 by 7.5 mm, female, 4.6 by 10.3 mm (Plate 17, H).

The biology of the redheaded sawfly was studied in Quebec by Daviault (1951a) and by Benjamin (1955) in the Great Lakes area of the United States.

The number of generations per year varies with latitude: one generation occurs in Canada and in northeastern United States, but there may be four or even five generations in the southern part of the United States. In Canada, most adults appear in June, although latecomers emerge until August. Shortly after emergence, females lay their eggs in shoe-shaped niches cut in needles with their ovipositor; each female lays from 100 to 140 eggs and up to 35 per needle (Plate 17, D). The eggs hatch within 4 to 5 weeks so that a great variety of larval age groups may be present throughout the summer. Larvae live in compact colonies (Plate 17, F), preferably on old needles; however, when old needles become scarce, they also attack new foliage and even the bark of young twigs. The young larvae eat only the edges of the needles, leaving a central spine which in time turns yellow. Larvae go through five instars and, from the third instar on, they devour the entire needle. Thus, a twig bearing a larval colony is rapidly defoliated, and the larvae move to another branch that is in turn defoliated. This continues from tree to tree. Any time from July to September, once they have finished feeding, the larvae fall to the ground where they spin cocoons in which they overwinter. Pupation normally occurs the following spring, but a small proportion of the population remains dormant in the ground, and the adults may emerge up to several years later.

Damage and diagnosis

Damage caused by larvae of the redheaded pine sawfly feeding on foliage and occasionally on the tender bark of young twigs can have serious consequences. Even a slight defoliation considerably reduces the aesthetic value of ornamental pines and spoils specimens intended for the Christmas tree market. Moderate to severe defoliation results in reduced growth, and those trees completely defoliated eventually die (Plate 17, A). Beal (1942) found that certain open-grown pines in United States could tolerate up to 75 percent defoliation, whereas in shaded areas other pines died after a 50 percent reduction in foliage. In Canada, however, open-grown trees are those most affected (Wilson and Reeks 1973).

The risk of a severe outbreak by the redheaded pine sawfly reduces the use of hard pines for reforestation.

Signs of an outbreak by this species on young hard pines differ with the seasons, and may be classified as follows:

- June to August: the presence of either eggs in needles or of old serrated and reddish foliage is an indication either of an imminent outbreak or the presence of young larval colonies;
- Summer and fall: larval colonies present in plantations and occasionally in natural stands indicate that an infestation is developing, whereas severe defoliation of the old foliage signifies damage by old larvae; and
- Fall: the presence of young, dead hard pines next to other pines with normal crowns is the sign of a declining infestation; the presence of sound and empty reddish brown cocoons in the litter at the base of young pines is a sure indication that an outbreak is underway and will continue through the following year.

Natural control

Fifty-eight species of parasites and predators have been identified as enemies of the redheaded pine sawfly on the North American continent. The most important are an egg parasite, *Closterocerus cinctipennis* Ashm., and two larval parasites, *Spathimeigenia spinigera* (Tns.) and *Neophorocera hamata* A. & W. (MacAloney 1957). In Canada, Daviault (1951a) recovered 24 species of parasites through rearings in Quebec, whereas in Ontario, Raizenne (1957) reported 12, of which 7 had already been obtained in Quebec. A Canadian effort to strengthen the parasite complex against this species led to the importation of nine new species (McGugan and Coppel 1962). Daviault also observed predation by two species of Hemiptera and by ants on larval populations; MacAloney (1957) reported extensive predation by small mammals on populations of larvae and prepupae in cocoons in the litter.

Entomopathogenic microorganisms also play an important role in the control of this sawfly, and according to MacAloney (1957), they are a major element in the decline of its populations. The action of a disease was recorded in Quebec as early as 1937 (Daviault 1951a). Experimental testing carried out with a virus in Quebec and Ontario in 1970 showed encouraging results, and subsequent aerial applications of this virus in Ontario were successful.

Climatic factors also play an important role in the control of populations of this sawfly. According to MacAloney (1957), prolonged periods of high temperatures in summer, as well as cold waves or wet snowstorms in the fall significantly reduce larval populations. Bird (1971b) stated that rapid population declines are usually associated with high temperatures coupled with dry periods.

Artificial control

Serious damage by the redheaded pine sawfly may be prevented by simple silvicultural measures consisting in a judicious choice of plantation sites and the careful maintenance of young trees. Isolated trees may be protected by shaking them to dislodge larvae, or by hand picking and destroying the larvae. When infested trees are numerous, foliage should be treated with a stomach insecticide during the larval feeding stage. If large areas are involved, it may be preferable to apply the insecticides by aircraft.

Also recommended is a method of control that has been used successfully in Ontario and Quebec in which affected plantations are treated with a suspension of a virus to promote the development of a disease in the larval population (Bird 1971b).

References

Beal 1942; Benjamin 1955; Bird 1971b; Daviault 1951a; MacAloney 1957; McGugan and Coppel 1962; Middleton 1921; Raizenne 1957; and Wilson and Reeks 1973.

Jack pine budworm
Plate 18

The jack pine budworm, *Choristoneura pinus pinus* Free., is, from a systematic viewpoint, so close a relative of the spruce budworm, *Choristoneura fumiferana*, that the two species were long believed to be one and the same; they were only recognized as distinct species in 1953. The jack pine budworm is a solitary defoliator native to North America whose range coincides almost exactly with that of its preferred host, jack pine. In Canada, it is found from New Brunswick to British Columbia, and to date has caused most damage in Ontario, Manitoba, and Saskatchewan.

History of outbreaks

In Quebec, since 1969, local outbreaks of the jack pine budworm have been reported for short durations. Elsewhere in eastern Canada, only small numbers of the insect have been reported, but the insect has been collected on 10 species of conifer. Very common on jack pine and Scots pine, it is fairly rare on other pines and is found occasionally on fir and larch where these are associated with jack pine. This budworm is of concern to foresters because of the damage it causes to natural stands of jack pine and to plantations of Scots pine both in central Canada and around the Great Lakes in the United States.

Description and biology

Studies on the biology of the jack pine budworm have been carried out mainly in the United States. This budworm closely resembles the spruce budworm, not only in its external morphology but also by its life cycle and behavior. The two species are not easily distinguished, and should be positively identified by a specialist. There are, however, characteristics distinctive of the growth stages of both insects that may guide foresters wishing to make a preliminary identification in the field. They are summarized in the following descriptions based on Campbell (1953) and Freeman (1953).

In eastern Canada, the jack pine budworm is univoltine and development occurs about 2 weeks later than that of the spruce budworm. Eggs are deposited in July and August on needles in the upper crowns of host trees. They are laid in clusters in which two rows overlap like shingles on a roof (Plate 18, A). Incubation lasts about 10 days; after hatching, the young larva does not feed, but crawls to a crevice in the bark of the host and spins a silken web as a measure of protection for the winter. At the beginning of the following June, the larva leaves its winter shelter in search of food. Prior to the appearance of new foliage, which is its preferred food, the young larva may feed on cones, staminate flowers, bark of twigs, or old needles (Plate 18, B). The greater part of the larval development takes place inside a shelter made of needles from a few adjacent twigs and

Stage	Characteristics	Jack pine budworm	Spruce budworm
Adult	Basic color	tawny brown, never gray	generally gray
	Wingspan	15-24 mm	21-30 mm
Egg	Number of rows per cluster	always 2	2-4
	Average number per cluster	37	19
	Preferred host	jack pine	balsam fir and white spruce
Pupa	Color of abdominal segments	dark gray or dark brown	yellow to reddish brown

loosely tied with a web. The needles are not entirely consumed, and the uneaten parts remain attached in the web along with larval excreta. This waste gradually takes on a reddish brown tinge that finally becomes the dominant color of the infested stands.

Pupae form mainly in July, and the pupal stage lasts about 10 days (Plate 18, C). The latest larvae complete their development in August. Moths are present on trees from July until September (Plate 18, D).

Damage and diagnosis

Larvae of the jack pine budworm are responsible for all the damage that is visible mainly in the upper crowns of dominant and codominant trees (Plate 18 E and F). Occasionally, following repeated severe attacks, entire trees die, but most often only the upper half of the crown is destroyed. A reduction in tree increment may also occur during the years following a severe outbreak, and recovery of the tree usually takes many years.

Infestation by the jack pine budworm can be recognized at several stages:

● June to August: presence on jack pine of larvae, abnormal elongation of new twigs, and defoliation of new shoots;
● August to September: presence of egg clusters particularly on jack pine needles; the eggs are green before larval hatching and silk white thereafter; the number of egg clusters indicate the intensity of the outbreak for the coming year; and
● Fall and winter: current year foliage of the dominant and codominant jack pines affected, is reddish brown in color.

Natural control

Several species of parasites attack the jack pine budworm at all stages of its development. Sixteen species have been reported in Canada (Bradley 1974; Walley 1953) and 26 in the United States (Allen et al. 1969; Kulman and Hodson 1961), many of which are known parasites of the spruce budworm.

Predators of the jack pine budworm include several insects, spiders (Allen et al. 1970), and a number of birds.

In spite of their great abundance, these natural enemies are not always successful in checking outbreaks of this insect. From a detailed study carried out in Michigan, Folz et al. (1972) concluded that climatic conditions can be important in the rise and decline of outbreaks. According to these authors, favourable weather during the period of larval and adult dispersal can be linked to the onset of outbreaks. On the other hand, Hodson and Zehngraff (1946) believed that infestations of this budworm are linked closely with abundance of staminate flowers in jack pine stands, although inclement weather and food depletion appear to be key factors responsible for bringing outbreaks to an end.

Artificial control

Long-term measures aimed at preventing outbreaks of the jack pine budworm, or reducing their effect, consist of eliminating mature trees that are likely to produce flowers and cones. When an outbreak is actually in progress, chemical insecticides may be used in an attempt to protect stands that are severely threatened. In Canada, research has been aimed at improving control methods by experimental tests with chemical insecticides applied both from the ground and from the air. Encouraging results were obtained from laboratory and field tests carried out in both Manitoba and Ontario with several chemical stomach and contact insecticides, to prevent serious defoliation by this species (Deboo and Hildahl 1971; Nigam 1970). Also, aerial application of chemical insecticides was carried out with success in Quebec thus preventing the spread of a new outbreak to huge surrounding stands of jack pine.

It is hoped that, in the near future, biological insecticides may prove effective in controlling this pest.

References

Allen et al. 1969, 1970; Bradley 1974; Campbell 1953; Deboo and Hildahl 1971; Foltz et al. 1972; Freeman 1953; Hodson and Zehngraff 1946; Kulman and Hodson 1961; Nigam 1970; and Walley 1953.

Jack pine budworm, *Choristoneura pinus pinus* Free.

A. Egg cluster on jack pine needle.
B. Larva on flower-bearing jack pine shoot.
C. Pupa in natural position, near its last larval molt.
D. Newly emerged moth near pupal case.
E. Moderately defoliated jack pine stand.
F. Severe defoliation on dominant jack pine trees.

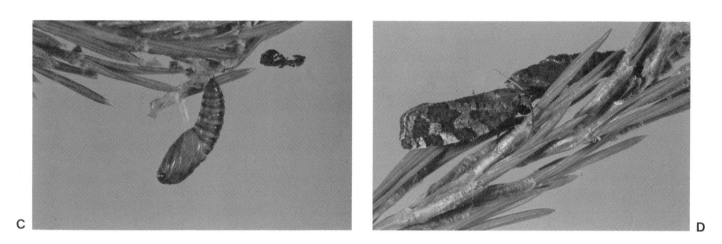

Jack pine sawfly
Plate 19

The jack pine sawfly, *Neodiprion pratti banksianae* Roh., is an important defoliator of jack pine. It is native to North America and was first reported in 1921. It is found in all the provinces of Canada with the exception of Newfoundland, but is most common in Ontario. In the United States, its presence has been reported only in Minnesota, Wisconsin, and Michigan. Jack pine is the preferred host and is the only species to which it causes serious damage, but it also attacks red pine and Scots pine where these grow mixed with jack pine.

History of outbreaks

The first reported outbreak of the jack pine sawfly in Canada goes back to 1930 by which time, together with two other sawflies, it had been attacking jack pine stands in Ontario and Quebec for several years. Since then, local outbreaks of this insect have occurred periodically in mature jack pine stands in these two provinces and the three states already mentioned.

Description and biology

Adult. Wasp-like; female brown (Plate 19, C and D), male black with feathery antennae (Plate 19, I). Lengths: 8 and 6 mm respectively.

Egg. Ovoid; white. Length: 1 mm.

Larva. Cylindrical in shape and elongated; head black, basic body color greenish yellow with black lines running longitudinally. Length when full grown: 25 mm.

Pupa. Cocoon cylindrical, rounded at both ends; brown. Length: 6-9 mm depending on the sex (Plate 19, J).

Although the jack pine sawfly is common in Canada, the biology of this species has not yet been studied thoroughly.

The insect has one generation per year. Adults leave the cocoons in September. Shortly thereafter females lay their eggs in egg-slits made with their ovipositor in needles (Plate 19, E and F); three

to six eggs are laid per needle at a distance of two to three times their own length. Eggs may be laid in 20 to 30 needles of the same twig. After their emergence the following spring, the larvae aggregate in clusters of about 50 and immediately attack the old foliage without touching that of the current year (Plate 19, G). Larval development takes about 4 to 5 weeks (Plate 19, H); there are five or six instars. Once it has finished feeding, each larva drops to the ground and spins its cocoon in the litter.

Schedl (1930) found that jack pines exposed to sunlight were generally most affected. Graham (1952) observed that outbreaks usually develop in large areas having high concentrations of mature or almost-mature jack pine.

Damage and diagnosis

All damage by the jack pine sawfly is caused by the larvae. Severe infestations (Plate 19, A) may lead to complete destruction of the old foliage in 2 years or more, without causing widespread tree mortality, because the new foliage is left intact (Ewan 1957) (Plate 19, B). However, severely defoliated trees undergo a more or less pronounced reduction in increment and this damage, although not visible from the outside, causes wood losses that, unfortunately, have not yet been evaluated.

An outbreak of the jack pine sawfly can be detected by various signs, depending on the observation period:

- May to July: colonies of young larvae present on old needles, especially in the upper part of mature and almost-mature jack pine trees; gradual defoliation of the old foliage;
- July to September: jack pine crowns more or less stripped of their old foliage; sound golden brown cocoons relatively abundant in the litter beneath affected trees; and
- September on: unhatched egg clusters present on current year's needles in upper crowns of mature or nearly mature jack pines; predominantly opened or empty cocoons abundant in the litter.

Natural control

Parasites although abundant, cannot arrest an infestation of the jack pine sawfly (Graham 1952). In an attempt to reinforce the action of native parasites, five species of parasites were imported from 1910 to 1958 (McGugan and Coppel 1962). In rearings carried out in Ontario from 1938 to 1957, Raizenne (1957) obtained 16 species of hymenopterous parasites, two of them foreign in origin. Seven species were recovered to date in Quebec, five of which had been introduced and already reported in Ontario. The relative importance of each species in controlling this sawfly is not yet known.

In the United States, several hymenopterous and dipterous parasites are considered to be the most important factors in the biological control of this sawfly, because they attack before the larvae can inflict any serious damage (Ewan 1957).

A

B

C

D

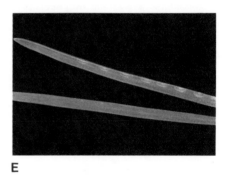

E

G

H

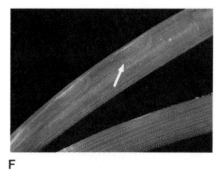

F

I

J

51

No reference has been found in the literature on the role played by predators of this sawfly, but small insectivorous mammals undoubtedly destroy part of the population in the cocoon, as is the case for the Swaine jack pine sawfly.

According to Graham (1952), climate, acting in a number of ways, is important in controlling populations of this sawfly. Late frosts in the spring may destroy a large proportion of the larvae when they hatch, or young larvae may be dislodged from crowns by heavy spring rains. Also, it has been observed that, periods of damp and cold weather followed by high temperatures can provide favorable conditions for the development of a larval disease that has already checked an outbreak in the past.

Artificial control

As a preventive measure of control against the jack pine sawfly, maturing and mature jack pine stands, as well as isolated and open-grown jack pines, should be harvested.

As a curative measure, it is important to develop a method favouring the use of the pathogen responsible for the disease already mentioned, so that it might be used as a means of biological control against outbreaks in limited areas.

Trees of high commercial value may be protected successfully by spraying with a stomach or contact insecticide, either from the ground or from the air, while the larvae are feeding.

References

Atwood and Peck 1943; Ewan 1957; Graham 1952; McGugan and Coppel 1962; Raizenne 1957; and Schedl 1930.

Other jack pine sawflies
Plate 20

The redheaded jack pine sawfly, *Neodiprion rugifrons* Midd., and the brownheaded jack pine sawfly, *N. dubiosus* Schedl, have always been difficult to identify because the first descriptions were unfortunately faulty. Thus, specimens collected in Canada have been identified successively as *N. rugifrons* Midd. (Middleton 1933), *N. dubiosus* Schedl (Schedl 1935), *N. virginiana* (Ross 1951) and *N. virginianus* complex (Ross 1955). However, following the well-documented study by Becker et al. (1966), only the first two names remain valid.

Both species are native to North America. In Canada, they are found mainly in Quebec and Ontario; in the Prairies and the Maritimes, the specimens collected were identified as *N. virginianus* complex, which means that they could be either species. In the United States, they are present in Wisconsin. Jack pine is the preferred host of both species, but the redheaded jack pine sawfly also attacks red pine and eastern white pine.

Description and biology

Redheaded jack pine sawfly, *N. rugifrons*
Adult. Wasp-like; male black, female brown. Lengths: 5-6 mm and 8-10 mm, respectively (Plate 20, D and E).
Egg. Ovoid; light colored initially, then turning gray.
Larva. Cylindrical and elongated; color at maturity: head varying from orange brown to bright orange, body yellowish green to olive green with two continuous dorsal lines and dotted lateral lines from the thorax to the ninth abdominal segment (Plate 20, C).
Cocoon. Cylindrical, rounded at both ends. Dimensions correspond to those of the inhabiting adult (Plate 20, F).

Major studies on the taxonomy of both these sawflies have been carried out by D. R. Wallace in Ontario, but the results have not yet been published. The following information is based on data collected on the biology of the redheaded jack pine

sawfly by Becker et al. (1966) in Wisconsin, in the southernmost part of its range, and by Martineau (1959) in Quebec, located at the northern edge of its range. These data also apply, at least in part, to the brownheaded jack pine sawfly, which has a very similar biology (Plate 20, G to I).

The redheaded jack pine sawfly has one generation per year in the northern part of its range, whereas farther south if weather conditions are favorable, two may occur, one in the spring and one in the summer.

In the one-generation area, the first adults emerge at the end of June, whereas in the two-generation area they appear in mid-May. Shortly after leaving the cocoon, females of the single generation, and those of the spring generation, lay their eggs in old needles. The eggs are laid singly in slits, 6-8 per needle, very close to one another and occasionally touching. They are found normally in colonies of about 90 on a few twigs scattered throughout the crown (Plate 20, B). Incubation lasts from 20 to 30 days. Upon hatching, the larvae of the same colony gather at the base of the twig on which

PLATE 20

Redheaded jack pine sawfly, *Neodiprion rugifrons* Midd., and brownheaded jack pine sawfly, *Neodiprion dubiosus* Schedl

A. Jack pine defoliated by *N. rugifrons*.
B. Colony of very young *N. rugifrons* larvae on jack pine twig.
C. Mature *N. rugifrons* larva.
D. *N. rugifrons*, adult male.
E. *N. rugifrons*, adult female.
F. Male and female cocoons of *N. rugifrons*.
G. Young larvae of *N. dubiosus*.
H. Mature *N. dubiosus* larva.
I. Lateral view of *N. dubiosus* female.

A

B

C

D

E

F

G

H

I

53

the eggs were laid and, as soon as their head-capsule has hardened sufficiently, they begin to attack the needles. The young larvae feed in groups of two or three, each with its head facing the distal end of the needle and progressing backwards. They feed only on the edges of the needles, leaving the central filament intact; as they grow older, they become solitary and consume the entire needle down to the sheath. Larval development extends over a period of 4 to 6 weeks. The male goes through five instars and the female through six; at the last instar, the larvae stop feeding and drop to the ground where they spin cocoons at a depth reaching 8-10 cm into the litter. They remain in the cocoon from 1 to 9 months, depending on whether there are two generations per year or only one.

Individuals of the summer generation follow the same pattern as those of the first, except that the eggs are laid in the new needles and the larvae use this new foliage for food.

Damage and diagnosis

In Wisconsin, most outbreaks of the redheaded jack pine sawfly occur in plantations of jack pine on trees 6 m high at the most, whereas in Quebec, they are found in natural forests and mainly on fully grown jack pine up to 10 m in height.

Damage resulting from the egg-laying process is negligible, whereas the larval feeding may have serious consequences. However, even during serious outbreaks, defoliation by larvae of the first generation does not kill trees, because they attack only old needles, and thus they rarely affect more than 60 percent of the foliage. At most only the tree growth increment is reduced. In the two-generation regions, however, larvae of the second generation attack new needles, so that trees may be stripped of both old and new foliage and death may result (Becker et al. 1966).

Various signs help in recognizing an outbreak of the redheaded jack pine sawfly depending on the time of year and the location:

- July and August (June to August in two-generation areas): egg colonies laid in a single row, generally in old needles of young pines; eggs of the second generation present in new needles.

- July and August (June to September in two-generation areas): larval colonies present on old foliage of young pines; defoliation of old needles by the first generation, and of old and new needles by the second generation.

Natural control

Several species of parasites attack the redheaded jack pine sawfly. Becker et al. (1966) obtained a total of 16 species through rearings in Wisconsin. Two of these are parasitic on the eggs, whereas the remaining ones attack the cocoon. These authors estimated that 75 percent of the individuals were destroyed in the cocoon. Martineau (1959) recovered nine species of parasites from experiments in Quebec; the two most important species were *Diplosthicus hamatus* A. & W. and *Perilampus hyalinus* Say, both of which were included in Becker's list. Both species were also among four obtained by Raizenne (1957) in Ontario. Neither of two foreign species introduced into Canada around 1940 to reinforce the action of native parasites, was recovered.

According to Becker et al. (1966), a high percentage of the eggs were destroyed in Wisconsin by a bug of the miridae family of the genus *Pilophorus*, whereas larval populations were greatly reduced by a stink bug, *Podisus maculiventris* (Say). Also, as with other sawfly species in natural jack pine forests in Canada, it is likely that cocoons are preyed upon by small insectivorous mammals and beetles living in the litter.

Abiotic control factors were of little importance in reducing egg and larval populations in the outbreaks studied in Wisconsin. In Quebec, on the other hand, Martineau (1959) observed in the field that a large proportion of the eggs did not hatch and, also, that a large proportion of the larval population had been destroyed within the 21 days following the hatching, by an undetermined cause.

Artificial control

In regions with only one generation, natural factors usually succeed in keeping populations of the redheaded jack pine sawfly within reasonable limits, and infestations are thus of short duration and remain local. Damage is generally light, and artificial methods of control are unnecessary.

In two-generation areas, on the other hand, damage may be very serious, and planting of jack pine in pure stands is not recommended. During widespread outbreaks when the life of the tree is threatened, the trees may be protected by spraying with a stomach or contact insecticide. Such treatment destroys the larvae of the spring generation and prevents the production of a summer generation, thus protecting the current year's foliage.

References

Becker et al. 1966; Martineau 1959; Middleton 1933; Raizenne 1957; Ross 1951, 1955; Schedl 1935; and Wilkinson et al. 1966.

European pine needle midge
Plate 21

The cause of premature needle drop on some pines in Canada remained unidentified for many years. This damage on red pine was temporarily attributed to an insect of the genus *Contarinia* by Reeks (1954b), but it was clearly established some 20 years later that, on Scots pine in south-central Quebec, this phenomenon was due to a miner, the European pine needle midge, *Contarinia baeri* (Prell), (Deboo and Laplante 1975; Martineau 1973a). There is reason to believe that the insect observed by Reeks belonged to the same species. This insect is native to Europe, where it is known by the very descriptive name of needle bending midge; its introduction to Canada apparently took place about 20 years ago. In North America, it occurs at present only in Canada, in Ontario, Quebec, and New Brunswick, where its known hosts are Scots pine and red pine. In Europe, apart from Scots pine, it is found on spruce and fir.

History of outbreaks

The outbreak observed on Scots pine in Quebec was of short duration (Deboo and Laplante 1975), whereas the one followed by Reeks (1954b) on red pine lasted for 7 years.

Description and biology

Adult. Gnat-like, with long legs and long antennae; brown black.
Length: 1 mm (Plate 21, E).
Larva. Rounded and tapering at both ends; yellow to orange.
Length: 2.2-3.2 mm.
Pupa. Spindle-shaped; brown (Plate 21, D and H).

Little is as yet known in North America about the biology of the European pine needle midge, and the scanty information that follows was collected in Quebec during a control program aimed at protecting severely infested Scots pine plantations.

There appears to be only one generation per year. The insect hibernates in a cocoon in the litter at the base of infested trees. From mid-June to mid-July, it leaves the litter as an adult and immediately flies to the upper portion of the crown, where the females lay their eggs in the needle sheaths. Upon hatching on Scots pine, the larva bores through the inner side (Plate 21, G) of a needle where it feeds on internal tissue for the greater part of its growing period. Reeks (1954b) observed that, on red pine, up to 25 larvae could live on the same needle cluster. On Scots pine, two or even more larvae may live on one pair of needles, but normally only one individual survives. When the needle cluster drops, towards the end of July or early August, the larva is still inside the needle although it has finished feeding, and is thus carried to the litter, where it spins a cocoon and transforms first to a pupa and then to an adult.

Damage and diagnosis

All damage by the European pine needle midge is caused by larval feeding on foliar tissue inside the sheath (Plate 21, I), causing one needle to wither and eventually to lean away from the other and to turn brown (Plate 21, F). This damage can result in a considerable loss of new foliage that is generally limited to the upper part of the crown, but may affect the whole crown (Plate 21, A, B and C). Trees rarely succumb to attacks by this insect, because damage is generally confined to the destruction of lateral and terminal shoots.

Needle drop from new shoots does, however, considerably lower the aesthetic value of infested trees, to the point where forest owners, in particular Christmas trees producers, hesitate to plant red pine and Scots pine, fearing that their trees may lose value or be refused on the market.

In early August, affected foliage begins to drop, and the pair of detached needles in their sheath, one brown and the other green, are easily seen because these are usually caught in the foliage remaining on the tree.

In the fall, it can be seen that part of the current year's foliage has disappeared from the upper part of the crown, although it remains intact on the lower part. After several years of repeated attack, crowns become more or less defoliated and occasionally deformed.

Natural control

A hymenopterous parasite of the genus *Tetrastichus* is the only insect known to reduce populations of the European pine needle midge in Quebec and Ontario. In certain years, it has destroyed up to 90 percent of the larval population.

Artificial control

Pruning the current year's shoots may improve the condition of trees lightly or even moderately infested with the European pine needle midge. Some protection may also be obtained by spraying the foliage with a contact insecticide while eggs are being laid, or by soaking the litter at the base of contaminated trees with the same insecticide to destroy the adults as they emerge.

References

Browne 1968; Deboo and Laplante 1975; Canadian Forestry Service 1973; Reeks 1954b; and Canada Department of Forestry 1962.

Pine leaf adelgid
Plate 22

The pine leaf adelgid, *Pineus pinifoliae* (Fitch), is a sucking insect belonging to an homopterous group whose biology is complicated because the life cycle extends over a period of 2 years and involves five different forms and two hosts. It occurs in all provinces of Canada and in the states of Maine, New Hampshire, Vermont, and New York. Its primary hosts are red spruce and black spruce, and its secondary hosts are generally eastern white pine and occasionally, red pine, Scots pine, and Austrian pine.

History of outbreaks

In eastern Canada, the pine leaf adelgid has been a major pest only in New Brunswick and Nova Scotia. The first outbreak started in 1942 and within 10 years all stands of red spruce and eastern white pine in most of New Brunswick were infested. In 1948, populations declined unexpectedly and only local infestations have been recorded since then. In Que-

bec, the insect was collected in three widely separated regions, namely, the part of Gaspé Peninsula bordering New Brunswick, the Eastern Townships, and south of La Vérendrye Park. In Ontario, only one small local outbreak has been reported.

Description and biology

Some knowledge of the biology of the pine leaf adelgid was obtained in the course of studies carried out in New Brunswick by Balch and Underwood (1950), and later in the state of Maine by Dimond and his colleagues (Deboo et al. 1964; Dimond and Allen 1974; Ford and Dimond 1973; Howse and Dimond 1965).

Several aspects of the biology of this species are still not clear. It is known, however, that the pine leaf adelgid takes five different forms, that succeed one another in the following order: fundatrix, gallicola migrans, exulis, sexupara, and sexualis. The fundatrix hibernates at the base of spruce buds and becomes active in the spring before the buds swell, when it causes the formation of a gall (Plate 22, B); it then lays its eggs, which produce the gallicola migrans. The nymphs of the gallicola migrans develop at the base of the needles and transform themselves into winged adults about mid-June (Plate 22, D and E), when they migrate to old pine needles. During an outbreak, they may be found lined up on needles, with their mouth parts attached to the stomata (Plate 22, C) and their heads facing the base of the needle. They remain in this position to lay their eggs and stay attached even after dying until well into the winter. The exules, that is the nymphs hatched from eggs laid by the gallicola migrans, crawl to the axis of new pine shoots about mid-July, attach themselves, and remain dormant until the following spring. In May, development is resumed and they produce either other wingless exules that reproduce on pine, or the sexuparae, which are winged adults that migrate at the end of May and settle on old needles of spruce, this time with their heads turned towards the distal end of the needle. These adults lay eggs under their wings, and the young nymphs, yellow orange at first then dark red, line up in a double line behind their mothers with their mouth parts inserted into the stomata of

the needle. Nymphs emerging from the preceding form develop into sexed adults that move, presumably about the end of June to new spruce shoots where they begin their cycle again.

Damage and diagnosis

On spruce, the damage by the pine leaf adelgid consists of the formation of cone-shaped galls that disfigure but do not affect the health of the trees because the percentage of galled shoots is never sufficient to cause a reduction in growth or permanent damage (Plate 22, A).

On pine, damage may cause mortality of shoots and even of the tree. A lightly damaged shoot bends at its base and eventually shows a reduction in length. If the attack is quite severe, the distal part of the shoot droops and, by mid-summer, the needles become reddish; if the outbreak is very virulent, some of the damaged pines may die.

Various symptoms indicate an outbreak by this species particularly the presence of:
- Elongated cone-shaped galls on spruce;
- Gallicola migrans on the old pine needles, from July to May of the following year;
- Exules on the axis of new pine shoots, from July to May; and
- Abnormally shaped, drooping, or dead lateral shoots on pine from mid-summer on.

Natural control

During the 1943-1948 outbreak in New Brunswick, Balch observed that mortality of pine leaf adelgids was due to well-identified natural phenomena: first, the death of the young shoots on which the insects depended for their survival, and secondly, temperatures below -35°C during the winter. He also observed mortality due to an unknown cause, apparently related to difficulty in egg-laying by the sexuparae.

PLATE 21

European pine needle midge, *Contarinia baeri* (Prell)

A. Scots pine branches at onset of an outbreak.
B. Scots pine crown losing current year's needles.
C. Scots pine branches partially stripped after 1 year of attack.
D. Pupa.
E. Adult, lateral view.
F. Pair of Scots pine needles, one affected, the other intact.
G. Pair of needles spread to show position of larva.
H. Pupa outside a damaged needle.
I. Appearance of damage at base of affected needle.

58

Artificial control

Large-scale experiments in control of the pine leaf adelgid using systemic insecticides on both spruce and pine, have not been successful. Some success may, however, be achieved on ornamental spruces by hand collecting galls and burning them before mid-June (Rose and Lindquist 1973). Infested pines may also be sprayed with a contact insecticide in July, when nymphs are exposed on the needles or on the shoots.

References

Balch and Underwood 1950; Deboo et al. 1964; Dimond and Allen 1974; Ford and Dimond 1973; Howse and Dimond 1965; and Rose and Lindquist 1973.

PLATE 22

Pine leaf adelgid, *Pineus pinifoliae* (Fitch), ragged spruce gall adelgid, *P. similis* (Gill.), and red spruce adelgid, *P. floccus* (Patch)

A. Red pine infested with *P. pinifoliae*.
B. Branch of white spruce bearing galls of *P. pinifoliae*.
C. *P. pinifoliae* adults attached to a pine needle by their mouth parts.
D. and E. Dorsal and lateral views of *P. pinifoliae* adults.
F. Living *P. similis* adult on spruce needle.
G. Recent damage by *P. similis* on spruce shoot.
H. *P. similis* adult dead near its eggs.
I. Damage caused by *P. similis* on several needles of a spruce shoot.
J. Appearance of a spruce shoot several months after damage by *P. similis*.
K. Woolly *P. floccus* adelgids on spruce shoot.
L. Appearance of a spruce shoot several months after attack by *P. floccus*.

Jack pine resin midge
Plate 23

Along with the other midges harmful to forests and ornamental trees, the entomological literature has little information on the jack pine resin midge, *Cecidomyia resinicola* (O.S). The lack of information about this midge is mainly because it attacks jack pine, a tree that has not been in great demand by the forest industry until recent years, and also because the insect prefers small trees with no commercial value. Over the past decade, however, jack pine has assumed a greater importance because of its use for reforestation of waste lands and for Christmas trees.

History of outbreaks

In Canada, outbreaks of the jack pine resin midge have been reported every year since 1963. The insect probably occurs over the entire range of jack pine, but sampling suggests that it is abundant only in Quebec and Ontario. The jack pine resin midge has attacked plantations in central Quebec and south-central Ontario and natural stands in western Quebec; its presence has also been reported in the western plains and in the Great Lakes states of the United States.

Description and biology

Adult. Resembles a tiny gnat, with transparent wings and orange body (Plate 23, J and K).
Larva. Rounded body, tapered at both ends; orange. Length: about 4 mm (Plate 23, F).
Pupa. Spindle-shaped; head and wings black; body orange (Plate 23, H and I).

The jack pine resin midge overwinters as a partially developed larva and transforms to a pupa in the spring. Adults appear in May and may be seen until mid-June. Eggs are laid on the needles or on the bark of new shoots. The larvae feed in pitch masses that seep naturally at the surface of new shoots of jack pine; this feeding irritates the young tissues and stimulates the flow of pitch until it eventually forms a ball about 10 mm in diameter (Plate 23, D and E). This pitch ball contains a small chamber in which several larvae may develop and eventually transform into pupae. (Plate 23, G)

Damage and diagnosis

Damage caused by the jack pine resin midge may be serious enough to kill young jack pines (Plate 23, A). Trees of larger diameter are less seriously affected and only their shoots are destroyed. The most frequent damage is the mortality of new shoots (Plate 23, B) and they are easily identified in the crown by their reddish yellow color. After several years of repeated attack, trees that survive become stunted and lose their decorative value.

Injured trees may be easily recognized, from fall to spring, by the presence of reddened shoots with a pitch mass at their base.

Natural and artificial control

No information has as yet been published on what might limit the proliferation of the jack pine resin midge in the forest. It may be eliminated from isolated trees or from small-scale plantations by cutting infested shoots so as to include all pitch masses, and by burning them.

No chemical insecticide treatment has been developed to date.

References

Rose and Lindquist 1973; Stein and Kennedy 1972; and Wilson 1977.

60

White pine weevil
Plate 24

The white pine weevil, *Pissodes strobi* (Peck), is native to North America and occurs throughout the range of eastern white pine. It was found for the first time in North America in 1817, but only since the beginning of this century has it been considered a constant threat to forest resources. Host trees are eastern white pine, jack pine, Scots pine, red pine, and Mugho pine, as well as white spruce, black spruce and Norway spruce. Tree damage is important because both the volume and the quality of the wood are reduced. The insect attacks the terminal shoot and, for this reason, it has sometimes been given the characteristic name of terminal twig borer. It was previously thought that weevil attacks decreased greatly once the tree had reached about 30 years of age or about 8 m in height. However, data collected by Ostrander (1957) and by Harman and Wallace (1971) have thrown some doubt on this accepted belief. In any case, damage is certainly more difficult to observe once the tree has reached a certain height.

History of outbreaks

In eastern Canada, damage caused by the white pine weevil varies from region to region. In Newfoundland, it has been reported only occasionally. In the Maritime provinces and Quebec, it was first collected in the few small eastern white pine and white spruce plantations that existed around 1920. With the constant increase in the number and size of plantations, however, the insect became a common species both on natural regeneration and in plantations. This weevil has been particularly harmful in Ontario, where outbreaks have been reported almost every year since 1930. For the past 20 years, outbreaks have been widespread, more tree species have been affected, and infestation rates have been very high in certain years.

Description and biology

Adult. Looks like a miniature elephant, oblong in shape; light to dark brown. Length: 5 mm (Plate 24, E).
Egg. Ovoid; pearl white. Length: 1 mm (Plate 24, H).
Larva. Legless and thick bodied; head brown, body yellowish white. Length at maturity: 7 mm (Plate 24, C).
Pupa. Resembles a folded adult; entirely white (Plate 24, D).

Several studies have been conducted in Canada and the United States on the biology and ecology of the white pine weevil to discover practical and effective methods of control.

This weevil has one generation per year, and overwinters in the adult stage. It leaves its winter shelter when the eastern white pine buds break in the spring and it flies or crawls towards the terminal shoots to feed on the bark and to mate. Eggs are laid in feeding punctures or in holes specially bored for that purpose, mainly found in the upper half of the terminal shoot. A female may lay eggs on more than one shoot, and several females may lay on the same shoot. Each lays an average of 100 eggs, at the rate of one to three per puncture. The egg-laying period lasts about 1 month, and the egg hatches after 1 to 3 weeks. Upon hatching, the young larvae bore under the bark to feed on the phloem towards the base of the stem. If the larvae are sufficiently numerous, they eventually girdle the stem, which then dies. Larval growth takes from 1 to 6 weeks and, once it reaches maturity, each larva bores a deeper chamber in the stem for pupation which lasts about 2 weeks. The adults appear in August and September and feed for a short time, preferably on the lateral shoots of the upper part of the crown. When cold weather arrives in the fall, they seek a shelter in which to spend the winter, most often in the ground beneath the affected tree.

Damage and diagnosis

Damage by the white pine weevil is caused by the feeding of both adults and larvae. The damage inflicted by the adult, being only small punctures in the bark,

PLATE 23

Jack pine resin midge, *Cecidomyia resinicola* (O.S.)

A. Young jack pines infested.
B. Damaged new shoots on a jack pine branch.
C. Jack pine branch with tip completely destroyed.
D. Recently attacked jack pine shoot with new pitch mass near terminal bud.
E. External appearance of pitch mass harboring larvae at the base of a jack pine twig.
F. Larvae extracted from pitch mass (length: about 4 mm).
G. Natural position of newly formed pupa in pitch mass.
H. Pupae out of pitch to show their appearance.
I. Empty pupal cases in pitch after emergence of adults.
J. Lateral view of adult male.
K. Dorsal view of live adult.

each covered with fresh or hardened droplets of pitch, is negligible in itself but these wounds may nevertheless have serious consequences, because they allow fungal pathogens to enter the tree. The damage resulting from the activities of larvae under the bark is more serious. The larvae attack shoots of the previous year, but damage appears first on shoots of the current year, which droop and then take on a reddish brown color (Plate 24, A). As a result, the two youngest shoots are often destroyed. The tree does not necessarily die, but its shape is seriously affected when it is young; it becomes forked or develops several leaders. Trees of all diameters are attacked, but open-grown trees less than 8 m tall are supposedly the most affected.

Damage caused by this weevil to eastern white pine of marketable size, as well as to lumber, results in a loss in height and in a reduction in volume varying from 3 to 20 percent. Also, the market value of this wood is considerably reduced; the quantity of Class 3 wood increases to the detriment of wood of the higher Classes 1 and 2, which results in an important monetary loss (Brace 1971).

PLATE 24

White pine weevil, *Pissodes strobi* (Peck), and northern pine weevil, *P. approximatus* Hopk.

A. Abnormal eastern white pine terminal shoot attacked by *P. strobi*.
B. Wood chips covering *P. strobi* larval chamber.
C. *P. strobi* larva in chamber.
D. *P. strobi* nymph in chamber.
E. *P. strobi* adult.
F. *P. strobi* adult exit holes.
G. Holes chewed by adult in the stem for egg-laying.
H. Eggs in natural position.
I. Larvae of predator *Lonchaea corticis* Taylor under bark.
J. Lateral view of adult predator.
K. Scots pine trunk severely damaged by *P. approximatus*.
L. Appearance of *P. approximatus* adult.

An attack by this weevil may be recognized by a number of signs, depending on the season, notably:

- Spring: adults present on 1-year old leader of young pines and spruces;
- Summer: pitch flows from punctures made by adults, and from damage caused by larvae on previous year's stems on pine and spruce. Particular attention should be paid to any abnormal development of new shoots, that take the shape of a shepherd's crook and eventually die; and
- Fall and winter: presence of crooked, forked, cabbage-shaped, or otherwise deformed trees.

Natural control

Parasites and predators of the white pine weevil are numerous and varied. Almost half a century ago, Taylor (1929, 1930) reported that *Eurytoma pissodis* Birault was the most effective parasite, and according to Baker (1972), the rate of parasitism by this species was 50 percent of the population in certain outbreaks. Research conducted in 13 locations in the state of Virginia by Harman and Kulman (1968) led to the recovery of nine species of parasites, whose effectiveness reached 16 percent. The most important parasites were *Bracon pini* (Mues.) and *Coeloides pissodis* (Ashm.). The same authors also collected three species of insect predators, of which the most common was *Lonchaea corticis* Taylor (Plate 24, I and J). The particular role of this predator in limiting populations was studied at length and published by Harman and Wallace (1971).

Birds also prey on larvae in the stem, and small insectivorous mammals attack them in the litter. Two entomopathogenic fungi should also be mentioned, that is *Beauveria bassiana* (Bals.) Vuill. and *Metarrhizium anisophiae* (Metachni Koft) Sorokin, because they are believed to participate in the control of this weevil.

Climate also plays an important role in the fluctuations of populations of this species (Sullivan 1960, 1961). Unfortunately, however, the combined action of all these natural factors is not always successful in holding populations down to tolerable levels, and it is often necessary to resort to artificial methods for prevention and control.

Artificial control

With the existing knowledge of the biology and ecology of the white pine weevil, the following methods are suggested to prevent or limit tree damage:

- Avoid planting host trees near contaminated areas;
- Avoid planting the most vulnerable tree species in pure stands or in close proximity to one another;
- Plant susceptible species along with fast-growing hardwoods so that a cover is created in as short a time as possible;
- Around mid-July, cut and burn the infested part of the stem plus the next green shoot; some lateral shoots should also be pruned to encourage development of a new leader; and
- Treat infested trees with a chemical stomach insecticide so as to kill adults during the egg-laying period in the spring, or when they emerge in the fall. In the spring, this treatment could also be applied at the ground level before adults leave their hibernation shelter.

Another species, known as the northern pine weevil, *Pissodes approximatus* Hopk., is sometimes found in large numbers in pine plantations (Plate 24, K and L). Its biology is quite similar to that of the foregoing insect, but damage is mainly confined to the base of the stem. To keep populations at tolerable levels, tree trunks should be treated with a stomach insecticide to render them unfit for egg-laying.

References

Baker 1972; Belyea and Sullivan 1956; Benoit 1976; Brace 1971; Harman 1971; Harman and Kulman 1968; Harman and Wallace 1971; Ostrander 1957; Philip 1978; Rose and Lindquist 1973; Sullivan 1960, 1961; and Taylor 1929, 1930.

Pitch nodule maker
Plate 25

The pitch nodule maker, *Petrova albicapitana* (Busck), is a solitary feeder so named because its larva, in making its tunnel, causes an outflow of pitch that accumulates on the trunk or branches in a more or less rounded mass. In North America the insect occurs throughout the range of jack pine and the southeastern part of the range of lodgepole pine. Its main host is jack pine, but it is often found on Scots pine and lodgepole pine and, occasionally, on red pine and Mugho pine. The insect was first collected in Canada in 1931, at which time it was known as a pest of young plantations of jack pine. For several years now, however, it has also been found in natural forests where it causes damage on older trees.

History of outbreaks

In eastern Canada particularly in the Maritime provinces and Ontario, local outbreaks of the pitch nodule maker have occurred occasionally in plantations, hedges, and nurseries. In Quebec, the insect attracted hardly any attention before 1959 but, since that time, outbreaks in plantations of jack pine have been reported almost every year. In 1968, the insect was also found to be abundant in jack pine in natural forests, even in stands approaching maturity. A special survey carried out in 1971 showed that stands of some 500 km^2 of jack pine in the upper St. Maurice valley were under serious attack by the pitch nodule maker and by a second species, *P. metallica* (Busck), representing 10 percent of the nodule maker population. Light to moderate infestations were also found in an additional 7500 km^2 north of Lake St. John. During the following 4 years, the insect continued its progress, but, in 1975, the population started to dwindle to the point at which, in 1978, it was difficult to find.

Description and biology

Adult. Small brown moth. Wingspan: 20 mm (Plate 25, J).

Egg. Shaped like a flattened tear; lemon yellow. Diameter: 0.5 mm.

Larva. Elongated; head yellow brown, body reddish. Length at maturity: 15 mm (Plate 25, F and H).

Pupa. Spindle-shaped; head and wings dark up to black, body reddish (Plate 25, I).

Major studies on the biology of the pitch nodule maker were carried out in jack pine plantations and on natural regeneration in Manitoba (Turnock 1953) and in mature stands in central Quebec (McLeod and Tostowaryk 1971). Unfortunately, neither the life cycle nor the ethology of *P. albicapitana* is as yet well known.

The life cycle of this lepidoptera covers a period of 24 months spread over 3 years. It begins with the appearance of the moth, that flies from early to mid-July. Females lay their eggs on terminal shoots (Plate 25, B). Upon hatching, the newborn larva chews the bark near the egg site (Plate 25, C). By September, it has succeeded in digging a circular hole that it then transforms with silk and pitch into a sort of little chamber in which it feeds until fall and then passes the winter. The following spring, that is, at the beginning of the second year, the larva enlarges the chamber begun the preceding fall and builds its first small nodule (Plate 25, D). In June, it leaves this first nodule (Plate 25, E) and crawls along the branch to the junction with another branch, where it begins to dig a second hole in the bark, this time covering it with a silken tent some 10 mm in diameter; once covered with pitch, this tent becomes the second nodule. Once this second nodule has reached its full size of 25-40 mm (Plate 25, G), it serves as a shelter in which the larva spends its second winter. In the spring of the third year, the larva pupates and transforms to an adult. The moth leaves the nodule through a thin silken wall constructed by the larva before it pupated.

Damage and diagnosis

All damage is caused by the larvae of the pitch nodule maker when they feed. Although it is of little consequence during the first year, it becomes more serious during the second year (Plate 25, A). When the larva attacks the current year's shoots, these may become girdled and die. Needles on these shoots turn brick red in color indicating that a nodule is probably present, and the twig finally breaks near the nodule. When the stem is attacked, the tree shows a reduction in height and becomes forked. Open wounds left by the larvae are vulnerable to infection by pathogenic fungi.

Infested trees may be easily recognized by the presence of brown pitch masses about 25-40 mm in diameter at the junction of two branches. The second nodule is the easiest to find; in winter and spring it contains a pink larva or reddish pupa. The first nodule is always smaller than the second and is harder to see; it may be found on new shoots near the bud. Both types of nodules are sometimes found on the same shoot. Once the adult has left, the second nodule blackens and, with time, disintegrates. Twigs located above a first nodule may die, whereas those located above a second nodule first die and then break off.

PLATE 25

Pitch nodule maker, *Petrova albicapitana* (Busck)

A. Young jack pine damaged by nodule maker.
B. Location of eggs on terminal shoot of jack pine (diameter: 0.5 mm).
C. Newly hatched larvae near eggs.
D. Appearance of a first nodule in the fall of the first year.
E. Appearance of a first nodule in the spring.
F. Larva inside a first nodule.
G. Second nodule in July of second year.
H. Second nodule opened to show mature larva (length: 15 mm).
I. Pupa.
J. Pinned adult (wingspan: 20 mm).

Natural control

Even though the larvae of the pitch nodule maker are protected by their nodule during most of their development, they still do not escape attack by their enemies. Turnock (1953) reported 11 species of parasites, the two most common being *Calliephialtes comstockii* (Cress.) and *Macrocentrus cuniculus* Walley. Parasitism by all species combined is considered slight, varying from 2 to 17 percent of the total population of the host. Raizenne (1952) and Bradley (1974) each reported two of the parasites mentioned by Turnock. Four species were obtained in Quebec, of which the two most common had also been reported by Turnock.

Artificial control

To prevent attacks by the pitch nodule maker, it is recommended to plant more resistant pines, to isolate new plantations from existing centers of infection, and to avoid locating plantations in formerly contaminated areas.

On isolated ornamentals, the insect may be destroyed by picking off the nodule at the beginning of the second year, before the larva has caused any serious damage. No practical method of control, using chemical insecticides has yet been developed. It might be possible to apply a contact insecticide during two vulnerable periods, i.e., either when the moths fly, with a view to preventing egg-laying, or at the beginning of the second year to kill the larvae when they leave the first nodule and move into the second one.

References

Bradley 1974; Canadian Forestry Service 1971; McLeod and Tostowaryk 1971; Prentice 1965; Raizenne 1952; Rose and Lindquist 1973; and Turnock 1953.

European pine shoot moth
Plate 26

The European pine shoot moth, *Rhyacionia buoliana* (Schiff.), begins its larval development as a leaf miner and then becomes a borer of the shoots. This species was probably introduced to North America on ornamentals imported from Europe. At present it occurs throughout eastern North America, from the Atlantic Ocean as far as the state of Iowa in the United States and as far as Ontario in Canada, between the 40th parallel and the 29°C isotherm (Pointing and Miller 1973); in the West, it occurs at the southern end of British Columbia. All species of pines may be attacked, but the preferred host is red pine. Scots pine, Austrian pine, ponderosa pine, jack pine and Mugho pine are moderately susceptible, whereas pitch pine, Virginia pine, and eastern white pine are relatively resistant.

History of outbreaks

The European pine shoot moth was first reported in 1914 in the state of New York. The following year, it was found in nine additional states, and it then spread gradually towards the interior of the continent. In Canada, this insect was first reported in 1925, both in Nova Scotia and Ontario, where it had probably been established for several years. It was found in Quebec in 1931, at first in the Montreal area and then in several large towns in the southern part of the province. In 1952, it was first collected in Newfoundland, at St. John's in the eastern part of that province and at Corner Brook in the western part. In the same year, it was reported for the first time in Prince Edward Island, and one year later in New Brunswick.

At first damage was limited to ornamentals, but populations gradually increased and by 1948, the insect was considered the most serious pest on red pine, Scots pine and jack pine of southern Ontario, and foresters for a time held doubts as to the future of red pine in reforestation. Fortunately in 1953 populations began to decline and by 1967,

---

PLATE 26

European pine shoot moth, *Rhyacionia buoliana* (Schiff.)

A. New red pine shoots: (left) damaged shoot; (right) normal shoot.
B. Adult at rest on red pine needles (wingspan: about 20 mm).
C. Eggs at base of red pine needles (length: about 1 mm).
D. Young larva on red pine needles.
E. Longitudinal cut of red pine shoot to show mature larva (length: about 15 mm).
F. Pupa amongst red pine needles (length: about 10 mm).

A

B

C

D

E

F

damage by this insect was no longer of major interest. Since that time, however, the insect has regained some of its importance.

In Quebec, the population began to decline in 1951 and since that time, population levels have remained low; nevertheless the insect gradually extended its range, reaching the Magdalen Islands in 1972.

Description and biology

Adult. Small moth; forewings orange marked with silvery lines.
  Wingspan: 20 mm (Plate 26, B).
Egg. Oval-shaped; cream in color turning orange brown and then gray.
  Length: 1 mm (Plate 26, C).
Larva. Elongated; light brown initially, becoming darker with age.
  Full length: 15 mm (Plate 26, E).
Pupa. Yellow brown, thorax varying from brown to gray.
  Length: about 10 mm (Plate 26, F).

One generation of the European pine shoot moth is produced per year. The adult appears in June, and lives for about 4 weeks. Moths emerge at sunrise, but are hardly seen before sunset, when females occupy open spaces and attract males by emitting a particular odor. After mating, the female lays eggs singly or in small groups on twigs or on sheaths of new needles. The larva leaves the egg 2 weeks later. The first two larval instars are spent in a tunnel bored by the larva in new needles; with the end of the third instar, it moves to an opening bud to feed (Plate 26, D). By the month of August, the larva has completed half of its larval development and goes into hibernation.

The following spring, the larvae leave their winter quarters and head for buds or new shoots where they complete their development before transforming to pupae. Pupation takes place inside the buds or in pitch masses; the pupal stage lasts about 2 weeks and occurs between May and July.

Damage and diagnosis

All damage is caused by the larva of the European pine shoot moth. It starts by mining the new needles, which, once hollowed, turn brown, break off, and fall to the ground. Later the larva attacks the terminal bud, thus damaging the stem; repeated destruction of the terminal bud causes the formation of many lateral shoots and, consequently, stem deformity. Damage caused in the spring is generally permanent, and crooked stems considerably reduce the aesthetic value of ornamental trees.

The first sign of an outbreak is the presence of a few dead needles hanging from the terminal shoot in July. A little later in the season, pitch accumulations may be seen at the base of buds, or pitch masses may be found containing young larvae. In May, infested trees may be recognized easily by the presence of dead shoots (Plate 26, A).

Natural control

In Canada, besides the 17 species of native parasites obtained from the European pine shoot moth, 13 foreign species have been introduced, 5 of which have become well established. Pointing and Miller (1973) claimed that the combined action of all parasites causes a reduction in the host population of about 10 percent. *Orgilus obscurator* (Nees) is apparently highly effective when the host population is small, and, in certain areas, parasitism by this species would have reached 92 percent (Syme 1971). Several predators also play a role in reducing populations of this pest (Rose and Lindquist 1973).

The most important natural factor is undoubtedly climate. It has been clearly established that during certain winters, low temperatures are responsible for the death of many larvae on trees not protected by snow, and this would explain the major declines in population observed in the eastern part of the insect's range in Canada from 1950 on (Béique 1960; Green 1962).

Artificial control

Although their action is sometimes quite effective, natural factors are rarely successful in preventing serious damage by the European pine shoot moth; when protection of the aesthetic value of trees is desired, the following methods may be used:

- Cut and burn attacked shoots on slightly infested trees, during the month of May;
- If only a few trees are to be protected, the insects may be exposed to cold for a few days during the winter, by removing the protective snow cover from affected trees;
- Pruning of pines planted for the Christmas tree market often helps to reduce the population of this insect to acceptable levels; and
- At the end of June, or when the new needles of red pine are about half the length of the old needles, affected trees may be treated with a contact insecticide, and the treatment repeated about 10 days later.

References

Béique 1960; Canada Department of Agriculture, 1940-1952, 1953-1960 and 1959; Canada Department of Fisheries and Forestry, 1969; Canada Department of Forestry, 1961-1966; Canada Department of Forestry and Rural Development, 1967-1968; Canadian Forestry Service, 1970-1971, 1972-1981 and 1974a; Green 1962; McGugan and Coppel 1962; Pointing and Miller 1973; Rose and Lindquist 1973; and Syme 1971.

Table 3. Other insects harmful to pine — Other insects that are regarded as pests of pine are listed in this table. For some insects, their characteristics are described in the chapter that applies to their primary host, and in such cases, that chapter (in Roman numerals) and the appropriate plate numbers are given. For other insects, a plate number alone is shown; and for the remaining insects, this table provides the only information.

Common and scientific names	Hosts (chap.)	Plate no.	Type of insect	Destructive stages	Period of activity	Importance*
Eastern pine shoot borer *Eucosma gloriola* Heinr.	Jack pine, pine	32	Borer	Larva	June to Sept.	B
European pine sawfly *Neodiprion sertifer* (Geoff.)	Pine	30	Defoliator	Larva	May and June	B
Fir cone worm *Dioryctria abietivorella* (Grote)	Spruce (I)	4	—	—	—	C
Introduced pine sawfly *Diprion similis* (Htg.)	Eastern white pine, Scots pine, pine	31	Defoliator	Larva	May to Oct.	C
Large spruce weevil *Hylobius piceus* (DeG.)	Spruce (I)	8	—	—	—	B
Northeastern sawyer *Monochamus notatus* (Drury)	Conifers	—	Borer	Adult and larva	April to Nov.	B
Northern pine weevil *Pissodes approximatus* Hopk.	Pine	24	Borer	Larva	May to Oct.	A
Nursery pine sawfly *Gilpinia frutetorum* (F.)	Scots pine	—	Defoliator	Larva	May to Aug.	C
Pales weevil *Hylobius pales* (Hbst.)	Pine, conifers	—	Borer	Adult and larva	April to Oct.	A
Pine bark adelgid *Pineus strobi* (Htg.)	Pine, spruce	—	Sucker	Nymph	May to Oct.	C
Pine engraver *Ips pini* (Say)	Pine, spruce	—	Borer	Adult and larva	April to Nov.	B
Pine needleminer *Exoteleia pinifoliella* (Cham.)	Jack pine, pine	35	Miner	Larva	May to Oct.	B
Pine needle scale *Chionaspis pinifoliae* (Fitch)	Pine, conifers	27	Sucker	Adult and nymph	May to Nov.	C
Pine needle sheathminer *Zelleria haimbachi* Busck	Jack pine, pine	—	Miner	Larva	May to Aug.	C
Pine root collar weevil *Hylobius radicis* Buch.	Scots pine, pine	—	Borer	Adult and larva	May to Oct.	B
Pine spittlebug *Aphrophora parallela* (Say)	Scots pine, conifers	—	Sucker	Adult and nymph	May to Aug.	B
Pine tortoise scale *Tourmeyella parvicornis* (Ckll.)	Jack pine, Scots pine, pine	34	Sucker	Adult and nymph	May to Sept.	A
Pine tube moth *Argyrotaenia pinatubana* (Kft.)	Eastern white pine	—	Binder	Larva	May to Oct.	C
Ragged spruce gall adelgid *Pineus similis* (Gill.)	Spruce, pine, larch	22	Sucker	Adult and nymph	May to Oct.	C
Red pine cone beetle *Conophtorus resinosae* Hopk.	Red pine, jack pine	28	Borer	Adult and larva	May to Sept.	C
Red pine needle midge *Thecodiplosis piniresinosae* Kearby	Red pine	33	Gall-maker	Larva	Aug. to Oct.	C
Red spruce adelgid *Pineus floccus* (Patch)	Spruce, pine	22	Sucker	Adult and nymph	June to Aug.	C
Spruce budworm *Choristoneura fumiferana* (Clem.)	Balsam fir (IV)	36	—	—	—	A
Spruce spider mite *Oligonychus ununguis* (Jac.)	Spruce (I)	—	—	—	—	B
White pine sawfly *Neodiprion pinetum* (Nort.)	Eastern white pine	29	Defoliator	Larva	June to Sept.	C
Whitespotted sawyer *Monochamus scutellatus* (Say)	Balsam fir (IV)	43	—	—	—	B
Zimmerman pine moth *Dioryctria zimmermani* (Grote)	Pine	—	Borer	Larva	May to Oct.	C

*A: Of major importance, capable of killing or severely damaging trees.
 B: Of moderate importance, capable of sporadic and localized injury to trees.
 C: Of minor importance, not known to present a threat to trees.

A

B

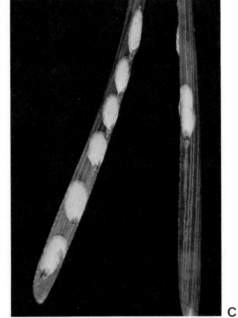

C

D

E

PLATE 27

Pine needle scale, *Chionaspis pinifo-liae* **(Fitch)**

A. Mugho pine shoots severely damaged.
B. Scale on Austrian pine needles.
C. Close-up of the scale.
D. and E.   Scale content: eggs and dead adult.

A

B

C

D

E

PLATE 28

Red pine cone beetle, *Conophtorus resinosae* Hopk.

A. Young jack pine with several damaged shoots.
B. Resin flow near adult entrance hole.
C. Mass of resin mixed with adult excrement.
D. Adult near exit hole.
E. Longitudinal cut of a tunnel showing content.

PLATE 29

White pine sawfly, *Neodiprion pinetum* (Nort.)

A. Eastern white pine shoots severely damaged.
B. Female adult on eastern white pine needles.
C. Eastern white pine twig used for egg laying.
D. Close-up of eggs.
E. Larval colony on eastern white pine shoot.
F. Damage by young larvae.
G. Dorsal view of mature larva.
H. Eggs of predator (*Anatis mali* (Say)) laid on pine needles.
I. and J.   Larva and adult of same predator.

PLATE 30

European pine sawfly, *Neodiprion sertifer* (Geoff.)

A. Mugho pine shoot showing defoliation on previous year needles.
B. Adult female at rest on jack pine foliage.
C. Adult male near its cocoon shell.
D. Middle-aged larvae on Scots pine foliage.
E. Dorsal view of mature larva.

A

B

C

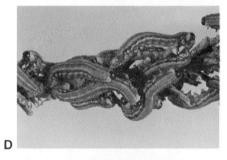

D

E

D

C1

C2

A

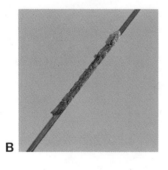

B

E

F

Introduced pine sawfly, *Diprion similis* (Htg.)

A. Female laying eggs.
B. Eastern white pine needle showing eggs scars.
C. Young larvae on pine needles, 1) in August and 2) in September.
D. Crown of eastern white pine severely defoliated.
E. Larval excrement under severely defoliated eastern white pine.
F. Lateral view of larva and of a cocoon; the cocoon is sometimes spun in the crown.

Eastern pine shoot borer, *Eucosma gloriola* **Heinr.**

A. Plantation of injured Mugho pine.
B. Adult at rest.
C. Damaged Mugho pine twig showing the larval boring.
D. Position of larva inside the twig.
E. Opening bored by the larva in red pine twig.
F. Damaged Mugho pine twig.
G. Damaged Scots pine twig.
H. Pupa.
I. Adult female.

A

B

C

D

◄ PLATE 33

Red pine needle midge, *Thecodiplosis piniresinosae* Kearby

A. Red pine plantation severely damaged.
B. Larva in needle sheath of red pine.
C. Red pine branches severely damaged.
D. Red pine branches partially stripped of their needles after an attack.

PLATE 34 ►

Pine tortoise scale, *Toumeyella parvicornis* (Ckll.)

A. Young jack pine seriously affected.
B. Close-up of damaged twig.
C. Young nymphs at the base of a jack pine twig.
D. Wax covering nymphs body.
E. Long, narrow, flat, white shields protecting the males.
F. Old damage.
G. Larva of predator (ladybug).
H. Black mushroom developing on female sugared secretions.

A

B

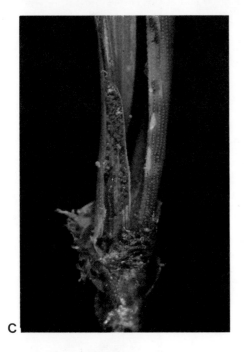

C

D

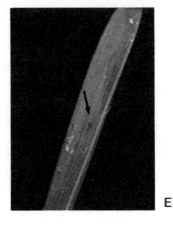

E

F

G

H

PLATE 35

Pine needleminer, *Exoteleia pinifoliella* **(Cham.)**

A. Damaged jack pine twig.
B. Close-up of jack pine twig showing needle pairs, one brown, the other still green.
C. Longitudinal cut of damaged needle showing damage at sheath levels.
D. Larval excrement thrown out of the tunnel through a hole in the needle wall.
E. Current year needle mined by the larva before hibernation in the fall.
F. Larva outside the mined needle.
G. Moth showing front wings spread.
H. Longitudinal cut of damaged needle showing place of pupation and appearance of pupa.

CHAPTER IV
Insects harmful to fir

The genus *Abies* is represented in Canada by four species: balsam fir (*A. balsamea* (L.) Mill.), alpine fir (*A. lasiocarpa* (Hook.) Nutt.), amabilis fir (*A. amabilis* (Dougl.) Forbes), and grand fir (*A. grandis* (Dougl.) Lindl.). The first species is common in Canada, being found in all provinces, whereas the range of the other three is limited mainly to British Columbia. In eastern Canada, balsam fir is the most common. In fact, it ranks second in abundance among conifers, after the spruces, and it characterizes eastern landscapes. Also, some exotic firs are used for ornamental purposes. The main concentrations of balsam fir are located in the eastern parts of Ontario and Quebec and throughout New Brunswick, Nova Scotia, and Newfoundland. The gross merchantable volume of balsam fir known in eastern Canada is now estimated at 1 345 million m^3 (Bonnor 1982). Of that volume, 72.6 percent is found in Quebec, followed by Ontario with only 11.7 percent. From a commercial point of view, this tree species has long been considered a second-class conifer, however, it has attracted favorable markets since the 1930s.

The balsam fir is a very attractive conifer; conical in shape, it grows to about 20 m in height and 50 cm in diameter. It is less demanding than spruce and is frequently encountered both in damp areas and on well-drained slopes. It is often found in pure stands as well as mixed with spruce, trembling aspen, birch, and other hardwoods.

Its wood is light, moderately flexible, and uniformly white, and hence it has commercial value in eastern Canada for timber and pulpwood. Its resin is used in the preparation of a number of laboratory products, and its characteristic silhouette, the color, and the odor of its needles make it popular as a Christmas tree or as an ornamental tree.

Balsam fir does not have many insect enemies, but it is very susceptible to those that do attack; damage caused by certain species in eastern Canada, particularly the spruce budworm, is well known. The most serious pests are members of the phyllophagous group, but damage by certain sucking and wood-boring insects is frequently encountered.

Spruce budworm
Plate 36

The spruce budworm, *Choristoneura fumiferana* (Clem.), is native to North America, where it is considered the most destructive pest of fir and spruce forests. Its importance is due to its cyclic epidemics through forests in eastern Canada. The insect occurs throughout almost the entire range of fir. In Canada, this budworm is found on 25 conifer species; that is, eight spruces, six pines, five firs, three hemlocks, two larches, and one juniper. Fir is the preferred host, but white spruce and red spruce are also seriously affected. Its common name of spruce budworm comes from the fact that, prior to 1900, spruce was the conifer most sought after by the forest industry, and no attention was paid to the pests of fir. It was only later, when fir became accepted as a substitute for spruce, that it was realized that balsam fir was the most seriously affected of the conifers. In Canada, more has been published on this insect than on any other, and most of these publications are easily accessible.

History of outbreaks

Little information is available about outbreaks of the spruce budworm over the past centuries, but Blais (1964, 1965, 1968) determined, through methodical study of the growth rings of very old firs and spruces, that seven outbreaks had occurred in the northeastern part of the continent between 1704 and 1877, with an average interval of 29 years between each.

Three other outbreaks have occurred since then in eastern North America, and it has been possible to follow them closely (Table 4).

The first outbreak, which raged from 1909 to 1920, ended leaving no indication as to the cause of the population's decline. The second outbreak, which began around 1937, ended in 1958 in Quebec due to the combined action of natural factors and large-scale spraying with chemical insecticides that had been used from 1954 on. Meanwhile in New Brunswick, some centers remained active until the following outbreak, in spite of treatments begun in 1952. In 1967, populations increased again in all regions of eastern Canada. This latest outbreak began to subside in western Quebec in 1976, but has persisted in many areas further east, and it is not known when it will end. To protect forests from damage by this insect, widespread aerial spraying has been carried out, using mainly chemical, but also biological insecticides. Despite these treatments, fir and spruce losses already covered more than 5 million ha in Quebec in 1977, and this mortality is likely to continue to increase for several years to come.

Description and biology

Adult. Medium-sized moth; gray brown in color speckled with white. Wingspan: 22 mm (Plate 36, C).

Egg. Overlapping one another to form a flattened, silky mass; apple green turning brown and silk white after hatching (Plate 36, E and F).

Larva. Cylindrical in shape; brown spotted with white. Length: about 25 mm when full grown (Plate 36, G).

Pupa. Obtected; reddish. Length: about 20 mm (Plate 36, D).

The life cycle of the spruce budworm is relatively simple in eastern Canada, where one generation is produced per year, as compared to higher regions in western Canada where its development is spread over 2 years. In eastern Canada, the moths emerge in July and are present until the beginning of September. The females lay their eggs on the needles, preferably on shoots exposed to sunlight. The eggs are laid in masses of 10 to 20 on the surface of the needle, overlapping one another like shingles on a roof. Incubation lasts from 7 to 10 days. Upon hatching, the newborn larva moves towards the interior of the crown seeking a favorable site in which to spend the winter; that is, in crevices of the bark, amongst lichens, or in the cupules of staminate flowers. Once it has found a suitable site, the larva spins a shelter with silken webs and, after going through a first moult, becomes dormant for the winter.

In the early days of spring, the larva returns to the exterior of the crown seeking food. It prefers new staminate flowers but, if these are not present, it will mine one or more old needles and thus survives until buds open. As soon as the buds begin to expand, the larva attacks the young, developing needles. Once the shoots have reached a certain size, the larva moves into a sort of shelter built with two neighboring shoots attached with silken threads where it can then feed in complete safety. If disturbed, it abandons its shelter and drops at the end of a silken thread that it spins as needed; it may thus settle at a lower level of the crown or else be carried by the wind, sometimes over great distances. When new needles become scarce due to overpopulation, the larva will feed on old needles. Towards the end of June or the beginning of July, the larva transforms to a pupa, attached either to dead needles and waste material by silken threads, or to a support by its abdominal tip. Moths emerge about 10 days later, and the cast pupal case remains in place for some time before being carried off either by the wind or destroyed during bad weather.

PLATE 36

Spruce budworm, *Choristoneura fumiferana* (Clem.)

A. Severely defoliated, 50-year old balsam fir stand in July.
B. Appearance of 25-year old balsam fir stand almost killed by budworm attack.
C. Light-colored moth at rest (wingspan: 22 mm).
D. Light-colored pupa in natural position (length: 20 mm).
E. Sound egg mass on balsam fir needle (seen from above).
F. Mass of hatched eggs on fir needle (side view).
G. Mature larva on fir twig (length: 25 mm).
H. Close-up of severely defoliated balsam fir twig.
I. Defoliation of a balsam fir that survived budworm attack.

Damage

Damage is caused by the spruce budworm larvae feeding and is most serious during the last larval instar. The larva is known to prefer needles of the current year, eating them completely or partially, depending on the size of the insect population. Often, during periods of high population, all new shoots are consumed early in the season, that is, as soon as the buds open. Destruction of a single year's foliage does not normally have serious consequences, because enough needles remain in the crowns to keep the trees alive. Evergreens are known to keep each season's foliage for a period of many years; in the case of fir, this period is about 7 years. The situation becomes more critical (Plate 36, H) if defoliation is repeated over several consecutive years, because the foliage is increasingly thinned out. Firs generally begin to succumb after 4 consecutive years of severe defoliation (Plate 36, B), and, even after the end of an epidemic, mortality gradually increases over the next 5 years to an average level of 50 percent (McLintock 1955).

Mortality of fir is accelerated and intensified when insect populations become so large that the larvae also attack old needles. In such cases, larvae fall in large numbers onto young firs growing as underbrush, and these are often destroyed well before the larger trees. If, due to reduced insect populations, there is a break of 1 or 2 years in the defoliation, balsam fir buds that escaped destruction will develop normally, and one or two lateral buds may replace the destroyed terminal bud (Plate 36, I). The crown then takes on a bayonet shape, characteristic of the passage of the spruce budworm.

Repeated defoliation also reduces incremental tree growth. For example, in balsam fir, there is an interval of 3-6 years between the first severe defoliation and a reduction in growth increment and, according to McLintock (1965), this reduction may reach from 60 to 75 percent after a period of 5 years.

Diagnosis

In the spring, an on-going epidemic of spruce budworm may be identified by a number of signs, such as an abnormal spreading of new fir twigs and an early defoliation of some shoots. Also, at the lightest shock to a twig, many larvae spin down on silken threads. The number of larvae on tree crowns may help to predict the extent of damage that will be caused.

In the summer, infested fir stands take on a reddish color due to the presence of dead needles held by strands of silk (Plate 36, A). In the fall, most of these needles are carried off by wind or rain, and the stands become grayish. At that time, larvae, pupae, or their empty pupal cases may be found on the crowns.

At the end of the summer and in the fall, sound and hatched egg masses on the underside of needles indicate that young larvae are already hidden in the crown or are on the way to doing so; the counting of egg masses may enable a prediction to be made of the defoliation likely to occur the following spring.

Following an outbreak, damaged stands may be recognized by the presence of bayonet-shaped stems, the deformity being present at about the same level on all damaged stems. The number of years passed since an outbreak may easily be established by counting the number of whorls present above the bayonet-level or by examining the growth rings on discs cut from the trunk.

Natural control

Factors that may check proliferation of the spruce budworm are numerous and varied. Among the biological factors are entomophagous parasites, of which there are about 70 species. One of these, *Trichogramma minutum* Riley, attacks the egg and destroys a large proportion of them in some years. Several parasitic species attack the larvae, some acting on the full-grown larvae, whereas yet others attack the pupae. The most active and numerous species are *Apanteles fumiferanae* Vier., *Glypta fumiferanae* (Vier.), *Diadegma acronyctae* (Ashm.), and *Meteorus trachynotus* Vier.

During the second-last outbreak, parasites were introduced from British Columbia and Europe to reinforce the action of native parasites, but the results were not encouraging.

Many predators also exist, such as spiders, insects, and birds, that feed on eggs, larvae, pupae, and adults. Sometimes birds may eat large numbers of larvae and pupae and contribute to holding populations down to low levels for a number of years, but there comes a time when they are no longer able to keep up, and then a new outbreak of spruce budworm develops.

A number of microorganisms, including microsporidia, bacteria, viruses, and fungi, infest various stages of the spruce budworm, but their importance varies with the type of environment and the various elements of the climate.

The most important natural factor in controlling populations of the spruce budworm is probably the climate. Rapid increases in population clearly result from three or four successive seasons of favorable weather, and declines in population often result from certain unfavorable climatic factors. For example, late frosts in the spring may kill large numbers of early larvae, as was the case in the region north of Montreal in 1944. Similarly, the first fall frosts may interfere with egg-laying or kill newborn larvae before they have prepared their hibernacula, as was observed in Gaspé in 1957 and in western Quebec in 1976. The most significant losses, however, take place during the time at which the young larvae disperse either to seek shelter in the fall, or to find food early in the spring. Lastly, during their flights, large numbers of moths are carried over great distances by the wind and land in unfavorable sites.

The combined action of all these factors varies considerably not only during an outbreak, but also during different periods of the life cycle of the spruce budworm. Life tables have been developed that permit an evaluation of the action of the various factors during a given season (Table 5).

Artificial control

The cyclic appearance of outbreaks of the spruce budworm is in itself proof that natural factors provide insufficient control. The organization of a control program against the spruce budworm is a complex matter, but control work would be made

Table 4. Summary of three spruce budworm outbreaks

Type of data	Outbreak periods		
	1909–1920	1937–1958	1967–present
Starting point	Southwestern Quebec	Eastern Ontario	Southwestern Quebec and southeastern Ontario
Main directions	East	East and west	East and west
Known longitudinal limits	Western border of Quebec to Cape Breton Island	Eastern Manitoba to Cape Breton Island	Center of Ontario to Newfoundland
Extreme latitudes	46° to 50°N	45° to 50°15'N	45° to 51°30'N
Total distance covered	1 500 km	2 800 km	2 700 km
Known duration	11 years	21 years	15 years
Total area affected	300 000 km^2	1 100 000 km^2	900 000 km^2
Approx. losses of fir and spruce (m^3) (Quebec only)	540 000 000* 360 000 000**	66 000 000† 125 000 000†† 180 000 000††	Not yet determined
Use of artificial control	—	Quebec and New Brunswick	Ontario, Quebec, New Brunswick and Newfoundland

  * Shierbeck 1922.
 ** Piché, in Swaine and Craighead 1924.
  † Royer 1958.
†† Martineau, R. 1975. Tordeuse des bourgeons de l'épinette; historique des épidémies antérieures à 1967. Symposium sur la tordeuse des bourgeons de l'épinette. Unpublished report.

Table 5. Factors controlling spruce budworm populations

Stage of development	Natural factors	Mortality during the stage (%)	Survival rate for the stage (%)	Total survival at stage end (%)
Egg	Parasites and predators	19	81	81
Larval instar 1st and 2nd	Dispersion	82	18	14.5
3rd to 6th	Parasites and disease	86	14	2
Pupa	Parasites and predators	34	66	1.3

easier if certain preventive measures were taken. For example, it is well known that the greater the percentage of mature firs in a stand, the more vulnerable is the stand, and this vulnerability increases with the height of the trees and the extent and density of the stand. Thus, it would be advantageous to harvest the stands before they reach maturity and to develop cutting methods that would favor mixed and uneven-aged stands.

During an outbreak, however, a realistic approach would be to try and keep the trees alive until the insect populations decline. This is done by attempting, right from the beginning of the outbreak, to predict how it will develop based on the experience of past outbreaks, and to determine which areas are likely to be attacked. Cutting programs can then be devised to harvest threatened stands before they are destroyed by the insect. Stands that cannot be harvested in time may be kept alive for several years by aerial applications of insecticides. This method was used for the first time in 1927 with little success. It was tried again, successfully, in Gaspé and in New Brunswick around 1950. Large-scale programs for aerial spraying have been carried out in eastern Canada, particularly since 1970 in Quebec, where up to 3.5 million ha of forests have been treated every year. The application of insecticides over such vast areas necessitates the use of larger and larger aircraft with sophisticated navigation systems. In the majority of cases, chemical insecticides were used, but a biological insecticide, *Bacillus thuringiensis* Berl., has also been tested in small areas.

Before going ahead with any treatment, it is important to study carefully the conditions of the stands to be protected, and to choose the method most likely to produce the desired result. If the primary aim is to protect an already thin foliage from destruction, it is best to apply the product as early as possible in the season, whereas a late treatment would ensure the destruction of a greater number of insects. Both objectives may be attained by carrying out two applications, one early and one late, during the same season.

In recreational forests, the use of a biological insecticide such as *B. thuringiensis* is recommended, although, because of its slower action, it should be applied fairly early in the season to obtain the desired effect.

When only a few isolated trees need protection, larvae may be dislodged by shaking the trees vigorously, and, from smaller trees, larvae may simply be collected by hand. Larvae may also be dislodged by spraying crowns with a strong stream of water. Application of either a contact, stomach, or biological insecticide at the first signs of defoliation also gives satisfactory results.

References

Blais 1964, 1965, 1968; Dorais 1977; McLintock 1955; Miller 1963; Morris 1963; Prebble 1975; Royer 1958; Schierbeck 1923; Swaine and Craighead 1924; and Zon 1903.

Hemlock looper
Plate 37

The hemlock looper, *Lambdina fiscellaria fiscellaria* (Guen.), is an insect defoliator native to North America, that occurs from the Atlantic coast westward to the province of Alberta and the state of Iowa. In the eastern provinces, the main host of this looper is balsam fir (Plate 37, F), whereas in the west it is hemlock. If, however, during an outbreak, these two preferred hosts are in short supply, the insect feeds on many other conifers, and even on hardwoods. In Quebec, as an example, it has been collected on all native conifers and on hardwoods such as birch, maple, and poplar. It has attracted particular attention in its eastern range by sudden outbreaks that have usually developed in over-mature fir stands growing in damp areas and near large bodies of water.

History of outbreaks

The hemlock looper has been a particular pest in Newfoundland where, since the first outbreak in 1912, five waves of epidemics, lasting from 3 to 6 years, have occurred at intervals of 10 to 15 years. The two outbreaks recorded from 1947 to 1954 and from 1959 to 1963 caused the loss of 3.6 million m^3 of balsam fir, and the following one, that lasted from 1966 to 1970, seriously damaged an additional 10 million m^3.

In the Maritime provinces, outbreaks have been less frequent than in Newfoundland, occurring mainly in Nova Scotia and Prince Edward Island. In 1960, large populations were observed for the first time in the Maritime provinces since 1930 and, 2 years later, large numbers of balsam fir were killed during that outbreak. Attacks were also reported in 1969 and 1975, but were confined to a small area.

In Quebec, six waves of epidemics were observed between 1928 and 1977; these occurred at intervals of about 10 years and lasted about 3 years each time. Their degree of intensity varied considerably, and most of them occurred in areas bordering the Gulf of St. Lawrence. The most important ones were the 1928 outbreak that caused losses of 3.6 million m^3 of balsam fir on the north shore of the St-Lawrence River; the epidemic that spread from the Rivière-à-Claude watershed to Gaspé in 1947, destroying all the balsam fir over an area of some 400 km², and the last outbreak on Anticosti Island in 1970 that destroyed balsam fir over an area of 800 km².

In Ontario, outbreaks have been local in scope and occurred mainly in stands of hemlock and balsam fir located on islands. The most serious ones were reported between 1953 and 1956 and destroyed up to 90 percent of the hemlock in the affected areas.

Description and biology

Adult. Medium-sized moth; creamy beige with forewings crossed by two thin, brown, and broken lines; hindwings crossed by a single line in the prolongation of the more distal line of the forewings. Wingspan: 32 mm. (Plate 37, B).

Egg. Ovoid; light green initially, turning coppery brown after a few days. Length: about 0.9 mm (Plate 37, C).

Larva. Cylindrical and having the characteristic form of looper larvae, with three pairs of abdominal prolegs; first instar larva dark gray, taking on as it matures various colors varying from yellow to black. Full length: about 32 mm (Plate 37, D).

Pupa. Spindle-shaped; honey yellow. Length: about 20 mm (Plate 37, E).

Research on the biology of the hemlock looper has been carried out in Quebec and Newfoundland. It has only one generation per year and overwinters in the egg stage. Upon hatching in June, the newborn larvae, because they are positively phototropic, immediately move towards the tender needles of the new shoots; this food is absolutely necessary to their survival. Should this food be lacking, they may eat one another. As they grow older, the larvae feed on older needles, and for that reason they are found in the interior of the crown whereas the younger larvae usually stay on the outside. Defoliation may be irregularly spread in the crown as well as in the forest; thus, during an outbreak in a given area, severely defoliated stands may be found next to unaffected stands. Larval development is completed in July and August, and a drastic change takes place. The larva becomes negatively phototropic and seeks a shaded area for pupation.

For that reason pupae are most often found in bark crevices, lichens, under dead leaves or bark debris, or under other such waste. The pupal stage lasts from 15 to 20 days. The first adults appear in August, and may be seen around the trees until September. The flight capabilities of moths are fairly poor; they are low fliers and, when they alight on a tree trunk, it is usually within the lower 3 m. Moths may be seen at any time of the day, but particularly in the evening, when the male seeking the female is attracted by light. Both sexes appear to be equally attracted to damp areas.

Eggs may be found from the month of July until the following spring, in groups of two or three, in a wide variety of locations, from the litter right up to the twigs. Lichens, bark crevices, moss growing on stumps, and the trunks and branches of host trees are preferred sites for egg-laying.

Damage and diagnosis

Damage by the hemlock looper is mainly found in pure stands of balsam fir or those mixed with white spruce and occasionally black spruce. Apart from defoliation, damage consists in growth reduction and mortality of affected parts of trees. This damage is increased by the fact that the larvae waste part of the foliage. The young larvae eat the edges of the needles, leaving a central filament that eventually dries, curls, and yellows. The older larvae move from one needle to another, nibbling rather than eating the whole needle, and often feeding only at its base, causing the distal part of the needle to redden and die (Plate 37, G). In severe outbreaks, totally bare twigs are liable to dry out, because they are no longer protected from wind and sunlight.

When severe outbreaks occur on balsam fir, all needles may be eaten during the summer (Plate 37, H), and trees thus defoliated generally die during the winter or the following spring (Plate 37, I). If defoliation is partial and no defoliation occurs the following year, the tree will survive, but its annual increment will be reduced. Defoliation on white spruce is generally less important, except on trees of small diameter growing under severely affected balsam firs. In very severe outbreaks, however, such as that which occurred between 1947 and 1950 in the Gaspé Peninsula, all spruce trees even-

tually die. On Anticosti Island, 12 percent of white spruce trees were killed during the 1970-1972 outbreak. Black spruce is generally less defoliated and damage is less important.

In winter, in a forest containing stands of balsam fir and white spruce the presence of completely defoliated areas next to stands that have undergone little or no attack indicates an attack by this looper; the other conifers may also be affected, but to a lesser extent.

In summer, trees infested by this insect may be recognized by the presence of looper larvae of various colors, feeding on the current year's needles as well as those of previous years, on fir and spruce and, to a lesser degree, on many other tree species including hardwoods.

In July, August, and September, especially in the evening and at low altitudes, the sudden appearance of multitudes of creamy-beige moths in balsam fir and spruce stands indicates that an infestation will occur in the following year.

Natural control

From research conducted in Newfoundland, Otvos (1973) showed that natural factors play a major part in controlling the hemlock looper. Two fungi appear to be the primary agents in the control of infestations. The fungal infection in the larval population develops gradually, during a 3-year period, in several centers within the infested territory; finally it spreads to the whole territory and causes populations to decline. Temperatures between 15° and 20°C, along with high humidity, favor the development of this disease. Parasites are also quite effective; one species destroys up to 23 percent of the eggs, whereas 12 others recovered on larvae and on pupae cause population reductions of about 79 percent. Otvos also recorded 19 species of birds feeding on the larvae of the hemlock looper, but their role is not very important.

In Quebec, all known outbreaks seem to have disappeared as suddenly as they appeared, and none lasted longer than 2 or 3 years. In the north shore outbreak, Watson (1934) attributed the population drop to excessive humidity during the summers of 1928 and 1929. In his research on Anticosti Island, Jobin (1973), collected 12 species of parasites, that is, 4 very active dipterous species and

PLATE 37

Hemlock looper, *Lambdina fiscellaria fiscellaria* (Guen.)

A. Severely defoliated balsam firs in July.
B. Adult at rest (wingspan: 32 mm).
C. Eggs on stem of balsam fir twig (length: about 0.9 mm).
D. Mature larva on balsam fir twig (length: 32 mm).
E. Dorsal and ventral views of pupa (length: 20 mm).
F. Young larva on balsam fir needle.
G. Close-up of severely defoliated balsam fir twig.
H. Severely defoliated balsam fir forest in July.
I. Balsam fir forest killed by severe outbreak.

8 species of hymenoptera, responsible for a mortality estimated at 49 percent. As previously, this last outbreak died out suddenly over the entire affected area due to the action of natural factors. In certain sectors treated with chemical insecticides, the process was greatly accelerated, which prevented the destruction of large quantities of wood.

Artificial control

Isolated trees may be protected from hemlock looper attack by using a strong spray of water on the crowns to dislodge larvae at the beginning of their active period. This treatment would also raise the humidity and thus would favor the development of disease in the larval population.

Clear-cutting, in winter, of infested stands and those adjacent plays a considerable role in lowering insect populations by reducing the amount of food available to newborn larvae when they hatch in the spring.

Widespread outbreaks may be avoided, or their intensity at least reduced, by a management plan providing not only for the removal of mature balsam fir trees using appropriate cutting methods, but also for the prevention of the regeneration of this tree species in pure and dense stands over large areas.

It was also demonstrated, during recent outbreaks on Anticosti Island and in Newfoundland that aerial spraying with chemical insecticides while larvae are feeding may help to bring about sharp population drops before too much damage has been caused. It is to be hoped that some day it might be possible to replace chemicals by biological insecticides such as *Bacillus thuringiensis* Berl.; these should be applied as early in the outbreak as possible, to destroy populations before they increase too much.

References

Benoit and Desaulniers 1972; Canada Department of Agriculture 1960; Canada Department of Forestry, 1963; Canadian Forestry Service, 1971; Carroll 1956; Carroll and Waters 1973; Daviault 1949b; Jobin 1973; Lambert 1941a; Lambert 1942; Otvos 1973; Otvos and Bryant 1972; Prebble 1975; Smirnoff 1974; Smirnoff and Jobin 1973; and Watson 1934.

Balsam fir sawfly
Plate 38

Even though the presence of the balsam fir sawfly, *Neodiprion abietis* (Harr.), was recorded in North America as early as 1910, the only study devoted to its biology was carried out by Strubble (1957) during an infestation on white fir (*Abies concolor* (Gord. and Glend.)) in the state of California. In the United States, this defoliator was long thought to attack white fir and also red fir, *A. magnifica*. In Canada, the insect has been reported every year, in varying numbers, since its discovery in 1936. As early as 1939, Brown called attention to the presence of this diprionid on balsam fir and on various species of spruce across Canada, often in considerable numbers in the East. It was subsequently determined that in Canada the principal host of this species is balsam fir, although it is often found on white spruce and black spruce and, less frequently, on red spruce.

History of outbreaks

In eastern Canada, the balsam fir sawfly has been most active in the Newfoundland region, where local outbreaks have been reported in various places almost every year since 1945. Outbreaks occur every 3 or 4 years in that province, and last for equivalent periods. Damage recorded has normally been on balsam fir and spruces. On the former species, cases of mortality were recorded following defoliation if a second pest, such as the eastern blackheaded budworm (*Acleris variana*) was also involved in causing the damage.

In the Maritime provinces, outbreaks have been less frequent; damage has been caused only in Nova Scotia, during the periods of 1942 to 1945, 1959 to 1961, and 1967 to 1969. Outbreaks are of short duration, as is the case in Newfoundland, but with longer intervals between them.

In Quebec, local infestations of large numbers of insects have been reported on several occasions, particularly in Garthby and Risborough townships in 1941; on the north shore of the St-Lawrence River, in the north of Montreal region, and in the Ottawa valley in 1950; and in the basin of the lower Gatineau River and its tributaries from 1967 to 1977.

Similar infestations were observed in Ontario during various periods, and the insect caused particular damage in the southeastern part of that province, especially in the Ottawa valley. Outbreaks took place during four distinct periods; that is, from 1939 to 1944, 1950 to 1954, 1961 to 1963, and 1967 to 1974. As in Quebec, the last outbreak was of longer duration than the preceding ones.

Description and biology

Adult. Resembles a small wasp, with four membranous wings; female brown, male black. Lengths: 6-8 mm and 4-5 mm, respectively (Plate 38, A).
Egg. Oval-shaped; white (Plate 38, C).
Larva. Cylindrical, elongated; initially green, taking on a blackish color as it matures. Length at full development: 20 mm (Plate 38, D).
Pupa. Enclosed in an oval cocoon; dimensions slightly larger than adult.

The entomological literature gives little information on the biology of the balsam fir sawfly, and the only detailed study was carried out on white fir in the southern United States (Strubble 1957). It is well known that the behavior of an insect species varies greatly with its host and with climatic conditions, and it would therefore be useful to study the ethology and life cycle of this species on balsam fir and in the northern part of its range. Because this information is not available at present, the basic data given is that provided by Strubble (1957) with some additional observations made in Quebec over the years.

The balsam fir sawfly overwinters in the egg stage in a slit made by the female's ovipositor in the leaf cuticle. The eggs are normally laid one per needle, all on the same branch, most commonly on the current year's growth, but occasionally on that of previous years (Plate 38, B). The first larvae leave the eggs when buds open in the spring. As they emerge, the larvae form colonies of 30 to 100, scattered in small groups on adjacent needles. They feed on old needles, beginning with those of the previous year, then attacking older ones, but rarely touching the current year's foliage (Plate 38, E).

The larvae strip the outside of the needles, leaving a central filament that in time shrivels, yellows, and finally takes on a brick red color. The larva goes through six instars and takes about 1 month to reach its full development. As it matures, the larva becomes solitary. Once its growth is completed, it drops to the ground to spin its cocoon, generally in the ground litter and, more rarely, on the surface. Larvae may be found occasionally on foliage. The collecting of cocoons of this insect in the field is quite difficult, even in heavily infested areas. During 1940 and 1941, 2 years of heavy infestation, the first cocoons were obtained in the laboratory in mid-June, and the first adults emerged about 1 month later. This observation indicates the possibility of two generations per year. If this is the case, it is likely that some individuals from the second generation do not have time to complete their development before fall comes. In the United States, only one generation per year has been reported to date.

PLATE 38

Balsam fir sawfly, *Neodiprion abietis* (Harr.)

A. Female and male adults near their respective cocoons (lengths: 6-8 mm and 4-5 mm respectively).
B. Current year's growth, showing many needles bearing egg-slits.
C. Close-up of egg outside of egg-slit.
D. Mature larva on fir twig (length: 20 mm).
E. Fir twig defoliated by this diprionid: (1) the current year's needles are intact; (2) 1-year old needles are chewed and reddened; and (3) 2-year old needles have disappeared.
F. Fir stand showing several reddened crowns following an outbreak lasting several years.
G. Close-up showing reddened fir crown following an outbreak.

Damage

Middle-aged forest stands of medium-to-thin density, where balsam fir dominates, are the hardest hit in Quebec. Damage reported to date has all been caused by larvae and takes three forms, namely defoliation, reduced growth, and slight mortality of balsam firs.

Defoliation is the first symptom of a balsam fir sawfly infestation. Once the larvae have finished feeding, defoliation is evidenced by the red coloring of 1 year-old needles, although this may be partly hidden by the lighter green of the current year's growth (Plate 38, F and G). In time, however, the red foliage finally drops, and the most heavily affected part of the crown appears as a silhouette surrounded by a thin layer of green foliage.

Strubble (1957) observed a considerable reduction in growth increment from the very first years of an outbreak on white fir and, after 3 years of continuous severe defoliation, mortality was estimated at approximately 1 percent. In Quebec, a slight degree of mortality was noted among isolated balsam firs that had been severely defoliated for 5 or 6 consecutive years in the lower Ottawa valley; however, it was impossible to establish the extent to which the sawfly was responsible, because these firs had been attacked previously by the spruce budworm.

Diagnosis

During the winter months, it is easy to identify trees attacked by the balsam fir sawfly during the preceding months by examining the upper part of fir crowns. By then, they are bare of all or part of their foliage except on the current year's growth; on closer examination, eggs may be present on the current year's foliage.

In July, the crowns of firs infested by feeding larvae can be identified by the presence of yellow or brick red needles on the inside part; at that time of year the larvae can be made to drop down the tree by striking the trunk sharply with a blunt instrument.

In the fall, the presence of a few sound or empty golden cocoons in the ground litter is a sure indication of the insect's presence.

Natural control

Balsam fir sawfly populations are highly susceptible to various natural factors. A number of species of parasites have been reared in the laboratories in the provinces of eastern Canada. Raizenne (1957) lists 14 species for Ontario; 5 species have been identified in Quebec, and 9 in the Maritime provinces. In Newfoundland, the population decline observed in 1959 and 1961 is at least in part attributable to the action of parasites. In California, Strubble (1957) mentioned 12 species of parasites and 10 species of predators, half of which have been identified to the species. In 1952, a program of biological control was organized in Canada that consisted of introducing predators into Newfoundland. Of the seven species introduced prior to 1959, several are now well established.

Strubble also mentioned the action of a virus that caused drastic reductions in larval populations during the outbreak he studied. The population decreases observed in Newfoundland and the Maritime provinces were also partly attributed to the action of an unidentified disease. It is probable, too, that a viral disease was, to a large degree, responsible for the decrease in populations of this diprionid in eastern Ontario.[1] A polyhedrosis virus appeared in 1971 among larvae reared in the laboratory in Quebec, but its role in reducing populations has not yet been clearly determined. There are reasons to believe that this virus helps to keep the population under control. The presence of a microsporidia was also detected in samples taken in Ham-Nord, Quebec, in 1972.

[1] F.T. Bird, personal communication.

Artificial control

Natural factors regulating the balsam fir sawfly, in particular parasites and a disease of unknown nature, are normally successful in keeping populations of this diprionid down to reasonable levels in eastern Canada, and the real damage which may result from outbreaks is thus negligible. For this reason, direct control measures have so far not been necessary. If such action were found to be necessary, a stomach insecticide, applied when the larvae are feeding, would be most appropriate.

References

Canada Department of Agriculture, 1940-1952, 1953-1960 and 1959; Canada Department of Fisheries and Forestry, 1969; Canada Department of Forestry, 1961-1966; Canada Department of Forestry and Rural Development 1967-1968; Canadian Forestry Service, 1970-1971, 1972-1981 and 1974a; Raizenne 1957; and Strubble 1957.

Eastern blackheaded budworm
Plate 39

The eastern blackheaded budworm, *Acleris variana* (Fern.), is a microlepidopterous defoliator distributed throughout the surveyed area of Canadian forests. The insect has been collected on 20 conifer species, the preferred ones being balsam fir, white spruce, and western hemlock. In the northern part of the continent, this budworm is a greater threat in the west and in Alaska, where a number of outbreaks occurred in recent years. It is, however, quite possible that, in some outbreaks reported in western Canada, this insect was confused with another species recently identified as *A. gloverana* (Wlshm.), commonly called the western blackheaded budworm.

History of outbreaks

In eastern Canada, past outbreaks of eastern blackheaded budworm may also have been confused with those of a more common species, the spruce budworm, *Choristoneura fumiferana*. The first outbreak identified with certainty occurred in the Maritime provinces from 1929 to 1934. In 1937, another short-term outbreak developed in eastern Quebec. A few years later, that is from 1945 to 1950, a series of outbreaks swept Newfoundland, the Maritime provinces, and Quebec, without invading Ontario. The situation was particularly disastrous in Quebec, where the largest moderate-to-severe infestation covered an area of 25 000 km^2 in the central and eastern sections of Gaspé Peninsula. Stands of balsam fir and white spruce were completely stripped of their foliage and eventually died. Two other less important centers were discovered covering a total area of 4 000 km^2; the first one in the St. Maurice River watershed and the second near Drummondville in the Eastern Townships.

Description and biology

Adult. Medium-sized moth with very diversified coloring, predominantly gray and brown with highly varied designs. Wingspan: about 15 mm (Plate 39, E to H).

Egg. Orange and hidden under a layer of gray hairs.

Larva. Rather pale initially; body rapidly taking the color of the surrounding foliage, whereas the head becomes black. Full length: 12 mm.

Pupa. Basically brown, often with green wings (Plate 39, C).

Despite the importance of the eastern blackheaded budworm, the literature contains little information on its biology.

This insect has only one generation a year, and overwinters in the egg stage. Eggs are laid singly on the underside of the needles. Hatching begins by mid-May, and peaks in early June. Upon hatching, the young larva moves towards an opening bud where it penetrates and builds a shelter by spinning a silken web around several needles (Plate 39, B). It develops there in safety during the first two larval instars and part of the third one, before leaving its shelter to complete its development in the open. When disturbed, the larva drops at the end of a thread that it uses to try and reach another source of food. Larvae initially feed on new needles but when these become scarce on fir, particularly during outbreaks, they also attack old needles.

PLATE 39

Eastern blackheaded budworm, *Acleris variana* (Fern.)

A. Young larva on fir shoot.
B. Mature larva in silken shelter on foliage.
C. Pupa reared in laboratory.
D. Pupa formed in natural environment.
E. Adult at rest.
F. G. H.   Pinned adults to show some variations in design and color of the forewing (wingspan: 15 mm).

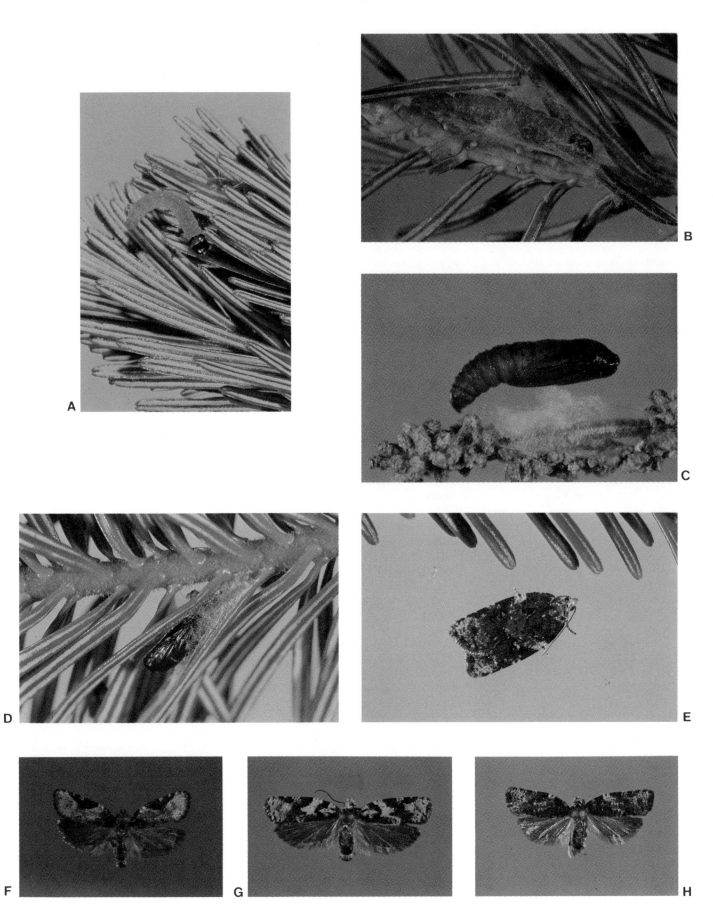

Once its development is completed, the larva transforms into a pupa that may be seen from June to September with a peak around the end of July, attached to needles by its anal tip. The pupal stage lasts about 10 days, and moths are present from the beginning of July until the end of September.

Damage and diagnosis

Damage caused by the eastern blackheaded budworm consists mainly in the destruction of needles of the current year, especially on fir and white spruce, but during an epidemic, the old fir needles are also seriously affected. During a larval migration, firs of all ages are defoliated completely in a single season.

A reduction in growth increment also results from the defoliation as secondary damage, and affected trees eventually begin to die. A single year of severe defoliation is sufficient to cause fir mortality. Balch (1932) stated that on white spruce the old needles are not affected and buds are not destroyed, thus limiting damage on this tree species; also black spruce and red spruce apparently suffer only a slight defoliation.

In June and July, on new needles of balsam fir and white spruce, small green larvae with brown to black heads may be seen dangling on silken threads when disturbed. During July and August, small brown pupae with green wings can be found together with their exuviae, hanging by their anal tip from twigs or dead needles (Plate 39, D). From August to the end of September, small grayish brown moths, with wings of various designs and often of very bright colors, may be seen flying around the defoliated crowns of fir and white spruce. An egg-sampling method developed on hemlock in western Canada could easily be adapted to the east to evaluate the population density and to make predictions on the intensity of the outbreak the following spring.

Natural control

Data collected by FIDS include a total of 14 species of entomophagous parasites of the eastern blackheaded budworm in Canada (Bradley 1974). After Lambert (1949), the sudden population decline often noted in Quebec, was apparently due to the action of an unidentified disease. The sudden disappearance of many of the outbreaks reported in other provinces may indicate the action of factors other than parasites or predators; in western Canada, climate seems to be of major importance (Schmiege 1966; Silver 1960, 1963).

Artificial control

When only a few isolated trees need protection, an attempt should be made to encourage the development of diseases caused by pathogenic microorganisms in the larval population of the eastern blackheaded budworm by spraying the affected crowns copiously with water several times during the larval development. In the forest, appropriate silvicultural methods may help the stands to become less vulnerable to attack by this insect by preventing the development of pure balsam fir stands and encouraging the regeneration of black spruce or red spruce.

While an outbreak is in progress, populations in infested stands may be destroyed by aerial spraying with chemical stomach or contact insecticides at the time the larvae leave their winter shelter and feed greedily, but before they can cause serious damage.

In areas where the use of chemical insecticides is dangerous to the environment or in confined areas, a biological insecticide could eventually be used against this species, as is done for the spruce budworm.

References

Balch 1932; Bradley 1974; Canada Department of Agriculture, 1949; Prentice 1965; Roy 1948; Schmiege 1966; and Silver 1957a, 1960, 1963.

Balsam woolly adelgid
Plate 40

The balsam woolly adelgid, *Adelges piceae* (Ratz.), a sucking insect of European origin, was discovered first in 1908 in the state of Maine in the United States. Its importance has long been known on this continent because of its threat to balsam fir forests, and especially since the balsam fir became an important source of supply for the pulp and paper industry. The insect also attacks several other fir species and causes serious damage to amabilis fir, alpine fir, and grand fir. Its range in North America is confined to the Atlantic and Pacific coastal regions. In the East, infestations of this insect occur in a limited sector of North Carolina and in a strip of land along the Atlantic coast that includes six New England states, from Connecticut to Maine; in Canada its range covers an area of over 100 000 km² in the Maritime provinces, Newfoundland, and eastern Quebec.

History of outbreaks

In eastern Canada, the balsam woolly adelgid was first observed in southern Nova Scotia in 1910. It had probably been established there for quite some time. From this entry point, it spread gradually across the other Atlantic provinces, where by 1948, it was present in all counties except Madawaska and Restigouche. In Newfoundland, the insect was first observed in 1949 over an area of several hundred hectares but 20 years later the affected area had increased to about 16 000 km². The insect was discovered in Quebec in 1964 in the Magdalen Islands and in the eastern part of the Gaspé Peninsula, where it had apparently caused damage for about 15 years. In 1978, the epidemic had made little progress in the Gaspé Peninsula, and the affected area was estimated at about 2 500 km². In the west, its distribution is limited to part of the states of Washington and Oregon in the United States and to an area of 10 000 km² in southern British Columbia in Canada.

In all the provinces of eastern Canada where infestations of the balsam woolly adelgid have occurred, the outbreaks were generally quite severe and lasted long enough to cause balsam fir mortality in certain areas. Over the past 15 years, however, no notable change has been observed in the range and harmfulness of this species in areas where it is known as a pest.

Description and biology

The balsam woolly adelgid is a tiny sucking insect, normally covered with a thick white coat of waxy material; its life cycle is made up of three stages: adult, egg, and nymph.

Adult. Wingless; unisexual. Length: about 1 mm.

Egg. Tiny, ovoid; pale yellow turning to reddish brown with time.

Nymph. Ellipsoid; orange when young and mobile, black when attached to the bark.

Detailed studies on the biology of the balsam woolly adelgid were conducted in New Brunswick by Balch (1952) and in Newfoundland by Bryant (1971, 1976).

The life cycle of this adelgid is simpler than that of most other adelgids because all stages are found on the same host, reproduction is parthenogenetic and winged forms are rare. Figure 3, adapted from Bryant (1976), shows the life cycle as it occurs in Newfoundland; it is probably similar in Quebec.

The balsam woolly adelgid may have two or three generations per year, depending on which forms develop (Bryant 1976). It overwinters in the sistens stage and may subsequently develop into either of two forms; the sistens or the progrediens. The first form predominates, being present year round and in all generations, whereas the second form represents only a small part of the population and exists only in the first generation (June and July).

Immediately upon hatching, the young nymph of any generation has a very active phase called "crawler" during which it seeks a favorable site in which to settle permanently. Once settled, the adelgid becomes stationary by inserting its stylets into the bark to suck out the juices on which it feeds, while injecting an irritating substance into the tissues of the host.

This adelgid may be found on all parts of the bark, from the trunk to the twigs. In Newfoundland, according to Bryant (1976), 95 percent of the adelgids are found in crevices of branches, under the scales of the previous year buds, and amongst or in staminate flowers, the majority of the population being located within the last 3 years growth. Those mature balsam fir left standing after cutting operations are usually the most seriously affected. This adelgid may also be found in unharvested middle-aged stands, in which case, even trees regenerating under or near the stands are affected.

Damage and diagnosis

The balsam woolly adelgid causes two types of damage. The first results from stem attack by white woolly adelgids lined up vertically in bark crevices; and when the attack is severe, they may be found from the tree's collar up to its largest branches (Plate 40, E and F). After being punctured by the adelgid, the affected parts of the tree become swollen and its diameter often increases to the point at which it masks the tapering. As the adelgid population increases, the whole crown turns brick red and needles fall to the ground in a relatively short time (Plate 40, B). During a severe and persistent attack, the tree may die within a period of 3 to 4 years (Plate 40, C). The attack also causes the formation of compression wood that reduces the quality of the fibre for pulp and paper and the value of logs destined for sawmills.

The second type of damage is related to twig attack in which adelgid activity brings on the swelling (Plate 40, H) and distortion of twigs (Plate 40, A), a condition commonly known as gout. In a prolonged attack, bud formation is inhibited, and upward growth is retarded, and the tree begins to die from the top. This process takes about 25 years to complete (Plate 40, D and G).

In spring and summer, especially at the end of the summer season, it is easy to identify the trees under attack by the white streaks at the base of balsam fir trunks of large diameter, occasionally extending up into the large branches. Under their woolly coating, one can see one or more stages of the insect. Gout, if present at the top of fir crowns, is easily seen throughout the year, even from

a distance, using binoculars. The first symptom of gout consists in the presence of swellings on twigs that eventually become distorted; on careful examination, the affected branches show an irregular distribution of the needles and sometimes a white secretion is present where the adelgid is attached.

Natural control

In Canada, the balsam woolly adelgid is not attacked by known entomophagous parasites, but it has many species of insect predators. Between 1933 and 1958, to reinforce the action of these predators, 13 more species were introduced into Canada and 4 of these are well established (McGugan and Coppel 1962). However, their role in reducing the insect population has remained insignificant in

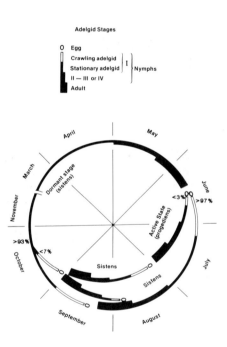

Figure 3. Life cycle of the balsam woolly adelgid in Newfoundland. (Adapted from Bryant 1976)

A

B

C

D

E

F

PLATE 40

Balsam woolly adelgid, *Adelges piceae* (Ratz.)

A. Appearance of mature balsam fir forest after several years attack on crowns.
B. Old balsam fir showing red needles after severe attack on stems.
C. Old balsam fir killed by severe attack on stems.
D. Top of balsam fir crown following several years of severe attack on crown.
E. Balsam fir stem covered with white woolly substance secreted by adelgids.
F. Close-up of white woolly substance covering adelgids.
G. Top of balsam fir crown broken off following severe attack and showing characteristic development of top branches.
H. Characteristic swelling of twigs bearing adelgids after recent attack on crown.

G

H

areas where the twig attack predominates. This adelgid occasionally falls victim to entomopathogenic fungi, one species of which was discovered in Quebec (Smirnoff 1970); to date however their effect has been negligible. The most important factor in limiting populations is the climate, particularly low temperatures in winter. Greenbank (1970), found that ice formation in wood tissues is fatal to the adelgid. The rate of fatality increases as the temperature reaches $-20°C$ and all individuals die at $-37°C$. However, temperatures of $-37°C$ are rare along the Gaspé coast, where the insect is well established; also, the adelgid is usually protected from cold by a thick layer of snow that covers the lower part of the trunks and even accumulates in dense crowns, so that some individuals can survive. Significant reductions in population as a result of cold have been observed, however, during particularly severe winters.

Artificial control

Control by artificial methods is very difficult because the balsam woolly adelgid is protected during its entire existence under the swellings on the twigs. It is thus difficult to reach the insect using chemical products. Failing direct control, the following preventive measures may be used to limit the damage:

- Cut affected trees during the winter to prevent the outbreak from spreading, because during that season the adelgids are dormant and attached to the tree by their stylets anchored in the bark;
- Section the logs within the infested area before the spring thaw and burn the waste on the spot to eliminate the danger of subsequent contamination; and
- Bark any fallen trees before moving them from the affected zone to areas known to be still uninfested.

References

Balch 1934, 1952; Balch and Mitchell 1973; Bryant 1971, 1976; Clark et al. 1971; Greenbank 1970; McGugan and Coppel 1962; and Smirnoff 1970.

Balsam twig aphid
Plate 41

The balsam twig aphid, *Mindarus abietinus* Koch, is usually not a forest pest, because it prefers ornamental and edge trees, or plants in nurseries and plantations. It occurs throughout Europe and North America. On the North American continent, this aphid is found throughout the range of fir, from the Atlantic to the Pacific ocean. Balsam fir and white spruce are the only hosts in Canada, but elsewhere this aphid has been found on four other species of fir and on juniper.

History of outbreaks

In Canada, outbreaks of the balsam twig aphid generally develop on balsam fir; these are always of a short duration and are small in scale, although occasionally they occur in several pockets scattered over a large area. In eastern Canada, the insect was first reported in the 1930s. In Newfoundland, it has been collected periodically since that time throughout the province, but no serious damage has been caused, except in the Bay d'Espoir area in 1972. In the Maritime provinces, local and short-term outbreaks are recorded every 3 or 4 years; 1967 was a year of great abundance, marked by many severe outbreaks in southern New Brunswick, central and southwestern Nova Scotia, and Prince Edward Island, but by early in 1968 populations had declined significantly. In Quebec, the insect began to attract attention from 1964 on, because, with the exception of a few years, it was present constantly, although usually in small numbers. In 1972, the insect populations developed at an extraordinary rate throughout the province south of the 50th parallel, and then, just as suddenly, became sparse again the following year. In 1978, the insect population again increased in the same area and, on many fir trees, up to 90 percent of the shoots were attacked.

In Ontario, except in 1946 when it was abundant, the insect has usually been found in small numbers throughout the province without any major damage being reported.

In spite of their small size and short life cycle, outbreaks of this aphid cause serious concern to Christmas tree producers, because they may spoil large fir plantations to the point at which part of the annual production cannot be marketed until a year later.

Description and biology

The biology of the balsam twig aphid is not yet well understood because the ephemeral nature of its epidemics do not allow study of the insect for more than a year at a time.

This aphid has three, and even four, generations each year, one after the other within a 2-month period, i.e., from the beginning of May to the beginning of July. The numerous forms encountered during that period are difficult to tell apart, complicating the study of its annual life cycle. The generations develop more or less as follows:

The insect overwinters in the egg stage, from which emerges the first generation, called the fundatrix; this generation goes through its entire development on old needles near the buds and causes little damage. During the first 2 weeks of June (Plate 41, A), the larvae of this first generation grow into wingless adults (Plate 41, C) and each female lays between 40 and 60 eggs (Plate 41, B). With the hatching of these eggs begins the second and main generation, followed closely by a third one that resembles the second in many ways. These two generations live on new shoots and feed by sucking the sap from the needles, which causes the needles to become distorted. The larvae have a woolly covering and secrete large quantities of honeydew. During the last 2 weeks in June, the larvae of the third generation transform into naked but winged adults and fly to new hosts on which they lay about 10 eggs, from which emerge the fourth generation. Incubation of these eggs lasts about a week.

Individuals of the fourth generation are wingless and include both males and females. They secrete a small amount of wool and cause little damage. The adult females of this fourth generation lay one or two black eggs near the buds, and these eggs preserve the species through the winter.

Damage and diagnosis

New fir shoots are attacked and punctured by the balsam twig aphid as soon as they open in the spring, and as a result, the shoots become distorted and the needles curve inwards until their dorsal part becomes visible (Plate 41, D). Later on, both shoot growth and bud formation may be visibly reduced. Occasionally, the tip of the shoot dies and, naturally, produces no needles the following year.

The shape of the shoots, with needles curled inward, is characteristic of damage by this species (Plate 41, F). Also, on examination of shoots thus distorted, colonies of aphids are found covered with bluish white woolly substance and secreting a fair amount of honeydew.

Damage by this insect on spruce is less known.

Natural control

The larvae and adults of several coccinellid beetles, as well as larvae of a syrphid fly (Plate 41, G and H), are known predators on the balsam twig aphid (Amman 1963). A syrphid fly was also responsible for the drop in population during the 1978 outbreak in Quebec.

Artificial control

Because the balsam twig aphid has a predilection for open-grown trees, young trees may be protected, as a preventive measure, by favoring their development under forest cover. From a remedial point of view, it is neither practical nor necessary to organize the control of this species around the forest edges. Control, however, is necessary to ensure a normal growth and to encourage the formation of an attractive crown in plantations of balsam fir destined for the Christmas tree market, in nurseries, and on ornamentals. A certain amount of success may be obtained by applying a chemical contact or systemic insecticide when the buds are expanding and before any damage appears in the spring.

References

Amman 1963; Canada Department of Agriculture 1948, 1949 and 1960; Canadian Forestry Service 1974b; Kerr 1952; and Quednau 1966.

PLATE 41

Balsam twig aphid, *Mindarus abietinus* Koch

A. Balsam fir shoot showing aphids feeding actively in June.
B. Appearance and location of eggs.
C. Adult at rest.
D. Needles on new balsam fir shoots after attack.
E. Healthy new balsam fir shoots.
F. Severely damaged balsam fir branches in nature.
G. Pupa of a predator, the Lapland syrphid fly, *Metasyrphus lapponicus* (Zett.), on fir needles.
H. Adult of same predator at rest.

Balsam gall midges
Plate 42

According to the literature, the first observations on galls of fir needles go back to 1888 and, up until recently, it was thought that these galls were due to activities of the false balsam gall midge, *Dasineura balsamicola* (Lint.). In 1977, however, Osgood and Gagné (1978) showed that a second species, the balsam gall midge, *Paradiplosis tumifex* Gagné, was the real cause of these needle swellings. The gall results from the mechanical or chemical irritation of leaf tissues caused by the activities of a larva growing inside. The life of the tree is not affected by the presence of these galls, but the galled needles do fall prematurely, which reduces the aesthetic and market value of affected trees, particularly those intended for the Christmas tree market, as such trees may be graded lower or even rejected.

History of outbreaks

Both balsam gall midges are present throughout the range of balsam fir and Fraser fir, *Abies fraseri* (Pursh) Poir.; extraordinary proliferation occurs periodically on the first tree species and occasionally on the second. The first mention of such galls in eastern Canada goes back to 1938, and they have been observed practically every year since. In Newfoundland, the presence of these galls was reported only in 1959 and 1963, whereas in the Maritime provinces, local outbreaks were reported in 1938-1939, 1945-1946 and, over much larger areas, from 1956 to 1960 and from 1965 to 1968. Populations have since declined and have stabilized at lower levels.

In Quebec, galls were noted first in 1939 and then almost every year since then; fortunately, outbreaks are usually of a local nature and last only a few years. For instance, in 1940, Lambert reported that stands in Gatineau and Labelle counties were infested, but a year later this outbreak was over. Subsequent increases in populations were noted between 1966 and 1969, and two small but severe outbreaks were recorded, one in 1971 and the other in 1972. In 1975, outbreaks varying in intensity from light to severe were observed in a number of locations in the lower St. Lawrence River valley and in the Gaspé Peninsula; in 1976 these outbreaks continued, and new ones developed in southern Quebec.

In Ontario, severe outbreaks were reported in fairly limited areas in a few districts, but only between 1959 and 1963.

Description and biology

The adults of both balsam gall midges are small two-winged insects that look like orange gnats. Their larvae may be distinguished by the texture of their integument that is rough in the false balsam gall midge and smooth in the balsam gall midge. They also differ slightly in color, young larvae of the first species being yellow and taking on an orange color as they grow older, whereas those of the second species are white at first and gradually turn yellow orange.

Both species have one generation per year and their life cycles are almost identical. The adult is present during the second half of May and the eggs from mid-May to early June (Plate 42, B). Larvae of both species go through three instars, but the duration of the second larval instar lasts 5 months in the case of the false balsam gall midge and only 3 months for the balsam gall midge. Both species overwinter as larvae in their third instar and reach the pupal stage in May of the following year (Osgood and Gagné 1978).

The galls are caused by the larvae of the balsam gall midge (Plate 42, A). Shortly after their formation, the galls are invaded by the larvae of the false balsam gall midge that not only settle in them permanently, but also most often cause the original occupant either to die or to develop abnormally. In the fall, the larvae of whichever species completed their development leave the gall and drop to the ground where they spend the winter. The galled needles slowly turn yellow and most of them drop off the twig in October or November (Plate 42, E). Out of 507 galled needles observed in Quebec in 1977, 54 percent had fallen by October 31, 89 percent by November 30, and 99 percent by May 1978. Healthy needles generally remain on the tree for about 7 years.

Damage and diagnosis

The gall is about the only damage that can be attributed to attack by the balsam gall midges (Plate 42, C and D); however, the literature mentions that, during very severe and repeated outbreaks, trees may suffer a reduction in growth. The number of galls per needle varies and, during a widespread outbreak, up to six were observed on a single needle (Plate 42, F). The average dimensions of the gall are 2.5 mm long by 1.5 mm wide, but they may vary in the case of multiple galls. The epidemic stage is reached when more than 1 percent of the twigs are affected. The intensity of an epidemic is determined by the percentage of affected twigs, based on the following categories: low 1-5 percent, medium 6-40 percent, and high 41-100 percent.

The study of gall distribution produced several interesting facts: first, galls are only produced on the current year's needles; secondly, they are generally concentrated on a certain number of twigs, and up to 95 percent of the needles on a given twig may be contaminated; and finally, these insects show a predilection for terminal twigs.

The conditions under which an outbreak is likely to develop are found in thin or open-growing stands on trees less than 8 m in height showing signs of abnormal growth or weakened vitality, as well as in stands growing on soils having a pH higher than 5.0.

Eggs are difficult to detect, but galled needles are easy to spot from the end of June until the fall. Later, leaf scars indicate the place occupied by galled needles before they dropped. The numbers of remaining galls and of leaf scars give some idea of population levels.

Natural control

Insect parasites seem to play a very important role in reducing populations of balsam gall midges. In their research conducted in Wisconsin, Giese and Benjamin (1959) recovered two species of parasites, *Tetrastichus whitmani* (Grlt.) and *T. marcovitchi* (Cwftd.) that destroyed over 80 percent of the larval populations in the areas studied. A total of nine species of parasites, including the two mentioned, were obtained in Maine by Osgood and Dimond, but in their rearings, the two most important species were *Tetrastichus* sp. near to *solidaginis* and *Platygaster* sp. A fungus from the rust group, *Milesia marginalis* Faull and Wats., occasionally destroys part of the population when a mass of hyphae fills the gall chamber. These gall midges are also killed by an unidentified predator (Strubble and Osgood 1976).

Artificial control

Direct control of balsam gall midges is occasionally justified when it is important to preserve the appearance of valuable ornamental trees in parks or gardens, or to protect the foliage of trees planted for the Christmas tree market. In the latter case, however, if marketing of damaged trees can be postponed, it is preferable to avoid the application of costly treatments, because all traces of damage will have disappeared 3 years after the end of an outbreak, and trees that had deteriorated will again become acceptable for the market.

Chemical control is complicated because it is difficult to reach the larva inside the gall. A systemic insecticide that filters into the tissues of the plant must be used; also, the treatment should be applied as soon as the needle begins to swell, and care must be taken to cover the foliage thoroughly (Dimond and Osgood 1970).

References

Canadian Forestry Service 1974d; Dimond and Osgood 1970; Giese and Benjamin 1959; Lambert and Genest 1940; MacGown and Osgood 1972; Osgood and Dimond 1970; Osgood and Gagné 1978; and Strubble and Osgood 1976.

A

B

C

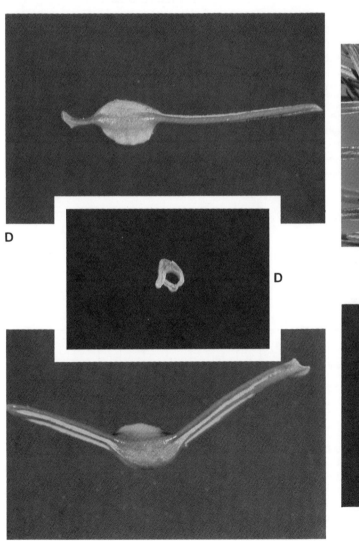

D

D

D

E

F

PLATE 42

False balsam gall midge, *Dasineura balsamicola* (Lint.), and balsam gall midge, *Paradiplosis tumifex* Gagné

A. Two balsam fir twigs seriously infested by balsam gall midges, placed side by side to show the galls on both sides of the twig.
B. *D. balsamicola* adult (length: about 2 mm).
C. *D. balsamicola* larva near its gall.
D. Various positions of galls on balsam fir needle, with cross section of a gall showing larval chamber.
E. Galled needles of balsam fir about to drop in the fall.
F. Balsam fir needles bearing two galls; appearance of a galled needle in summer and in fall.

Whitespotted sawyer
Plate 43

The whitespotted sawyer, *Monochamus scutellatus* (Say), is normally included in the insect group referred to as secondary, because it ordinarily attacks weakened, dying, or dead trees and rarely healthy ones. It is a regular resident of conifer forests in North America, and its damage is well known to foresters. Its hosts are eastern white pine, jack pine, Norway pine, white spruce, black spruce, red spruce, balsam fir, and occasionally, larch. The insect finds ideal conditions for breeding in trees weakened by either age, a forest fire, a windfall, or an infestation of defoliating insects. It is also found in slash, piles of softwood left in the forest during the summer, and in the walls of cabins built with unbarked logs.

History of outbreaks

In eastern Canada, the presence of the whitespotted sawyer in conifer forests is considered to be a normal phenomenon. It has been observed annually since 1936, although reported only in some regions and only when populations reached abnormal proportions. In Newfoundland, for instance, damage of commercial importance was reported in 1963 in stands damaged by fire. In Quebec and Ontario, spectacular damage by adults has been reported occasionally near huge stretches of forests devastated by the spruce budworm, *Choristoneura fumiferana,* and the Swaine jack pine sawfly, *Neodiprion swainei.*

Description and biology

Adult. Large beetle, completely black except for a white shield at the base of the elytra. Length: about 25 mm; antennae twice as long as body on the male, of the same length on the female (Plate 43, I and J).

Egg. Oval in shape; white. Dimensions: 0.9 mm by 3 mm.

Larva. Legless, elongated and slightly flattened; body dirty white with amber brown head. Length when full grown: 40-50 mm.

Nymph. Resembles a curled-up adult, white. Length: 20-25 mm.

The numerous studies conducted on the biology of the whitespotted sawyer, both in Canada and the United States, were aimed mainly at finding adequate methods of preventing or limiting its damage.

The life cycle of this insect usually covers a 2-year period; in the southern part of its range, it may be completed in 1 year only, whereas it may take 3 years in the north. The 2-year cycle is shown in Figure 4.

Adults are active mainly during sunny days and are rarely visible during overcast days. After feeding for about 10 days they mate. The females lay their eggs in bark crevices or in slits made by their strong jaws in partly shaded areas of the bark. This habit explains why more eggs are generally found on the sides and bottom, rather than on the top of logs. Incubation of the eggs lasts an average of 12 days.

Once hatched, the young larva begins to bore a tunnel through the phloem, reaching the cambium in 2 or 3 days; it extends its tunnel therein without damaging the surface of the wood, and completes its first instar in a period of 2 to 3 weeks. During the second instar, equal in duration to that of the first one, the larva extends its tunnel by enlarging it at the surface of the cambium, causing slight marking of the wood surface. When populations are large, surface tunnels may cross each other during the first instars, and the meeting of larvae results in cannibalism.

By September, the larva has reached the third instar and begins to tunnel towards the interior, returning occasionally to the surface to feed, and thus severely marking the wood surface. At the end of September, almost all larvae are located in interior tunnels, where they overwinter in a dormant state.

Early in the spring of the second year, the larvae become active again and extend their tunnels towards the interior. During the summer, part of the sawdust produced by boring is pushed out of the tunnel to enable the larva to return to the surface. By midsummer, the larva has reached its greatest depth into the wood and reorients its tunnel towards the surface.

By the end of September, the larva is about 5 mm from the surface of the log or trunk, and there builds a pupal cell isolated from the rest of the tunnel by the last bits of sawdust.

The pupal stage occurs in the spring of the 3rd year and lasts about 15 days. Shortly after, the adult forms, and leaves the tunnel by chewing a perfectly circular exit hole at right angles to the wood surface.

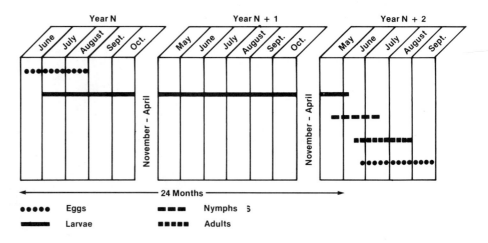

Figure 4. Two-year life cycle of the whitespotted sawyer.

Damage

The first form of damage is caused by the adult whitespotted sawyer feeding on tender bark (Plate 43, A and B), usually on the underside of young twigs; this normally causes the tip of the twig to die, and its needles then to turn brick red (Plate 43, C and D). Such damage has little effect on the tree itself, except in the case of massive attacks, during which damage to large areas of bark endangers the life of the tree. During the summer of 1977 in Quebec, for example, in the vicinity of areas heavily infested by the spruce budworm, great swarms of adults seen flying towards healthy trees ate the bark of twigs, probably causing the trees to die.

Tunnels bored by young larvae close to the surface of the wood are of little consequence, even for the production of lumber, because these are eliminated with the slab during the sawing (Plate 43, F and G). On the other hand, the large tunnels dug inside the wood by larvae of the third instar and older are much more damaging (Plate 43, E) because they remain after sawing and often host the growth of a fungus that gives a blue color to the tunnel walls. Boards from logs damaged in this way usually contain many holes that greatly reduce the market value.

The importance of the damage caused by this insect varies with the use to be made of the affected wood; according to Wilson (1962b), losses were about 5 percent by volume in wood destined for pulp and 35 percent of the cash value in logs sawn into lumber.

Diagnosis

The beginning of an infestation of the whitespotted sawyer is easy to recognize in the summer by the presence of adults in softwood forests during sunny weather, and by red twigs that look like red flags.

Infested timber is easily located by small, conical piles of sawdust at the base of trees or alongside cut logs left in the forest. The color of this sawdust may indicate the larval activity: brown sawdust is a sure sign that larvae have stopped feeding.

The circular holes at the bark surface, bored by emerging adults marks the end of damage by the insect (Plate 43, H).

Safranyik and Raske (1970) developed a method by which the intensity of attack by this insect on lodgepole pine may be determined simply by counting the larvae on some logs; with a few minor adjustments, this method could be adapted to conifers of eastern Canada.

Natural control

Cannibalism amongst young larvae at tunnel junctions may sometimes be an important factor in reducing populations of the whitespotted sawyer.

Three species of parasites have been found in the United States, but their role in control appears negligible. In studies conducted in northwestern Ontario between 1952 and 1954 on severely damaged balsam fir logs, Rose (1957) estimated the cumulative natural death rate from the egg stage to adult emergence at over 95 percent. Similarly, Wilson (1962b) estimated natural mortality from the newborn larva to adult emergence at about 70 percent, without identifying the various natural factors involved in this mortality.

Woodpeckers are known to consume large quantities of sawyer larvae, but this action does not contribute significantly to the reduction of the populations of this pest.

Artificial control

The knowledge accumulated on the biology of the whitespotted sawyer led to the development of several methods for the protection of cut logs against its attack. The choice of method depends on the importance of wood defects in the intended market. In cases where defects are of great importance, as with timber cut from very valuable trees, attack may be almost completely eliminated by the adoption of the following methods:

- Bark logs immediately after cutting;
- Cover piles of logs thoroughly with a layer of balsam fir branches (30-50 cm thick) to protect them during the egg-laying season, that is, from June to September; and
- Spray piles of valuable logs continually with water during the egg-laying period.

It is not necessary to use such extreme measures in the case of pulpwood, and damage may be minimized by using the following methods:

- Carry out operations between September and January so that attacks are limited;
- Use logs promptly that were exposed to egg-laying or else immerse them before the second year's activities begin;
- Locate log piles so that they are protected from the sun by standing trees;
- Make large piles rather than numerous small ones so as to limit the bark surface exposed to the sun and thus attractive as egg-laying locations; and
- Apply a contact insecticide to log piles during periods of adults' activity.

In the long term, the abundance of sawyers is reduced by eliminating conditions that favor its development. Mature or overmature trees should thus be removed at the first signs of decay, and trees damaged by fire, or windblown, should be cut and used within 1 year. In the same way, slash from cutting should be used or destroyed to prevent its use for egg-laying.

References

Cerezke 1975; Daviault 1948a; Gardiner 1957; Gray and Mol 1969; Raske 1973b; Rose 1957; Safranyik and Raske 1970; and Wilson 1962b.

A

C

B

D

E

F

G

I

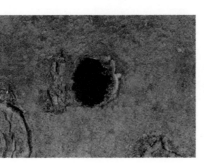

H

J

PLATE 43

Whitespotted sawyer, *Monochamus scutellatus* (Say)

A. Adult seeking for tender bark on young stem of eastern white pine.
B. Close-up of wound on a stem of eastern white pine.
C. Dead foliage of balsam fir after adult attack on the twig.
D. Close-up of wound on balsam fir.
E. Longitudinal cut through a larval tunnel.
F. Appearance of wood surface, once barked.
G. Oval entrance hole at wood surface.
H. Circular adult exit hole at bark surface.
I. Adult female (length: 25 mm).
J. Adult male.

Table 6. Other insects harmful to balsam fir — Other insects that are regarded as pests of balsam fir are listed in this table. For some insects, their characteristics are described in the chapter that applies to their primary host, and in such cases, that chapter (in Roman numerals) and the appropriate plate numbers are given. For other insects, a plate number alone is shown; and for the remaining insects, this table provides the only information.

Common and scientific names	Hosts (chap.)	Plate no.	Type of insect	Destructive stages	Period of activity	Importance*
Balsam fir aphid *Cinara curvipes* (Patch)	Balsam fir	—	Sucker	Adult and nymph	July to Oct.	C
Balsam fir false looper *Syngrapha rectangula* (Kby.)	Conifers	—	Defoliator	Larva	May to Aug.	C
Balsam shootboring sawfly *Pleroneura brunneicornis* Roh.	Balsam fir	—	Defoliator	Larva	May to Aug.	C
Chameleon caterpillar *Anomogyna elimata* (Guen.)	Conifers	—	Defoliator	Larva	May to Aug.	C
Dashlined looper *Protoboarmia porcelaria indicataria* (Wlk.)	Conifers	—	Defoliator	Larva	May to Oct.	C
Eastern spruce gall adelgid *Adelges abietis* (L.)	Spruce (I)	6	—	—	—	B
False hemlock looper *Nepytia canosaria* (Wlk.)	Conifers	—	Defoliator	Larva	May to Sept.	C
Filament bearer *Nematocampa limbata* (Haw.)	Balsam fir, conifers	—	Defoliator	Larva	May to Sept.	C
Fir coneworm *Dioryctria abietivorella* (Grote)	Spruce (I)	4	—	—	—	C
Fir harlequin *Elaphria versicolor* (Grote)	Balsam fir, conifers	—	Defoliator	Larva	June to Sept.	C
Hairskirted caterpillar *Tolype laricis* (Fitch)	White spruce, balsam fir, larch	—	Defoliator	Larva	June to Sept.	C
November moth *Epirrita autumnata henshawi* Swett	Balsam fir, spruce	—	Defoliator	Larva	May to Sept.	C
Redlined conifer caterpillar *Feralia jocosa* (Guen.)	Conifers, hardwoods	—	Defoliator	Larva	June to Aug.	C
Rusty tussock moth *Orgyia antiqua* L.	Maple (VIII)	72	—	—	—	C
Saddleback looper *Ectropis crepuscularia* (Denis and Schiff.)	Conifers, hardwoods	—	Defoliator	Larva	May to Oct.	C
Spruce coneworm *Dioryctria reniculelloides* Mut. and Mun.	Spruce (I)	4	—	—	—	C
Spruce-fir looper *Semiothisa signaria dispuncta* Wlk.	Spruce, balsam fir	—	Defoliator	Larva	May to Oct.	C
White pine bark miner *Marmara fasciella* Cham.	Pine, balsam fir	44	Miner	Larva	May to Oct.	C
Whitemarked tussock moth *Orgyia leucostigma intermedia* Fitch	Maple (VIII)	71	—	—	—	C
Yellowlined conifer looper *Nyctobia limitaria* (Wlk.)	Conifers	—	Defoliator	Larva	May to Aug.	C

*A: Of major importance, capable of killing or severely damaging trees.
 B: Of moderate importance, capable of sporadic and localized injury to trees.
 C: Of minor importance, not known to present a threat to living trees.

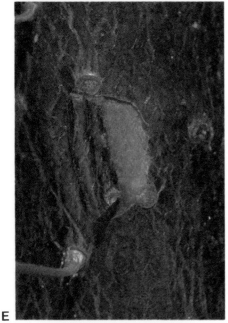

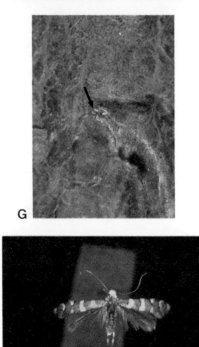

PLATE 44

White pine bark miner, *Marmara fasciella* Cham.

A. Opened tunnel showing appearance and location of larva.
B. Larval tunnel seen through balsam fir bark.
C. Mature larva close to exuviae inside tunnel.
D. Opened tunnel showing egg parasites.
E. Swelling and bursting of external wall of balsam fir bark at time of pupation.
F. Pupa inside cocoon shell spun by the larva in its tunnel.
G. Pupa exuviae at bottom of tunnel after adult emergence.
H. Adult at rest near the tunnel.
I. Pinned adult.

CHAPTER V
Insects harmful to arbor-vitae

The genus *Thuja* is known throughout eastern Canada by one of its representatives, erroneously called either cedar, white cedar, or eastern white cedar; this tree is actually the arbor-vitae (*T. occidentalis* L.). True cedars belong to the genus *Cedrus* and grow in North Africa and in Asia. The genus *Thuja* includes six tree species, only two of which are found in Canada, the arbor-vitae and the giant arbor-vitae (*T. plicata* Donn), also mistakenly called western red cedar. The other arbor-vitae found in eastern Canada are of foreign origin. Arbor-vitae has become popular in Canada due to the durability of its wood and also for its repellent properties used in dwellings to keep insects away. For these reasons, there is a considerable demand for this tree species.

Arbor-vitae is found in all provinces of eastern Canada except Newfoundland, and from the United States border to latitude 50° 15' N; it has attained a commercial importance in southern Ontario and Quebec, and in northwestern New Brunswick. The gross merchantable volume of arbor-vitae in eastern Canada is estimated at 157 million m^3 (Bonnor 1982), of which the province of Quebec has the highest proportion at 44.8 percent, and Ontario follows with 30.9 percent. This tree species grows mainly in damp areas such as swamps and along streams, on steep slopes, and in old pastureland; it grows isolated or in pure stands.

Arbor-vitae is a conifer having a conical shape and reaching an average height of 15 m and diameter of 50 cm, although these dimensions may be doubled under favorable growing conditions. Its foliage is dense; on isolated trees, the crown reaches to the ground, whereas in the forest it stops about halfway down. Among the outstanding qualities of this tree are the shape of its crown, the beauty and permanence of its foliage, and the durability, lightness, and odor of its wood. This species is popular as an ornamental tree, whereas its foliage is used for decorative purposes or in the fabrication of fine oils. The wood is used for articles coming in contact with the ground or in damp conditions, and as sawtimber.

Because arbor-vitae is valued for its foliage and its trunk wood, damage to either reduces its value. It is commonly believed that few insects would attack arbor-vitae; in fact several insects are detrimental to this tree species. Usually, these insects are specific to *Thuja*, and most belong to the miners group.

Arbor-vitae leafminers
Plate 45

Compared to other forest trees of eastern Canada, arbor-vitae has relatively few enemies. The most important pests attack the foliage even though it is strongly aromatic and is often used as a repellent to other insects. Over the past two decades, however, a group of four miners have caused severe damage to arbor-vitae growing in forests or planted as ornamentals. Damage caused by each of the four species is so similar that it has initially been all attributed to the first species identified, which subsequently proved to be the most important, the arbor-vitae leafminer, *Argyresthia thuiella* (Pack.). This species was first reported in the state of Connecticut in 1921. It was soon realized, however, that other species were involved in the damage, and three have been identified to date that is *Argyresthia canadensis* Free., *A. aureoargentella* Brower, and *Pulicalvaria thujaella* (Kft.) (Plate 45, G to J). These four species occur in most of the range of their preferred host in North America, arbor-vitae. They have been most active in southern Ontario and Quebec, western New Brunswick, and in Prince Edward Island. The first published reports on damage to arbor-vitae foliage attributed it only to the arbor-vitae leafminer, but the other species gradually began to be blamed as well.

History of outbreaks

In Ontario, the first infestations of arbor-vitae leafminers were reported around 1940 and short-lasting outbreaks struck in 1946 and 1951. A third one began in 1963 and diminished only 10 years later, after destroying a large number of branches and even stems. In Quebec, a first outbreak, of a short duration, was reported in 1962; a second one, more serious began in 1967 and lasted until 1973. This latter outbreak caused the death of such a large number of stems that, in the southern part of the province, stands had to be cut prematurely to avoid a total loss. In the Maritime provinces, the first outbreak lasted from 1949 to 1953,

and a second one from 1963 to 1974, both of them resulting also in local tree mortality.

Description and Biology
Arbor-vitae leafminer, *A. thuiella*

Adult. Small moth; forewings basically pale gray, marked with brown. Wingspan: 8 mm (Plate 45, G).

Egg. Irregular in shape, inserted between two adjacent leaves; greenish yellow. Length: 3 mm.

Larva. Elongated in shape; body light to dark green, tinged with red, head black. Length: 5 mm (Plate 45, D).

Pupa. Body leaf green with brown head. Length: 3-4 mm (Plate 45, F).

Literature on the arbor-vitae leafminers is as yet scarce, although research was conducted both in New Brunswick and in Quebec in an attempt to elucidate their biology.

There is one generation of arbor-vitae leafminer per year. Moths appear between mid-June and mid-July and a few days later the females lay from 1 to 25 eggs under the edges of the current year's scale-like leaves, at a short distance from the tip or on the twig itself. Incubation lasts 11 to 20 days, the first larvae appearing towards the end of June. Upon hatching, each larva begins to bore a mine, or tunnel (Plate 45, D), inside the leaflets in which it will develop. Damage occurs progressively from the exterior to the interior of the crown. In the fall, once the larva has reached the fifth instar, it pushes its excrement to one end of the tunnel, and there it overwinters. When buds begin to open in the spring, the larva becomes active once again, first eliminating its excrement and then extending its tunnel towards the interior of the crown. Once fully grown, that is between the end of May to the end of June, the larvae change to pupae and then to adults (Plate 45, E).

Argyresthia canadensis Free., *A. aureoargentella* Brower, and *Pulicalvaria thujaella* (Kft.)

A

C

D

E

F

G

H

I

J

The biology of the other three leaf-miners found on arbor-vitae is less well known; however, data collected in recent years permit some distinctions. The life cycles of *A. canadensis* and *A. aureoargentella* are similar to that of *A. thuiella* already described, but their habits differ in many respects. The first two species, for example, mine only half of the three leaflets or scales that constitute the width of the twig, whereas in the case of *A. thuiella* the mine occupies the whole width. Also, *A. canadensis* and *A. aureoargentella* bore several mines rather than one and do not evacuate their excrement to the outside.

The life cycle of *Pulicalvaria thujaella* (Plate 45, J) differs from that of *Argyresthia* species mainly in that its larvae overwinter in the second or third instar rather than in the fifth. In the spring, its larvae begin their feeding 2 or 3 weeks later than those of *Argyresthia* species, and its adult emergence happens that much later. Also, most individuals complete their entire development in a single mine, although a few may begin a second one.

Damage and diagnosis

Trees of all ages are subject to attack by the arbor-vitae leafminer but young, fast-growing trees and those growing in the shade seem to be less attractive. Initial damage is easily recognizable by the presence of foliage that turns gradually from straw-colored to brown (Plate 45, A); when examined in front of a source of light, this foliage is seen to contain a tunnel, beginning near the end of one twig and continuing either into a second twig or along the main twig. As the mining progresses, the flow of sap towards the apical part of the twig more or less stops, and the dried leaflets eventually turn brown and die. This damage worsens with cold weather in the fall. Damaged foliage falls during the following year, and twigs become bare (Plate 45, B). A severe attack lasting for several consecutive years results in considerable defoliation and eventually kills a certain percentage of the twigs.

In fall and winter, twigs with brown tips and showing signs of mining may be found on the exterior of arbor-vitae. At this time of year, the tunnels contain brownish larvae and excrement whereas, in the spring, after the excrement has been ejected, the larva or pupa inhabits an empty tunnel.

A preliminary distinction among the four arbor-vitae leafminers can be made using data shown in Table 7.

During the off-season, collect one or more tunnels, examine their shape and contents, and compare with the data shown in the table concerning larvae, width of tunnel and the presence or absence of excrement. The result of this preliminary examination may be confirmed by a second examination carried out in early June of the following year, referring to the data of the same Table but this time concerning the appearance and location of the pupa. Positive identification is necessary in the case of *P. thujaella* if an attempt is made to control this species with insecticides because the various stages appear later than the other species.

Natural control

Parasites constitute the most important factor in reducing populations of the arbor-vitae leafminers. Twenty-seven species were reported for the Maritime provinces (Silver 1957) and 10 for Ontario prior to the publication of a study by Bazinet and Sears (1979), in which 15 species are listed. In the latter province, the decline of the 1946 and 1951 epidemics appears to have been due to the action of a chalcid, *Pentacnemus bucculatricis* Howard. In Quebec, 32 species of parasites were recovered through rearings of the four species of leafminer from arbor-vitae stands near Sherbrooke in 1970 and 1971; it was then established that the overall population reduction reached between 10 and 14 percent the first year and 40 percent the second year. The most important species were *P. bucculatricis* Howard, *Dicladocerus westwoodii* Westwood, and *Chrysonotomyia* sp. The last named species also acts as a hyperparasite of the first two (Brillon 1971).

Artificial control methods

Because of the abundance of parasites, artificial control of the arbor-vitae leafminers should be undertaken on a small scale and mainly on ornamental trees. On isolated trees and during a light infestation, damage may be kept down by eliminating infested twigs during the off-season.

Action may also be taken against females of the arbor-vitae leafminer to prevent egg-laying by spraying trees at 3-week intervals, between the beginning of June and the middle of July, with a repellent that will keep females away. It is also possible to use a systemic insecticide to destroy larvae in their mines, but, in such cases, the advice of an experienced entomologist should be sought.

When an outbreak has been going on for several years with no end in sight, it is recommended that the most severely affected stands be cut to recover the wood before it dries out, taking care to burn all slash.

Control methods proposed for *A. thuiella* may also be used against the other three leafminers; however, in the case of *P. thujaella*, the treatment used to repel moths should be delayed by about 2 weeks, because adult emergence happens later.

References

Bazinet and Sears 1979; Brillon 1971; Britton and Zappe 1921; Brower 1940; Collingwood and Brush 1964; Freeman 1967, 1972; Johnson and Lyon 1976; Laviolette and Juillet 1976; Prentice 1965; and Silver 1957b, 1957c.

Table 7. Comparison of four species of arbor-vitae leafminer found in Quebec

Date	A. thuiella	A. canadensis	A. aureoargentella	P. thujaella
Relative abundance 1968-1971				
Southern Quebec	Very abundant	Abundant	Rare	Relatively rare
Sherbrooke area	Common	Rare	Rare	Rare
Adult emergence				
Maritimes	Mid-June to mid-July	Mid-June to mid-July	Mid-June to mid-July	End June to end July
Larva				
Colour	Gray to brown	Yellow green to green	Light to dark green	Reddish
Overwintering instar	5th	—	—	2nd or 3rd
Pupa				
Appearance	Bare (no cocoon)	In white cocoon spotted with brown	In all-white cocoon	Bare (no cocoon)
Location	In tunnel	Generally under foliage	On foliage	In tunnel
Damage				
Number of tunnels	Usually 1 (summer tunnel extended in spring)	Usually 2 (summer tunnel and new tunnel in spring)	Usually 2 (summer tunnel and new tunnel in spring)	Usually 1 (summer tunnel extended in in spring
Width of tunnel	Usually all 3 scales	Very often 1-1/2 scale	Very often 1-1/2 scale	Usually all 3 scales
Position of beginning of tunnel	From 1st to 9th scale from tip of twig	—	Farther from tip of twig than A. thuiella	Most often at the end of twig
Excrement	Present in summer tunnel, but cleaned in spring	Always present in tunnel	Always present in tunnel	Present in summer tunnel, but cleaned in spring

Table 8. Other insects harmful to arbor-vitae — Other insects that are regarded as pests of arbor-vitae are listed in this table. For these insects, this table provides the only information.

Common and scientific names	Hosts (chap.)	Plate no.	Type of insect	Destructive stages	Period of activity	Importance*
Arbor-vitae weevil *Phyllobius intrusus* Kono	Arbor-vitae, juniper	—	Borer	Larva	June to Aug.	C
Bagworm *Thyridopteryx ephemeraeformis* (Haw.)	Arbor-vitae, conifers	—	Defoliator	Larva	June to Oct.	C
Cedar sawfly *Monoctenus fulvus* (Nort.)	Arbor-vitae, juniper	—	Defoliator	Larva	May to Sept.	C
Fletcher scale *Lecanium fletcheri* Ckll.	Yew, arbor-vitae, juniper	—	Sucker	Adult and nymph	May to Oct.	C

*A. Of major importance, capable of killing or severely damaging trees.
 B: Of moderate importance, capable of sporadic and localized injury to trees.
 C: Of minor importance, not known to present a threat to living trees.

CHAPTER VI
Insects harmful to birch

Of the 50 known species of birch (*Betula*) in the northern hemisphere, 10 are found in Canada, and only 5 in the eastern provinces; they are white birch (*Betula papyrifera* Marsh.), yellow birch (*B. alleghaniensis* Britton), grey birch (*B. populifolia* Marsh.), cherry birch (*B. lenta* L.), and Alaska birch (*B. neoalaskana* Sarg.). White birch is the most common, being found through most of the territory, whereas the four others occur in much more limited areas. Yellow birch comes second, being found in all provinces but only south of the 48th parallel. Grey birch is in third place, growing in southern Ontario, southern Quebec, and the Maritime provinces. The other two species are less well distributed, being found only in limited areas, cherry birch in eastern and southeastern Ontario and southwestern Quebec, and Alaska birch only in western Ontario.

The gross merchantable volume of birch in eastern Canada is estimated at about 883 million m^3 (Bonnor 1982). The greater proportion of this volume, 54.7 percent, is found in Quebec and Ontario comes next with 38.2 percent.

Only the first three birch species are of interest insofar as insect damage is concerned. The first, white birch, is a very attractive tree that grows both in the open and in the forest. As a forest tree, it has a slender, tapered trunk and a narrow, thin, oval-shaped crown, whereas in the open the crown becomes thicker and covers the greater part of the trunk. It grows in a wide variety of locations, but preferably on well-drained ground, both in pure and mixed stands, and often it reproduces by means of sprouts from the trunk. It grows to a height of 25 m and a diameter of over 50 cm. Bark is smooth, thin, inflammable, reddish brown in color initially, becoming chalk white. The wood is white, hard, and strong, although it deteriorates rapidly in contact with the ground. It is used for several purposes, particularly for turnery, pulpwood, plywood and veneer, and as an ornamental tree.

The second species, yellow birch, is another attractive hardwood. In the forest, its crown is short and rounded, whereas in the open, it increases in length and in width. It grows on rich and moist soil, in pure or mixed stands, and reaches slightly greater dimensions than white birch. Its bark is dark red, becoming yellow or bronze with time. The wood is heavy, hard, strong, white in color and polishes well. It is used in cabinet-making, flooring, and for veneer and plywood.

The last species, grey birch, is less attractive than the other birches; it normally grows in clumps and can reproduce by means of sprouts from the trunk. The crown is straight, conical, irregularly open and has drooping twigs. It grows on various soils, mainly in pure stands. It is short-lived and seldom grows to more than 12 m in height and 15 cm in diameter. The smooth bark is reddish brown initially but becomes chalky white with time. The wood is soft and deteriorates easily; it is of little value and is used mainly for fuel. This birch is also planted as an ornamental.

Phyllophagous insects, both defoliators and miners, are the main pests on birch, which is also attacked by a few wood and bark borers.

Gypsy moth
Plate 46

The gypsy moth, *Lymantria dispar* (L.), is a very common pest on all continents with the exception of the islands of the Pacific. The insect is of European origin and was introduced into the state of Massachusetts in 1869 by a French naturalist seeking a silkworm that could adapt to the North American climate. In 1870, the insect accidentally got loose and, within 20 years, had multiplied over a vast area estimated at 900 km^2. Its present range in North America covers some 180 000 km^2. In the United States, it is found in all New England states, the eastern half of New York state, and in two small pockets located further to the west, one in Pennsylvania and the other in Michigan.

History of outbreaks

In Canada, the first reported damage by gypsy moth was confined to the localities of Henrysburg, Lacolle, Stanstead, and Milltown in southern Quebec in 1924, and then to St. Stephen, New Brunswick in 1936. These first two outbreaks were completely wiped out in 2 years through the implementation of vigorous methods of control. In 1959, a new centre was discovered in southern Quebec, from where the insect spread in various directions. Today, the known area of infestation in Quebec covers some 8 000 km^2, covering all surrounding counties located west, south, and east of Montreal Island and reaching almost as far east as the city of Sherbrooke. In Ontario, the insect was first found in 1969 and its distribution now covers an area of about 1 800 km^2 located to the northeast of Lake Ontario.

Since its introduction into Massachusetts, more than $100 million have been spent in the United States to limit damage by gypsy moth and to check its spread towards the south and the west. Gypsy moth is extremely polyphagous and attacks over 500 different plant species including trees and shrubs (Mosher 1915) (Plate 46, A and B). Few tree species are spared when an outbreak develops in a given area but they may be grouped into the following categories:

- Preferred species: oak, white birch, grey birch, larch, linden, willow, Manitoba maple, poplar, apple, and speckled alder to which should be added beech, hemlock, pine, and spruce which become attractive once the larvae are half-grown;
- Species accepted but not sought after: other birches, cherry, elm, hickory and other maples; and
- Rejected species: ash, walnut, locust, plane-tree, and tulip-tree.

Description and biology

Adult. Moth displays marked sexual dimorphism. Male with narrow, brown body; forewings brown crossed with irregular darker lines; Wingspan: 35 to 40 mm (Plate 46, I). Female with large, heavy body covered with buff hairs;forewings almost white with irregular blackish lines; wingspan: reaches 65 mm (Plate 46, J).

Egg. Pink at first, then dark gray; laid in a flattened, relatively oval mass measuring 25-40 cm at its widest point; egg mass almost always covered with buff-colored hairs from the female's abdomen, giving it the appearance of a small sponge (Plate 46, D).

Larva. Very hairy; head yellow with black markings; dorsum with double row of large tubercles from the head to the tip of the abdomen, i.e., six blue pairs followed by five red pairs; stiff hairs grow from each of these large tubercles as well as from other smaller ones scattered over the entire body. Length when full grown: 40-65 mm (Plate 46, K).

Pupa. Light to dark brown with a few yellowish hairs; female much larger than male (Plate 46, H).

Many studies have been carried out on gypsy moth, both in Europe and in the United States. In Canada, recent research is aimed principally at the discovery of factors that might check populations in climatic conditions specific to Canada.

One generation of gypsy moth is produced per year. In North America, moths are present from mid-July until the end of August and sometimes later. The males are good fliers and, on warm days, they can be seen flying in a zig-zag manner a short distance from the ground in search of females. The latter, on the other hand, fly only rarely and drag themselves with difficulty, mainly by crawling, a short distance away from their pupation site all the while emitting a particular odor that attracts the males. Soon after mating, the female lays a mass of 100 to 800 eggs in various locations such as on trunks or branches, in bark crevices as well as in cavities, under rocks, and in other secluded spots where they are visible throughout the winter and even into the following year (Plate 46, C). Embryo development takes 4 to 6 weeks, and the insect overwinters in the egg, as a partly developed larva.

PLATE 46

Gypsy moth, *Lymantria dispar* (L.)

A. and B. Stands of grey birch, and apple severely defoliated by *L. dispar*.
C. Egg masses on tree trunk.
D. Close-up of (1) egg mass with (2) single egg in medallion.
E. Young larvae on egg mass shortly after hatching.
F. Single young larva on sugar maple leaf.
G. Half-grown larva.
H. Pupa.
I. Adult male (wingspan: 35-40 mm).
J. Adult female (wingspan: up to 65 mm).
K. Mature larva (length: 40-65 mm).

The young larvae emerge the following spring, about the time oak leaves unfold (Plate 46, E). The newborn larvae feed at the base, or on the surface, of leaves by chewing small holes about the size of a pinhead. They often drop down on a thread of silk to reach other leaves and, at that time, are often carried over long distances by the wind. Older larvae devour leaves completely, starting at the edge and working inward. They feed mainly during the night and rest during the day in a shaded spot, often going down into the litter at the base of infested trees. When food becomes scarce, starving larvae leave in groups in search of new sources of food. Feeding lasts 6 to 8 weeks, during which time the male larvae go through five larval instars and the females through six. Once they are fully grown, around the end of June, the larvae scatter in search of an appropriate location to pupate, generally on trunks, branches, stones, and various forest debris.

Damage and diagnosis

All damage is caused by the larvae, especially during the last 2 weeks of feeding, i.e., in June. During severe outbreaks, all trees and shrubs in the infested area are completely stripped of their foliage. In spite of their ability to produce new foliage during the season, hardwoods suffer a reduction in growth; however, these trees may survive 2 or 3 years of total defoliation. Conifers such as hemlock, pine, and spruce, on the other hand, die within the first year. Loss of foliage also causes a reduction in the quality of the site and in the aesthetic, recreational, and faunal value of the area. An attack by gypsy moth is easily identified by the presence of egg masses on trunks and branches. Also, the size of the egg masses gives an idea of both the intensity and age of the outbreak; they are larger in the early stages but diminish from year to year.

Natural control

When gypsy moth was introduced onto the North American continent, the only natural factors that could check its spread were those related to climate, particularly temperature. Indeed, a large proportion of the young larvae that wintered in eggs unprotected by snow or other cover succumbed. Experiments showed that at temperatures of $-25°C$, 20 percent of them died within one day and 95 percent after 5 days; all larvae died after 24 hours at $-32°C$. Also, newborn larvae emerging early in the spring are often killed directly by late frosts or indirectly when these frosts destroy the young foliage on which they depend for their survival (Anderson 1960).

Certain insect-eating predators adapted gradually to this new prey and, in some cases, succeeded in destroying large numbers of larvae and pupae. The insect was, however, neglected by native parasites and, from 1905 on, the American government actively imported parasites and predators from Europe and Asia to fill this gap. Of 45 imported species, about 10 became established in the infested areas of New England, and some of these have since spread into Canada.

Gypsy moth is also attacked by several pathogenic microorganisms, notably fungi, protozoa, and bacteria, but the most important is undoubtedly a virus, *Borrelinavirus reprimens*, that sometimes decimates larval populations over vast areas.

Finally, during severe outbreaks, when trees are completely stripped of their foliage, huge larval populations starve to death.

Artificial control

As soon as the gypsy moth appeared on the North American continent, attempts were made to prevent it from spreading to areas as yet untouched by establishing wide quarantine zones around infested areas. Within these zones, during the off-season, egg masses were surveyed and destroyed by painting them with creosote or a sticky substance to prevent the young larvae from emerging in the spring. When populations are very large, larvae may be destroyed by spraying the foliage during the feeding period with a chemical stomach insecticide either from the ground or the air. Similarly, an aqueous preparation of *Bacillus thuringiensis* Berl. may be applied in the spring after the hatching of the young larvae. It is also possible to use a suspension of the virus *Borrelinavirus*

reprimens to cause disease among larval populations. To this end, it is recommended that large quantities of the virus be gathered in areas where an outbreak is diminishing and to preserve it in an appropriate manner for use as needed.

Research is now going on into ways of sterilizing males to prevent the fertilization of females; however, the results obtained to date have not been encouraging.

When only a few trees need protection, direct methods of control give satisfactory results, in particular by taking advantage of the fact that the larvae take refuge in the litter at the base of infested trees during the day. They can be prevented from climbing back up into the crowns, and thus destroyed, either by attaching a tarpaper collar to the base of the trunk or by trapping them on sticky material which can be renewed every 10 days.

Various silvicultural practices have been tried with a view to reducing populations by cutting a certain percentage of the preferred hosts, but results have not been very satisfactory. It is finally recommended that dead litter be left in infested woodlands to promote the activity of insect-eating predators that attack older larvae when they come down to the ground in the daytime.

References

Anderson 1960; Baker 1972; Benoit and Béique 1978; Campbell 1974; Dowden and Blaisdell 1959; Herrick 1935; Johnson and Lyon 1976; Lewis and Daviault 1973; Mosher 1915; Novak 1976; and O'Dell 1959.

Birch casebearers

Among the numerous enemies of birch are five species of casebearers, two of which are found in eastern Canada: the birch casebearer, *Coleophora serratella* (L.), and the lesser birch casebearer, *C. comptoniella* (McD.).

Birch casebearer
Plate 47

The birch casebearer, *C. serratella* (L.), is a solitary defoliator long designated by the scientific names of *C. fuscedinella* Zell. and *C. salmani* Heinr. Its country of origin is uncertain, but it appears that it came from Europe and was introduced to the eastern United States around 1920. In Europe, it attacks various species of birch, alder, and elm. In North America, its preferred host is white birch but, during severe outbreaks, it also attacks grey birch and yellow birch, alder, apple, and hawthorn, as well as many other hardwoods.

History of outbreaks

Since its discovery in the state of Maine in 1927, the birch casebearer has spread north and west, reaching the Maritime provinces in 1933. It caused serious damage in New Brunswick from 1937 to 1952 and in Nova Scotia from 1949 to 1954. Since then, its presence has been reported every year in those provinces, with significant fluctuations in populations. It was introduced into Newfoundland on ornamental trees in 1953 and caused heavy damage in the western part of the island in 1962 and 1963. By 1971, it had spread across the other regions of the island and is now considered the most serious pest of birch. In Quebec, the birch casebearer was found first in 1957, and a major outbreak raged throughout the eastern part of that province from 1963 to 1969. The insect then spread gradually into the western part of the province,

where it is still fairly rare. The first mention of this casebearer in Ontario goes back to 1944 and, although it now occurs throughout the entire province, it is still relatively rare.

Description and biology

Adult. Small triangular moth; gray-brown; wings bordered with fringe of hairs of the same color. Length: 6.5 mm; wingspan about 12 mm (Plate 47, H).

Egg. Oval, opaque; yellow orange at time of laying, then becoming darker; chorion slightly dimpled and longitudinally ribbed. Length: 0.5 mm.

Larva. Small, almost hairless larva, living hidden between the two epiderms of the leaf or at the surface of the lamina in a small, slightly curved, cigar-shaped case, constructed with the leaf epiderm; head black, body translucid yellow initially, gradually taking on the color of the chlorophyll. Length when full grown: 5 mm (Plate 47, D).

Pupa. Spindle-shaped, enclosed in larval case generally attached to leaf. Length: 6.5 mm (Plate 47, G).

Major studies were carried out on the birch casebearer in the state of Maine and in Newfoundland and Quebec.

It has one generation per year and its life cycle necessarily varies with local climatic conditions of the various regions. In the northeastern part of the continent, moths are present from mid-June to the beginning of August; females lay their eggs singly in tufts of hair at rib junctions, under the lamina of the leaf. Incubation lasts 20 to 30 days and, on hatching, the larva penetrates directly between the two epiderms of the leaf and makes an irregularly shaped mine. The second larval instar is reached about 2 weeks later. Almost all of this instar is spent in building a case, or sheath; the larva cuts the two epiderms of the leaf along the outside of the mined part and attaches them together so as to form a case in which it encloses itself. It then moves along the surface of the leaf dragging its case and feeding by gnawing on the epidermis. Shortly before leaves drop in the fall, the encased larva leaves the foliage in search

of a suitable spot in which to pass the winter, i.e., near buds, in bark crevices, or in the axil of a twig (Plate 47, B). Most larvae have, by this time, reached their third instar, but individuals hatched from eggs that were laid later are still in their second instar; in such cases, the larval cycle has only four instars instead of five.

As soon as leaves appear in the spring, the larva, still with its case, abandons its winter quarters and settles on new foliage to resume feeding (Plate 47, F). By mid-June, it is full grown and, after attaching its case firmly, it transforms to a pupa and, about 20 days later, to an adult.

Damage and diagnosis

All damage is caused by larval feeding; and is particularly severe during spring when the larvae of the birch casebearer attack buds and young leaves (Plate 47, E). The larva feeds by chewing the surface of the leaf in irregular patches that are gradually increased in size until they finally cover the whole laminar surface. The damaged parts turn brown, dry up, and fall to the ground. When defoliation is severe, many twigs may die (Plate 47, A), but the trees generally survive due to the fact that birch grows throughout the season. Their crowns have a certain respite at mid-summer during pupation of the casebearer, and heavily damaged birch may even replace their foliage during this period. However, leaves produced at this time are generally less numerous, smaller, and sometimes in tufts.

The most practical criterion for recognizing an attack by the birch casebearer is the presence, on birch and alder, of small cigar-shaped cases not flattened at the distal end; they are attached at right angles to the lamina in summer and on the surface of twig bark in fall and winter. This initial diagnosis may be confirmed during the summer season by the presence of hatched eggs in the pubescence along leaf ribs.

Bryant and Raske (1975) developed, in Newfoundland, a method for estimating the size of populations of this casebearer either on isolated trees or in stands, on the basis of the number of cases per unit of leaf surface.

Natural control

Populations of the birch casebearer are kept in check by a number of regulating factors. Parasites are particularly active, and some 40 species have been reported in North America. An egg parasite, *Trichogramma minutum* Riley, has destroyed about 4 percent of the eggs in Quebec and 12 percent in Maine. Larvae and pupae are also preyed upon by many parasitic species, and Reeks (1951) reported 7 species as being responsible for the decline of an outbreak in the Maritime provinces. Cochaux[1] obtained 17 species in central and eastern Quebec, of which the most common was *Itoplectis conquisitor* (Say). Later on, Guèvremont and Juillet (1975) reported for the Sherbrooke area of Quebec and the years 1971 and 1973, parasitism rates of 25 to 36 percent in casebearers on white birch and 43 to 56 percent of those on grey birch, due to a group of 19 hymenopterous species headed by *Orgilus coleophorae* Mues. In 1974, on the other hand, Raske reported 19 parasites native to Newfoundland and estimated that they were effective in reducing populations only by about 3 percent.

Insect-eating predators also play a major role in limiting populations of this casebearer. Over 50 years ago, Salman (1929) and Gillespie (1932) reported that eggs were destroyed by these predators. In 1974, Raske reported almost total egg destruction by a spider, *Triophydeus triophtalmus* (Ouds.).

Two species of the genus *Campoplex* were introduced into Newfoundland in 1971 and 1972 in an attempt to check the spread of the birch casebearer; one of the two species has been recovered, but it is too early to tell how effective it is.

Among other natural factors, Guèvremont and Juillet (1975) mentioned premature leaf drop (which dislodges casebearers), trophic factors, cold, and arrested growth. They were able to develop life tables and to show that, during their research period, only 7 percent of the population survived. Likewise, in Newfoundland, Raske (1975c) estimated that, during the winters of 1971, 1972, and 1973, populations were reduced by rates of 59, 62, and 58 percent respectively.

Collecting cases by hand or brushing them off twigs in the fall or in early spring are simple, low-cost methods that may be used on a small number of trees. Leaves may even be removed by hand before they begin to yellow in the fall, thus removing larvae before they can migrate to twigs.

Chemical control presents great difficulties because the larva is almost constantly protected by its case; however it is possible to reach the young larvae during their first week of activity in the spring or around the third week of August when they begin to move about. A contact insecticide should then be sprayed on the foliage. Trunks may also be painted with a systemic insecticide.

[1]1969: unedited report.

PLATE 47

Birch casebearer, *Coleophora serratella* (L.), and lesser birch casebearer, *C. comptoniella* McD.

A. White birch severely defoliated by *C. serratella*.
B. Young cases of *C. serratella* attached to bark for the winter.
C. New, undamaged white birch foliage.
D. Case opened to show larva.
E. New white birch foliage attacked by *C. serratella* in the spring.
F. Mass of *C. serratella* cases on white birch foliage before emergence of adult in June.
G. Lateral and ventral views of *C. serratella* pupa.
H. *C. serratella* adult (wingspan: 12 mm).
I. *C. comptoniella* adult.
J. *C. comptoniella* case and adult resting near its case.

The lesser birch casebearer, *Coleophora comptoniella* (McD.) is fairly rare. It is also a solitary, leaf-eating insect, and its known hosts are white birch and yellow birch. It has always been collected in limited quantities in eastern Canada, very often in association with the birch casebearer. It is also found in North Carolina.

History of outbreaks

The lesser birch casebearer had only been collected in Ontario up until 1976, when it was discovered for the first time in Quebec in the Ottawa valley. Later on it was collected in several localities in the western part of that province.

Description and biology

Adult. Small, triangular moth; wings bordered with a fringe of ochre-yellow hairs, lighter on the sides; head same yellow as sides of wings, body reddish brown. Length, about 7 mm (Plate 47, I).

Case. Brown, cigar-shaped, flattened in the shape of a fish-tail at the distal end. Length: about 8 mm (Plate 47, J).

The biology of the lesser birch casebearer is similar to that of the birch casebearer with some differences in dates of appearance of the various stages in the life cycle. Larval development is characterized also by the presence of two forms quite distinct from one another. During the first instar, the larva feeds by mining the leaves, whereas from the second instar on it comes out of the tunnel and becomes a surface defoliator. The larva is found in June and the moth in July.

Damage and diagnosis

Initial damage by the lesser birch casebearer consists mainly in small circular tunnels made by the larva as it feeds on the parenchyma contained between the two epidermis of the leaf. Because the insect is relatively rare, damage caused to date has been negligible.

The cigar-shaped cases flattened at their distal end on either white birch or yellow birch leaves during the summer, and on the bark of twigs during the fall and winter, best indicate an outbreak of this species.

Natural control

Natural factors keeping populations in check are not well known and to date, only two species parasitic on lesser birch casebearer have been reported in Ontario (Raizenne 1952).

References

Bryant and Raske 1975; Clark and Raske 1974; Gillespie 1932; Guèvremont and Juillet 1974, 1975; Martineau 1974; Raizenne 1952; Raske 1973a, 1974a, b, 1975b, c, 1976; Reeks 1951; and Salman 1929.

Birch skeletonizer
Plate 48

The birch skeletonizer, *Bucculatrix canadensisella* Cham., is native to North America, where it is considered to be one of the most serious pests of birch. This microlepidopteron is a skeletonizer that attacks all species of birch, but prefers white birch and grey birch. In Quebec, it has also been collected on alder and has been known to attack red oak when other food becomes scarce.

It is known to occur all across Canada and, in the United States, from Maine to Minnesota and towards the south as far as North Carolina. Throughout this huge territory, populations rise dramatically from time to time, usually every 9 to 10 years, causing outbreaks that cover vast areas; after a few years, populations return to endemic levels.

History of outbreaks

Four separate outbreaks of birch skeletonizer were reported during the period from 1890 to 1925, although no precise details are given (Friend 1927); however, since the inception of the FIDS in 1936, several outbreaks have been followed closely in eastern Canada.

The first of these outbreaks lasted from 1939 to 1943, over a vast area including the Maritime provinces, southern Quebec, and eastern and western Ontario. From 1952 to 1955, a second outbreak covered part of Newfoundland, the Maritime provinces, the southern tip of Quebec, and the northeast and western tip of Ontario. Several years later, from 1960 to 1965, a third outbreak developed in the Maritime provinces, Quebec, and central and southwestern Ontario. A fourth outbreak occurred in 1970, in central and eastern Newfoundland, western and central Quebec, and northern and northwestern Ontario, although the Maritime provinces were untouched until 1974. Populations disappeared from Ontario in 1975 and from Quebec in 1976.

Description and biology

Adult. Small brown moth; head with a tuft of piliform scales, brown in the middle and white on the sides; body brown above, lighter below; forewings brown with white transversal bands; hindwings gray with fringe of long, darker gray hairs. Length: about 3 mm; wingspan: 7 mm (Plate 48, G and H).

Egg. Oval, flattened, translucid white when freshly laid, becoming opaque after several days of incubation; chorion bears well-defined hexagonal markings. Length: 0.25 mm (Plate 48, C).

Larva. Characterized by two distinct forms, the first legless, flattened dorsoventrally, translucid white and adapted to life inside tissues; the second is cylindrical in shape with well-developed, functioning legs, brown head, greenish yellow body having piliferous discs. Length when full grown:6 mm (Plate 48, B).

Pupa. Spindle-shaped, robust; brown; enclosed in ribbed cocoon orange yellow initially, turning darker with time. Length of pupa: 3 mm (Plate 48, F).

The birch skeletonizer has been well known for some time, and was the object of a very detailed study by Friend (1927). It produces one generation per year in

PLATE 48

Birch skeletonizer, *Bucculatrix canadensisella* Cham.

A. Severely defoliated white birch stand.
B. Young larvae and damage on white birch leaf.
C. Close-up of a larva and of eggs on a portion of a white birch leaf.
D. and E. Second and first tents; close-up of second web tent showing position of larva inside.
F. Cocoon spun by larva on dead leaf.
G. Pinned adult (wingspan: 7 mm).
H. Close-up of adult at rest.
I. Section of birch twig filled with webs.

A

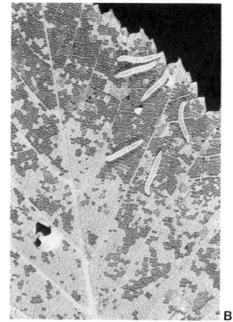

B

C

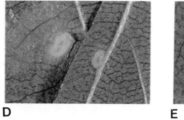

D

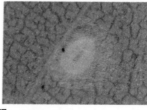

E

F

H

G

I

eastern North America and possibly two in British Columbia. In eastern regions, the moth is present during June and July. Shortly after emerging, females lay their eggs singly and at random either on the upper or lower side of the leaves. Incubation lasts about 2 weeks, and the larvae hatch around the end of July and during August. On hatching, the young larva penetrates directly into the leaf and mines a tunnel in which it spends 2 to 5 weeks, by which time it has reached the middle of the third larval instar.

The larva then leaves the tunnel and wanders for several hours on the underside of the leaf before spinning a web tent of white silk, generally near the main rib. This web is oval-shaped and measures about 1.5 mm in diameter at the widest point (Plate 48, D). Here the larva molts and goes into its fourth instar. After this transformation, it leaves the web to feed on the parenchyma for several days. It then spins a second tent similar to the first, but slightly larger, about 2.5 mm in diameter at the widest point, in which it molts for the fourth time and goes into the fifth instar (Plate 48, E, and I). Once it is fully grown, normally around September, the larva drops on a thread of silk to the ground where it spins a cocoon under dead leaves, rocks, or other debris littering the soil. The insect overwinters in the pupal stage inside the cocoon and resumes its development the following spring.

Damage and diagnosis

All damage attributable to the birch skeletonizer is caused by the larva when it tunnels inside the leaf and when it feeds on the parenchyma on the underside. The tunnels formed by the young larvae may be up to 20 mm long, and it is not uncommon to count 25 to 40 per leaf. Feeding is confined to the underside of the leaf, and the ribs are untouched. During severe outbreaks, leaves are quickly reduced to their skeletons, dry, turn brown, and fall, sometimes leaving the crown completely bare (Plate 48, A). This type of damage may be observed both on isolated trees and on large stretches of forest, but it is generally more spectacular than detrimental, except where trees undergo severe defoliation for several consecutive years. Destruction of foliage normally does not have serious conse-

quences, because it occurs late in the season; however, some reduction in growth and the death of a few twigs at the top of the crown may be observed on the most heavily damaged trees.

In summer and fall, skeletonized birch leaves and the presence of tiny, oval-shaped white webs on the underside of the leaves are signs by which an attack by the birch skeletonizer may be easily recognized.

Natural control

Friend (1927) claimed that parasites and insect-eating predators play a major role in controlling populations of birch skeletonizer. In his rearings of larvae and pupae of this insect in Connecticut, Friend obtained 10 species of parasites belonging to the ichneumonid and chalcid groups. In rearings carried out by the FIDS in Quebec, 4 species of ichneumonids and 3 species of chalchids were obtained, 2 of which were included in Friend's list.

The most important enemies, however, are the predators, particularly various species of ants and other insects that capture and devour the larvae when they drop to the ground to pupate. Several species of birds have also been seen eating larvae, but their action is less important. Friend (1927) also mentioned a fungus of the genus *Verticillium*.

Climate also plays an important role, especially in the spring, because the pupae die from dry weather (Blais and Pilon 1968).

Artificial control

On isolated trees the severity of the attack by the birch skeletonizer may be reduced considerably by burning in the fall the dead litter in which the pupae take shelter at the base of affected trees. In other cases, trees may be protected by spraying a residual-action chemical insecticide on the foliage when the first mines appear in the leaves in the summer, taking the precaution of covering both sides of the leaf and repeating the operation as often as required.

References

Blais and Pilon 1968; Cochaux 1965; Daviault 1937; Friend 1927; and Prentice 1965.

PLATE 49

Birch tubemaker, *Acrobasis betulella* Hulst

A. Larva feeding on white birch leaf.
B. First tube formed by larva (length: 19.3 mm).
C. Completed tube in natural surroundings (dimensions: 7-8 mm by 8-10 mm).
D. Isolated tube and tube opened so as to show the pupa inside.
E. Pinned adult (wingspan: 21-25 mm).
F. Adult at rest.

A

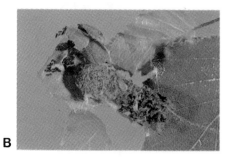

B

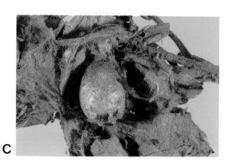

C

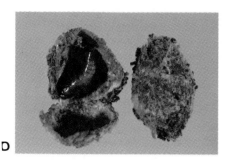

D

E

F

Birch tubemaker

Plate 49

The birch tubemaker, *Acrobasis betulella* Hulst, is a solitary leaf-eater that lives constantly hidden inside a silken shelter. First described in 1890, this species is found all across Canada, although most frequently in Ontario and Manitoba. In the United States, it occurs from the Atlantic Ocean to the central state of Colorado, but also farther west, in California. White birch is its preferred host, although it is occasionally found on other birches and sometimes on alder and dogwood. Although it is very common in eastern Canada, no serious damage has yet been reported.

Description and biology

Adult. Medium-sized moth; body and forewings ochre-brown; hindwings brownish gray. Wingspan: 21-24 mm (Plate 49, E and F).

Egg. Ellipsoidal, flattened; chorion uniformly white at time of egg laying, then developing a number of irregularly shaped pink spots. Dimensions: 0.3 mm by 0.5 mm.

Larva. Pinkish-white on hatching, turning dark gray after a few days; at maturity, body light to very dark gray, head very dark reddish brown. Dimensions: 3.4 mm by 19.3 mm (Plate 49, A).

Pupa. Obtect; light brown. Dimensions: 3-5 mm by 9-10 mm (Plate 49, D).

Cocoon. Ovoid; dusky gray. Dimensions 7-8 mm by 8-10 mm.

A detailed study of the birch tubemaker was carried out by Daviault (1937) in Quebec, but many points of its biology still remain to be cleared.

This tubemaker has only one generation per year, with the various stages appearing at different dates throughout its range. In Quebec, moths appear at the end of June and are present until the end of August. Shortly after emerging, the females lay their eggs at random throughout the tree in clusters of varying size, with the eggs overlapping each other slightly like shingles on a roof. The eggs hatch in about 1 week. On hatching, the larvae move to young twigs where they feed on young foliage while spinning a tubular silken shelter spotted with blackish excreta (Plate 49, B). By fall, the larva has reached a quarter of its length and drops to the ground with the leaves, overwintering in the dead litter.

In the spring, the larva leaves its shelter and crawls up the trunk to feed on the newly-formed foliage while spinning a new tube in which to continue its development (Plate 49, C). It is during this period that most known damage occurs. The larva reaches maturity around mid-June and then transforms to a pupa in the widest part of its tube, having first closed off the two ends. The pupal stage lasts about 2 weeks.

Damage and diagnosis

Most damage by the birch tubemaker is caused by the larva during the spring of the second year. At that time, it not only devours numerous leaves, but also wastes many others by tying them together to make a sort of nest. This damage is never serious enough to cause the death of trees, but it does spoil considerably the appearance of ornamental trees.

The presence of dark brown moths in crowns in June and July is a good indication of attack by this tubemaker. On careful examination of the foliage, clusters of white eggs bearing pink spots will probably be found. Later on, the first tubes containing larvae may be seen and, when leaves drop in the fall, tubes will be found among other debris lying on the ground.

In the spring, small gray larvae may be seen crawling up birch trunks towards the crown. Shortly thereafter, tubes and nests may be seen here and there on the foliage.

Natural control

To date, eight species of entomophagous parasites have been obtained from the birch tubemaker in Canada. Daviault (1937) also mentioned one species of diptera and five of hymenoptera, two of which, *Itoplectis conquisitor* (Say) and *Meteorus indigator* Riley, are very common. Three species of hymenoptera

have been reported by the FIDS, including *I. conquisitor* (Say) (Bradley 1974). In his report, Daviault also mentioned having observed two entomophagous predators, although these were definitely of secondary importance.

Artificial control

The literature contains no information on methods of control of the birch tubemaker. On the basis of its biology the following methods are suggested:
- Collect and burn fallen leaves at the base of infested trees, in the fall or before buds open in the spring, or spray the surface of the ground with a residual light-oil-based insecticide;
- Early in the spring, apply a sticky coat of tanglefoot around the trunk of trees infested the previous year, to trap the larvae as they climb towards the crown; and
- Spray the trunk and crown of infested trees with a stomach or contact insecticide in the spring, when larvae are exposed to the air and before they have made their second tube.

References

Bradley 1974; Daviault 1937; Forbes 1923; Prentice 1965; and Winn 1912.

Birch Leafminers

Of the many birch defoliators, a certain number fall into the group designated as leafminers, because their larvae devour the parenchyma between the two leaf surfaces. In eastern Canada, four species in this group are singled out for attention. The damage they cause is so similar that it is most often attributed to the commonest species, the birch leafminer, *Fenusa pusilla* (Lep.). Two other species, the late birch leaf edgeminer, *Heterarthrus nemoratus* (Fall.) and the ambermarked birch leafminer, *Profenusa thomsoni* (Konow), may occasionally become extremely abundant in eastern North America. There is also a fourth species, the early birch leaf edgeminer, *Messa nana* (Klug), which was discovered on this continent in 1966 and whose territorial distribution is as yet quite limited.

Birch leafminer
Plate 50

The birch leafminer, *Fenusa pusilla* (Lep.), was imported from Europe and became established in the northeastern United States around 1923. Although considered fairly harmless in Europe, this species has become a serious pest on birch in eastern North America. It is found on all species of birch, but shows a preference for grey birch, white birch, and silver birch, whereas black birch and cherry birch are hardly affected; yellow birch is sometimes slightly damaged in the spring.

History of outbreaks

In Canada, the birch leafminer was first observed in south-central Quebec in 1929 where, in all probability, it had been for several years. This leafminer then spread through the eastern provinces of Canada, no doubt due to the abundance of its preferred hosts. In Newfoundland, where only white birch favored its spread, the insect was not reported until 1954, but it spread rapidly and, by 1965, it was common throughout the province, causing major damage every year on ornamental birches and those along roads and in camping grounds. In the Maritime provinces, where white birch and grey birch are plentiful, outbreaks have followed one another almost without interruption since 1939, occasionally covering very large areas. In Quebec, outbreaks have been reported almost every year since 1942, particularly in the southern part of the province, where grey birch is abundant. In Ontario, white birch is common everywhere, although grey birch is confined to the southeastern part. The first outbreak was reported in 1939 in southern Ontario, and the insect remained confined to that area until 1955, but from 1963 on, it spread northwards and around 1966 into the northwest. Thus, by 1974 and 1975 moderate to severe infestations were reported provincewide.

Description and biology

Adult. Resembles a tiny four-winged fly; jet black; female larger than male. Length: 3 mm, wingspan: 7 mm (Plate 50, H).

Egg. Ovoid; thin, uniform membrane, translucid when laid, then gradually turning opaque white.
Dimensions: 0.24 mm by 0.45 mm.

Larva. Flattened dorsoventrally, becoming cylindrical at the fifth instar; head brown, body almost uniformly white in the early instars, but bearing four black spots on the underside, one on each of the three thoracic segments and one on the first abdominal segment; organs of locomotion primitive and hair almost absent. Length on leaving leaf, 6.9 mm. (Plate 50, D).

Pupa. All white initially, head gradually turning brown and body light yellow. Length: 3.3 mm (Plate 50, E). Enclosed in oval cocoon (Plate 50 F); length: 4 mm.

Numerous studies have been carried out on the birch leafminer in the United States and in various provinces of Canada.

One complete generation lasts about 35 days, and thus the insect may have two to four generations per year depending on the weather conditions, the year, and the host. In Newfoundland, for example, two complete generations and a partial third occur, whereas in Quebec there are three complete and one partial generation. There is, however, one generation less on old birch trees, due to the absence of young foliage in midsummer.

In the field, the adult is normally present on trees from May until September, but in Newfoundland, it does not appear until June, which explains the absence of one generation. Eggs are always laid on tender leaves, never on hardened leaves, in such a way that they may swell more easily. They are laid in a uniform manner on the central part of the leaf, inserted singly in the parenchyma under the upper surface (Plate 50, G). Freshly laid eggs are hard to locate without a magnifying glass, but their outline may be seen by holding the leaf up to the light. Shortly after being laid the eggs swell, and this shows up as a small protuberance on the upper surface of the leaf, while the injured parts take on a grayish tinge. Incubation of the eggs lasts 5 to 8 days.

The larva goes through five instars and, during the first four, feeds on the parenchyma of the leaf with the ventral part of its body against the upper surface of the leaf. Young larvae at first move along the main vein; as they grow older, they may take any direction. Tunnels formed by the young larvae are very small and reniform, whereas later on, they are circular (Plate 50, B). Initially, the tunnels formed by different larvae are quite distinct, but, as they become more numerous, they join together to cover half of the leaf surface or even more.

When the larvae reach the last instar, they stop feeding and drop to the ground where they burrow down to a depth of 2.5-5 cm and construct a cell by pushing away soil particles. Once the cell is formed, they stick the largest particles of soil together with secretions and finish the cell by lining the interior with silk.

Damage and diagnosis

Initial damage is caused by the female during egg-laying; wounds bring about a temporary halt in development of leaf tissues located around the slit, and these take on a gray color. More serious damage is caused by the larvae, which feed on the parenchyma between the two surfaces of the leaf. One or two larvae do not cause too much harm to the leaf, but five or more may destroy the parenchyma completely (Plate 50, C). From the second generation on, however, only the leaves at the tips of the shoots are attacked, because this is the only place where new foliage may be found.

Destruction of foliage rarely causes the infested tree to die, but it does considerably diminish the aesthetic value of individuals planted as ornamental trees (Plate 50, A). Leaves bearing eggs are easily recognized by the many gray spots due to wounds inflicted by the female during egg-laying. Those that harbor larvae display tunnels of various sizes full of excreta, which is characteristic of this species. If the larva is still present, the species may be identified: the ventral side of the insect body bears four characteristic black spots on a white background.

Natural control

When introduced to this continent, the birch leafminer had absolutely no parasite or predator enemies, but certain species have adapted gradually to this new prey. Friend (1933) obtained four native species of chalcids in his rearings in Connecticut, and Daviault (1937) mentioned one species of this same group. Twenty years later, however, Cheng and Leroux (1966, 1969, and 1970) obtained 22 species of hymenopterous parasites, 10 species of insect predators, and 3 bird predators. Although very numerous, parasites do not play an important role in reducing populations of this leafminer, whereas predators, such as birds, wasps, and ants, destroy about 20 percent by preying on eggs and on the young larvae still in their tunnels. Predators are most harmful during the last larval instar, after the larvae drop to the ground, when 80 percent of the surviving larvae are destroyed before they can burrow into the ground.

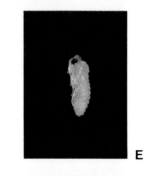

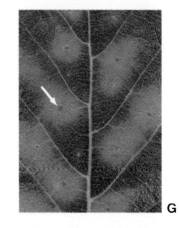

A

B

C

D

E

F

G

H

The most important factor, however, is that eggs laid in leaves that are over-mature, hardened, or dried are destroyed; this factor becomes more important as the season advances and the quantity of young foliage suitable for egg-laying diminishes. Hardening of leaves also has a disastrous effect on young larvae, who are unable to chew the hardened leaf tissues.

Artificial control

Numerous methods have been tried in an attempt to set up a control program against the birch leafminer, which is very difficult to fight due to the fact that its development occurs inside the leaves and also because it has several generations per year. Control using chemical insecticides has not given satisfactory results. Repellent products were first tried in an attempt to prevent egg-laying. Later on, attempts were made to destroy the larva in the tunnel, either by spraying with a contact insecticide or indirectly, using systemic insecticides in three different ways: either by spreading granules on the ground surface, by painting the trunk, or by spraying leaves. To date, the results of these attempts remain uncertain.

During the period 1970-1973, two species of European parasites were introduced into Newfoundland in an attempt to reinforce the action of natural factors. One parasite has apparently become established, but it is too early to determine its effect in reducing populations.

Protective measures against this leafminer should mainly be aimed at protecting the young foliage, because this is the only foliage suitable for egg-laying. In the spring, all leaves are subject to attack, whereas later on only the foliage on adventitious shoots is acceptable to the females.

References

Cheng and Leroux 1965, 1966, 1968, 1969, 1970; Daviault 1937; Friend 1933; Jones and Raske 1976; Lindquist 1959; Raske and Jones 1975; Scheer and Johnson 1970; and Schread 1960, 1964.

PLATE 50

Birch leafminer, *Fenusa pusilla* (Lep.)

A. Severely defoliated white birch crowns.
B. Isolated mine on grey birch leaf.
C. Birch leaf almost totally mined by several larvae.
D. Ventral and dorsal views of a larva (length: 6.9 mm).
E. Pupa (length: 3.3 mm).
F. Cocoons (length: 4 mm).
G. Close-up of section of birch leaf containing eggs.
H. Adult at rest (length: 3 mm).

Late birch leaf edgeminer
Plate 51

The late birch leaf edgeminer, *Heterarthrus nemoratus* (Fall.), formerly known as *Phyllotoma nemoralis* (Fall.), is a less serious menace than the birch leafminer, *Fenusa pusilla*. Of European origin, this species was first discovered on this continent in 1905 in Nova Scotia; from there it spread very rapidly across North America. It caused major outbreaks up until 1941, but very few since then. This species attacks all birches, showing a preference for white birch and grey birch. It occurs throughout most of eastern Canada and causes some damage in all provinces.

History of outbreaks

The late birch leaf edgeminer was first established in the Maritime provinces, where serious outbreaks occurred until 1940, but it has become much less abundant since then. In Newfoundland, this leafminer was first reported in 1944, and it was present in sufficient numbers to cause overall browning on some trees. Since 1959, it has normally been found there together with the birch leafminer, which outnumbers it, causing annual damage to birch. In Quebec, a severe outbreak, lasting several years, ended in 1937 having caused widespread damage in the eastern part of the province but, since that time, the insect has never again been reported in large numbers. In Ontario, only local outbreaks have been recorded, particularly in 1941, 1952, 1955-1957, and in 1959.

Description and biology

Adult. Resembles a tiny fly with four transparent wings; jet black. Length: 4.5 mm (Plate 51, A). Egg. Oval in shape, flattened; white. Length: 0.5 mm.

Larva. Body elongated, straight, flattened dorsoventrally, hairless except for a few hairs on the head; cream white with small brown spots, the most characteristic being found on the head, on the dorsal and ventral sides of the prothorax, and in the middle of the ventral side of the mesothorax and of the metathorax. Length in sixth instar: 10 mm (Plate 51, D and E).

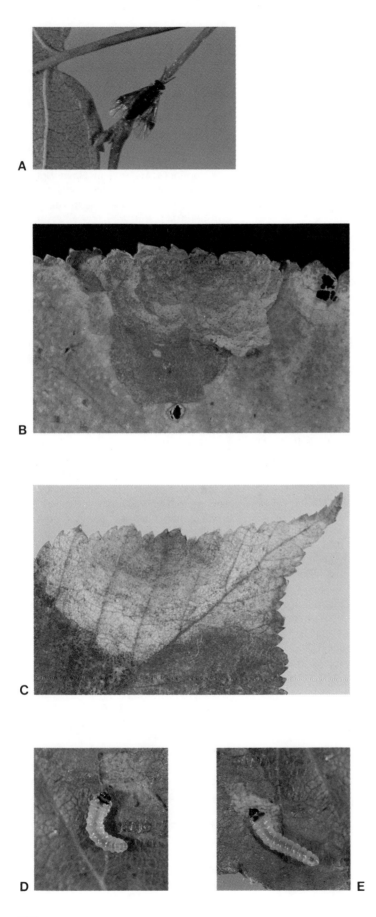

A

B

C

D

E

Pupa. Elongated, white initially gradually turning black. Length: 6.5 mm; enclosed in bean-shaped hibernaculum about 7 mm long.

The late birch leaf edgeminer is less well known than the birch leafminer, but studies of its habits have been carried out in the eastern United States and in Canada (Peirson and Brower 1936; and Daviault 1937).

This leafminer is of particular interest because only the female is known and because it can reproduce by thelytokous parthenogenesis. In North America, the insect produces only one generation per year, whereas in certain regions of Europe there are two. The adult is present for about a month, normally from mid-June to mid-July. Soon after emerging, the female lays her eggs singly in the large serrations bordering the edges of normal, old birch leaves. She avoids leaves damaged in any way, whether chewed by insects, covered with honeydew, or only partially developed. The eggs hatch in about 20 days.

Larvae generally go through seven instars and feed by mining between the upper and lower surface of the leaf. The larva is very clean and clears its tunnel of all excreta as they are produced, which is a distinctive characteristic of this species. Larvae hatch in July and feed actively until cold weather in the fall; they then construct individual circular, flattened cocoons and drop with the leaf to the ground where they overwinter, transforming to pupae and adults the following spring.

PLATE 51

Late birch leaf edgeminer, *Heterarthrus nemoratus* (Fall.)

A. Dorsal view of adult.
B. Appearance of tunnel in green leaf.
C. Old damage.
D. Dorsal view of larva (length: 10 mm).
E. Ventral view of larva.

Damage and diagnosis

All damage by the late birch leaf edgeminer results from destruction by larvae of the parenchyma between the two surfaces of the leaf (Plate 51, B and C). Tunnels, starting from the egg located at the edge of the lamina, initially appear as distinct brownish spots; however, if there are several tunnels in the same leaf, they usually run together by the end of the season. In early summer, damage is not too apparent, but later on, the leaves, reduced in most cases to their two surfaces, turn yellow, dry up and fall. This phenomenon can be seen in August, and, when the outbreak is widespread, birch trees may be damaged in this fashion over huge areas.

Defoliation, even if severe, rarely kills birch trees, but does bring about a noticeable reduction in growth the year following the outbreak and for several years thereafter. However, the worst damage consists in diminished aesthetic value of trees planted as ornamentals.

An attack by this leafminer can be distinguished from that of other related species because the tunnel is clear of larval excreta, pupation takes place inside the tunnel in the leaf, and characteristic spots are present on both dorsal and ventral sides of the thorax of the larva.

Natural control

Peirson and Brower (1936) stated that predators are mainly responsible for the destruction of the late birch leaf edgeminer. Birds consume large quantities of larvae and pupae in the crowns and at ground level; chrysopid larvae, ants, and wasps feed in the crowns; and shrews, ground beetles, click beetle larvae, and ants eat individuals that drop to the ground with the leaves. In their rearings, these authors obtained 20 species of parasites that destroyed up to 25 percent of the eggs and 28 percent of the larvae in some areas.

Some physical factors are also responsible for reducing populations of this leafminer, particularly drought, which prevents eggs from hatching and thus kills the unhatched larvae; also, early frosts in the fall may cause leaves to drop prematurely thereby killing larvae by depriving them of their food.

Another important factor is competition among the various pests for occupancy of the leaf, particularly other miners and certain defoliators such as the birch skeletonizer, *Bucculatrix canadensisella*. Because damaged or abnormal leaves are unacceptable to the late birch leaf edgeminer as egg-laying locations, it often happens during widespread outbreaks by a number of leaf-eating insects that the female of this species fails to find suitable leaves in which to lay her eggs.

Between 1930 and 1934, attempts were made in the United States to introduce European parasites to this continent. The two species imported, *Chrysocharis laricinellae* (Ratz.) and *Phanomeris phyllotomae* Mues., are now well established, but their action is quite negligible.

Artificial control

The methods already suggested for controlling the birch leafminer may also be used against the late birch leaf edgeminer, provided that care is taken to adjust dates for applying treatment according to the life cycle of this second species.

Another method of control is to collect and to burn the leaves when they drop in the fall, because the larva overwinters in its tunnel.

References

Daviault 1937; Dowden 1941; Gobeil 1937; Lindquist 1955, 1959; and Peirson and Brower 1936.

Ambermarked birch leafminer
Plate 52

The ambermarked birch leafminer, *Profenusa thomsoni* (Konow), has been known in Europe for quite a long time. In Canada, this leafminer was unfortunately confused with the birch leafminer for some time, and only in 1955 was its true identity established. Its range is considered as holarctic, and its known hosts are white birch, yellow birch, and grey birch. Its presence has been reported in six states of the United States, i.e., Massachusetts, New York, New Hampshire, Maine, Illinois, and Wisconsin. In Canada, the species has been collected from the Maritime provinces to Manitoba.

History of outbreaks

In the Maritimes, the ambermarked birch leafminer was only reported during 1957 and 1959. In Quebec, the insect was observed for the first time in 1959, after which it was discovered that it had been established for several years; from 1969 to 1972, an outbreak raged through a huge area in the northwestern part of the province, and again in 1977 and 1978 (Plate 52, E). In Ontario, the insect was observed from 1948 on, and in 1955, it was realized that this leafminer was already common throughout the northeastern part of the province. By 1958, it had reached the north and central parts of Ontario and, by 1973, it occurred throughout the province, although it did not cause any appreciable damage.

Description and biology

Adult. Resembles a tiny wasp with four transparent wings; color black. (Plate 52, F).

Egg. Translucid initially, gradually turning brown. Length: 0.5 mm.

Larva. Cylindrical, elongated, tapering at both ends; head beige, body translucid white allowing food to be seen in the digestive tract; ventral side of thorax bears three amber-colored spots, the largest on the prothorax and two smaller, oval-shaped ones on the mesothorax and the metathorax. Maximum length of body during the fifth and last feeding instar: 7 mm (Plate 52, D).

Pupa. Enclosed in a cocoon covered with soil particles; head translucid white; body light yellow initially, turning to bluish grey and then to black with age. Length: about 4 mm.

The information available on the habits of the ambermarked birch leafminer comes mainly from studies carried out in Ontario (Lindquist 1955, 1959; and Martin 1960).

Only one generation is produced per year. Adults are present during July and part of August. Females lay their eggs preferably in totally or partly shaded leaves, on branches less than 1.5 m above the ground; however, during outbreaks, all locations are acceptable. Eggs are inserted singly under the surface in the medial part of the leaf, normally close to a rib (Plate 52, A). Incubation of the eggs lasts about 10 days.

Larvae may be found from mid-July until October. They go through six larval instars and, during their lives, they consume about 5.3 cm^2 of leaf parenchyma. Thus, each leaf may easily support five or six individuals (Plate 52, B and C), but more are generally found, sometimes up to 40 insects. When the green matter is exhausted, all the larvae drop to the ground, whatever their stage of development. The insect overwinters in the prepupal stage at depths of 2 to 10 cm underground. In the spring, pupation takes place followed by the adult stage about 8 days later.

Damage and diagnosis

All damage is caused by the larva during its feeding period and is similar to that of the leafminers described previously, with a few differences. First, only small-diameter trees are attacked, except during an infestation when all trees may be affected (Plate 52, E). Secondly, eggs are laid on the upper surface of the leaf along a rib, where their location is surrounded by a little white ring. Lastly, the tunnel spreads out from the rib; initially it is narrow, sinuous and easy to find because the larval excrements appear as a dotted line; but later the tunnel widens and gradually takes on the form of a swelling within which excreta are scattered at random. The tunnel is irregular in shape, slightly raised, and eventually turns light brown. Diagnosis may be confirmed by the distinctive characteristics of the larva.

Natural control

A number of factors for natural control were observed by Martin (1960) during his research in Ontario. He observed first that adults are attacked by spiders and ants in the spring, as soon as they appear at ground level and also while they lay their eggs in the crowns. Control is also exerted on the eggs, of which about 50 percent do not develop due to the drying of the leaves.

The greatest mortality, however, takes place during the larval stage when available food in a leaf is insufficient for the number of larvae present. Larvae lacking food in this way drop to the ground in search of a new food source and starve to death or are killed by predators. In the fall, predators also feed on larvae that have reached maturity and have dropped naturally to the ground to spin their cocoons.

The role played by parasites has not yet been determined. In Ontario, however, hymenopterous parasites have been observed to lay their eggs in larvae, causing some mortality in the larval and prepupal stages (Martin 1960).

Artificial control

The chemical insecticide treatments suggested for the birch leafminer may also be used against the ambermarked birch leafminer, bearing in mind that the period of larval activity and location may differ.

References

Lindquist 1955, 1959; MacGillivray 1923; Martin 1960; and Watson 1959.

PLATE 52

Ambermarked birch leafminer, *Profenusa thomsoni* (Konow)

A. Tunnels and developing eggs on white birch leaf.
B. White birch leaves containing several tunnels.
C. Tunnel containing several larvae.
D. Tunnel opened showing ventral side of larva (length: 7 mm).
E. Aerial view of damaged white birch forest.
F. Dorsal view of adult.

A

Early birch leaf edgeminer
Plate 53

The early birch leaf edgeminer, *Messa nana* (Klug), presumed to be of European origin, was first reported in North America in the states of Maine and New York in 1966. In Canada, it has been identified in only two provinces, in Ontario in 1967 and in Quebec in 1973. In Quebec, it now occurs from the Ontario border to the lower North Shore region on the St. Lawrence River. In Ontario, the insect is as yet confined to the southern part of the province, but as populations increase, severe outbreaks occur, as was the case at Orono from 1972 to 1974. Its preferred host is white birch, but it is occasionally found on yellow birch and grey birch.

Description and biology

Adult. Resembles a tiny wasp with four transparent wings.

Egg. Ovoid; translucid white; chorion thin, smooth and colorless. Length: 0.6 mm.

Larva. Elongated, flattened dorsoventrally; head pale yellow, body greenish gray covered with dark, irregularly disposed small markings; large brown spot on dorsum of prothorax; dorsum of mesothorax and of metathorax divided by a sort of fissure separating two narrower spots; ventrum charac-

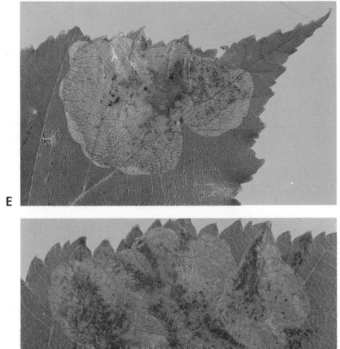

E

C

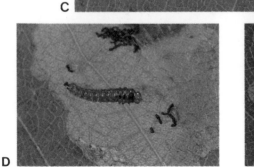

D

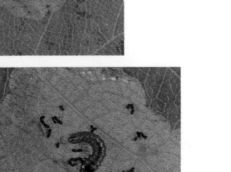

E

terized by the following: (1) dark, distinctly segmented thoracic legs; (2) four lighter brown spots, the largest on the prothorax, two others smaller, trapezoid-shaped ones on the mesothorax and the metathorax and one smaller, rounded one on the first abdominal segment; and (3) one pair of dark brown tubercles on the ninth abdominal segment (Plate 53, D and E). Length: about 7 mm.

Pupa. Enclosed in a cylindrical cocoon rounded at both ends and covered with soil particles.

Little is now known on the biology of the early birch leaf edgeminer; the data that are available come from studies carried out in Ontario (Lindquist and Thomson 1970).

Only one generation occurs per year. Adults appear from mid-May to early June, and eggs are present from mid-May until the end of June. Eggs are laid one to three to a leaf, but sometimes as many as ten; they are placed in a sort of pocket that the female makes with her ovipositor near the serrations around the edge of birch leaves. This cut causes the formation of an oval protuberance that is clearly visible on the underside of the leaf.

The larva feeds on the parenchyma, with its ventral side against the upper surface of the leaf; it mines from the edge of the leaf towards the inside of the blade (Plate 53, B). From the outside, the tunneled section appears as a swelling on the upper surface of the blade. Larvae are solitary and feed from the end of May until July; during their development, they molt five or six times. Once they are full-grown, each of them makes an opening in the upper side of the tunnel and drops to the ground where it spins an individual cocoon in which to pass the winter. Pupation occurs in the following spring.

Damage and diagnosis

All damage by the early birch leaf edgeminer is caused by the larva as it feeds inside the leaves (Plate 53, A). The first sign of an outbreak is the appearance on the underside of the leaves of small protuberances corresponding to the position of eggs; a little later in the season, tunnels may be seen to extend from these protuberances (Plate 53, C). The diagnosis may be confirmed by examining the larva carefully for the distinctive characteristics listed previously.

Natural control

Little is known about the natural factors that limit the spread of the early birch edgeminer in North America. To date, no parasites have been obtained from eggs and only three species from larvae; furthermore, their effectiveness is slight, not exceeding 3 percent.

It is likely that predators play a part by destroying not only larvae when they drop to the ground in the fall but also adults when they emerge, but no data are available as yet.

Artificial control

The chemical insecticides recommended for the birch leafminer may also be used against the early birch leaf edgeminer, adjusting the treatment period to correspond to the appearance of its various stages.

References

Lindquist and Thomson 1970; Maine Forest Service 1968; and Smith 1964.

Bronze birch borer
Plate 54

The bronze birch borer, *Agrilus anxius* Gory, is rightly considered to be a serious pest of white birch in North America. It is native to North America, occurring in all provinces of Canada and in all the states between Maine and Idaho. It is a wood and bark borer that attacks almost all species of birch. It was once thought to be a pest of declining trees, or of residual forest trees left after conifers were cut, but around 1925 it was believed to be responsible for a notorious anomaly that destroyed birch in the northeastern part of the continent, known as dieback. However, it was recognized later that the bronze birch borer was not responsible for this dieback and that it only attacks trees already weakened.

Description and biology

Adult. Small beetle, elongated in shape; olive green to black with bronze reflections. Length: female, 7-11 mm, male smaller (Plate 54, D).
Egg. Ovoid but flattened on two sides; creamy white when laid, gradually turning yellow. Length: 1.3-1.5 mm.
Larva. Elongated, narrow, and flattened; legless; white with head deeply embedded in prothorax and last abdominal segment bearing two chitinous, forceps-like spines. Length at full growth: 37 mm.
Pupa. Creamy white initially, gradually taking on adult coloring (Plate 54, C).

Major studies have been carried out on the biology of the bronze birch borer in New Brunswick and in the eastern United States (Barter 1957; Barter and Brown 1949; MacAloney 1968).

Depending on climate conditions of the area, the life cycle of this insect lasts 1 or 2 years, generally taking in two winters. Adults appear in early June and are visible into August; they live about 3 weeks and feed on birch leaves. They are good fliers and move about rapidly in search of places suitable for egg-laying, notably in open stands, cut areas, and on damaged or declining trees.

A

C

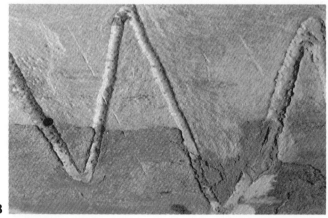

D

B

F

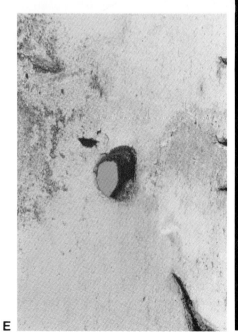

E

G

H

PLATE 54

Bronze birch borer, *Agrilus anxius* Gory, and bronze poplar borer, *A. liragus* B. and B.

A. Dying white birch affected by *A. anxius*.
B. Typical tunnel of *A. anxius* at the wood surface.
C. Pupa of *A. anxius*.
D. Adult of *A. anxius*.
E. Adult exit hole of *A. anxius*.
F. Tunnel of *A. liragus*.
G. Larval of *A. liragus*.
H. Adult of *A. liragus*.

Eggs are laid in crevices in the bark of the trunk and hatch in about 2 weeks. On hatching, the larva penetrates directly through the bark to the cambium and begins to construct meandering tunnels between the wood and the bark, occasionally penetrating into the wood either to molt, to hide from enemies, or to avoid unfavorable weather conditions. The tunnel takes various directions, often heading against the grain of the wood; it is usually filled with digested and solidly packed particles of wood (Plate 54, B). The first section is sometimes covered with new wood. The entire larval development takes place inside the tunnel. At the end of its tunnel, the larva digs a pupal cell in which pupation takes place in the spring. After some time, the adult insect abandons the tree by cutting a D-shaped exit hole (Plate 54, E).

Damage and diagnosis

The bronze birch borer attacks aerial parts of trees of all ages and diameters, although it prefers weakened trees, because the larva has difficulty surviving in a healthy tree. The slight damage caused by adults feeding on the leaves is of little importance; the most serious damage results from the construction of tunnels at the surface of the wood. These tunnels often girdle the branches or trunk, thus cutting off the flow of sap.

The attack usually begins in the upper crown, on branches measuring about 20 mm in diameter and, each year, the insect moves gradually downward. Wood usually dies just above the level of attack. The seriousness of the damage depends on the larval population and the distribution of tunnels in the tree. During a severe outbreak, there is a more or less pronounced reduction in annual growth, and some trees eventually die (Plate 54, A).

The following symptoms indicate an attack by the bronze birch borer: sparse and chlorotic foliage; raised welts on the bark of branches; death of some branches; and death of the entire crown. This diagnosis is confirmed if, by peeling the bark below the level of dead branches, meandering tunnels filled with packed, digested sawdust and sometimes covered with new wood are found at the surface of the wood. By following one of these tunnels, it is possible to locate a white, ribbon-like larva. Once the outbreak is well underway, the adults' semicircular, D-shaped exit holes may be seen here and there on the surface of the bark.

Natural control

Although they spend their lives hidden in their tunnels, larvae of the bronze birch borer are not immune to attack by certain enemies. In a study carried out in New Brunswick, Barter (1957) observed that a large number of larvae are destroyed by woodpeckers and that about 9 percent are killed by five species of entomophagous parasites. The egg is the most vulnerable stage, however, and Barter calculated that 55 percent of the eggs were destroyed by two species of parasites. He also observed that, during widespread outbreaks, populations may be wiped out by the abortion of eggs laid in healthy trees where they cannot develop.

Artificial control

The best way of protecting trees from attack by the bronze birch borer is to keep them healthy and strong by fertilizing them and watering them copiously. The spread of this insect may be prevented by cutting and burning weakened branches slightly below the dead wood level or by destroying dead trees before adults emerge in the spring, that is around mid-May. Crowns and trunks of lightly infested host trees can also be sprayed with a stomach or contact insecticide in June, to kill adults while they are feeding, and to prevent egg-laying.

References

Appleby et al. 1973; Barter 1957; Barter and Brown 1949; Daviault 1946a; Huard 1929; Johnson and Lyon 1976; Johnson and Zepp 1979; Kotinsky 1921; and MacAloney 1968.

Table 9. Other insects harmful to birch — Other insects that are regarded as pests of birch are listed in this table. For some insects, their characteristics are described in the chapter that applies to their primary host, and in such cases, that chapter (in Roman numerals) and the appropriate plate number are given. For other insects, a plate number alone is shown; and for the remaining insects, this table provides the only information.

Common and scientific names	Hosts (chap.)	Plate no.	Type of insect	Destructive stages	Period of activity	Importance*
Birch-aspen leafroller *Epinotia solandriana* L.	Poplar (X)	95	Defoliator	—	—	B
Birch bark beetle *Dryocoetes betulae* Hopk.	Birch, beech	—	Borer	Adult and larva	May to Oct.	C
Birch sawfly *Arge pectoralis* (Leach)	Birch	58	Defoliator	Larva	June to Sept.	B
Birch witches broom mite *Eriophyes betulae* Steb.	Birch	—	Spider	Adult and nymph	May to Oct.	C
Dusky birch sawfly *Croesus latitarsus* Nort.	Birch	58	Defoliator	Larva	June to Sept.	C
Forest tent caterpillar *Malacosoma disstria* Hbn.	Poplar (X)	91	—	—	—	A
Fruittree leafroller *Archips argyrospila* (Wlk.)	Hardwoods	57	Defoliator	Larva	May to Aug.	C
Linden Looper *Erannis tiliaria* (Harr.)	Maple (VIII)	67	—	—	—	B
Lintner's scale *Chionaspis lintneri* Comst.	Hardwoods	—	Sucker	Nymph	May to Oct.	C
Miner of birch petiole, a *Apagodiplosis papyriferae* (Gagné)	Birch	56	Miner	Larva	June to Sept.	C
Mite, a *Acalitus rudis* (Canestrini)	Birch	55	Spider	Adult and nymph	May to Oct.	C
Pinkstriped oakworm *Anisota virginiensis virginiensis* (Drury)	Oak, hardwoods	—	Defoliator	Larva	June to Aug.	B
Spearmarked black moth *Rheumaptera hastata* (L.)	Birch, hardwoods	59	Defoliator	Larva	June to Sept.	C
Yellownecked caterpillar *Datana ministra* (Drury)	White birch, hardwoods	—	Defoliator	Larva	July to Sept.	C

*A: Of major importance, capable of killing or severely damaging trees.
 B: Of moderate importance, capable of sporadic and localized injury to trees.
 C: Of minor importance, not known to present a threat to trees.

A

B

C

D

E

PLATE 55

A mite, *Acalitus rudis* (Canestrini), and aspen leaf mite, *Aceria dispar* (Nal.)

A. White birch severely damage by *Acalitus rudis*.
B. *A. rudis* young damage.
C. Close-up of old damage by *A. rudis*.
D. *Aceria dispar* damage at a distance.
E. Close-up of damage by *A. dispar*.

135

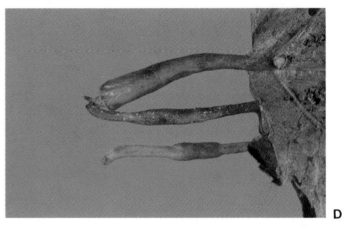

PLATE 56

A miner of birch petiole, _Apagodiplosis papyriferae_ (Gagné)

A. Appearance of a few affected white birch.
B. Adult.
C. Sound white birch leaf.
D. Affected white birch leaf petioles.
E. Larva out of the tunnel in the petiole.

136

A

B

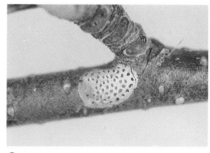

C

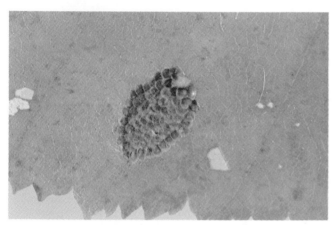

D

E

F

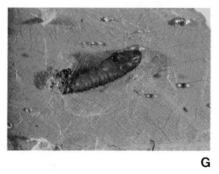

G

H

I

PLATE 57

Fruittree leafroller, *Archips argyrospila* (Wlk.)

A. Adult at rest on a cherry leaf.
B. Unhatched eggs on red oak trunk.
C. Hatched eggs on white birch branch.
D. and E. Eggs hatching on white birch leaf.
F. Lateral view of larva.
G. Pupa.
H. Pinned male adult.
I. Pinned female adult.

A

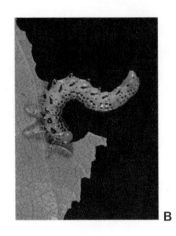

B

C

E

D

F

G

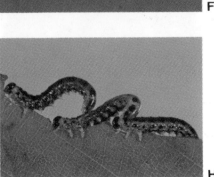

H

PLATE 58

Birch sawfly, *Arge pectoralis* (Leach), and dusky birch sawfly, *Croesus latitarsus* Nort.

A. Colony of *A. pectoralis* larvae on a white birch leaf.
B. Mature *A. pectoralis* larva feeding on a white birch leaf.
C. *A. pectoralis* cocoons on white birch leaves.
D. *A. pectoralis* adult.
E. Mature *C. latitarsus* larva.
F. *C. latitarsus* cocoons.
G. *C. latitarsus* adult near cocoon.
H. Young *C. latitarsus* larvae.

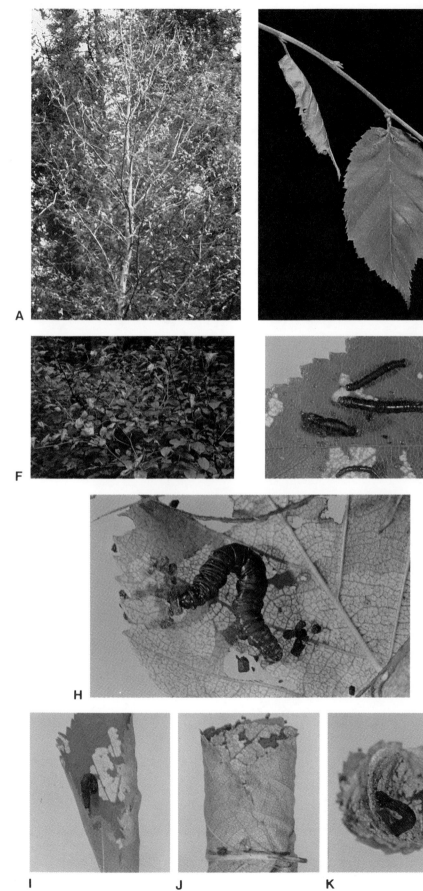

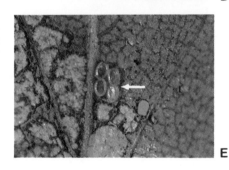

PLATE 59

Spearmarked black moth, *Rheumap-tera hastata* **(L.)**

A. Young white birch severely damaged.
B. Normal and damaged white birch leaves.
C. Dorsal and ventral views of pupa.
D. Moth.
E. Hatched eggs on white birch leaf.
F. Damaged alder foliage.
G. Young larvae feeding on white birch leaves.
H. Mature larva.
I. and J. Various forms of rolled leaves.
K. Larva inside a rolled leaf.

CHAPTER VII
Insects harmful to oak

Some 75 to 80 species of oak (*Quercus*) are native to North America, and 10 of these are found in Canada. Nine species grow naturally in eastern Canada but are not found in all eastern provinces and no oaks are found in Newfoundland. Five species are exclusive to southern Ontario: chinquapin oak (*Q. muehlenbergii* Engelm.), chestnut oak (*Q. prinus* L.), black oak (*Q. velutina* Lam.), pin oak (*Q. palustris* Muenchh.), and dwarf chinquapin oak (*Q. prinoides* Willd.). White oak (*Q. alba* L.) and swamp white oak (*Q. bicolor* Willd.) are found only in southeastern Ontario and southwestern Quebec; bur oak (*Q. macrocarpa* Michx.) and red oak (*Q. rubra* L.) grow in the southern part of Ontario and Quebec and throughout New Brunswick, but only red oak grows in Nova Scotia. Several species imported from Europe as ornamentals are also seen occasionally in eastern Canada.

The gross merchantable volume of oak is, unfortunately, not presented in the annual reports of the Canadian Forestry Service.

Among the hardwood species, the oaks have always been considered to be very robust and long-lived trees. Oaks in eastern Canada vary in height from one species to another: some, like white oak, may grow as tall as 30 m with a diameter of more than 1 m, whereas the smallest, dwarf chinquapin oak, never grows taller than a shrub. The majority of the species grow between 12 and 24 m in height. Most oaks may grow either in the open, in which case the trunk is generally short and stout and the crown well developed, or as forest trees, either in pure or mixed hardwood stands, in which case the trunk is long and straight and the crown is somewhat reduced.

With the exception of pin oak, which prefers damp soil, and bur oak, which grows best in low areas with deep soil, oaks in eastern Canada grow in well-drained, rocky or gravelly ground.

In general, oak wood is hard, heavy, and very strong; its color varies from one species to another, and annual growth rings are normally well defined. Today, oak is used for many purposes, particularly in cabinet-making, flooring, woodwork, barrels, and carpentry; in the early colonial days, it was also used in ship construction. Some species are planted as ornamentals, especially red oak, because of the beauty of its foliage in the fall and a sturdiness that enables it to grow even in unfavorable city conditions. Although production of oak in eastern Canada is rather low, it continues to be very much in demand because of the exceptional qualities of its wood.

Among the hardwoods used as shade trees, oak is the least vulnerable to attack by insects. In eastern Canada, its best known enemies attack the foliage; others suck the sap, cause the formation of galls, mine fruits or bark, or attack the wood itself. All these pests have a certain importance, but few of them succeed in killing the tree.

Oak leafshredder
Plate 60

The oak leafshredder, *Croesia semipurpurana* (Kft.), is a solitary leaf roller and is considered to be one of the most serious defoliators of oak in northeastern North America. Its preferred host is red oak, but it also attacks other species of the same genus, particularly white oak, pin oak, and black oak. It occurs throughout the eastern United States as well as southern Canada, from Ontario to the Maritime provinces. The harmfulness of this pest has increased progressively since 1955 and epidemics have occurred periodically throughout its range.

History of outbreaks

The first outbreak in eastern Canada was reported in Ontario in 1944, and between 1957 and 1975 the oak leafshredder caused heavy damage to red oak in various parts of the province. In Quebec, the insect was first observed in 1945, and a major outbreak lasted from 1957 to 1966 around Quebec city, from where the insect spread to the southern and western parts of the province. In the Maritime provinces, where red oak is its only host, the insect was first reported in 1963, but local outbreaks have been reported every year since, except in 1967 and 1968.

Description and biology

Adult. Tiny moth; sulphur yellow forewings covered with brown spots and uniform beige hindwings. Wingspan: 12-15 mm (Plate 60, F and G).

Egg. Oval flattened; chorion smooth and shiny; pale orange then becoming dull and hard to distinguish. Length: 1 mm (Plate 60, B).

Larva. Elongated; head black and body yellow-brown on hatching; at maturity, head pale with dark lines on the sides; body dirty white to pale yellow. Length: 18 mm (Plate 60, D).

Pupa. Obtect; pale yellow green to brown; wings lighter; spines on each abdominal segment (Plate 60, E).

The biology of the oak leafshredder is fairly well known through studies carried out in Connecticut in 1961 and 1962, and in Quebec between 1957 and 1966 (Beckwith 1963; Cochaux 1968).

Only one generation occurs per year. Moths appear in June and are present until the end of July. During the day, they remain motionless on the undersides of leaves in the undergrowth, flying away at the slightest disturbance. Eggs are laid singly in crevices or rough spots in the bark of twigs aged two years or more, mainly around the nodes (Plate 60, C). They remain in diapause for about 10 months. The young larvae hatch when the oak buds begin to open in the spring and enter the buds where they mine the tissues of developing leaves. Once the leaves are completely open, the larvae feed on them from the outside, under a little silk web attaching the edge of the blade to one or two main ribs. The larval stage lasts about a month, with four instars. Once they are fully grown, the larvae drop down a thread to the ground where they pupate in the folds of leaves or between two dead leaves. A small number of larvae transform in the crown, in rolled up edges of leaves. The first pupae are formed around mid-June, and pupation lasts about 10 days.

Damage and diagnosis

Initial damage by the oak leafshredder consists in the destruction of leaves, first noticeable when the leaves open already full of tiny holes. When the population is very large, all foliage may be destroyed (Plate 60, A), but it is usually replaced by a new generation of foliage. In Quebec, after several years of heavy defoliation, trees were observed to decline and some of them eventually died. In certain regions of the United States, loss of foliage for three or more consecutive years caused a reduction in annual growth, and then significant mortality of oak (Nichols 1968).

Signs of an imminent attack by this leaftier are the presence of sulphur yellow moths flitting about oak crowns in summer, or of eggs found on twigs in fall or near buds in winter. In the spring, unopened buds are perforated with tiny holes made by larvae. Later on, when the leaves open, they are shot through with

holes and larvae are hidden in slight folds in the leaf. Damage, however, could be the work of any of a number of defoliators, and it would be best to consult a specialist for positive identification.

Natural control

Little is known about the natural enemies of the oak leafshredder. Schaffner (1959) mentions two species of insect parasitic on it in the northeastern United States, and a third was reported by Raizenne (1952) in southern Ontario. In Quebec, 36 species of parasites were obtained from rearings, 12 of which were reported by Cochaux (1968); however, in spite of the large number of species collected in Quebec, the parasitism rate among the larval population of the oak leafshredder has always remained low. It was slightly higher among the small group of pupae that transform in the crown and that are mainly parasitized by *Itoplectis conquisitor* (Say).

Cochaux (1968) also reports predation by ants and spiders on pupae in the crown.

Artificial control

Before setting up a control program against the oak leafshredder, data should be obtained as to the degree of infestation of the trees in the area concerned either by physically counting eggs, or by counting the number of larvae hatched from eggs incubated in the laboratory, that had been found on branches collected early in the spring. When populations are large, major damage may be prevented by applying a chemical contact or systemic insecticide to the foliage early in the spring before the buds open, so as to kill the larvae as soon as they hatch and before they enter buds. When leaves are already open, a stomach insecticide may be used to kill older larvae feeding freely on green leaves, but the results are often deceptive.

References

Beckwith 1963; Bradley 1974; Cochaux 1968; Kegg 1966; Nichols 1968; Prentice 1963; Raizenne 1952; Schaffner 1959; and Smirnoff and Juneau 1973.

Oak skeletonizer
Plate 61

The oak skeletonizer, *Bucculatrix ainsliella* Murtf., is native to North America. It occurs throughout the range of oak in eastern Canada and in United States, it extends south to the state of Mississippi. This insect attacks all species of oak, but is most frequent on red oak. It is found both on shade and forest trees and can cause damage over large areas. In eastern Canada, outbreaks have been reported periodically in various parts of Ontario since 1961 and in Quebec during 1968 and 1979. In the Maritime provinces, only the presence of the insect has been reported.

Description and biology

Adult. Tiny, delicate moth; forewings beige marked with black spots; hindwings beige and pectinated. Wingspan: 8 mm (Plate 61, I and J).

Egg. Ovoid, flat; cream white.

Larva. Elongated; greenish yellow. Length: 6 mm (Plate 61, B).

Pupa. Dark-colored, enclosed in longitudinally ribbed white cocoon. Length: pupa 2 mm; cocoon 3 mm.

Normally, two generations of the oak skeletonizer occur per year, but due to unfavorable weather conditions, the second generation occasionally does not occur, as was the case in Quebec in 1957 (Cochaux and Ducharme 1963). In normal years, the moths that produce the first generation are present in April and May. The females lay their eggs on the underside of the leaves near the ribs (Plate 61, A). Incubation lasts about 10 days. On hatching, the larvae penetrate between the two surfaces of the leaf where they tunnel during the first instar and molt to the second instar.

The larvae return to the surface of the leaf about 10 days later and there molt a second time under a little silken tent spun especially for that purpose (Plate 61, C and D). They then continue to feed on the underside of the leaves, which are quickly reduced to skeletons. When they are disturbed, the larvae drop down on a thread of silk and settle in a lower part of the crown. Once fully grown, the larvae

---

pupate in a cocoon attached to the foliage (Plate 61, H). The adults fly in July and August and produce the second generation. Eggs at this time are laid closer to the center of the leaf than those in the spring. The larvae issued from these eggs are fully grown by October and spin cocoons on the bark of infested oaks or in the undergrowth where they overwinter.

Damage and diagnosis

Damage is caused entirely by the larvae of the oak skeletonizer. They begin by making tunnels in the leaves, some winding, others blistered, and cause their premature decoloration. From the third instar on, the larvae feed on the lower surface (Plate 61, E) and the two parenchyma layers of the leaf, leaving the upper surface and the rib system intact. During heavy epidemics, leaves are reduced to their upper surface only; they become transparent and eventually dry out. Trees that are heavily defoliated for several successive years show a reduction in growth, and sometimes part of the crown dies.

PLATE 61

Oak skeletonizer, *Bucculatrix ainsliella* Murtf.

A. Eggs on red oak leaf.
B. Young larva.
C. Silk tents spun by the larva before molting.
D. Close-up of tent with larva inside.
E. Damage on underside of red oak leaf.
F. Pupation cocoons (length: 3 mm).
G. Cocoon opened to show pupa inside.
H. Adult about to leave cocoon.
I. Adult out of its cocoon.
J. Pinned adult (wingspan: 8 mm).
K. Slightly defoliated oak.

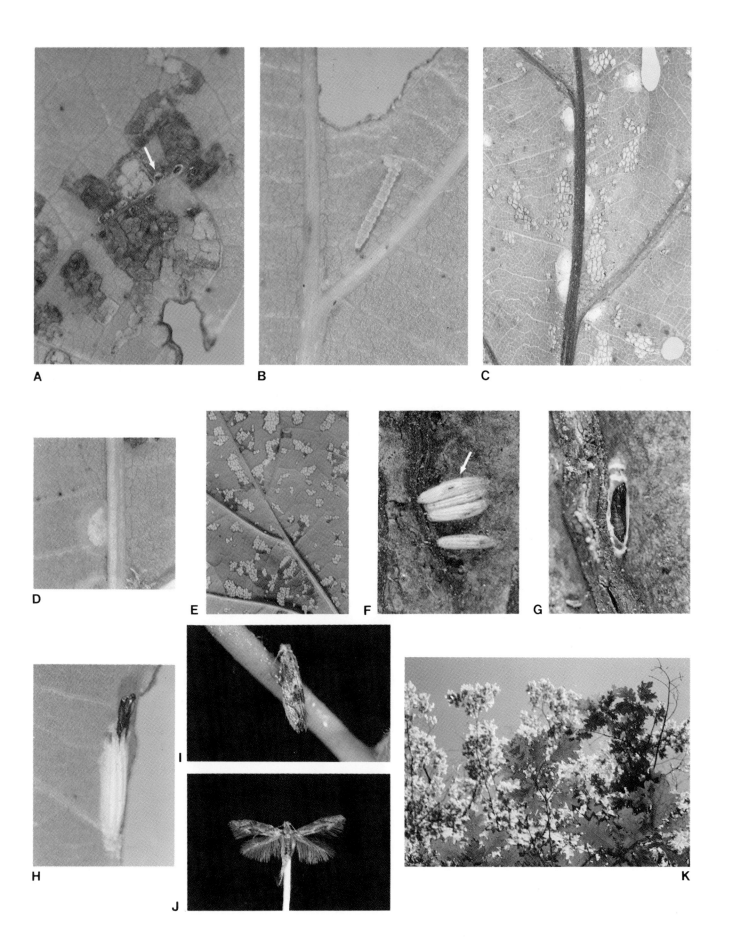

An outbreak by this insect may be recognized by the presence of tiny tunnels in oak leaves and, later on, by the appearance of little white silk tents and greenish yellow larvae on the underside of the leaf. In early summer, a good indication of attack is the presence of leaves that have kept their shape but that have transparent or brownish patches or are even reduced to the skeleton. Later on, the presence of ribbed white cocoons attached to leaves or bark constitute another easily recognizable symptom.

Natural control

Little information has been gathered on the natural factors that regulate the oak skeletonizer. Cochaux and Ducharme (1963) obtained only two species of parasites in their rearings carried out in Quebec, whereas Gibbons and Butcher (1961) reported three for Michigan. In the latter case, it was observed in 1959, that 20 percent of second-generation prepupae died in the fall.

Artificial control

Although there is no need to control the oak skeletonizer in forests, isolated trees or those growing in clumps may be successfully protected by spraying foliage with a stomach or contact insecticide when the larvae are feeding freely on the outside of the leaves. A systemic insecticide in solid form may also be mixed with the soil at the base of affected trees.

If trees are not too tall, they may be protected by destroying the cocoons stuck to the bark, during the off-season.

References

Cochaux and Ducharme 1963; New York State College of Agriculture and Life Science 1978; Gibbons and Butcher 1961; Johnson and Lyon 1976; and Turner et al. 1975.

Other oak defoliators

A number of other leaf-eating insects belong to the oak-pest complex, but most of them are much less harmful than the oak leafshredder and the oak skeletonizer. Five of them should, however, be mentioned because of the extent of epidemics they have caused on oak in Quebec from 1957 to 1965. These are the oak leaffolder, *Anchylopera burgessiana* Zell., the oak webworm, *Archips fervidana* (Clem.), the two leaftier, *Psilocorsis cryptolechiella* (Cham.), the flat leaftier, *P. reflexella* Clem., and the oakleaftier, *P. quercicella* Clem. The biology of these five species has as yet been only partly explained. The data that follow are necessarily incomplete, and they are based in part on studies carried out by Cochaux (1965) in the Quebec region and Carroll et al. (1979) in the United States. Unfortunately, no method of artificial control has been developed against these species.

Oak leaffolder
Plate 62

The oak leaffolder, *Anchylopera burgessiana* Zell., is a solitary defoliator that causes small-scale outbreaks in Quebec and Ontario on red oak and beaked hazelnut.

Description and biology

Adult. Tiny moth; forewings having a very distinct dark brown area at base and light brown spots at apex; hindwings grey beige and fringed.
Wingspan: 13 mm (Plate 62, D).

Egg. Leaf green, becoming lighter with age; chorion transparent.
Length: 0.89 mm.

Larva. Yellowish green; head amber-colored during last instars (Plate 62, B).

Pupa. Obtect; pale brown.
Length: 5-7 mm.

PLATE 62

Oak leaffolder, *Anchylopera burgessiana Zell.,* Bethune miner, *Cameraria bethunella* Cham., and Solitary oak leafminer, *Cameraria hamadryadella* (Clem.)

A. *A. burgessiana* damage on red oak leaf.
B. *A. burgessiana* larva found under the silk.
C. Another type of *A. burgessiana* damage.
D. *A. burgessiana* adult (wingspan: 13 mm).
E. *C. bethunella* larva and damage on red oak leaf.
F. Beginning of *C. bethunella* tunnel on red oak leaf.
G. *C. bethunella* adult.
H. *C. hamadryadella* larva and damage on white oak leaf.
I. *C. hamadryadella* pupa at tunnel exit on bur oak leaf.
J. *C. hamadryadella* adult.
K. Severe *C. hamadryadella* damage on oak.
L. *C. hamadryadella* damage on oak leaf.

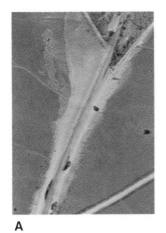

A

B

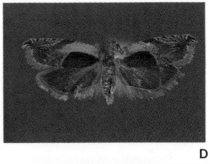

C

D

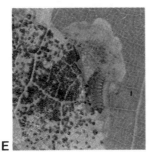

E

F

G

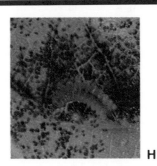

H

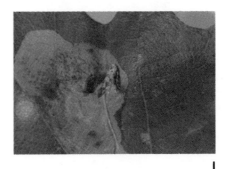

I

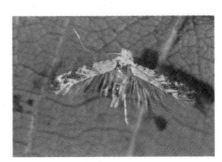

J

K

L

147

Only one generation of the oak leaffolder occurs per year in Canada. Adults fly in May or June. Eggs are normally laid on the upper surface of leaves, one per leaf and preferably along the main ribs. Larvae are present from mid-July to September. On hatching, they move to the underside of the leaf and construct individual tents between the main rib and a secondary rib, where they feed. Their life cycle includes six instars and takes place entirely on the same leaf, with the larvae enlarging their tents as required, so that the lamina of the leaf eventually curls and rolls up. In the fall, the larva pupates and the insect overwinters in this stage.

Damage and diagnosis

Damage is caused entirely by the oak leaffolder larvae, which graze on the parenchyma inside their tents without touching the upper leaf surface and ribs (Plate 62, A). A single larva chews about 350 mm^2 of the leaf surface. During an outbreak, the appearance of trees planted as ornamentals is spoiled considerably by the deformed leaves and white silk tents (Plate 62, C).

Infested trees are easily recognized by the white webs under rolled oak leaves, as well as by the color of the larvae they contain.

Natural control

Studies carried out on the oak leaffolder in Quebec revealed the presence of 18 species of insect parasites; some of the best known are *Trichogramma minutum* Riley, a tiny chalcid that can destroy over 60 percent of the eggs and *Oncophanus americanus* Weed, which attacks the larvae.

Oak webworm
Plate 63

The oak webworm, *Archips fervidana* (Clem.), is a gregarious insect that attacks various species of oak and occasionally choke cherry and trembling aspen. Its range in eastern North America corresponds to that of oak in southern Canada, and the northeastern and central United States.

Description and biology

Adult. Small moth; forewings yellow brown with dark spots; hindwings dark brown with lighter fringe.
Wingspan: 16-25 mm (Plate 63, E).
Larva. Elongated; head black and body dark green with black spots.
Length: 20 mm (Plate 63, A).
Pupa. Obtect; pale brown.
Length: 10 mm (Plate 63, D).

The oak webworm has only one generation per year in Canada. Adults emerge during July and August and lay eggs that overwinter without hatching. Larvae begin to appear at the end of May and may be found until mid-August. They live in groups (Plate 63, B) and feed inside silken tents that tie together the foliage of several branches and may reach 45 cm in length (Plate 63, F and G). Pupation takes place inside the tents (Plate 63, C), during July and August, and the adult emerges some time later.

Damage and diagnosis

Damage by the oak webworm consists mainly in the presence of unsightly tents, which incidently enable affected trees to be easily identified.

Natural control

In Quebec, Cochaux (1965) obtained from his rearings five species of insect parasites that destroyed about 25 percent of larvae; the most important was the well-known ichneumid fly, *Itoplectis conquisitor* (Say). Two additional species are included in the list published by Bradley (1974).

Two leaftier
Plate 64

The two leaftier, *Psilocorsis cryptolechiella* (Cham.), erroneously identified as *P. quercicella* Clem. by Cochaux (1965), is a solitary leaftier that has been reported on white oak, red oak, chinquapin oak, and bur oak. In Canada, it is found from Ontario to the Maritime provinces; and in the United States its range from Maine to Florida extends westerly to Arkansas and Texas.

Description and biology

Adult. Small moth; forewings basically beige with two darker crosswise lines, one at the apex and the other, often less pronounced, in the centre; hindwings solid gray beige and fringed. Wingspan: 12-15 mm (Plate 64, C).
Egg. Translucid, white becoming red with age, longitudinally undulated and transversely striated.
Larva. Elongated, head solid black and smooth, body delicate green (Plate 64, B).
Pupa. Obtect; dark brown. Length: 8 mm (Plate 64, D).

PLATE 63

Oak webworm, *Archips fervidana* (Clem.)

A. Larva on heavily damaged red oak leaves (length: 20 mm).
B. Group of larvae in nature.
C. Pupa in nature (length: 10 mm).
D. Pupa out of its damage.
E. Adult at rest (wingspan: 16-25 mm).
F. and G. Heavily damaged red oak; close-up of tent spun by larva.

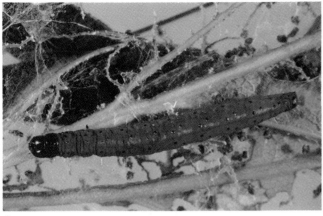

A

B

C

F

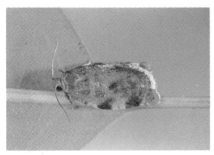

D

E

G

Carroll et al. (1979) reports that the two leaftier is bivoltine in the United States, but in Canada the insect has only one generation per year. In Canada the moths are present near the end of June, and the first larvae appear in mid-July and can be seen until October. Eggs are laid on the underside of leaves or between two leaves already tied by oak webworms. The larvae go through five instars and feed on the parenchyma of leaves in the same manner as skeletonizers; they move from one place to another in tunnel-like structures made of white silk covered with leaf debris and blackish larval excreta (Plate 64, A). Around mid-September, the earliest-born larvae stop feeding and, a few days later, transform to pupae in the litter for the winter.

Damage and diagnosis

All damage is caused by the larvae of the two leaftier, which feed on the parenchyma of leaves and build their characteristic silken corridors.

Natural control

In Quebec, there are, as yet, few parasites of the two leaftier. In 1963, for example, parasitism was practically non-existent, and the following year about 6 percent of larvae and 5 percent of pupae were parasitized (Cochaux 1965). To date, seven different species have been obtained from rearings carried out by the Quebec Region FIDS, and two additional species were reported by Bradley (1974). Carroll et al. (1979) listed 21 species of parasites, and to these the 9 species found by Cochaux (1965) erroneously on the oak leaftier should be added.

Flat leaftier
Plate 64

The flat leaftier, *Psilocorsis reflexella* Clem., is often found on oak, but also on other hardwoods such as white birch, yellow birch, maple, beech, willow, trembling aspen, and various other species of poplar. Its distribution in eastern North America corresponds more or less to that of the two leaftier.

Description and biology

Adult. Small brown moth; forewings beige thickly speckled with brown; hindwings solid gray beige and fringed. Wingspan: 18-25 mm (Plate 64, F).

Egg. Form and appearance similar to the two leaftier. Length: 0.5 mm.

Larva. Elongated, head amber to dark brown and rough; body green yellow, very well segmented; presence of dark anal plate (Plate 64, G and H).

Pupa. Obtect; pale brown. Length: 9 mm (Plate 64, E).

In Canada the biology of the flat leaftier presents many similarities to that of the two leaftier, except for the fact that the adult is apparently present earlier in the spring and that all other stages appear earlier. In the United States this species has only one generation per year.

Natural Control

Carroll et al. (1979) reported that 29 parasites were recovered from this leaftier and 17 of them had been mentioned by Cochaux (1965).

Oak leaftier
Plate 64

The oak leaftier, *Psilocorsis quercicella* Clem., is another leaftier, found on various species of oak and a few other hardwoods. Its range is similar to those of the two leaftier and the flat leaftier. It is univoltine in Canada and bivoltine in the United States.

Description and biology

Adult. Small moth; brown; forewings beige irregularly marked with dark spots. Wingspan: 10-15 mm (Plate 64, I).

Egg. Form and appearance similar to the two leaftier and the flat leaftier.

Larva. Elongated; head amber to dark brown; mesothorax and metathorax with black pigmentation (Plate 64, J and K).

Pupa. Brown red. Length: 6 mm.

The biology of the oak leaftier closely resembles that of the two leaftier.

Natural control

Carroll et al. (1979) have listed 23 species of parasites for this species including 9 species mentioned for Canada by Cochaux (1965) that should be eliminated due to an error of identification.

References

Baker 1972; Bradley 1974; Carroll et al. 1979; Cochaux 1965; Cochaux and Ducharme 1963; Prentice 1965; and Raizenne 1952.

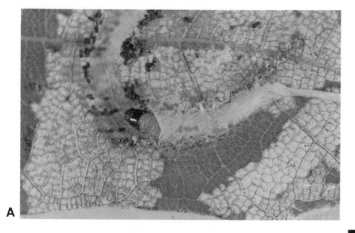

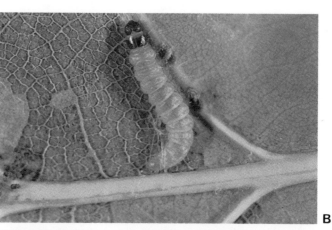

A

B

C

D

E

F

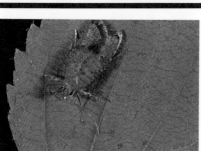

G

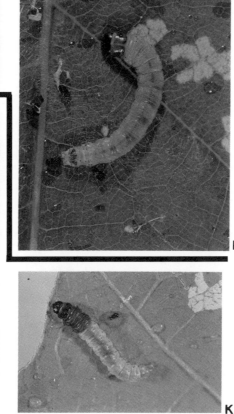

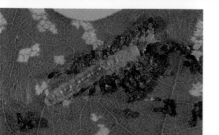

I

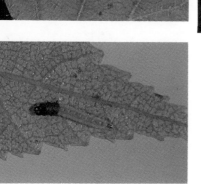

J

H

K

PLATE 64

Twoleaf tier, *Psilocorsis crypto-lechiella* (Cham.), flat leaftier, *P. reflexella* Clem., and oak leaftier, *P. quercicella* Clem.

A. *P. cryptolechiella* larva under its silk.
B. *P. cryptolechiella* mature larva.
C. *P. cryptolechiella* pinned adult.
D. Ventral and dorsal views of *P. cryptolechiella* pupa (length: 6 mm).
E. Dorsal and ventral views of *P. reflexella* pupa (length: 9 mm).
F. *P. reflexella* pinned adult (wing-span: 18-25 mm).
G. Young *P. reflexella* larva in its silk.
H. Mature *P. reflexella* larva.
I. *P. quercicella* adult at rest (wing-span: 12-15 mm).
J. Young *P. quercicella* larva.
K. Mature *P. quercicella* larva and its damage.

Table 10. Other insects harmful to oak — Other insects that are regarded as pests of oak are listed in this table. For some insects, their characteristics are described in the chapter that applies to their primary host, and in such cases, that chapter (in Roman numerals) and the appropriate plate numbers are given. For other insects, a plate number alone is shown; and for the remaining insects, this table provides the only information.

Common and scientific names	Hosts (chap.)	Plate no.	Type of insect	Destructive stages	Period of activity	Importance*
Bethune miner *Cameraria bethunella* Cham.	Oak	62	Miner	Larva	July to Sept.	C
Fall cankerworm *Alsophila pometaria* (Harr.)	Maple (VIII)	69	—	—	—	A
Fall webworm *Hyphantria cunea* (Drury)	Elm (IX)	84	—	—	—	B
Forest tent caterpillar *Malacosoma disstria* Hbn.	Poplar (X)	91	—	—	—	A
Gypsy moth *Lymantria dispar* (L.)	Birch (VI)	46	—	—	—	A
Hickory twig pruner *Elaphidionoides parallelus* (Newman)	Oak, hickory	66	Borer	Larva	June to Aug.	C
Large oak apple gall *Amphibolips inanis* (O.S.)	Oak	65	Gallmaker	Larva	May to July	C
Linden looper *Erannis tiliaria* (Harr.)	Maple (VIII)	67	—	—	—	B
Oak gall wasp *Dryocosmus palustris* (Ashm.)	Oak	65	Gallmaker	Larva	May and June	C
Oak lecanium *Lecanium quercifex* Fitch	Oak	66	Gallmaker	Larva	May to Aug.	C
Oak olethreutid leafroller *Pseudexentera cressoniana* Clem.	Oak	60	Defoliator	Larva	May and June	C
Orangestriped oakworm *Anisota senatoria* (J.E. Smith)	Oak	—	Defoliator	Larva	June to Oct.	A
Pinkstriped oakworm *Anisota virginiensis virginiensis* (Drury)	Oak, hardwoods	—	Leaf roller	Larva	June to July	B
Solitary oak leafminer *Cameraria hamadryadella* (Clem.)	Oak	62	Miner	Larva	July and Aug.	C
Spring cankerworm *Paleacrita vernata* (Peck)	Elm (IX)	87	—	—	—	C
Tortricid oakworm *Argyrotaenia quercifoliana* Fitch	Oak	—	Leaf roller	Larva	May to July	C
Whitemarked tussock moth *Orgyia leucostigma intermedia* Fitch	Maple (VIII)	71	—	—	—	C
Yellownecked caterpillar *Datana ministra* (Drury)	Hardwoods	—	Defoliator	Larva	June to Sept.	C

*A: Of major importance, capable of killing or severely damaging trees.
 B: Of moderate importance, capable of sporadic and localized injury to trees.
 C: Of minor importance, not known to present a threat to living trees.

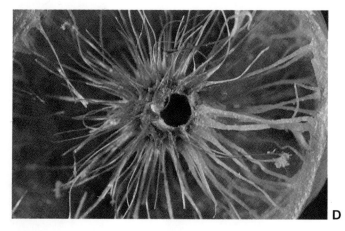

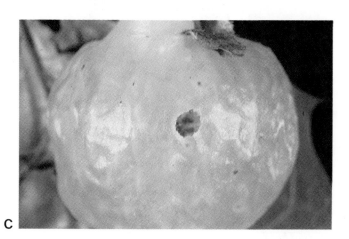

PLATE 65

Large oak apple gall, *Amphibolips inanis* (O.S.), and oak gall wasp, *Dryocosmus palustris* (Ashm.)

A. *A. inanis* gall early in the season.
B. Transversal cut of same gall.
C. Mature *A. inanis* gall showing adult exit hole.
D. Transversal cut of same gall.
E. and F. *A. inanis* male and female adults.
G. *D. palustris* pinned adult.
H. *D. palustris* gall on red oak leaves.
I. Transversal cut of *D. palustris* gall.

Oak lecanium, *Lecanium quercifex* Fitch., and hickory twig pruner, *Elaphidionoides parallelus* (Newman)

A. Dead oak branch killed by *L. quercifex*.
B. Red oak stem severely damaged by *L. quercifex*.
C. Young *L. quercifex* on red oak trunk.
D. Mature *L. quercifex*.
E. *E. parallelus* larva inside tunnel in red oak twig.
F. *E. parallelus* pupa.
G. and H. *E. parallelus* female and male adults.

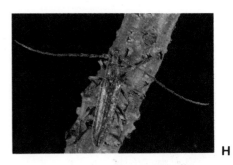

CHAPTER VIII
Insects harmful to maple

Of the 150 species of maple (*Acer*) known throughout the world, only 10 are native to Canada. Maple, however, has been such an important resource, right from the earliest days of settlement on this continent, that its leaf was chosen as the emblem of Canada. Seven species are found in the eastern provinces, but only three of these, sugar maple (*A. saccharum* Marsh.), silver maple (*A. saccharinum* L.), and red maple (*A. rubrum* L.), are currently used as a source of supply of maple wood and thus are of concern to foresters. These three species are found most commonly in southern Ontario, Quebec, and New Brunswick. Only sugar maple and red maple are found in Nova Scotia and Prince Edward Island, and red maple alone is found in Newfoundland. Much less important are the four other species of which black maple (*A. nigrum* Michx. f.) and Manitoba maple (*A. negundo* L.) are not particularly abundant and are little known due to their limited range, in Quebec and Ontario. The two others, striped maple (*A. pensylvanicum* L.) and mountain maple (*A. spicatum* Lam.), attract little attention because they rarely grow taller than shrub size. Of several foreign maples the most frequent is Norway maple (*A. platanoides* L.)

The gross merchantable volume of maple surveyed in the six eastern provinces is estimated at 493 million m^3, of which 47.7 percent is in Quebec and 28.1 percent in Ontario.

Sugar maple is one of the most attractive trees in Canadian hardwood forests. As a forest tree, it has a long, straight trunk and a narrow, rounded crown, whereas in the open the trunk is short and the crown wide and full. The average dimensions of maple are from 25 to 27 m high and 60 cm to 1 m in diameter. It grows best on deep, fertile, moist yet well-drained soils, in pure stands or mixed with other hardwoods or even with conifers.

It is known throughout eastern North America for maple syrup and sugar production.

Silver maple is of interest because of its shape and rapid growth. The trunk is normally short, dividing into several main limbs. It grows in rich soil particularly along streams, and reaches about the same size as sugar maple. It is mainly grown as an ornamental tree.

Red maple is best known for the red coloring of its leaves in the fall. As a forest tree, it has a long trunk and a narrow crown, whereas in the open the trunk branches out near the ground and the crown becomes deep and dense. It grows to an average height of 27 m and a diameter of over 1 m. Not only does it grow well in moist soils, but also it tolerates dry and even rocky soils.

Maple wood is generally hard and strong and, for this reason, the wood of a number of its species is used in making furniture, flooring, woodwork, veneer, and plywood. It is also used for making crates and boxes and as a fuel. Silver maple is weaker and is used in pulpmaking.

Maples are generally not very susceptible to damage by insects, and easily resist those that infest them from time to time. Defoliators are the most numerous but there are also sucking and wood-boring insects.

Linden looper
Plate 67

The linden looper, *Erannis tiliaria* (Harr.), is a defoliator native to North America. It occurs throughout a vast area stretching from the Atlantic Ocean to the Rocky Mountains in the United States and Canada. This species is polyphagous and feeds on a great variety of hardwoods of which 23 different species have been identified in Canada. Its most common hosts are basswood, elm, white birch, sugar maple, hickory, oak, and apple.

History of outbreaks

Severe outbreaks of the linden looper occur occasionally in the eastern part of the continent. In eastern Canada, Newfoundland has reported only the presence of this looper, although in the Maritime provinces one light outbreak was observed in 1955. In Quebec and Ontario, outbreaks were reported in the southern hardwood sectors from 1941 to 1944, in 1953 and 1954, from 1959 to 1963, and from 1974 to 1976.

Description and biology

Adult. Adult moths show very marked sexual dimorphism: only the males have fully developed wings, whereas females have only rudimentary wings. Male medium sized with buff-colored forewings crossed by two wavy brown bands; hindwings uniformly pale. Wingspan: 42 mm (Plate 67, F). Female practically wingless, pale gray to brown with two rows of black spots on the back. Length: 12 mm (Plate 67, E).

Egg. Oval; orange yellow with chorion marked with a network of wavy lines (Plate 67, A).

Larva. Cylindrical, elongated; head rust brown, body bright yellow with 10 black lines running down the dorsum; colors vary in intensity; three pairs of legs and two pairs of prolegs. Length: 37 mm (Plate 67, B and C).

Pupa. Conical, elongated; glossy brown. Length: 12 mm (Plate 67, D).

Few studies have been published on the biology of the linden looper, but observations made during the 1961 outbreak in Quebec yielded interesting data on its behavior in maple groves.

Only one generation occurs per year. Moths of both sexes emerge during October and November, males slightly earlier than females. Males are most active at dusk, flying about at low altitudes seeking females that are crawling upon tree trunks. Eggs are laid singly or in small clusters under partially loose bark or in crevices of the trunk and large branches where they overwinter. Eggs hatch in April or May at about the time that the buds open. Larvae are solitary and move about considerably, especially during the last larval instar. When disturbed, they drop down on a thread of silk into foliage lower on the tree. The larval stage lasts about 1 month and includes five instars in the case of males and six in that of females. Once fully grown, the larvae drop to the ground and burrow to a depth of about 25 mm, where they construct individual cells in which they immediately pupate.

Damage and diagnosis

All damage is caused by the larvae of the linden looper, which feed on the leaves, devouring them completely except for the petiole (Plate 67, G). It has been determined that each larva needs three to four sugar maple leaves to reach its full growth, and that the average maple tree has 30 000 to 35 000 leaves. Hence huge populations are necessary to strip trees of their foliage during an outbreak. Because, many hardwood species are able to produce new foliage before the end of the summer, and outbreaks are normally short-lived, it is rare that hardwoods die from defoliation by this looper.

Attack by this looper is normally easy to recognize in the spring by the presence of larvae of a very characteristic yellow color that move about by arching their backs like cats. In late fall and even after the first snowfalls, moths may still be observed, the wingless females crawling up the base of trunks towards the branches and the males flying about close by. The identity of the species may be established positively by the orange color of eggs obtained by pressing the abdomen of the female between the fingers.

Natural control

Outbreaks of the linden looper are generally short-lived, because the insects are kept in check by their natural enemies. To date, 14 species of entomophagous parasites have been found on this looper in North America, 9 in Ontario (Raizenne 1952) and 5 in Quebec, 3 of which were previously reported in Ontario. Three additional parasitic species have been reported: the first by Bradley (1974) in Canada, the two others by Baker (1972) in the United States.

By far the most effective natural factor is a disease caused by *Baculovirus tiliaria*, a polyhedrous microorganism that breaks out when larval populations become very large (Smirnoff 1962). Larvae that have developed this disease stop feeding and move about constantly; their bodies soon take on a brown color, become flaccid, and, at the slightest touch, give off a brownish liquid. A pronounced reduction in the larval population coincided with the onset of this disease during the 1961 outbreak in Quebec, and it was probably responsible for the rapid and unexplained decline of at least one previous infestation.

Artificial control

The existence of such an effective disease in natural populations of the linden looper normally eliminates the need for direct methods of control. If it should happen that artificial control becomes necessary to protect isolated trees, a sticky band encircling the trunk will capture the wingless females when they crawl towards the crown in the fall, or a contact insecticide can be used directly on tree trunks. Once the leaves have opened or when larvae start feeding in the spring, the larvae may be killed by spraying the foliage with a stomach or contact insecticide.

A

D

Lastly, disease among larval populations can be provoked by spraying crowns with a suspension of polyhedrous virus either collected in an infested area where the disease is already active or else obtained during previous epidemics.

References

Baker 1972; Bradley 1974; Herrick 1935; Johnson and Lyon 1976; Johnson and Zepp 1978; Martineau 1961; Prentice 1963; Raizenne 1952; and Smirnoff 1962.

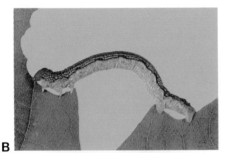

B

C

E

F

G

Linden looper, *Erannis tiliaria* **(Harr.)**

A. Eggs laid in bark crevices on red maple trunk; yellow eggs are freshly laid, brown eggs are already developing.
B. Side view of a larva (length: 37 mm).
C. Dorsal view of a larva.
D. Pupa.
E. Female adult (wingless) crawling up a maple trunk (length: 12 mm).
F. Male adult resting on maple trunk (wingspan: 42 mm).
G. Severely damaged maple grove, seen from a distance.

Bruce spanworm
Plate 68

The Bruce spanworm, *Operophtera bruceata* (Hulst), is a defoliator native to North America, where it periodically causes major damage in certain parts of the United States and Canada. Its distribution in Canada is transcontinental; in the United States, it stretches from the Atlantic Ocean to the Great Lakes. Its presence was first reported in Canada in 1903 and, since that time, the insect has been collected on 16 hardwood species; in eastern Canada, its preferred hosts are sugar maple and beech, whereas in the West they are trembling aspen and willow.

History of outbreaks

The first epidemics of the Bruce spanworm that attracted the attention of foresters broke out in western Canada and the most recent, which occurred in 1957, covered an area of some 250 000 km^2. In eastern Canada, the most damage was reported on sugar maple in Quebec, where serious outbreaks, lasting from 1962 to 1965 and from 1969 to 1973, caused extensive defoliation in maple groves (Plate 68, A and B). The first Quebec outbreak spilled over into the Maritime provinces, where no other outbreaks have been reported since. In Ontario, the insect is considered of secondary importance, although local outbreaks were reported in 1951, 1963, and 1973.

Description and biology

Adult. Moth with marked sexual dimorphism, only the male having well-developed wings. Male medium-sized with light brown body; forewings fringed, semi-transparent with crosswise brown or gray bands on beige background; hindwings solid beige but occasionally crossed with faint lines. Wingspan: 25-30 mm (Plate 68, C). Female wingless; overall color brown, body spotted with white and covered with scales giving it a rough appearance. Length: 6-7 mm (Plate 68, D).

Egg. Ovoid; green when laid, gradually turning orange as winter approaches; chorion covered with a network of deep waves. Dimensions: 0.55 by 0.96 mm.

Larva. Body tapering at both ends; hairless and bright green, sometimes darker, with three white lines on sides, three pairs of legs, and two pairs of anal prolegs. Length when full grown: 18 mm (Plate 68, E, F and G).

Pupa. Obtect; golden to dark brown; enclosed in a cocoon shell covered with grains of sand or humus. Length: 6-7 mm (Plate 68, H).

The biology of the Bruce spanworm is quite well known through studies conducted during the most recent outbreaks in Alberta and Quebec.

It produces only one generation per year. Moths appear in October or November, that is, long after leaves have fallen and often when the first frosts occur or sometimes when the ground is already covered with a layer of snow. They leave their cocoons in late afternoon or early evening, the males usually 1-2 days later than the females.

The moths are active mainly at sunset. Females crawl up trunks while males fly about at low altitude seeking females with which to mate. Eggs are laid preferably in the lower part of the trunk, but may be found as high up as 12 m, in various places such as in lichens, under pieces of bark, or in bark crevices.

In a normal year, the hatching of larvae coincides with the opening of buds in the spring, but if this phenomenon is delayed for one reason or another, the buds are devoured by the young larvae. When the leaves have had a chance to open, the young larvae eat the green matter without touching the ribs. Larvae feed either on the underside of the leaf, or inside a shelter made of leaves folded and tied together with silk. They are not particularly active and often go unnoticed when populations are small. When food becomes scarce, the larvae drop down on a thread of silk which they spin as needed, onto leaves in the lower part of the crown. If they do not land on another branch, they may be carried by the wind to new areas often great distances away. Larvae reach maturity in 5 to 7 weeks, at around the end of June, and this is when damage reaches its peak. The larvae drop to the ground at the base of defoliated trees and spin individual cocoons in which they pupate. The insect remains in the pupal stage for the rest of the summer, and adults emerge after 4 to 5 months.

Damage and diagnosis

The degree of damage, which is caused entirely by larvae of the Bruce spanworm, depends both on the population density and the degree of development of the leaves at time of larval hatching. Each larva consumes about two maple leaves, but it always attacks a larger number. Defoliation can easily go unnoticed and attracts attention only when populations reach moderate-to-high levels. During an epidemic, defoliation may be greater than 90 percent of the leaves of maples over huge areas. No mortality of maples has as yet been reported and defoliation in maple groves has not been proven to affect the flow of sap adversely.

PLATE 68

Bruce spanworm, *Operophtera bruceata* (Hulst)

A. Undergrowth in an healthy maple grove.
B. Undergrowth in a severely defoliated maple grove.
C. Adult male on maple trunk (wingspan: 25-30 mm).
D. Adult female (wingless) laying green eggs in bark crevices (length: 6-7 mm).
E. Side view of a green larva (length: 18 mm).
F. Dorsal view of a green larva.
G. Dorsal view of a dark larva.
H. Pupa in open cocoon (length: 6-7 mm).

A

B

C

D

E

F

G

H

Following severe defoliation early in the season, several species of hardwoods including maple produce a new crop of foliage during the summer. This phenomenon generally occurs in July, so that from August on damage is less obvious. However, careful examination of the new foliage reveals that the leaves are smaller and less numerous than usual.

In early spring, the presence on maple or beech of little green larvae hidden under leaves or between two leaves tied together with silk is a good indication of attack by this spanworm. A preliminary diagnosis may be confirmed in the fall after leaf drop, and sometimes even after the first snow, by the appearance of the pale brown male moths flying around trunks and of the brown wingless females crawling up the trunks. Positive identification of the species may be made by pressing the abdomen of females gently to see the green color of the eggs.

The intensity of an imminent attack can be forecast by counting the number of females captured on a sticky collar placed around the trunk base in the fall.

Natural control

In Canada, the first observations of parasites attacking the Bruce spanworm were made in Alberta by Brown (1962), who recovered seven species of hymenopterous parasites in his larval rearings, but none of them was abundant enough to control this pest. According to the FIDS, however, the decline of several local outbreaks observed in Ontario in 1966 could be attributed, at least in part, to a high degree of parasitism on eggs and larvae.

Predators also play an important part in checking populations of the Bruce spanworm and, in Quebec, FIDS personnel observed a number of bird species feeding on the larvae. The sudden decline of outbreaks, however, usually follows the appearance of a viral disease, possibly the same one that destroyed populations during the 1962 outbreak in New Brunswick. The last two outbreaks in Quebec maple groves are known to have ended suddenly following the action on larvae of a disease caused by the virus *Baculovirus bruceata* (Smir.). The first symptoms

of this larval disease are an interruption in feeding, followed by a change in the color of certain abdominal rings which turn yellow; then, the larva becomes flaccid and, when touched, its body gives off a yellowish liquid (Smirnoff 1964).

Artificial control

Human intervention is rarely necessary to control the Bruce spanworm whose outbreaks are usually short-lived, because the trees are rarely damaged enough to die and also because most hardwoods can produce new foliage. However, occasionally it may be desirable to protect very valuable ornamental trees against severe defoliation. A practical and low-cost method is to place a sticky collar around the base of affected trees in the fall, to capture the females when they crawl towards the crowns and before they lay their eggs. Females may also be killed at this time by spraying trunks with a contact insecticide.

Stomach or contact insecticides may also be sprayed on crowns in the spring, shortly after the leaves open, to prevent severe defoliation.

Another low-cost method is to initiate the development of disease by spraying on trees to be protected a suspension of the virus obtained either from larvae infected in other areas where the disease is prevalent, or collected during a previous outbreak.

References

Baker 1972; Brown 1962; Martineau 1973; Martineau and Monnier 1967; McGuffin 1958; Prentice 1963; Smirnoff 1964; and Smith 1979.

Fall cankerworm
Plate 69

The fall cankerworm, *Alsophila pometaria* (Harr.), is so named because the moths do not appear until late fall. It is native to North America where it has been recognized as a serious pest in hardwood forests, on fruit trees, and on ornamentals since the early days of settlement. It occurs in Canada from the Maritime provinces west to Alberta and, in the United States, from the Canadian border to the Carolinas in the east and to California in the west. Fall cankerworm is found on almost all hardwood species in eastern North America where its preferred hosts are elm, basswood, red maple, silver maple, red oak, and apple; in the West, however, it prefers Manitoba maple. This spanworm is a solitary defoliator that periodically produces short-lived epidemics, usually confined to local areas but occasionally covering large areas.

PLATE 69

Fall cankerworm, *Alsophila pometaria* (Harr.).

A. Severely defoliated undergrowth in red maple stand.
B. Adult male on sugar maple trunk (wingspan: 25-35 mm).
C. Pupa in open cocoon (length: 10 mm).
D. Mass of mainly empty eggs, on maple twig.
E. Adult female (wingless) on basswood trunk (length: 12 mm).
F. and G. Larva showing parasite eggs on the dorsum and remains of larva once parasites have developed.
H. Side view of green larva showing the characteristic third pair of prolegs under abdomen (length: 25 mm).
I. Side view of dark-colored larva giving a clearer view of the third pair of prolegs.
J. Dorsal view of dark-colored larva.

History of outbreaks

In the Maritime provinces, the fall cankerworm has caused damage, mainly to elm, every year since 1938, often in association with other geometrids, notably with the winter moth, *Operophtera brumata,* in Nova Scotia. In Quebec, it has attracted attention mainly since 1958, more specifically in maple groves in the southern part of the province, and often in association with two other species: the linden looper, *Erannis tiliaria,* and the Bruce spanworm, *Operophtera bruceata.* In Ontario, damage by the fall cankerworm has been reported since 1938 in the south as well as in the forest regions of the western part of the province; populations have fluctuated greatly there as elsewhere, and outbreaks have been generally short-lived.

Description and biology

Adult. Moth with very pronounced sexual dimorphism, only the male having well-developed wings. Male brownish gray with glossy forewings decorated with two indented white bands; hindwings with tiny spots on the distal part. Wingspan: 25-35 mm (Plate 69, B). Female wingless, ash gray. Length: 12 mm (Plate 69, E).
Egg. Shaped like a flower pot, brownish gray (Plate 69, D).
Larva. Body elongated and very delicate; very light green to dark brownish green, with faint lines running down the back and three pairs of prolegs. Length when full grown: 25 mm (Plate 69, I and J).
Cocoon. Oval in shape; brown. Length: 10 mm (Plate 69, C).

No complete study has as yet been made on the biology and ecology of the fall cankerworm, probably because of the short duration of outbreaks.

This spanworm has only one generation per year. The moths emerge in late fall, between October and December, normally after the first heavy frosts. The males appear first and are active mainly at sunset; they may then be seen flitting around trees in search of females crawling up the trunks. Each female lays about 100 eggs, carefully lined up in a single layer, on the bark of twigs or branches.

The insect overwinters in the egg stage, and the larvae hatch around the end of April or beginning of May, when the buds burst. Young larvae feed on new leaves around the edges of the crown. At first they cut small holes in the leaves, but when they get older, they eat the leaves entirely, leaving only the main ribs. When food becomes scarce, the hungry larvae drop down on silken threads into the lower branches. The larvae develop in 5 to 6 weeks, reaching full growth around the end of June. They then drop to the ground, burrow to a depth of 25-50 mm, and spin a cocoon in which they pupate. The moths emerge 4 or 5 months later.

Damage and diagnosis

All damage is caused by the fall cankerworm larvae during feeding. When populations are low, defoliation is slight, but during severe outbreaks, trees over vast areas may be completely defoliated (Plate 69, A). When this phenomenon reoccurs for 3 or 4 years in a row, some trees may die. If defoliation occurs in early spring, however, many tree species have time to produce new foliage before the end of the summer, thus hiding the extent of damage. The presence of thousands of caterpillars searching for food in the vicinity of houses or in parks can be a nuisance to vacationers.

In the spring, early defoliation of many hardwood species may be recognized as an epidemic of this insect by the presence of spanworms having the three pairs of prolegs that are characteristic of this species. From fall on, masses of flowerpot-shaped eggs may be seen easily on the bark of twigs. The species may be identified before egg-laying by the brownish gray color of eggs obtained by pressing the abdomen of females found at the base of trees in fall. By counting the number of females crawling up trunks, a prediction may be made of the probable intensity of attack likely to occur the following spring.

Natural control

Most infestations of all cankerworm last only a few years. Populations are often destroyed by unfavorable weather conditions, such as late spring frosts that destroy the new foliage and deprive the young larvae of their only source of food.

During severe infestations, part of the population starves to death from lack of food. Outbreaks often decline due to the sudden appearance of a bacterial or viral disease that quickly wipes out most of the larval population.

Also, larvae are continually exposed to attack by parasites (Plate 69, F and G) and predators such as spiders and birds. Raizenne (1952) reports having obtained 13 species of parasites in his rearings carried out in Ontario. In Quebec, 19 species were reported only one of which was included in the Ontario group. However, the importance of the role played by these parasites has not as yet been determined.

Artificial control

Isolated trees can be protected with a band of sticky substance installed around the base of their trunks before the females crawl up into the crowns in the fall to lay their eggs. They may be killed also by spraying a contact insecticide on trunks.

Larvae may be destroyed when they hatch in the spring, before they have caused too much damage, by spraying the crowns with a chemical stomach or contact insecticide. The biological insecticide, *Bacillus thuringiensis* Berl., may even be used with success for this purpose, although because its action is normally slower than that of chemical insecticides it should be applied earlier.

A recent method that shows some promise consists in attempting to provoke an epizootic disease by injecting larval populations with a suspension of bacteria or virus collected during previous epidemics.

References

Bradley 1974; Jones and Schaffner 1939; Larson and Ignoffo 1971; Lyon and Brown 1970; Prentice 1963; Raizenne 1952; and Smith 1974b,

Greenstriped mapleworm
Plate 70

The greenstriped mapleworm, *Dryocampa rubicunda rubicunda* (F.) is a defoliator native to North America. It occurs in the eastern half of the United States and in Canada, in the Maritime provinces and the southern parts of Quebec and Ontario. In eastern Canada, only Newfoundland has not as yet reported its presence.

The greenstriped mapleworm attacks all species of maple and occasionally a few other hardwoods, but its preferred hosts are red maple and sugar maple. Occasionally its population multiplies excessively, sometimes over large areas, but usually in areas of less than 20 ha. Fortunately these epidemics rarely last longer than 2 or 3 years in a given location, and their decline is often associated with the action of microorganisms in the larval population.

History of outbreaks

The greenstriped mapleworm was collected for the first time in the Maritime provinces in 1930 and as early as 1937 a severe epidemic occurred over an area of some 4 ha in New Brunswick. A second epidemic covered around 100 ha in central Nova Scotia from 1971 to 1975. In Quebec, mainly local outbreaks were reported every year from 1939 to 1948, but from then until 1968 few if any were reported; from that date on however, the mapleworm was active again particularly in western Quebec, where persistent epidemics caused some mortality on red maple in certain areas. In Ontario, the insect was first reported back in 1938, and since that time it has been active almost every year, mainly in the southeastern part of the province; it was particularly injurious during two distinct periods; from 1946 to 1950 and from 1970 to 1975.

Description and biology

Adult. Heavy-bodied moth; dorsum yellow, ventrum and legs pink; forewings light pink with a large pale yellow central section; hindwings solid pale yellow. Wingspan, 40-50 mm (Plate 70, B).

Egg. Round, smooth, and slightly flattened dorsally; lemon yellow becoming amply spotted with red after a few days of incubation; chorion colorless and translucid. Diameter: about 1 mm (Plate 70, C).

Larva. Cylindrical, elongated; head cherry red; body light greenish yellow with seven dark green lines along the dorsum, two horns on the mesothorax, two rows of short spines on the sides of body segments, and four longer spines on the last abdominal segment. Length when full grown: 40-50 mm (Plate 70, E, F and G).

Pupa. Obtect with rigid surface; solid dark brown with straight spines on certain parts of the thorax and abdomen and forked spines on the anal part. Length: 24-32 mm (Plate 70, D).

The biology of the greenstriped mapleworm is well known from research carried out in the northern part of its range.

Only one generation occurs per year in the northern part of its range, although two are common in the southern part. In eastern Canada, the life cycle of this mapleworm is believed to be as follows: adults appear from the end of May until the end of July, with a peak in early July. Eggs may be found from the beginning of June until the beginning of August, and larvae from early June until the end of September. Pupae are present from mid-July until the following spring.

Being nocturnal, the moths rest during the day on the underside of leaves of host trees. Females produce between 150 and 200 eggs laid in clusters of 9 to 11, mainly on the distal half of the underside of maple leaves growing at the ends of branches. The eggs take 10 to 15 days to develop.

The young larvae feed in colonies, but, from the fourth instar on, they become solitary. They are highly voracious and devour the leaves completely. During an epidemic, they may strip the leaves from whole stands over wide areas. In regions where two generations occur per year, larvae may defoliate the same trees twice in a single season. The larval cycle includes five instars and lasts some 4-5 weeks, at the end of which time the larvae drop to the ground and pupate in the litter. Most individuals of the first gener-

ation remain dormant in the ground until the following spring, but, from time to time, in the more southerly regions, some individuals continue their development and produce a second generation, which can reach full growth before the winter.

Damage and diagnosis

All damage is caused by the larvae of the greenstriped mapleworm feeding on the foliage of trees, which they often manage to strip completely (Plate 70, A). This massive defoliation reduces the aesthetic value of those trees but generally does not endanger their life, because they are able to produce a second crop of leaves during the same season. However, if the phenomenon is repeated for 2 or 3 years consecutively affected trees may lose their resistance and some of them die.

An attack by this lepidoptera is easily recognized in summer by the presence of large yellow larvae with green stripes and having two horns in front and several spines on the sides of the body. In the spring, rose pink moths may be easily seen flying around maple crowns, and lemon yellow eggs may be found on the undersides of the leaves; eggs obtained by pressing the abdomen of females are of the same color.

Natural control

Because of their large size, the larvae and pupae of the greenstriped mapleworm are easy prey for birds in the crowns and predators on the ground. They are also susceptible to attack by entomophagous parasites of which Bradley (1974) reports two species for Canada (Plate 70, H). Allen (1976) has published a list of the 13 known parasitic species for Canada and the United States, 5 of which were obtained through his rearings; among these, *Eumasicera sternalis* (Coquillet) is considered the most important. Allen determined that these parasites are responsible for the destruction of 11 percent of the eggs and from 10 to 23 percent of the pupae. In Canada, larvae are apparently less affected by parasites, but they are more susceptible to diseases caused by three pathogenic microorganisms: a bacterium of the genus *Bacillus* and two fungi of the genera *Entomophthora* and *Isaria*.

163

PAGE C

Artificial control

Outbreaks of the greenstriped maple-worm are normally short-lived, so that it is rarely necessary to use artificial methods of control.

However, when prolonged outbreaks threaten to kill trees, the crowns of affected trees may be treated with a stomach insecticide in an aqueous solution, after the larvae have started feeding and before they have caused too much damage.

When only a few small trees need protection, the young larvae may be dislodged from the foliage of the crown by knocking the tree trunk.

References

Allen 1976; Bradley 1974; Canadian Forestry Service 1971; McGugan 1958; Raizenne 1952; Schaffner and Griswold 1934; and Wilson 1971.

PLATE 70

Greenstriped mapleworm, *Dryocampa rubicunda rubicunda* (F.)

A. Severely damaged red maple stand.
B. Adult at rest (wingspan: 40-50 mm).
C. Appearance of eggs (diameter: about 1 mm).
D. Side view of pupa (length: 24-32 mm).
E. Colony of young larvae on sugar maple leaf.
F. Dorsal view of mature larva (length: 40-50 mm).
G. Side view of a different mature larva.
H. Mature larva attacked by the parasite *Hyposoter fugitivus fugitivus*.

Whitemarked tussock moth
Plate 71

The whitemarked tussock moth, *Orgyia leucostigma intermedia* Fitch, is a native North American insect, found throughout the eastern half of the United States, and in Canada from Newfoundland west to Alberta. This highly polyphageous insect feeds on most species of hardwoods and many species of conifers. It is a pest in city parks rather than in forests, and outbreaks fortunately remain local and last only a few years.

History of outbreaks

The whitemarked tussock moth was first reported in 1937 in the Maritime provinces, and has been reported almost every year since. In Quebec, this lepidoptera was first observed in 1938, and following that, it was a particular pest during two distinct periods, in 1947 and 1948 and from 1975 to 1977. In Ontario, occasional outbreaks occurred in cities from 1938 to 1947, and once again in 1974.

Description and biology

Adult. Moth with marked sexual dimorphism, only the male having normal wings. Male, medium-sized, brown gray. Wingspan: about 31 mm (Plate 71, B). Female, wingless, covered with long hairs; gray to brown. Length: 12 mm (Plate 71, C).

Egg. Fairly large, rounded in shape and depressed at upper pole; laid in a flattened cluster covered with a mass of whitish foam (Plate 71, D).

Larva. Elongated, very hairy; head coral red, with two diverging pencils of long black hairs at the back; body with black and yellow lengthwise stripes; dorsal part of first four abdominal segments bears a tuft of short white hairs, whereas the sixth and seventh each have one red spot and the eighth a tuft of long black hairs; sides of body bear tubercles with radiating hairs. Length: 25-37 mm (Plate 71, E and F).

Pupa. Obtect; brown black; enclosed in a gray cocoon sprinkled with larval hairs (Plate 71, G and H).

One to three generations of white-marked tussock moth may occur per year depending on the climate; in eastern Canada, there is usually only one. Moths appear at the end of July and are present until the end of September. Eggs, covered with white foamy matter that hardens after a few days, are laid in a mass on host trees either near or on empty cocoons. The insect overwinters in the egg stage, and larvae hatch from mid-April on. The larvae begin their feeding on the surface of the leaf, but later they devour the leaf completely, leaving only the large veins and the petiole. They take 5 to 6 weeks to reach full development, although some may be seen until mid-October. Once the larval stage is completed, larvae spin individual cocoons made of loose threads of silk, normally on the bark of trunks or branches. The pupal stage lasts about 2 weeks, and the cycle begins again with the emergence of the adult.

Damage and diagnosis

Damage is caused by the larvae of whitemarked tussock moth, which devour leaves completely, often leaving crowns bare over large areas (Plate 71, A). Also the larvae occasionally chew the bark of twigs, sometimes resulting in twig mortality. Some people develop an allergic reaction on contact with larvae.

Attack by this insect is easily identified in summer by the very characteristic appearance of the larvae, and in winter by the presence of egg masses scattered at random on trunks or branches.

Natural control

In his research carried out in the northeastern United States, Howard (1897) was able to prove that many factors work to check the whitemarked tussock moth. He first observed that a certain proportion of the eggs aborted during their development and that a certain percentage of newborn larvae starved to death because they hatched too far away from their source of food. He also identified 21 species of entomophagous parasites, as well as 11 species of predators of the various stages of the insect; among these predators were several species of common birds that feed on young larvae.

PLATE 71

Whitemarked tussock moth, *Orgyia leucostigma intermedia* Fitch

A. Damage by larva on dogwood.
B. Adult male at rest (wingspan: 31 mm).
C. Adult female laying eggs (length: 12 mm).
D. Typical egg mass.
E. Side view of larva (length: 25-37 mm).
F. Dorsal view of larva.
G. Cocoon on trembling aspen twig.
H. Pupa in opened cocoon.

Raizenne (1957) reported 12 species of entomophagous parasites obtained from rearings of material collected in Ontario. Parasites were also mentioned as important factors in controlling outbreaks recorded in the Maritime provinces, but in many cases a viral disease was identified as the key factor that destroyed populations in the larval stage.

Artificial control

Isolated trees may be easily protected from attack by the whitemarked tussock moth with a simple and practical method consisting in finding egg masses when they are very obvious, either to destroy them by hand or to paint them with a creosote compound. In the spring, populations of young larvae may easily be killed by spraying infested crowns with a chemical stomach or contact insecticide. In areas where there is objection to the use of chemical insecticides, a biological insecticide such as *Bacillus thuringiensis* Berl. may be used with good results.

References

Howard 1897; Johnson and Lyon 1976; Prentice 1962; Raizenne 1957; Rose and Lindquist 1977; Smith 1974d; and Turner et al. 1975.

Rusty tussock moth
Plate 72

The rusty tussock moth, *Orgyia antiqua* L., is a foreign species introduced from Europe; this lepidoptera has also been known for quite some time in Asia. Its distribution is transcontinental in Canada and extends southward into the center of United States along the Atlantic coast and to northern California on the Pacific. Two subspecies have been recognized for some time on the North American continent, *O. antiqua nova* Fitch and *O. antiqua badia* Henry Edwards. The first occurs mainly in the eastern part of the continent, whereas the second is confined to the far western part and is not discussed in this text. The first subspecies is a highly polyphagous insect; it attacks most conifers and all hardwoods, and populations often reach excessive levels on conifers and occasionally on hardwoods.

History of outbreaks

In Newfoundland, a number of major outbreaks of the rusty tussock moth have been reported on fir and spruce since 1961, in areas also infested by the hemlock looper. In the Maritime provinces and Quebec, the only outbreaks reported have been short-lived and confined to small areas in both conifers and hardwoods. Populations of this insect have rarely caused serious damage in Ontario.

Description and biology

Adult. Moth with marked sexual dimorphism, only the male having well-developed wings. Male medium-sized, rusty brown; forewings crossed by two darker bands and bearing a white spot in the shape of a half-moon; hindwings solid rusty yellow edged with golden hairs. Wingspan: about 26 mm (Plate 72, H). Female wingless, almost oval in shape, gray. Dimensions: about 12 mm by 20 mm (Plate 72, G).

Egg. White with a light brown ring; rounded in shape but slightly flattened at upper pole.

Larva. Elongated, very hairy; head black, dorsal side of body dark gray and ventral side yellow; body has four to seven thick tufts of short hairs and five pencils of long black hairs, two in front, two others in the middle, that is, one on each side projecting outward at right angle from the body, and the last at the back. Length when full grown: 25 mm (Plate 72, C, D and E).

Pupa. Yellowish brown, enclosed in a dirty gray silken cocoon.

Only one generation of the rusty tussock moth occurs per year throughout the greater part of this insect's distribution, although a second may occasionally occur. Moths are present from the end of July until mid-September. Males are very active, whereas females move about with great difficulty. Females lay their eggs on their cocoon where they are left unprotected throughout the winter season (Plate 72, B). Larvae hatch in June and immediately move towards the leaves, on which they feed. They are full-grown between the end of July and the end of August, when they spin individual cocoons in the axil of two small branches (Plate 72, F), where they pupate and transform into adults.

Damage and diagnosis

Damage is caused only by the larvae of the rusty tussock moth during the feeding period. Although, one or more species of trees may be completely stripped in a limited area during an outbreak (Plate 72, A), the infestations are generally short-lived and, consequently, no great damage is done to the trees. Some people develop an allergy when in contact with the larvae, which poses a serious problem to loggers during cutting operations.

In the summer, this species is easy to identify, due to the typical appearance of the larvae. In the fall, a count of the number of egg masses on the cocoons gives some indication of the severity of the infestation to be expected the following year.

A

B

C

D

E

F

G

H

PLATE 72

Rusty tussock moth, *Orgyia antiqua* L.

A. Severely defoliated white birch.
B. Egg mass on female cocoon.
C. Young larva.
D. Half-grown larva on trembling aspen leaf.
E. Mature larva (length: 25 mm).
F. Cocoon attached to twig.
G. Newly hatched female near its cocoon (dimensions: 12 mm by 20 mm.)
H. Adult male (wingspan: 26 mm).

Natural control

The larvae of the rusty tussock moth are heavily parasitized. One egg parasite, Trichogramma cacoeciae March., destroys a large proportion of eggs in Poland and is recognized as being very effective (Nilmczyk and Olszak 1978). In Canada, 11 species of entomophagous parasites have been obtained from rearings of larvae in Ontario (Raizenne 1952), and 3 additional species were collected by FIDS personnel in Quebec.

Artificial control

It is usually unnecessary to organize a control program against the rusty tussock moth in the forest, since outbreaks are local and of short duration. If larvae occasionally become a nuisance on ornamental trees, they may be destroyed by spraying the foliage of affected crowns with a chemical stomach insecticide when leaves open in the spring.

Before the buds open in the spring, especially in the case of hardwoods, an attempt may be made to eliminate the insect by destroying the eggs, which are easily seen on the old cocoons of the females.

References

Anderson 1960; Bradley 1974; Daviault 1947; Ferguson 1978; Hughes 1976; Keen 1952; Nilmczyk and Olszak 1978; Prentice 1962; Raizenne 1952; and Rose and Lindquist 1977.

Maple leafrollers

Two leaf rollers belonging to the same genus are found on maple: the maple leafroller, *Cenopis acerivorana* MacK., and the maple-basswood leafroller, *C. pettitana* (Rob.). Formerly these two species were grouped under the name *Sparganothis pettitana* Rob., and it was only in 1952 that they were recognized as separate entities.

Maple leafroller
Plate 73

The maple leafroller, *Cenopis acerivorana* MacK., is found in the Great Lakes region of the United States and Canada, in southern Quebec and occasionally in the Maritime provinces. This insect has been reported on 11 hardwood species, but in Quebec it mainly affects maple.

Description and biology

Adult. Small moth, color differing according to sex; male with lemon yellow head and thorax; forewings of same color but marked with reddish brown, and particularly by a diagonal line running all the way across so as to form a perfect V when wings are folded; hindwings and abdomen white (Plate 73, H and I); female with head, thorax and forewings practically solid creamy yellow; hindwings and abdomen white (Plate 73, G). Wingspan for both sexes: 21-25 mm.

Egg. Oval in shape; green in color, although chorion appears silky white after hatching.

Larva. Elongated; head brown, body gray. Length when full grown: 25mm (Plate 73, E).

Pupa. Obtect, reddish brown. Length: about 12 mm (Plate 73, F).

Little is known on the biology of the maple leafroller, and the brief information presented here comes from observations made by FIDS personnel.

Moths are found from early June until mid-August. Females lay all their eggs in an irregularly shaped mass containing up to 50 eggs overlapping one another like shingles on a roof (Plate 73, C). These masses can be found easily on leaves and at many other places on the host tree or on other objects located nearby. The egg hatches before fall and the larva overwinters in a dormant state, probably in an hibernaculum, becoming active again when the leaves open in the spring. The larva first rolls a leaf and secures it with threads of silk to form its shelter, which it leaves only to feed (Plate 73, D). At the slightest disturbance, it drops down on a thread of silk. It also has the characteristic habit of cutting the middle rib of the leaf blade near the petiole, and, as a result, the blade hangs downwards for some time. Once full-grown, the larva constructs a second shelter inside the first one where it pupates. Pupae may be found from mid-June until the beginning of August.

Damage and diagnosis

Damage is caused, mainly on maple, by the larva of the maple leafroller which first rolls and then mutilates the leaf. Severely damaged crowns lose their attractiveness when affected leaves become distorted and and change color (Plate 73, A). This damage normally does not harm the tree permanently, although attack by this insect in some maple groves in Wisconsin led to the deterioration and death of a certain number of trees (Giese 1964).

In the spring, the maple leafroller attack is easily diagnosed by the presence of rolled leaves (Plate 73, B). Later in the season, the blade of certain leaves may be seen to hang down vertically, although still attached to the petiole. Examining the contents of rolled leaves reveals the presence of a gray larva or reddish brown pupa.

Natural control

To date, only two species of parasites have been obtained from the maple leafroller (Bradley 1974). Volney (1975) reported that leaves rolled by larvae provide a shelter for many small creatures, notably spiders, and it is likely that some of these play a role in controlling this insect.

B

D

C

E

F

G

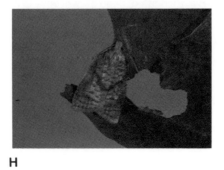

H

I

170

In Quebec, known predators are several unidentified species of birds that have often been observed searching into rolled leaves, no doubt in search of larvae to feed on.

Artificial control

The degree of damage caused by the maple leafroller rarely justifies the use of artificial measures. If this became necessary on small trees, the rolled leaves could be collected at the beginning of the summer and be burned while the larvae are still inside them. Tree crowns could also be sprayed with a contact or stomach insecticide when buds open and larvae become active in the spring.

PLATE 73

Maple leafroller, *Cenopis acerivorana* MacK.

A. Severely defoliated sugar maple stand.
B. Undergrowth of maple grove showing sugar maple leaves rolled and hanging down.
C. Mass of incubating eggs.
D. Young larva on sugar maple leaf.
E. Mature larva (length: 25 mm).
F. Pupa in pupal chamber (length: 12 mm).
G. Adult female (wingspan: 21-25 mm).
H. Adult male (wingspan: 21-25 mm).
I. Slightly different adult male.

Maple-basswood leafroller
Plate 74

The maple-basswood leafroller, *Cenopis pettitana* (Rob.), occurs over a much larger area than the maple leafroller. In the United States, it is found in all states along the Atlantic coast, from Maine to Florida; to the west it reaches the Mississipi River valley. In Canada, it is found from the Maritime provinces to the center of Saskatchewan. Local outbreaks have been reported frequently in the Maritimes since 1956, and occasionally in Quebec and Ontario. This pest feeds on a wide variety of trees and has been collected on 23 hardwood species, among which the most frequent are, in decreasing order of importance, basswood, red maple, and sugar maple. In Quebec, this insect is most harmful to basswood.

Description and biology

Adult. Male head, thorax and forewings yellow with silvery to pale yellow coloration; hindwings with reddish brown spots and a truncated diagonal line halfway down wing (Plate 74, F); female head, thorax and forewings pale yellow to white (Plate 74, G).
Larva. Elongated; yellowish green initially, gradually turning light yellow. Length when full grown: 21 mm (Plate 74, C and D).

Little is known about the maple-basswood leafroller, and the brief information presented here comes from observations made by FIDS personnel.

This species is easily confused with the maple leafroller and the two are often found together on the same trees and at practically the same dates. They can be differentiated by the color of the moth and of the larva.

The habits of this species are very similar to those of the maple leafroller. Moths appear in the summer and lay eggs (Plate 74, H and I); larvae hatch before fall, overwinter in the larval stage, and become active again the following spring. Pupation occurs in early summer (Plate 74, E).

Damage and diagnosis

Damage by the maple-basswood leafroller is seen most frequently on basswood and is similar to that caused by the maple leafroller, except that the central rib of the leaf is not cut so thus the leaf blade does not hang down (Plate 74, A and B).

An attack by this species may be determined, especially on basswood, by the presence of folded or rolled leaves containing a yellowish green larva. Rearing a few mature larvae or pupae will produce moths that can be easily identified.

Natural control

In Canada, several species of parasites were obtained from rearings of insects identified under the name *Sparganothis pettitana*, before the two species were distinguished, so that it is impossible to link them with one or the other. Raizenne (1952) thus reported 16 species of parasites for Ontario, whereas 7 other species were obtained between 1959 and 1963 in the Maritime provinces. Bradley's list (1974) added 2 more species to those already known in Canada.

In Quebec, birds have often been observed hunting for larvae in rolled leaves on basswood.

Artificial control

Control methods which may be used against the maple-basswood leafroller are the same as those given for the maple leafroller.

References

Baker 1972; Bradley 1974; Giese 1964; MacKay 1952; Prentice 1965; Raizenne 1952; Schaffner 1959; Simmons 1973; Smith 1974a; and Volney 1975.

A

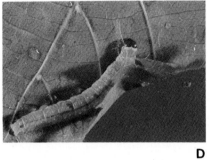

B

C

D

E

F

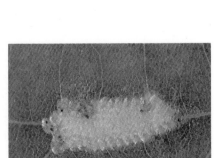

G

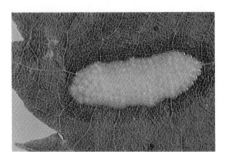

H

I

PLATE 74

Maple-basswood leafroller, *Cenopis pettitana* **(Rob.)**

A. Cluster of rolled basswood leaves.
B. Silk holding leaf rolled up.
C. Young larva.
D. Mature larva (length: 21 mm).
E. Pupa extracted from rolled leaf.
F. Adult male.
G. Adult female.
H. Mass of sound eggs.
I. Mass of hatched eggs.

Saddled prominent

Plate 75

The saddled prominent, *Heterocampa guttivita* (Wlk.), is a solitary defoliator native to North America. It occurs throughout the eastern half of United States and Canada, with the exception of Newfoundland. In Canada, it has been found on 24 hardwood species, with a preference for maple, birch and beech.

History of outbreaks

Since the turn of the century, periodic outbreaks of the saddled prominent have been reported at intervals of about 10 years in the northeastern United States. In Canada, sporadic and generally local outbreaks have been reported in the Maritime provinces, Quebec, and Ontario. The most severe outbreak occurred from 1967 to 1971 in southern Ontario, where it ravaged an estimated 2.5 million km^2.

Description and biology

Adult. Medium-sized moth; gray brown; wings with variable dark spots. Wingspan: 40-50 mm (Plate 75, F).

Egg. Semi-spherical; solid pale green initially, later turning reddish brown and then red; chorion translucid. Diameter: about 1 mm (Plate 75, G).

Larva. Elongated, bulging towards body center; color varying from pale green to reddish brown; back marked with lines of various colors and different patterns, the most common being a saddle-shaped, brownish red spot in the middle of the body. Length when full grown: about 40 mm (Plate 75, C, D and E).

Pupa. Obtect; dark brown. Length: about 20 mm (Plate 75, H).

The biology of the saddled prominent is well known through many studies carried out during outbreaks that occurred in the northeastern United States over the past decade.

In the northeastern part of the North American continent, this species has only one generation per year. Moths can be seen from the end of May until the beginning of July. Eggs are laid from the beginning of June into July. Usually they are laid singly on the underside of the leaf blade, but during outbreaks they may also be found on the upper side. Each female lays about 200 eggs, and interestingly, females that feed on the foliage of yellow birch are more fertile than others and their eggs are larger. The eggs take about 7-10 days to develop. Larvae pass through five instars and usually reach maturity in 5-6 weeks, but they develop more rapidly on beech than on sugar maple. At certain times during the summer, all stages of the insect may be found because of the prolonged period over which the adults emerge. Once the larva is fully grown, it drops to the ground where it pupates and overwinters.

Damage and diagnosis

All damage is caused by the larva of the saddled prominent. During the first three instars, the larva feeds on the underside of the leaf (Plate 75, B), but later may be found on the edge of the leaf or on the upper side, consuming it completely. During an outbreak, entire stands may be totally defoliated, often over vast areas (Plate 75, A). One year's defoliation causes little apparent damage to sugar maple growing in good locations, and damage may then be confined to the mortality of some twigs in the upper part of the crown. Two years of successive defoliation cause more serious damage to immature maples growing on poor sites. Repeated defoliation generally causes a decrease in annual growth.

In the summer, this species is easily recognized just by the appearance of the larvae. They can be found easily once they reach the third instar because of their characteristic coloring and, above all, the saddle-shaped spot on the back. It is even possible to predict at the beginning of the summer the damage to be expected by taking samples of foliage and counting the number of eggs or larvae.

Natural control

In a recent study, Allen (1972) listed 34 species of entomophagous parasites that may feed on the saddled prominent. In his own rearings, carried out in the northeastern United States, he obtained 17 parasitic species, of which 11 were new ones. One of the two parasites obtained from the egg stage, *Telenomus coelodasidis* Ashm., was particularly effective, causing mortality ranging from 20 to 76 percent. During his research carried out in Vermont on a group of defoliators including saddled prominent, Fisher (1970) noticed, in addition to parasites, the action of insect predators, birds, and even an entomophytous fungus of the Ascomycetes group.

Some authors also mentioned that, during outbreaks, saddled prominent populations are often drastically reduced by a disease that followed the starvation resulting from their complete destruction of the foliage.

Artificial control

When a few isolated trees need protection from the saddled prominent, defoliation may easily be prevented by dislodging the larvae once they reach the third instar by beating the branches with a pole.

On forest trees, a large proportion of the larval population may be destroyed by spraying the foliage of infested crowns with a stomach insecticide once the larvae have reached their third instar and have moved from the undersides of leaves to feed on the upper surface. A biological insecticide such as *Bacillus thuringiensis* Berl. may also be used for this purpose.

References

Allen 1972, 1973; Allen and Grimble 1970; Collins 1926; Fisher 1970; Prentice 1962; Raizenne 1952; Ticehurst and Allen 1973; and Wallner 1971.

PLATE 75

Saddled prominent, *Heterocampa guttivitta* (Wlk.)

A. Defoliation seen in a maple grove.
B. Dorsal view of young larva and its damage.
C. Side view of half-grown larva.
D. Dorsal view of mature larva.
E. Side view of mature larva.
F. Adult at rest (wingspan: 40-50 mm).
G. Eggs on maple leaf.
H. Pupa (length: 20 mm) and its cocoon.

Orangehumped mapleworm
Plate 76

The orangehumped mapleworm, *Symmerista leucitys* Francl., is a semi-gregarious leaf eater that is found in the United States, from Maine to Minnesota and, in Canada, in the southern part of Quebec and Ontario. Sugar maple is the preferred host, but the insect also occasionally attacks other hardwood species, such as beech, basswood, elm, and oak. This attractive lepidoptera sometimes reaches epidemic proportions over limited areas, and causes significant damage in maple groves, but fortunately outbreaks are always of short duration.

History of outbreaks

In Quebec, one severe outbreak of the orangehumped mapleworm lasted from 1950 to 1952 and a second occurred in 1969 and 1970, both in a few maple groves in the Eastern Townships. In 1962, a moderate-to-severe outbreak was reported in two counties in southern Ontario.

Description and biology

Adult. Medium-sized moth; ash gray; forewings marked with a long, narrow white spot at the costal margin; hindwings solid lighter gray.
Wingspan: 30-40 mm (Plate 76, F).

Larva. Cylindrical; head orange red; body yellow with black and purple stripes, with an orange red dorsal hump on eighth abdominal segment.
Length: about 30 mm (Plate 76, D).

Pupa. Obtect; dark brown.
Length 15-20 mm (Plate 76, E).

No detailed study has as yet been made on the biology of the orangehumped mapleworm, no doubt due to the sudden and short-lived nature of the outbreaks.

Only one generation occurs per year. The moth appears in the spring, and the female lays her eggs in masses on the underside of the leaves. Larvae may be found from July until September and, once they are fully grown, they drop to the ground where they transform to pupae and overwinter.

Damage and diagnosis

Damage is caused solely by larvae of the orangehumped mapleworm, which feed on the leaves and devour them completely. Initially, they simply chew the surface of the leaf, but later they consume it entirely, except for the main veins and the petiole (Plate 76, A and B). Defoliation takes place late in the summer, and thus the trees do not have time to produce a new crop of foliage. This type of damage causes less harm than spring defoliation and, during an epidemic, entire forests may be severely defoliated for 2 or 3 consecutive years without tree mortality.

In late summer, an outbreak of this species in maple groves is easily recognized by the characteristic coloring of the larva.

Natural control

Little information has been gathered on the natural factors that keep the orangehumped mapleworm in check. However, observations made during the outbreak that ravaged certain maple groves in the Eastern Townships of Quebec in 1969-1970 indicate that the abrupt decline in populations may have resulted from a disease of unknown origin, as well as a lack of food (Plate 76, C).

Artificial control

It is generally unnecessary to make long-range plans to control the orangehumped mapleworm, because damage is usually slight. When only a few trees need to be protected, larvae may easily be collected by hand and be destroyed, or be dislodged from foliage by hitting the branches with a pole.

In maple groves, larvae may be destroyed by spraying the foliage with a chemical stomach or a biological insecticide, such as *Bacillus thuringiensis* Berl., when the larvae begin to disperse, or else by using a suspension of the microorganism that causes the natural disease already mentioned which could be collected in centers already severely infested.

References

Franclemont 1946; Prentice 1962; and Raizenne 1952.

Maple leafcutter
Plate 77

The maple leafcutter, *Paraclemensia acerifoliella* (Fitch), is a tiny microlepidoptera native to North America. It is a defoliator whose larva first behaves like a miner and then remains inside the shelter of its case. Its distribution extends from southeastern Canada down to Virginia, and from the Atlantic Ocean west to the state of Illinois and to central Ontario. Sugar maple is its preferred host, but the insect is occasionally found on several other hardwood species. Periodically, it multiplies excessively and infests limited areas for several years, then disappears suddenly and becomes very rare again.

History of outbreaks

A number of outbreaks of the maple leafcutter have been reported in eastern Canada, notably in 1872, 1881, 1911, and 1923, about which little information is available (Hutchings 1925). The epidemic that broke out in 1939 is better known. It covered southern Quebec and eastern Ontario, and populations of the insect remained at high levels until 1947, when they began to decline and finally disappeared in 1950. An upsurge in populations of this insect was again recorded in the same two provinces in 1959, dying out in 1963 in Quebec and 2 years later in Ontario.

Description and biology

Adult. Tiny moth with delicate, narrow, tapering wings; forewings steel blue bordered with a fringe of black hairs; hindwings brown, translucid, and fringed with long brown hairs. Wingspan: 8.5-13 mm (Plate 77, E and F).

Egg. Ovoid; chorion membranous, transparent, and delicately reticulated. Dimensions: 0.23 mm by 0.33 mm.

Larva. Form varies with age; first instars correspond to the mining phase, with flattened body, wider at prothorax and tapering off towards the end of the abdomen; final instars correspond to surface-feeding phase, roughly cylindrical with brown head and flesh-colored body. Length at maturity: 6 mm.

A

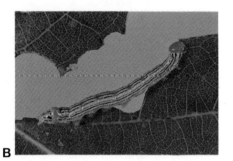

B

D

C

E

F

PLATE 76

Orangehumped mapleworm, *Symmerista leucitys* Francl.

A. Severely damaged maple grove.
B. Side view of immature larva feeding.
C. Larvae migrating because of lack of food.
D. Mature larva (length: 30 mm).
E. Pupa (length: 15-20 mm).
F. Pinned adult (wingspan: 30-40 mm).

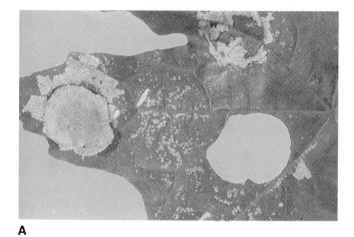

A

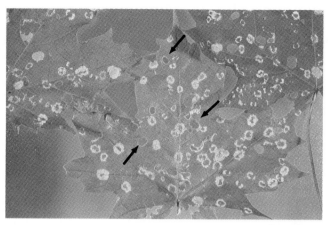

G

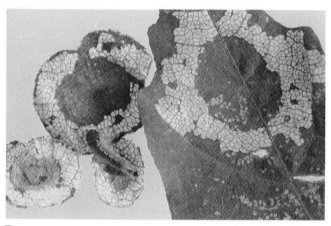

B

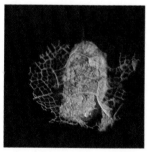

C

D

E

F

PAGE C

PLATE 77

Maple leafcutter, *Paraclemensia acerifoliella* (Fitch)

A. Hole cut in a maple leaf blade by *Paraclemensia acerifoliella* to get a disk to be used as a roof of the habitaculum.
B. Green foliage inside defoliated ring, seen after removing the habitaculum, and series of disks forming the habitaculum of *P. acerifoliella*.
C. Pupal case of *P. acerifoliella*.
D. Pupa of *P. acerifoliella*.
E. Living adult of *P. acerifoliella* at rest.
F. Pinned adult of *P. acerifoliella* (wingspan: 8.5-13 mm).
G. Series of holes made by larva of *P. acerifoliella* in a maple leaf blade.

177

Pupa. Enclosed in a cocoon; amber-colored; abdomen with short spines female larger than male. Length: 4.2-5.7 mm (Plate 77, C and D).

The biology of the maple leafcutter is fairly well known due to major studies carried out in Ontario (Ross 1958, 1962).

Only one generation occurs per year. Moths appear at the end of May, their emergence coinciding with the opening of maple leaves. About 2 days after emerging, the females begin to lay their eggs singly, in a small number of the many pockets they make with their ovipositor in the underside of the leaf. Incubation of the eggs lasts from 14 to 22 days. On hatching, the larvae begin constructing a tunnel, feeding on the parenchyma between the two leaf surfaces for 10-15 days, during which they complete their first instar and part of the second. At this stage, they make individual cases composed of two superimposed foliar disks, the first cut from the under surface of the lamina and the second, slightly smaller, immediately above it in the upper surface. The larva fastens the two disks together using silk, the larger disk on top, to form a case called an habitaculum, which it then transports and positions temporarily on the upper surface of the leaf. The larva uses the case as a shelter and feeds around its edges, with the result that, once the case has been moved away, the eaten part has the form of a gray ring around a green circle. After each molt, the larva cuts a new disk slightly larger in diameter to make a new roof for its case.

Larvae are present from mid-June until the end of September. Once the larva is full-grown, it drops to the ground with its case, in which it spins a loose silken cocoon, pupates, and overwinters.

Damage and diagnosis

Damage is of three types and results from the various activities of the larva of the maple leafcutter, either feeding or constructing its protective case. Initial damage is caused by the larva mining the leaf and then cutting two small oval-shaped disks with which to construct its first case. The second type of damage consists in the destruction of the upper surface of the leaf and takes the form of defoliated rings with the central part still intact; the diameter of these rings increases with the age of the larva. The third type of damage is the result of oval-shaped perforations of varying sizes cut in the leaf after each larval molt, to make new roofs for the habitaculum (Plate 77, G). The consequence is a gradual drying of the leaf, which occurs more rapidly where larval populations are large.

In summer, attack by this insect is easily recognized by examining damage to the leaf. The presence of oval-shaped holes of various sizes, clearly cut in sugar maple leaves (Plate 77, A), as well as defoliated rings with green centers, allow a preliminary diagnosis to be made. Cases composed of a series of superimposed foliar disks, and containing a developing larva, may also be seen on the leaf surface (Plate 77, B)

Natural control

Little information has been gathered to date on natural factors that keep the maple leafcutter in check, but the fact that populations drop to very low levels between outbreaks appears to indicate that natural factors play an important role. In his rearings of material collected in Ontario, Raizenne (1952) obtained eight species of entomophagous parasites, some of which seem to be key regulating factors.

Artificial control

When only a few ornamental trees need protection from the maple leafcutter, the hibernating population may easily be destroyed at ground level in the fall, by collecting and burning dead leaves. In maple groves, spraying foliage with a chemical stomach or a biological insecticide when larvae begin to feed on the leaf surface may yield good results.

References

Baker 1972; Bradley 1974; Hutchings 1925; Prentice 1965; Raizenne 1952; and Ross 1958, 1962.

Maple petiole borer
Plate 78

The maple petiole borer, *Caulocampus acericaulis* (MacG.), is an hymenoptera of European origin first reported in North America in Connecticut at the beginning of this century. Its present distribution extends to three states, Massachusetts, New York, and New Jersey, as well as to two provinces, Quebec and Ontario. Its preferred host is sugar maple, which is its only host in Canada; in the United States, however, the insect has been reported on several other species of maple.

History of outbreaks

In eastern North America, local outbreaks of the maple petiole borer have occasionally been serious enough to cause concern among maple growers. In eastern Canada, local outbreaks were observed in the southern part of Quebec and Ontario between 1962 and 1966, but populations have remained low since that time.

Description and biology

Adult. Small hymenoptera with four transparent wings; head, thorax, and antennae black; abdomen and legs honey yellow.
Larva. Cylindrical; head yellow, turning light brown; body whitish, turning straw yellow. Length at maturity: 8 mm.

Little research has as yet been done in North America on the biology of the maple petiole borer, and the information available is thus fairly incomplete.

Only one generation of this sawfly occurs per year. The adult appears in May and, shortly after emerging, the female lays her eggs singly at the base of the petiole of maple leaves. On hatching, the young larva tunnels into the petiole, heading toward the blade and leaving only the external wall (Plate 78, B). In about a month, the larva has hollowed out a good portion of the petiole and is normally between 6 to 12 mm from the leaf blade (Plate 78, C and D). It then cuts the petiole, and the leaf blade falls to the ground with the upper end of the petiole. The

A

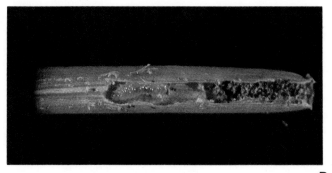

B

C

D

E

PLATE 78

Maple petiole borer, *Caulocampus acericaulis* (MacG.)

A. Appearance of healthy maple leaf at junction between petiole and veins.
B. Section of damaged petiole opened to show the position of the larva and its excrement.
C. Appearance of blade and petiole of maple leaf when the larva reaches the upper end of the petiole (upper side).
D. Appearance of the same leaf on other side (underside).
E. Similar type of damage caused by climate on maple leaf petiole.

larva remains in the portion still attached to the twig for about 10 days, and then drops to the ground. It burrows down about 50-75 mm into the ground, where it constructs a chamber in which it pupates in the fall. The insect overwinters in this stage and transforms to an adult the following spring.

Damage and diagnosis

The important damage consists in the defoliation caused by the larva of the maple petiole borer which, in the spring, tunnels through a good portion of the petiole of maple leaves and then cuts it. Outbreaks usually affect fairly limited areas, but the insects destroy 30 percent of the leaves on certain trees. This damage has a negligible effect on the condition of the tree, although the presence of many dangling leaves detracts considerably from the attractiveness of those trees planted as ornamentals.

An attack by this insect may be recognized in the spring by the presence on the ground of green leaves with cut petioles. Many dangling leaves about to fall from the crown may also be observed, as well as petioles in their normal position but without the leaf blades. When these petioles are opened, each one is seen to contain a small, developing larva.

Artificial control

If severe outbreaks of the maple petiole borer occur on valuable ornamental trees, a practical way of preventing the insect from spreading is to collect by hand the dangling leaves together with their petiole and burn them, before they fall to the ground.

Larvae may also be destroyed as they fall to the ground to pupate by collecting them on a sheet spread under the crown.

Note that collecting dead leaves when they have fallen to the ground is of no use because these larvae remain in the petiole on the tree for some time after the leaf blade falls.

References

Baker 1972; Connecticut Agricultural Experiment Station 1956; Herrick 1935; and Johnson and Lyon 1976.

Maple leafblotch miners

The larvae of several moths mine maple leaves and attract attention by the appearance of their damage. Two species are considered here: the maple leafblotch miner, *Cameraria aceriella* (Clem.), and the lesser maple leafblotch miner, *Phyllonorycter lucidicostella* (Clem.). Little is as yet known about their ethology and biology, but the first species is the most common.

Maple leafblotch miner
Plate 79

The maple leafblotch miner, *Cameraria aceriella* (Clem.), is found mainly on red maple but occasionally on sugar maple and mountain maple, in the southern part of Ontario and Quebec where local outbreaks occur occasionally. Its presence has also been reported in New Brunswick, and its distribution probably extends into the northeastern United States.

Description and biology

Adult. Tiny, delicate moth; forewings brown crossed with three straight diagonal white bands, two complete and one partial; hindwings solid silver gray, fringed with long hairs of same colour. Wingspan: 7-9 mm (Plate 79, E).

Larva. Elongated and flattened, with clearly designed segments; head brown, triangular, and flattened; thoracic segments wider and equipped with rudimentary legs; abdominal segments tapering gradually from thorax to anus; most segments marked with dark spots; larvae in last instar cylindrical with well-developed legs (Plate 79, D).

Pupa. Obtect; pale brown. Length: 4 mm.

Adults appear in the spring, and females lay their eggs on foliage. On leaving the egg, each larva tunnels under the upper surface of the leaf, normally working toward its edge. It feeds on the parenchyma from the end of July until mid-September. The tunnel is irregular and resembles a wide path, which remains flattened until the eighth larval instar. During this last instar the larva covers the detached part of the leaf surface with a circular silken web (Plate 79, B), visible from the outside, under which it pupates, partly in the fall and partly during the following spring.

Damage and diagnosis

All damage is caused by larvae of the maple leafblotch miner when they burrow into the leaf's parenchyma. This considerably diminishes the aesthetic value of trees (Plate 79, C) planted as ornamentals, especially as several tunnels may cover up to one-third of the leaf (Plate 79, A). Damage is more evident when the larvae have lined their tunnels with a layer of white silk. Its appearance on the upper surface of maple leaves is sufficient to identify an attack by this species.

Natural and artificial control

No information is available on natural factors that control the maple leafblotch miner. It is certain that the insect, which remains inside the leaf throughout most of its life cycle, is well protected against parasites and predators. For the same reason, direct control by artificial methods presents enormous difficulties. Because the larvae remain imprisoned inside dried leaves when they drop in the fall, however, a practical way of reducing populations is to collect and to burn the dead leaves.

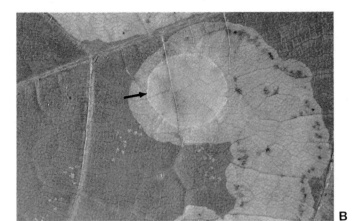

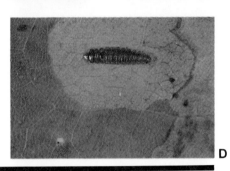

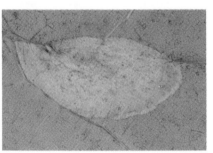

PLATE 79

Maple leafblotch miner, *Cameraria aceriella* (Clem.) and lesser maple leafblotch miner, *Phyllonorycter lucidicostella* (Clem.)

A. Damage by *C. aceriella* on sugar maple leaf.
B. Circular case constructed by full-grown larva of *C. aceriella*.
C. Appearance of old *C. aceriella* mine on sugar maple leaf.
D. Dorsal view of *C. aceriella* larva in its mine.
E. *C. aceriella* adult (wingspan: 7-9 mm).
F. Recent damage by larva of *P. lucidicostella*.
G. Old damage by larva of *P. lucidicostella*.
H. Young *P. lucidicostella* larva in opened mine.
I. Mature *P. lucidicostella* larva in opened mine.
J. *P. lucidicostella* adult (wingspan: 6.5-7 mm).

Lesser maple leafblotch miner
Plate 79

The lesser maple leafblotch miner, *Phyllonorycter lucidicostella* (Clem.), resembles the maple leafblotch miner, although it is less common. Its preferred host is sugar maple, and it may also attack other maples. Up to now in eastern Canada, its presence has only been reported in Quebec and in Ontario.

Description and biology

Adult. Tiny, delicate moth; forewings white decorated with gold designs on the distal third and a black spot near the apex; hindwings also white, fringed with long hairs of the same color. Wingspan: 6.5-7 mm.

Larva. Larvae in last instar elongated and cylindrical, with well-defined segments; pale yellow with digestive tract visible through the skin (Plate 79, H and I).

Pupa. Obtect; pale brown. Length: 4 mm.

The biology of the lesser maple leafblotch miner is very similar to that of the maple leafblotch miner. The larva remains inside a tunnel between the two leaf surfaces throughout its development and pupates there in the fall; however, unlike the maple leafblotch miner, the tunnel is located under the lower epidermis of the leaf. The detached part of the leaf surface is lined with white silk so as to form a sort of tent, which may take on various shapes but which often occupies all the space between two veins.

Damage and diagnosis

Damage by the lesser maple leafblotch miner is similar to that caused by the maple leafblotch miner, but tunnels can be seen on the underside of the leaves (Plate 79, F and G). Attack by this species can easily be identified by the appearance and location of tunnels in the leaves.

Natural and artificial control

Information given in this connection for the maple leafblotch miner also applies to the lesser maple leafblotch.

References

Baker 1972; Forbes 1923; Herrick 1935; and Prentice 1965.

Cottony maple scale
Plate 80

The cottony maple scale, *Pulvinaria innumerabilis* (Rathv.), is a member of the sucking insects group. Its common name refers to the female which, in summer, appears twice her normal size, because she is extended by an egg sac made of a mass of white cottony matter. This insect is mainly found on silver maple, sugar maple, and red maple, but also on other hardwoods. Its distribution is very wide in North America. It covers almost the whole area of the United States and, in Canada, it has been collected from Quebec to British Columbia. Local epidemics of this scale have occurred occasionally, mostly in Ontario but also in Quebec; these attacks rarely last more than 2 years in a given area, after which the insect becomes very rare again for long periods.

Description and biology

Adult. Oval-shaped and convex; yellow-brown to glossy brown; female wingless, very obvious in summer due to the presence of a bulky white egg sac which extends from the abdomen. Length 4-6 mm. Male winged and much smaller than female.

Egg. Elliptical, pearl white with waxy spots. Length: 0.3 mm.

Nymph. Oval-shaped; white initially becoming translucid and sometimes developing reddish brown spots on dorsum. Maximum length of female: 3 mm.

Only one generation of the cottony maple scale occurs per year. Fertilized but immature females overwinter on twigs where they are barely visible because the egg sac has not yet developed. The following spring, they start developing again and reach maturity by the beginning of June. They then lay hundreds of eggs in a huge mass which they cover with a cottony substance that extends the abdomen. Eggs hatch around the end of June; those laid by unfertilized females produce only males. The young nymphs crawl immediately towards the underside of the leaves where they feed on the sap by means of a sucker inserted lengthwise into the main veins. The males reach maturity in September; they mate and die off immediately. Immature females, whether fertilized or not, migrate to the bark of twigs before the leaves fall and there pass the winter.

Damage and diagnosis

The many punctures made for their feeding by the nymphs of the cottony maple scale cause the yellowing and premature drop of leaves, and sometimes mortality of twigs, but never the death of the entire tree. While feeding, the nymphs secrete a sweet liquid called honeydew, which soils leaves and nearby objects, and on which develops a smoky-colored fungus. This gives the leaves a dirty appearance, and considerably reduces the attractiveness of trees planted as ornamentals.

In the summer, the presence of cottony masses on maple twigs (Plate 80, K), particularly silver maple, as well as honeydew dropping on leaves and on objects beneath the crown, enables attack by this scale to be easily recognized.

Natural control

The fact that outbreaks of the cottony maple scale are always short-lived and that they occur at long intervals suggests that natural factors control its spread. In Ontario, McClanahan (1970) showed that about 55 percent of the females were destroyed by bad weather conditions during the winter months, and that an insect predator, *Hyperaspis signata* (Say), wiped out almost all survivors during the following summer. Another insect of the same genus was also very active during all the outbreaks reported in 1968 by the FIDS in Ontario.

Several other species of predators have been reported by other authors as important factors in the control of this scale (Baker 1972).

Artificial control

Given the sporadic nature of outbreaks, it is unnecessary to develop a control program against the cottony maple scale using artificial methods. Very valuable ornamental trees may be protected, however, and the dropping of honeydew on nearby objects prevented by spraying the foliage with a contact insecticide at the end of June or the beginning of July, when the nymphs are feeding. Care should be taken to thoroughly cover the underside of the leaves.

A superior oil may also be sprayed on branches before buds open in the spring, to kill immature females. Note, however, that this treatment is not recommended in the case of sugar maple and Japanese maple, which are highly sensitive to oil.

References

Baker 1972; Canada Department of Forestry and Rural Development 1968; Hutchings 1925; Johnson and Zepp 1979; McClanahan 1970; Phillips 1962; and Turner et al. 1975.

Maple gall makers

A number of species of insects and acarids cause on maple leaves ugly deformities commonly designated as galls and scientifically as cecidia. The causal organisms are extremely small and can be identified only with a binocular microscope, but the galls produced are so different from one another that it is often easy to identify them by their shape, their color, and their dimensions. Among the most common gall-making species are the insect called the ocellate gall midge, *Cecidomyia acericecis* (O.S.), and the three acarids called the maple bladdergall mite, *Vasates quadripedes* Shimer, the maple spindlegall mite, *V. aceris-crumena* (Riley), and an eriophyid, *Aceria regulus* (Hodge).

The biology of the three acarids is very similar. These species produce one or more generations per year and overwinter in the adult stage at the base of buds, on twigs or under bark scales. In the spring, the adults crawl to the opening leaves and begin feeding on the underside of the leaf, with the exception of *Aceria regulus* (Hodge), which is found on either the upper or the underside. In all cases, punctures or bites by the adult cause the formation of a gall on the opposite side of the leaf. Females lay their eggs in the developing gall where the larvae remain throughout their development period, leaving it only when they reach maturity, usually in July.

Each of these species also presents interesting particularities which should be emphasized, especially with respect to the gall.

Ocellate gall midge
Plate 80

The ocellate gall midge, *Cecidomyia acericecis* (O.S.), is an insect that causes the formation of a leaf gall that is easily confused with a damage caused by fungi. Its only host is red maple, and, in Canada, the midge has been reported in Ontario, Quebec, the Maritime provinces, and Newfoundland. In Quebec, it was first observed in 1942, and since 1960 it has been reported almost every year.

Description and biology

The larva of the ocellate gall midge is headless, conical in shape, colorless and measures about 1.5 mm when full grown. Little is yet known of the biology of this insect. From the distribution of the galls, it appears that the female lays her eggs singly on the underside of the leaf. On hatching, the larva attacks the closest cells, and a dark point appears on the upper side of the leaf, growing larger as time goes by. This gall eventually looks like a target about 8 mm in diameter, with a dark point in the center surrounded with a yellow ring which in turn is outlined in red. (Plate 80, A, and B). All the leaves on a given tree may be affected, and up to 50 galls may be found per leaf. Once the larva is fully grown, it drops to the ground and transforms to a pupa slightly below the surface.

Damage and diagnosis

Damage caused by the ocellate gall midge consists mainly in a deterioration of the appearance of the leaf. Attack by this diptera would be fairly easy to identify simply by the damage caused, were it not for the fact that the damage resembles certain spots caused by fungi. For this reason, it is necessary to have the diagnosis confirmed by a specialist.

Natural and artificial control

Information on the natural factors that regulate these gall makers is very scanty; and, although it is known that certain predators are very active, few authors have as yet given precise information.

Control of the ocellate gall midge might be planned if severe outbreaks threaten very valuable ornamental trees. The foliage should be sprayed with a chemical contact or systemic insecticide in the spring, before larvae take shelter inside the galls.

Maple bladdergall mite
Plate 80

The maple bladdergall mite, *Vasates quadripedes* Shimer, attacks silver maple and red maple. In Canada, this mite was first reported at the end of the 1930s, and local outbreaks have been reported almost every year in Ontario and Quebec. It is also found in part of the Maritime provinces, Newfoundland, and the eastern United States.

Description and biology

The gall produced by this mite can be seen on the upper side of the leaf and consists in an outgrowth having the form of a mushroom cap with a short stem, about 2 to 3 mm high (Plate 80, C). The surface of the cap is sometimes wrinkled, and its color varies with age, going from pale green to dark green with a slight pink or red tinge, then turning black (Plate 80, D,E and F). Galls may occur singly or in groups, and are often abundant enough to cause the blade to curl. On the underside of the leaf the initial puncture remains open, and the opening is protected by a number of hairs.

This mite may be found in the egg, larval or adult stages. The egg is ovoid in shape, colorless and translucid, measuring 0.06 mm in diameter. The larva has a wide, slightly curved, white body, and measures 0.08 to 0.1 mm long. The adult has a wide body, tapering sharply in front but more gradually towards the rear; it measures 0.17 to 0.2 mm long. The mite reaches its full growth in 8 to 10 weeks, or around the end of July; the tiny creature then leaves the gall and seeks a favorable location on the trunk, branches, or twigs where it passes the winter.

Natural and artificial control

Control of the maple bladdergall mite presents less difficulty, because it is not always protected inside the gall. Formerly young plants in nurseries or plantations were sprayed with lime sulphur in fall and winter, but the results were only fair. Nowadays, a superior oil is preferred; the treatment is applied by a spraying shortly before buds open in the spring, when all danger of frost is past. Note, however, that this is not recommended for sugar maple and Japanese maple, because both these trees are sensitive to oil-based treatments. Some success may also be obtained by using a miticide on buds and twigs when the leaves begin to open in the spring, or by treating the crowns or surrounding soil with a systemic insecticide in solid or liquid form at a time when circulation of sap is the greatest to reach the mites from inside the leaf.

PLATE 80

Ocellate gall midge, *Cecidomyia acericecis* (O.S.), maple bladdergall mite, *Vasates quadripedes* (Shimer), maple spindlegall mite, *Vasates aceris-crumena* (Riley), an eriophyid, *Aceria regulus* (Hodge), and Cottony maple scale, *Pulvinaria innumerabilis* (Rath.)

A. Maple leaves attacked by *C. acericecis*.
B. Close-up of *C. acericecis* galls.
C. Tuft of silver maple leaves infested by *V. quadripedes*.
D. Silver maple leaf showing immature *V. quadripedes* galls.
E. Appearance of older *V. quadripedes* galls.
F. Side view of *V. quadripedes* galls.
G. Side view of *V. aceris-crumena* galls.
H. Damage by *V. aceris-crumena*.
I. Tuft of sugar maple leaves infested by *A. regulus*.
J. Close-up of part of a sugar maple leaf attacked by *A. regulus*.
K. Appearance of *Pulvinaria innumerabilis* on a maple twig.

185

Maple spindlegall mite
Plate 80

The maple spindlegall mite, *Vasates aceris-crumena* (Riley), is less common than the above, and is found mainly on sugar maple and occasionally on silver maple and red maple. In Canada, its presence has been reported in the Maritime provinces, Quebec and Ontario, and its distribution also extends into some of the eastern United States.

Description and biology

As for the maple bladdergall mite, the gall of the maple spindlegall mite can be seen on the upper side of the leaf. This spindle-shaped gall is green in color and can take pink red tinges (Plate 80, G and H); it measures about 5 mm high and 0.05 mm wide.

Galls are normally located around the main veins, but may also be found all over the surface of the leaf. As with the maple bladdergall mite, the initial puncture made on the underside of the leaf remains open, and is protected by a tuft of hair.

The egg is spherical, colorless, and translucid and measures about 0.05 mm. The larva, also colorless and translucid, differs from the adult only by its size and the incomplete development of its genital organs. The adult has an annulated body, wide in the middle and tapered at the ends, yellow to pink in color, turning salmon pink during the winter; it measures 0.15 to 0.17 mm long by 0.05 to 0.06 mm wide.

Artificial control

The maple spindlegall mite can be controlled using the same methods as those outlined for the maple bladdergall mite.

An eriophyid
Plate 80

The last species is an eriophyid, *Aceria regulus* (Hodge) and attacks sugar maple, silver maple, and red maple; it occurs throughout eastern North America.

Description

The gall caused by this mite is usually located on the upper side of the leaves but, it may also be found on the underside, which distinguishes it from that of the maple bladdergall mite and the maple spindlegall mite. It takes the form of a little glossy oval or round mass; the galls are often found in clusters, forming irregularly shaped white or whitish yellow blotches that gradually turn dark red or purple (Plate 80, I and J). The adult mite is slightly smaller than the first two species mentioned and measures 0.12 to 0.17 mm.

Diagnosis

It is difficult to identify this eriophyid simply by examining the gall, because other types of mite produce similar outgrowths. For positive identification, it is best to refer to a specialist.

Artificial control

This eriophyid can be controlled using the same methods as those outlined for the maple bladdergall mite.

References

Agriculture Canada 1974; Herrick 1935; Hodgkiss 1930; Johnson and Lyon 1976; Johnson and Zepp 1979; Kecber 1946; Smith 1974c; and Turner et al. 1975.

Sugar maple borer
Plate 81

The sugar maple borer, *Glycobius speciosus* (Say), is without question the worst pest of maple in Canada. Its hosts are sugar maple, red maple, and silver maple, but it does not appear to attack Norway maple. It is probably native to North America, and its distribution corresponds almost exactly to the range of its hosts in the central and eastern provinces of Canada; it also extends down into the northeastern United States and southward to the tip of the Appalachians.

Ever since the early days of settlement on this continent, this longhorned beetle has been of serious concern to maple growers in the entire northeastern part of North America because of the extensive damage caused to the trunks of sugar maple.

Description and biology

Adult. Large blue black beetle; elytra marked with four narrow bright yellow bands, one of them in the form of a W; tip of elytron yellow except for one black spot; medium length antennae; body measuring about 27 mm (Plate 81, A).

Egg. Elongated; whitish. Length: about 2 mm.

Larva. Cylindrical, slightly flattened dorsoventrally, legless, pinkish red except for brown mouth parts. Length when full grown: about 50 mm.

Pupa. Similar to adult except for its whitish color.

PLATE 81

Sugar maple borer, *Glycobius speciosus* (Say)

A. Pinned adult (length: 27 mm).
B. Cleaned larval tunnel on sugar maple trunk.
C. Appearance of same sugar maple trunk, 5 years later.
D. Appearance of crown of same sugar maple, 5 years later.
E. Old damage caused by the insect in a maple grove.

A

B

C

D

E

The biology of the sugar maple borer has been known for some time, but many details of its ecology and the damage it causes have yet to be clarified.

The life cycle of the sugar maple borer lasts 24 months, covering part of three calendar years. Adults are present on trees from the end of June until September. The females lay their eggs during July and August; these are laid in bark crevices, under scales, near wounds, or in slits made by the female, generally in the lower 9 m of the trunk (Plate 81, B and C). On hatching, the larvae penetrate directly into the bark and construct individual tunnels at the surface of the sapwood and contrary to the grain of the wood; these tunnels are kept constantly clear of sawdust. In the fall, the larva builds a small cell in the wood where it spends the first winter. The following spring, it continues its tunnel along the wood surface, but this time following the grain, until the second fall, by which time it is nearing maturity. It then extends its tunnel to a depth of about 10 cm towards the interior of the wood and builds at the deepest end a second chamber where it spends the second winter. The following spring, it transforms to a pupa and then to an adult.

Damage and diagnosis

The main damage by the sugar maple borer is caused by the larvae, whereas the adults confine themselves to gnawing the tender bark of twigs. The larvae may measure up to 15 mm wide. Their tunnels are, for the most part, located in the most valuable part of the trunk. Moreover, because they run partly with the grain and partly against it, the tunnels inhibit sap circulation and cause a decrease in vitality of the tree and even some mortality of branches (Plate 81, D). Experience has shown that as few as three or four tunnels may kill a tree.

Affected trees are easily recognized by the presence of long, more-or-less voluminous swellings at the surface of the bark, which finally crack open and form an ugly, open wound (Plate 81, E). The onset of an attack may be detected by the presence of little heaps of sawdust soaked with sap, from freshly bored tunnels near areas where the eggs were laid.

Natural control

No information has as yet been published on factors that might check attacks by the sugar maple borer.

Artificial control

Direct control of the sugar maple borer presents great difficulties because of the habits of the larvae. Some simple silvicultural practices may, however, limit the possibility of attack. Inside maple groves, over-cutting should be avoided and animals should be prevented from grazing. On the other hand severely affected trees or branches should be cut as early as possible and should be burned before the adults emerge.

Valuable ornamental trees may be protected by attempting to kill the larva in its tunnel by inserting a wire into the entry hole and pushing it right to the end. Larvae may also be destroyed in tunnels by injecting a poisonous gas with a syringe, and then blocking the tunnel off with grafting wax or damp soil. It is more practical, however, to examine maple trunks in the summer to find new tunnels the location of which is revealed by an outflow of sap mixed with particles of bark; the larva can then be located by following the tunnel through the bark with a knife, and be destroyed.

Finally, one could prevent adults from laying their eggs in the trunks by applying a stomach or contact insecticide during the summer. Open wounds, particularly on aging maples, should not be neglected, but should be covered with grafting wax.

References

Baker 1972; Herrick 1935; Hesterberg et al. 1976; Johnson and Lyon 1976; Johnson and Zepp 1978; MacAloney 1971; Shigo et al. 1973; and Talerico 1962.

Table 11. Other insects harmful to maple — Other insects that are regarded as pests of maple are listed in this table. For some insects, their characteristics are described in the chapter that applies to their primary host, and in such cases, that chapter (in Roman numerals) and the appropriate plate numbers are given. For other insects, a plate number alone is shown; and for the remaining insects, this table provides the only information.

Common and scientific names	Hosts (chap.)	Plate no.	Type of insect	Destructive stages	Period of activity	Importance*
Basswood leafroller *Exartema nigranum* Heinr.	Maple	—	Defoliator	Larva	May and June	C
Boxelder leafworm *Chionodes obscurusella* (Cham.)	Maple, oak	—	Defoliator	Larva	May and June	C
Carpenterworm *Prionoxystus robiniae* (Peck)	Hardwoods	—	Borer	Larva	May to Oct.	C
Fall webworm *Hyphantria cunea* (Drury)	Elm (IX)	84	—	—	—	B
Forest tent caterpillar *Malacosoma disstria* Hbn.	Poplar (X)	91	—	—	—	A
Gypsy moth *Lymantria dispar* (L.)	Birch (VI)	46	—	—	—	A
Leafroller, a *Sparganothis xanthoides* (Wlk.)	Maple	—	Leafroller	Larva	May to Aug.	C
Lesser maple spanworm *Itame pustularia* (Guen.)	Maple	—	Defoliator	Larva	May to Aug.	C
Maple shoot borer *Proteoteras moffatiana* Fern.	Maple	82	Borer	Larva	May and June	C
Maple trumpet skeletonizer *Epinotia aceriella* Clem.	Sugar maple, red maple	83	Leafroller skeletonizer	Larva	July to Oct.	C
Obliquebanded leafroller *Choristoneura rosaceana* (Harr.)	Hardwoods	—	Leafroller	Larva	May to Sept.	C
Pitted ambrosia beetle *Corthylus punctatissimus* Zimm.	Maple	—	Borer	Adult and nymph	July to Sept.	B
Rearhumped caterpillar *Amphipyra pyramidoides* Guen.	Hardwoods	—	Defoliator	Larva	May to Aug.	C
Spring cankerworm *Paleacrita vernata* (Peck)	Elm (IX)	87	—	—	—	C
Woolly alder aphid *Paraprociphilus tessellatus* (Fitch)	Alder, maple	—	Sucker	Adult and nymph	May to Oct.	B

*A: Of major importance, capable of killing or severely damaging trees.
B: Of moderate importance, capable of sporadic and localized injury to trees.
C: Of minor importance, not known to present a threat to living trees.

A

B

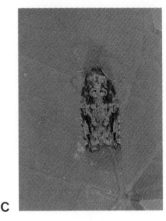

C

D

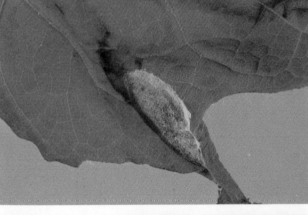

E

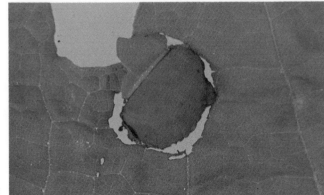

F

PLATE 82

Maple shoot borer, *Proteoteras moffatiana* Fern.

A. Young larva getting out of shoot.
B. Appearance of shoot after damage.
C. Moth at rest.
D. Pupa.
E. Cocoon spun by the larva in folded leaf.
F. Cocoon cut before leaf drop.

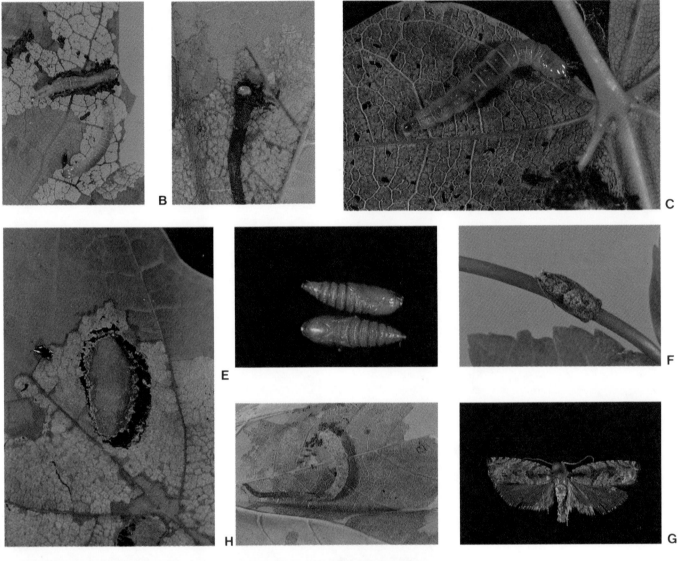

PLATE 83

Maple trumpet skeletonizer, *Epinotia aceriella* Clem.

A. Young larva.
B. Tube built by larva.
C. Mature larva
   (length: about 9 mm).
D. Pupal case seen from upper leaf surface.
E. Pupae out of their cases.
F. and G.   Moth newly emerged on sugar maple leaf and pinned adult (wingspan: 1.5 mm).
H. Close-up of damage.
I. Appearance of sugar maple leaves after damage.

CHAPTER IX
Insects harmful to elm

Eighteen species of elm (*Ulmus*) are native to North America. Three of these species grow in Canada and are all found east of the Rocky Mountains. Their ranges vary however; whereas all three species are found in southern Quebec and Ontario, none is present in the province of Newfoundland, and only white elm (*U. americana* L.), grows naturally in the Maritime provinces. White elm is the most common and has the widest distribution. Its range extends throughout the whole southern part of Ontario and Quebec, New Brunswick, Prince Edward Island, and Nova Scotia. Rock elm (*U. thomasii* Sarg.) is the second most common, with a range limited to part of the southeast tip of Ontario and extending east to the Montreal area in Quebec along a narrow band bordering the Ottawa River and the St. Lawrence River. Slippery elm (*U. rubra* Mühl.) is even less common and is confined to a thin strip stretching along the St. Lawrence River, from Lake Erie in Ontario to Île d'Orléans in Quebec. Besides these three, several species have been introduced from Europe and Asia for use as ornamentals.

As in the case of oak, the gross merchantable volume is not presented independently in the Canadian Forestry Service reports (Bonnor 1982).

White elm is a very elegant tree growing up to 38 m high and 2 m in diameter. Its trunk is straight, forking at a fair distance from the ground into three or four large limbs which, in turn, branch out and terminate in twigs that curve downward giving the overall impression of a huge umbrella. It is a very adaptable tree, and grows as well in damp areas as it does in well-drained ground, with the exception of sandy and dry soils.

The two other species of elm are less well known; they grow to a maximum of 20 m in height and 60 to 90 cm in diameter. Rock elm has an oblong crown and the trunk does not divide, but rather has branches almost up to the top that project horizontally. It grows in a variety of soils. Slippery elm, on the contrary, is similar in appearance to white elm, although its dimensions are smaller and twigs tend to be widespreading and point upwards. It grows well in rich soils along streams and tolerates dry, rocky ground.

Elm wood is hard, heavy, strong, and resistant to splitting. It is used for many purposes, notably in making barrels, furniture, boxes, crates, hockey sticks, railway ties, flooring, piano frames, boat frames, and dock fenders.

Before the outbreak of Dutch elm disease, this tree was highly sought after as an ornamental because of its attractive appearance and the quality of its shade; in fact, elm trees were the pride of many North American cities. Unfortunately, elm has many serious enemies, the most important of which is Dutch elm disease, caused by a fungus, *Ceratocystis ulmi* (Buism.) C. Moreau. Since this disease was discovered in Canada in 1944, elm has gradually lost its popularity as an ornamental because of its susceptibility and consequent destruction of huge numbers of trees. All species of elm are affected, although certain strains show some resistance to the disease. Scolytids have contributed to the decline of elm by spreading the fungus that causes the disease. A number of omnivorous insects, sap-suckers and wood borers also cause some spectacular damage, but their action does not generally have serious consequences.

Fall webworm
Plate 84

The fall webworm, *Hyphantria cunea* (Drury), is one of the rare native North American insects to have been accidentally introduced into Europe and Asia. Until recently, one race of this species was considered as a distinct entity and designated by the name *H. textor*, but it is now known that the difference in the coloring of the larvae by which the two races can be distinguished is simply the result of environmental factors. This insect occurs throughout North America, from the southern United States to the 55th parallel in Canada. In North America, more than 100 different tree species are known to be hosts of this insect, but its preferred hosts vary from region to region. In the Maritime provinces, the preferred species is alder, although it is also found on cherry, ash, Manitoba maple, apple, elm, poplar, birch, and willow. In Quebec, the insect has a predilection for elm and pin cherry.

History of outbreaks

Periodic outbreaks of the fall webworm occur in the eastern and central parts of North America. Morris (1964) states that 14 outbreaks of this gregarious tent caterpillar occurred between 1770 and 1961, at intervals of about 12 years, with an average duration of 5 years. Since the Forest Insect Survey (FIS) was created in 1936, four outbreaks have been recorded: that is, from 1939 to 1941, from 1946 to 1950, from 1956 to 1961 and from 1968 to 1975. In each case, all the eastern Canadian provinces were involved with the exception of Newfoundland.

Description and biology

Adult. Medium-sized moth; completely white, occasionally with black spots. Wingspan: 25-42 mm (Plate 84, E).

Egg. Globular, laid in irregular greenish masses covered with white hairs.

Larva. Cylindrical; basically pale yellow to greenish, with a dark medio-dorsal line and a yellow line running down each side; body covered with long gray hairs growing from black or orange tubercles. Length: 25 mm (Plate 84, B and C).

Pupa. Obtect; reddish brown; enclosed in a gray silken cocoon rounded at both ends and covered with hairs (Plate 84, D).

The fall webworm produces only one generation per year in Canada, which is in the northern part of its distribution, whereas it may have up to four in the south. In regions where one generation occurs per year, moths are present in the field from the end of May until the month of July. Eggs are laid next to one another in groups of 200 to 500, on the underside of leaves, and are covered with white hairs from the female's abdomen. Incubation lasts from 10 to 15 days. On hatching, newborn larvae from a given egg cluster begin to feed in a group on the leaf surface and, at the same time, spin a web of silken threads to protect themselves (Plate 84, A).The larvae extend the web as required, and eventually form a nest encompassing several branches and sometimes measuring 1 m in length. These webs are sometimes so numerous on a single tree that the crown seems to be enveloped in a veil. Larvae are present from June until October and develop in the web until the sixth and final instar. At this point, they cease to be gregarious, and leave the web in search of a place in which to spin individual cocoons, generally in bark crevices, in the litter, or in the soil at depths of up to 2 cm. The insect overwinters in the pupal stage in its cocoon and transforms to an adult during the following spring.

Damage and diagnosis

Damage by the fall webworm takes the form of webs spun by the larvae. The webs are especially numerous in hedges, open stands, and trees located along streets or roads (Plate 84, F and G), but are rare in dense forests, even where these contain the preferred host trees. Although sometimes spectacular, the damage generally has little effect on the vitality of the tree, because the loss of foliage occurs at the end of the season, when annual growth has ceased. The presence of unsightly tents containing excreta, exuviae, and dried leaves does, however, detract considerably from the appearance of those trees planted as ornamentals. Tents may be seen in August and September, and traces may be found on leafless trees even in winter.

An attack by this insect is easily recognized by the presence, in August and September, of large numbers of tents in the crowns of host trees. Examination of the contents of the tent reveals yellow-to-brown hairy larvae feeding on the green foliage of branches caught in the web. The intensity of attack may be predicted and population fluctuations followed from year to year using a technique developed by Morris and Bennett (1967) that consists in taking an annual count of the average number of tents seen along roadsides.

Natural control

Many studies have been carried out in an attempt to determine the causes of death of fall webworm larvae, both in Europe and North America. In North America, the number of predatory and parasitic species that attack this insect is close to a hundred, and there are probably as many in Europe. In a series of in-depth studies carried out in the Maritimes, Morris (1964, 1971, 1972a and b, 1976a and b; and Morris and Bennett 1967) showed that predators played an important role in the control, particularly birds and wasps. Larvae were also affected, although less seriously, by insect predators and spiders living right inside the web. Morris also observed that pupae in the ground were preyed upon by small insect-eating mammals. There are also a number of insect parasites that attack the fall webworm. Morris alone reported 13 species of insect parasites, although their action is hampered by the fact that some of them are highly polyphagous and also that the fall webworm has developed a certain resistance to others by building capsules around eggs and larvae. Raizenne (1952) obtained 16 species of parasites in his rearings in Ontario, and 14 species were obtained by the FIDS in the Quebec region. Further south, Nordin et al. (1972) reported that, in Illinois, five species of entomophagous parasites were responsible for destroying about 35 percent of the larval population.

A number of pathogenic microorganisms have also been found on this species, notably microsporidia and viruses. Nordin et al. (1972) determined that, in 43 percent of the colonies sampled, there were from one to four pathogens. In

PLATE 84

**Fall webworm, *Hyphantria cunea*
(Drury)**

A. Young larvae in the web.
B. Side view of larva.
C. Dorsal view of larva
   (length: 25 mm).
D. Pupa.
E. Moth at rest
   (wingspan: 25-42 mm).
F. Severely damaged mature ash.
G. Young ash tree covered with
   webs.

195

laboratory tests, Smirnoff (1976) succeeded in contaminating this species with certain microorganisms isolated from other lepidoptera.

Artificial control

The organization of control programs using artificial methods against the fall webworm is feasible only for small areas. On a few small trees, branches bearing webs may be cut and burned when the larvae are still young. As soon as tents are observed, the foliage may also be sprayed with a chemical or biological stomach insecticide having a residual effect, to kill the larvae before they cause too much damage. Once the larvae have left the web in search of a sheltered spot, it is usually too late.

Larvae may also be destroyed using one of the pathogenic microorganisms isolated from the fall webworm, which have proved effective in previous outbreaks. This is done by collecting infested material and making a watery mixture that is then poured onto the young larval populations.

References

Daviault 1950a; Durkin 1972; Kaya 1977; McGugan 1958; Morris 1964, 1971, 1972a, 1972b, 1976a, 1976b; Morris and Bennett 1967; Nordin et al. 1972; Raizenne 1952; and Smirnoff 1976.

Mourningcloak butterfly
Plate 85

The mourningcloak butterfly, *Nymphalis antiopa* (L.), also called the spiny elm caterpillar, is a gregarious defoliator and is very common in this country. It occurs throughout North America, as far north as the Arctic circle. Its preferred hosts are elm, willow, and trembling aspen, but other hardwoods are attacked during epidemics. This insect is of minor importance in forests, and is mainly a pest on trees planted as ornamentals on city streets and in parks. Short-lived outbreaks have been reported occasionally, mostly on elm, in all provinces of eastern Canada since the start of the Forest Insect Survey in 1936. In Newfoundland, willow and trembling aspen are the most affected hosts, because elm is not a species native to that province.

Description and biology

Adult. Large black-bodied butterfly; upper side of wings dark reddish brown ending in a yellow band following a line of blue spots; frontal part of the forewing marked with a broken line followed by two yellow spots. Wingspan: 60-80 mm (Plate 85, G).

Egg. Cylindrical; laid in clusters; golden yellow with concentric ridges (Plate 85, B and C).

Larva. Cylindrical; head bilobate and black; body black sprinkled with white spots and covered with many forked spines; dorsum of abdominal segments 1 to 7 and base of abdominal legs bear orange red dot. Length when full grown: 50-58 mm (Plate 85, F).

Chrysalid. Angular conch-shaped; light-colored with powder blue shades, double row of spines on the side (Plate 85, D).

In eastern Canada, the mourningcloak butterfly generally has only one generation per year, but a second generation is occasionally produced at the end of the summer, although it usually goes unnoticed, because it causes very little damage. It spends winter in the adult stage (Plate 85, A). The butterflies become active again during the first days of spring and lay their eggs during May and June. The eggs are laid neatly next to one another so as to encircle a small twig in a sort of ring that may be up to 50 mm long. Incubation lasts about 2 weeks and, on hatching, the larvae crawl to the leaves. They feed in tight clusters (Plate 85, E), first chewing the green matter of the leaves between the veins, and then devouring the entire leaf with the exception of the main rib. They consume all the leaves of one branch before moving to another. Defoliated branches are generally scattered throughout the crown, except during epidemics, when the entire crown may be stripped of its foliage. Towards the end of June, the larvae reach maturity; they stop feeding, disperse, and attach themselves to the lower part of a twig, branch, or other object where they transform to chrysalids. Two weeks later, the butterflies appear and may be seen flying about from July until fall. In certain areas, some butterflies lay eggs that give rise to a second generation. Adults present in early fall hibernate in places sheltered from bad weather.

PLATE 85

Mourningcloak butterfly, *Nymphalis antiopa* (L.)

A Butterfly on trembling aspen foliage (wingspan: 60-80 mm).
B. Sound eggs on twig.
C. Hatched eggs.
D. Chrysalid hanging with exuvia of caterpillar.
E. Young caterpillars on white elm leaf.
F. Side view of mature larva (length: 50-58 mm).
G. Adult resting on a flower.
H. Defoliation of willow by larva.

A

F

G

B

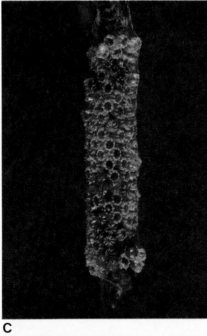

C

H

D

E

Damage and diagnosis

Initial damage by the mourningcloak butterfly consists in small holes or slits made in the leaves by the young larvae. Later they consume the entire leaf. When populations are small, only a few branches scattered through the crown are stripped, whereas during a severe outbreak crowns may be totally defoliated (Plate 85, H).

An attack by this lepidoptera is easily recognizable in early summer by the presence of branches or crowns that have been completely stripped by colonies of black caterpillars with red spots and many forked spines. Diagnosis may be confirmed by the presence of bands of hatched eggs on the twigs of defoliated branches. An attack may be predicted for the following year when free, naked chrysalids in the shape of angular conches are seen hanging from twigs.

Natural control

A number of regulating factors are usually able to check populations of the mourningcloak butterfly in a fairly short time. In the United States, Herrick (1935) observed five species of insect parasites. In Canada, Raizenne (1952) reported five additional parasites in Ontario; five species were also observed in Quebec, including three already mentioned by Raizenne. One of the species encountered in both Ontario and Quebec, *Compsilura concinnata* Meig., is a tachinid fly imported into Canada in 1912 and 1916 and now well established on a number of lepidoptera notably on the satin moth, *Leucoma salicis*.

Two insect and two bird species are mentioned as predators by Herrick (1935) for the United States. In Quebec, birds have often been observed feeding on larvae.

Artificial control

The best way of preventing damage by the mourningcloak butterfly on a few small trees is to crush the bands of sound eggs where they can be seen easily on branches. If caterpillars are confined to a few branches, these branches may be cut and the insects destroyed. When large, hard-to-reach trees must be protected, or when the outbreak is severe, it is recommended that foliage be sprayed with a chemical stomach, contact, or a biological insecticide, as soon as caterpillars appear in June and July.

References

Baker 1972; Becker 1938; Herrick 1935; McGugan 1958; Raizenne 1952; and Smirnoff and Juneau 1973.

Elm leaf beetle
Plate 86

The elm leaf beetle, *Pyrrhalta luteola* (Müll.), is of European origin and was first identified in North America in 1838. It now occurs throughout almost the entire range of elm in Canada and the United States. It lives on all native species of elm, but European species are usually more susceptible. This leaf beetle causes little damage in forests and is more of a pest on elms growing in cities and near houses.

History of outbreaks

In Canada, the elm leaf beetle was first recorded in southern Ontario in 1945 and, from that date on, local outbreaks were recorded almost every year up to 1960; the insect is now well distributed throughout southern Ontario. In 1949, four years after its discovery in Ontario, a severe epidemic broke out in a limited area of the Maritime provinces and lasted until 1951; since that time, only one outbreak, described as moderate-to-severe, occurred in five localities in New Brunswick and Nova Scotia. In Quebec, this insect first caused damage in a fairly large area in the southern part of the province in 1954, and since that time outbreaks have been reported in only a few localities.

Description and biology

Adult. Leaf beetle with greenish yellow body and a black band on the side of the elytra; antennae and legs yellow. Length: 6 mm (Plate 86, C).

Egg. Spindle-shaped; orange to yellow, laid in irregular-shaped clusters (Plate 86, D).

Larva. Elongated, rather wide body; basic color yellow with black tubercles and many black hairs; head and legs black. Length: 12 mm (Plate 86, F).

Pupa. Almost oval in shape; bright orange yellow. Length: 5 mm (Plate 86, B).

In the northeastern part of the continent, the elm leaf beetle may have one or two generations per year depending on temperature and location; further south, the number of generations increases and there are up to five in California.

A

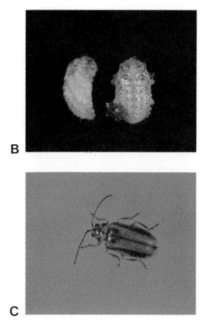

B

C

E

D

F

In eastern Canada, the insect normally has only one generation per year. It over-winters in the adult stage in various shelters, notably bark crevices, cracks in the ground, or inside buildings such as sheds, barns, and house attics. Occasionally, during winter thaws, the adults temporarily become active, but it is only when the elm buds open in the spring that they awake for good and fly to the crowns to feed on the leaves which they pierce with many tiny holes. The females lay all their eggs at the end of May or the beginning of June, in several small clusters of 5 to 25 eggs on the underside of the leaves. Incubation lasts about 1 week and on hatching the newborn larvae eat voraciously the under surface and the parenchyma of the leaves, leaving the upper surface and the ribs intact. The larvae feed for 2-3 weeks and, once they are fully grown, they crawl to the base of the trunk or drop to the ground where they gather and pupate on or near the trunk. About 10 days later, the adults appear and fly to the foliage where they feed for a time. During this time they seek a shelter in which to pass the winter. Certain years, however, when weather conditions are favorable, some of the adults lay eggs that give rise to a second generation of larvae, but they do not usually have time to develop fully before cold weather sets in.

PLATE 86

Elm leaf beetle, *Pyrrhalta luteola* (Müll.)

A. Crown of affected elm.
B. Pupa. (length: 5 mm).
C. Adult. (length: 6 mm).
D. Egg cluster on an elm leaf.
E. Young larvae and their damage on an elm leaf.
F. Mature larvae (length: 12 mm).

Damage and diagnosis

Damage is caused by both the adults and larvae of the elm leaf beetle (Plate 86, A). In the spring and fall the adults chew round or oval holes in the lamina of the leaves, but, because these holes are scattered about the lamina, they are usually of minor importance. Damage caused by the larvae, however, is much more serious (Plate 86, E), because they are extremely voracious and quickly reduce the leaves to their upper surface and ribs; the leaves dry, turn brown, and fall. In severe outbreaks, defoliation is often complete. Early in the season, trees do not suffer too much damage because they can produce a new crop of foliage, but if the second foliage is destroyed by a second generation of the pest, the health of the trees may be jeopardized. Fortunately, in eastern Canada, damage by a second generation is rare and often goes unnoticed.

Some adult beetles, which take shelter in house attics, occasionally become active during the winter and can be a nuisance.

An attack by the elm leaf beetle may be identified in the summer by the browning and drying out of elm leaves. Examination of the underside of the leaf blade reveals the presence of many feeding larvae. Later, large numbers of bright orange yellow pupae, or yellow to olive green adults, may be seen at the base of trunks or near the foot of elm trees.

Natural control

The natural enemies of the elm leaf beetle are fairly numerous. Among predators are toads, insect-eating birds, and many species of insect. In Oklahoma, in the south-central United States, Eikenbary and Raney (1968) observed 12 species of insect predators attacking all stages of the elm leaf beetle. Parasites seem to be less well known, and only one species deserves attention; this is a little chalcid fly, *Tetrastichus brevistigma* Gahan, commonly obtained from pupae in the northeastern United States. According to Herrick (1935) a fungus, *Sporotrichum proliferum,* may be responsible for mortality among pupae and adults in late summer, especially during damp seasons.

Artificial control

Various methods of control have been tested against the elm leaf beetle, especially in the southern United States, where several generations of the insect occur each year. The method most often recommended consists of spraying the foliage with a chemical stomach or contact insecticide in the spring, either to destroy adults during the feeding period before egg-laying, or to wipe out larvae when they are feeding. In the latter case, care must be taken to cover the underside of the leaves with insecticide.

Tests show that systemic insecticides applied by injection into the trunk or by soaking the trunks and the ground around the base of trees give protection which lasts several months. This treatment also has the advantage of not requiring complicated equipment.

Good results have also been obtained by destroying the larvae when they gather at the base of trunks to pupate, by spraying them with a chemical contact insecticide. Larvae may also be destroyed when they have become immobile or transformed to pupae simply by pouring boiling water or light oil on them.

It is also possible to eliminate those adults that shelter in buildings when they emerge in the springtime. This is done by covering most chinks and cracks with black paper and the remainder with transparent cellophane coated on the inside with a sticky substance.

References

Becker 1938; Brewer 1973; Eikenbary and Raney 1968; Herrick 1935; Saunders 1971; U.S. Department of Agriculture 1960; and Wene 1968, 1970.

Spring cankerworm
Plate 87

The spring cankerworm, *Paleacrita vernata* (Peck), is so called because of the early appearance of its moths, and is another native leaf eater known from the earliest days of settlement in Canada. This highly polyphagous insect attacks more than forty species of hardwoods, including forest trees, fruit trees, and ornamental shrubs, but its preferred hosts are elm, apple, and basswood. It occurs throughout a wide range stretching from Nova Scotia to Saskatchewan in Canada, and as far south as South Carolina and Colorado, and even into California, in the United States. Outbreaks take much the same form as those of the fall cankerworm (*Alsophila pometaria*) and are characterized by their sporadic appearance and short duration although the area covered may sometimes be large.

History of outbreaks

Outbreaks of the spring cankerworm have occurred in all the provinces of eastern Canada except Newfoundland. In the Maritime provinces, the insect has caused damage to elm almost every year since 1948, although in New Brunswick the first outbreak was reported only in 1966. In Quebec, the insect caused severe damage in maple groves around 1943, then the outbreak disappeared suddenly apparently due to a viral disease. Since that time, only a few very localized outbreaks have been reported, generally on elm. In Ontario, local outbreaks have occurred almost every year since 1941 on various deciduous species, elm in particular. In all regions of eastern Canada, this cankerworm is usually found together with other common loopers, particularly the fall cankerworm, so that it is often difficult to establish exactly to what extent each species is responsible for the damage caused.

Description and biology

Adult. Moth displaying very marked sexual dimorphism; male medium-sized with normal wings; forewings gray brown and hindwings ashen gray. Wingspan: 21-30 mm (Plate 87, A). Female wingless, covered with hairs ranging in color from gray to brown to black, with a black band down the middle of the back. Length: about 10 mm (Plate 87, B).

Egg. Oval in shape, slightly rippled; white to yellow with pink highlights (Plate 87, D).

Larva. Cylindrical, very delicate, varying from gray to brown to black; body sometimes striped with fine lengthwise lines; three central abdominal segments dorsally marked with a distinctive black X; abdomen with only two pairs of prolegs. Length: 18-30 mm (Plate 87 E, F and G).

Pupa. Obtect; body brown and wings greenish (Plate 87, C).

Only one generation of the spring cankerworm occurs per year. Moths appear in early spring, right after the ground has thawed, the males shortly before the females. On emerging, the females crawl up the tree trunks and lay their eggs in cracks in the bark; the males fly low around the trunk in search of females to fertilize. Each female may lay up to 400 eggs, in small clusters of a few dozen. Larvae hatch during the month of May and, on leaving the eggs, crawl towards the ends of branches. The first ones feed by chewing tiny holes in the buds and leaves. Once they have grown to a certain size, they eat the entire leaf with the exception of the main ribs. When disturbed, the larvae drop down on silken threads which they spin as they go, until they reach another place to feed. Larval development lasts 4-5 weeks, and in June the larva drops to the ground, burrows to a depth of 5 to 15 cm, and builds a pupation cell. The pupal stage begins in June, and the insect remains dormant until it transforms to an adult during the following spring.

Damage and diagnosis

All damage is caused by the larva of the spring cankerworm, which begins by perforating the buds and then feeds on the young foliage, eventually going on to consume most of the leaf blade (Plate 87, I). The partially devoured leaves dry and turn brown. During severe outbreaks, total defoliation may occur on the preferred hosts over wide areas. Trees stripped of their foliage for 2 or 3 successive years are weakened, but usually do not die. Because defoliation occurs early in the season, they are able to produce new foliage before the end of the growing season.

An attack by the spring cankerworm is easily recognized by the presence of gray brown moths flitting about trunks as soon as the first thaws occur in spring. Examination of the bark of trunks then reveals the presence of wingless females crawling up in search of a place to lay their eggs. Additional confirmation of this diagnosis is possible by examining the eggs, which may be recognized by their shape and color. If eggs have not yet been laid, they may easily be obtained by pressing the female's abdomen with the fingers. Once the larvae have begun to grow, the presence of black, X-shaped marks on the middle abdominal segments and the number of pairs of prolegs may be checked.

By counting the number of females crawling up the trunks of a certain number of trees, the intensity of an infestation can be predicted as soon as the adults appear in the spring.

Natural control

No major research has yet been undertaken on the factors which intervene to limit populations of the spring cankerworm, no doubt because of the difficulty of following fluctuations in abundance, the short duration of outbreaks, and the limited extent of damage. Because this looper appears very early in the spring, it is known that late frosts may kill young larvae while they are feeding, or else may destroy the foliage on which their survival depends. Parasites seem to be of secondary importance (Plate 87, H), and to date only one species has been obtained from rearings done in Ontario (Raizenne 1952). Pathogenic microorganisms, on the other hand, appear to play a very effective role, and it is known that, in Quebec, a severe outbreak that occurred during the 1940s was wiped out rapidly by the sudden appearance of a disease apparently of a viral nature.

Artificial control

Methods recommended to control the fall cankerworm may also be used against the spring cankerworm, using treatment dates appropriately modified.

References

Baker 1972; Herrick 1935; Jones and Schaffner 1953; Page et al. 1974; Prentice 1963; Raizenne 1952; and Stein 1974.

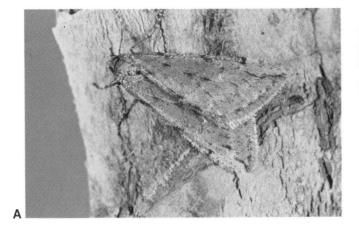

A

B

C

D

E

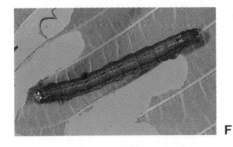

F

G

H

I

PLATE 87

Spring cankerworm, *Paleacrita vernata* (Peck)

A. Adult male at rest
   (wingspan: 21-30 mm).
B. Adult female laying eggs in bark
   crevice (length: 10 mm).
C. Pupa.
D. Row of eggs at the bottom of a
   bark crevice.
E. Dorsal view of light-colored larva, showing the three X-shaped
   marks on middle segments.
F. Dorsal view of dark larva.
G. Side view of larva
   (length: 18-30 mm).
H. Larva bearing hymenopterous
   parasite eggs.
I. Close-up view of affected elm.

Elm bark beetles

Since Dutch elm disease, one of the worst factors plaguing elm, was discovered in North America, insects that might serve as vectors of the fungus, *Ceratocystis ulmi* (Buism.) C. Moreau, responsible for this disease, have taken on enormous importance. In the United States, the disease was first observed in the state of Ohio in 1940, and in Canada near Sorel, Quebec, in 1944. Today, this disease covers a great portion of the geographical range of elm in North America.

Two bark beetles are the main carriers of this disease. In Canada, the one most responsible is the native elm bark beetle, *Hylurgopinus rufipes* (Eichh.), and in the United States, it is the smaller European elm bark beetle, *Scolytus multistriatus* (Marsh.). These two bark beetles, formerly considered of secondary importance in North America, are now recognized as very dangerous in all regions where elm grows as an important element of the environment.

Native elm bark beetle
Plate 88

The native elm bark beetle, *Hylurgopinus rufipes* (Eichh.), is native to North America. In Canada, it is found from Nova Scotia to Saskatchewan, and in the United States, its range covers all the northeastern states and some of the central and southern states. This beetle attacks all species of elm and occasionally basswood and ash.

Description and biology

Adult. Small beetle; cylindrical; brownish black, thinly clothed with short yellow hairs; peg top-shaped antennal club; frontal face of foreleg tibia terminated by a spine. Length: 2.5 mm (Plate 88, E).

Egg. Oblong; pearl white. Length: 0.6 mm.

Larva. Nearly cylindrical, legless, segmented, and curved; head yellowish brown and hard; body creamy white and soft. Length: 3.5-4.0 mm.

Pupa. Similar to adult; body white and soft; wings incomplete or folded under abdomen.

The life cycle of the native elm bark beetle is fairly complex and varies with the region, climatic conditions, and the year. In the Berthierville region of Quebec, Robert studied the species for a number of years (Robert 1948, 1949b, 1952a, b). Although, the insect overwinters in all stages except the egg, it is mainly the adults that hibernate. These adults are individuals hatched in July of the preceding year, most of which have already hibernated in the bark of healthy elms. They appear generally at the end of May, and eggs are laid until the month of July. After emerging, the adults mate in dead or dying trees, and subsequently feed and bore egg galleries in the bark of healthy trees, lightly marking the wood surface. These egg galleries are made up of two divergent sections, in the shape of a wide V (Plate 88, D), and extend against the grain of the wood on either side of the entrance hole. The eggs are distributed on each side of the gallery in niches prepared by the female. Incubation lasts from 6 to 12 days. The young larvae bore individual tunnels perpendicular to the egg gallery. The larval stage lasts about 40 days and usually includes five and sometimes six instars. Once the larva is fully grown, it transforms to a pupa in a tiny cell prepared for this purpose at the end of its tunnel. The pupal stage lasts about 8 to 12 days, and the first adults of the new generation, which appear in July, fly to healthy elms. They feed in galleries that they bore under the bark, before seeking dead or dying wood in which to establish their brood.

Most of these young adults feed until the fall and then move into their hibernation galleries. A few of them, however, construct an egg gallery in September and lay eggs that give rise to a second generation, but their larvae do not have time to reach full development before the winter and must hibernate in the larval stage. These larvae, along with late individuals from the first generation, make up the small percentage of the population that overwinters in the larval stage. All overwintering larvae produce adults in June of the following year, and their descendents reach the adult stage in September, early enough to dig hibernation tunnels.

Damage and diagnosis

Damage by the native elm bark beetle is made up of adult entrance and exit holes and of the system of egg galleries and larval tunnels that inhibit the circulation of the sap. When populations are large the consequences become serious. Robert (1948) stated that an elm of about 1 m in diameter could host more than 1 million of these beetles. Although the damage does not necessarily kill the tree, it is significant because the adult of this species is the main vector of Dutch elm disease in Canada.

The first visible sign of this insect's activity is the presence of red sawdust on the bark in the fall or early spring. To confirm the diagnosis, one has only to examine the inside of the bark; if egg galleries have two branches forming an obtuse "V" and extend across the grain of the wood, i.e., almost horizontally, the insect is surely the native elm bark beetle.

Natural control

Little research has been done on the factors that control the native elm bark beetle in North America. It appears, however, that climate, in particular low temperature, plays a major role in determining the number of generations and kills a large percentage of the hibernating individuals. Periods of drought during the summer may also have a disastrous effect on eggs in branches and logs. Competition between individuals of the same family and with other bark insects also reduces the populations, especially if these are large.

In Canada, the main parasite of the native elm bark beetle is the braconid, *Spathius canadensis* Ashm., but it is always rare. The predator, *Enocleris rufiventris* Spin., on the other hand, is very abundant in certain areas (Robert 1952a). Attempts have been made to introduce European species to complement this biological control, but no conclusive results have as yet been obtained.

Artificial control

Control programs against the native elm bark beetle are mainly directed to destroying adults to prevent the spread of the disease. Huge sums of money have been spent for this purpose in North America, especially in the United States, but most of the methods tested have given only partial or temporary results.

Preventive measures are intended to eliminate quickly any material in which the bark beetles could breed:

- Cut and burn all elms showing signs of infection;
- Prune elms of all material in which bark beetles could breed, burn the debris, and dress open wounds;
- Debark stumps and logs kept for fuel at the time of felling;
- Burn all elm wood that has not been debarked before the first of May;
- Treat all unburned or unbarked elm wood with a chemical insecticide having a residual action;
- Do not tolerate the presence of cut or damaged elm wood near live elms;
- Try to catch adults by using trap trees well selected and carefully watched: These trees are felled in time to make them attractive to adults when they fly, and are visited every week to see if insects are present and to take proper measures; and
- Prevent transfer of elm wood from a diseased area into other areas by applying measures for appropriate quarantine.

Finally an attempt may be made to protect healthy trees in a given sector by spraying them with an appropriate insecticide, taking care to treat all elms in a radius of 200 m from any known point of infection. The treatment consists in spraying a residual-action chemical on the bark, using adequate equipment and trained personnel, when the trees are still dormant in the spring.

The use of this method over a 20-year period in an area of New Brunswick where the native elm bark beetle was the only vector of the disease maintained the losses to the low level of 5 percent whereas 60 percent of the elm population was hit in neighboring untreated areas (Van Sickle and Sterner 1976).

Smaller European elm bark beetle
Plate 88

Unlike the native elm bark beetle, the smaller European elm bark beetle, *Scolytus multistriatus* (Marsh.), is an insect that was accidentally introduced into America. Its presence was first reported in Massachusetts, in the United States in 1909, and the insect is now fairly common in all states east of the Rocky Mountains as well as in several states farther west. In Canada, its presence was first reported in 1946 in Ontario, where its range is reported to have increased slightly every year. In Quebec, the insect was not reported until 1970 and appears to be progressing rather slowly. In the Maritime provinces, its presence is now suspected, because it has been captured in a trap set especially for that purpose.

The smaller European elm bark beetle is much more aggressive than the native elm bark beetle and when both species are established in a given region, the former gets ahead rapidly, as has been the case in the United States. In Canada, however, the insect has difficulty getting established under the harder climatic conditions.

Description and biology

Morphologically the smaller European elm bark beetle is similar to the native elm bark beetle. However, two characteristics distinguish the adults: first, the antennal club on the smaller European elm bark beetle is shaped like a pear rather than like a peg-top, and secondly, it is the back of the front tibia that ends with a spine (Plate 88, C).

The biology of the two species differ slightly. In Canada, the smaller European elm bark beetle produces one or two generations per year depending on weather conditions in the area. The insect overwinters in the larval stage under the bark of dead or dying elms, or on branches or felled logs. In the spring, the larvae transform into pupae and then into adults, which make up the so-called summer flight, seen during June and July. After their emergence, they fly from possibly contaminated elms to nearby healthy elms where they feed on the bark, usually in the crotches of twigs, but they

may reach the tissues of the wood and thus contaminate them. After feeding for some time, the females move to the trunks and bore individual egg galleries along the grain of the wood in weakened or damaged elms or in felled wood (Plate 88, B). Once each gallery is complete, the female lays her eggs on each side of it (Plate 88, F), and the larvae which hatch construct individual tunnels at right angles to the egg gallery (Plate 88, G). Some of these larvae do not have time to reach full development before the fall and immediately hibernate (Plate 88, H). The earlier larvae reach the adult stage by August or early September (Plate 88, I, J, and K). These adults, which make up the fall flight, may either produce a second generation, which reaches the larval stage before winter, or simply feed for a certain period of time and then die of cold.

Damage and diagnosis

Damage caused by the smaller European elm bark beetle resembles that of the native elm bark beetle except that the adults puncture the twigs rather than the trunk.

An attack by this insect may be recognized by the form and orientation of the egg galleries, which do not branch out and are parallel to the wood grain. It is also possible to find punctures made by adults in the bark of twig crotches.

Natural control

The smaller European elm bark beetle has had little research done on factors that control it in the natural state. However, it's known to be particularly susceptible to low temperatures. Few species of parasites have been obtained, and these only in small quantities.

Artificial control

The methods of controlling the smaller European elm bark beetle are the same as those described for the native elm bark beetle.

References

Barger and Hock 1971; Canadian Forestry Service 1974f; Cannon and Worsley 1976; Finnegan 1957; Kaston 1936, 1939; Robert 1948, 1949b, 1952a, 1952b; Van Sickle and Sterner 1976; Whitten 1958; and Whitten and Reeks 1973.

A

B

D

C

E

F

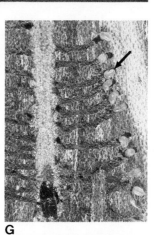

G

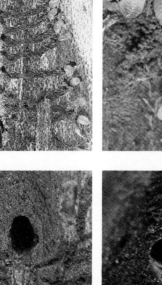

H

I

J

K

PLATE 88

Native elm bark beetle, *Hylurgopinus rufipes* (Eichh.), and smaller European elm bark beetle, *Scolytus multistriatus* (Marsh.)

A. Appearance of healthy elms.
B. *S. multistriatus* gallery on elm trunk.
C. Side view of *S. multistriatus* adult.
D. *H. rufipes* gallery on elm trunk.
E. Side view of *H. rufipes* adult (length: 2.5 mm).
F. *S. multistriatus* eggs on side of egg gallery.
G. Young *S. multistriatus* larvae in larval tunnels.
H. Mature *S. multistriatus* larvae.
I. *S. multistriatus* adult at gallery entrance.
J. and K. Appearance of *S. multistriatus* exit hole at wood surface and at bark surface.

205

Table 12. Other insects harmful to elm — Other insects that are regarded as pests of elm are listed in this table. For some insects, their characteristics are described in the chapter that applies to their primary host, and in such cases, that chapter (in Roman numerals) and the appropriate plate numbers are given. For other insects, a plate number alone is shown; and for the remaining insects, this table provides the only information.

Common and scientific names	Hosts (chap.)	Plate no.	Type of insect	Destructive stages	Period of activity	Importance*
Elm borer *Saperda tridentata* Oliv.	Elm	—	Borer	Larva	May to Oct.	C
Elm casebearer *Coleophora ulmifoliella* McD.	Elm	—	Defoliator	Larva	May to Sept.	C
Elm flea beetle *Altica ulmi* Woods	Elm	103	Defoliator	Adult and larva	July to Oct.	B
Elm lace bug *Corythucha ulmi* O. and D.	Elm	—	Sucker	Adult and nymph	June to Aug.	B
Elm leafminer *Fenusa ulmi* Sund.	Elm	—	Minor	Larva	May to Oct.	B
European elm scale *Gossyparia spuria* (Mod.)	Elm	—	Sucker	Adult and nymph	April to Sept.	C
European fruit lecanium *Lecanium corni* Bouché	Fruit trees, hardwoods	—	Sucker	Adult and nymph	May to Oct.	B
Fall cankerworm *Alsophila pometaria* (Harr.)	Maple (VIII)	69	—	—	—	C
Forest tent caterpillar *Malacosoma disstria* Hbn.	Poplar (X)	91	—	—	—	A
Gypsy moth *Lymantria dispar* (L.)	Birch (VI)	46	—	—	—	A
Linden looper *Erannis tiliaria* (Harr.)	Maple (VIII)	67	—	—	—	B
Oystershell scale *Lepidosaphes ulmi* (L.)	Fruit trees, hardwoods	—	Sucker	Adult and nymph	May to Oct.	B
Whitemarked tussock moth *Orgyia leucostigma intermedia* Fitch	Maple (VIII)	71	—	—	—	C
Woolly apple aphid *Eriosoma lanigerum* (Hausm.)	Elm, apple	90	Sucker	Adult and nymph	May to Oct.	C
Woolly elm aphid *Eriosoma americanum* (Riley)	Elm	89	Sucker	Adult and nymph	May to Oct.	C

*A: Of major importance, capable of killing or severely damaging trees.
 B: Of moderate importance, capable of sporadic and localized injury to trees.
 C: Of minor importance, not known to present a threat to living trees.

A

C

B

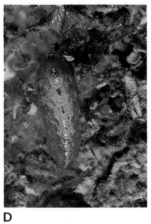

D

E

F

PLATE 89

Woolly elm aphid, *Eriosoma americanum* (Riley)

A. Typical distortion of a damaged elm leaf.
B. Female adult with young nymphs.
C. Group of winged aphids.
D. Larva of *Syrphus* sp. predator among aphids.
E. Adult of same predator near its cocoon.
F. Pupa of same predator.

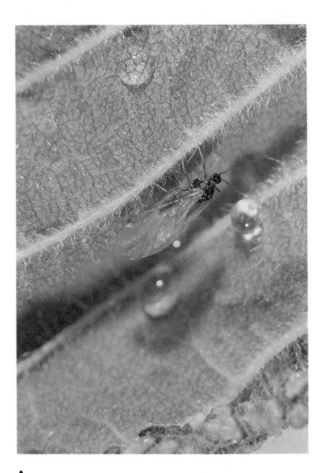

A

B

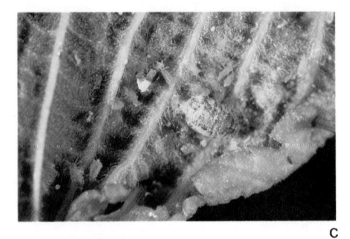

C

D

PLATE 90

Woolly apple aphid, *Eriosoma lanigerum* (Hausm.)

A. Lateral view of adult.
B. Dorsal view of adult.
C. Female adult with young nymphs.
D. Lower side of damaged elm leaves.

CHAPTER X
Insects harmful to poplar

Of six species of poplar, *Populus*, native to Canada, four are found in the eastern provinces. Two of these, trembling aspen (*P. tremuloides* Michx.) and balsam poplar (*P. balsamifera* L.) are distributed throughout, whereas large-tooth aspen (*P. grandidentata* Michx.) grows only in the southern parts of Ontario and Quebec and in the Maritime provinces. The range of eastern cotton-wood (*P. deltoides* Bartr.) is confined to a small area covering part of the upper St. Lawrence valley and the lower Ottawa River valley in Quebec, as well as three small pockets in Ontario, the first one adjacent to Lake Ontario, the second near Lake Erie, and the third near Lake of the Woods.

Besides the native species, a number of introduced poplars are grown in eastern Canada as ornamental trees or for the production of wood. The most common are European white, or silver poplar (*P. alba* L.), Lombardy poplar (*P. nigra* var. *italica* Muenchh.), and Carolina poplar (*P. × canadensis* Moench).

The gross merchantable volume of poplar is estimated at 907 million m^3 in eastern Canada (Bonnor 1982). The portion of this volume inventoried in Ontario and Quebec is 67.1 percent and 28.1 percent respectively.

Trembling aspen is the best known of all eastern poplars because of its abundance, and because its leaves attract attention to the crown by trembling in the slightest breeze. It is a slender tree with a straight trunk and a rounded crown. Its average dimensions are between 12 and 18 m in height and 20 to 30 cm in diameter, although under ideal conditions the tree may attain 27 m in height. This is an adaptable tree, which can grow in a wide variety of soils, although it prefers moist and well-drained sandy or gravelly loams. It grows both in pure stands and mixed with other hardwoods or conifers. In forests, trembling aspen is recognized as an aggressive tree with an astonishing capacity for colonizing cut-over or burned areas; however, it is not particularly tolerant and is succeeded quickly by trees growing in the understory. Its commercial range covers the southern parts of Quebec and Ontario.

Although its range is just as large as that of trembling aspen, balsam poplar is not as well known. It is less abundant in the provinces east of Ontario, where most of its commercial range in eastern Canada is concentrated. It is easily identified during the winter by its sticky, balsam-smelling buds, and in the summer by the color of its leaves; shiny dark green above and whitish green below. Its dimensions are somewhat larger than those of trembling aspen, and it grows in pure or mixed stands in moist, rich ground.

Large tooth aspen is less common than either trembling aspen or balsam poplar, but it is just as easy to identify in the summer, by the widely spaced teeth along its leaf margins. In the open, it has a short trunk and an irregular crown, but in dense forest the trunk lengthens, and the crown is then rounded. This species may grow up to 15 to 18 m high. It grows largest in moist, fertile soils, but tolerates dry, sandy or gravelly ground. Its commercial range in eastern Canada is in the southern parts of Ontario and Quebec.

Eastern cottonwood is not too well known in eastern Canada because of its limited range. In the open, its trunk is short and massive, whereas in dense stands, it has a long, straight trunk topped with a rounded crown. It may reach up to 30 m in height, and usually grows along streams, in pure or mixed stands.

Poplar wood is generally light, soft, and of uniform texture, within distinguishable growth rings. Although of low quality, it is used for a number of purposes. The best logs are used for veneer or lumber, and the rest is used for making crates, barrels, and small articles and for fuel. Poplars are also used as a windbreak because of their rapid growth. Several species are already used for pulpwood, and the prospects appear very good for producing hybrids with which to supply pulp mills in the future.

Poplars are known as quick-growing species, but they are fairly intolerant and have little resistance to unfavorable climatic conditions, with the result that they are short-lived.

Poplars are also susceptible to the action of several enemies, among which insects play a major role, subjecting the trees to attacks throughout the summer season, from the spring until leaves drop in the fall. The most common insects belong to the defoliator group, and certain species reach epidemic levels periodically and sometimes for several years' duration. Other insects include miners, and wood and bark borers.

Forest tent caterpillar
Plate 91

The forest tent caterpillar, *Malacosoma disstria* Hbn., is unquestionably the commonest leaf eater in North American hardwood forests. Its preferred host is trembling aspen, but during widespread outbreaks it attacks all hardwood trees, except red maple. This native North American insect is widely distributed, from coast to coast; the northern limit of its range approximates that of trembling aspen, and it is found as far south as the state of Louisiana.

History of outbreaks

Damage caused by the forest tent caterpillar has long been recognized, and the first outbreak to be positively identified goes back to the year 1791. Since that date, the records contain reports of periodic outbreaks at intervals of 10 to 12 years. Ontario, which has the most complete records on the subject in Canada, reported a total of 12 outbreaks since 1867. The most recent ones occurred at the end of the 1930s, at the end of the 1940s, and in the early 1960s; the last one began in 1972. These four outbreaks extended into Quebec at about the same time, except for the third, which began in 1965 and ended in 1969. In the Maritime provinces, outbreaks appeared at slightly different periods, that is from 1932 to 1935, from 1943 to 1953, and from 1962 to 1964; since 1968, a series of local, short-lived outbreaks have been recorded in various areas. The insect does not appear to be established permanently in Newfoundland as yet, although a few moths were collected in 1951 and 1975.

Description and biology

Adult. Stout-bodied moth; beige to buff brown, with forewings crossed by two darker diagonal lines or bands. Wingspan: 20-45 mm (Plate 91, J).

Egg. Shaped like a flowerpot, laid side by side so as to form a band 5-15 mm wide around small twigs; gray in color but covered with a brown substance resembling varnish (Plate 91, C).

Larva. Cylindrical, very hairy; black during first instars, becoming dark brown at full growth, with a blue band on each side and a row of keyhole-shaped white spots on the back. Length: 45-55 mm (Plate 91, F and G).

Pupa. Brown to black; enclosed in a cocoon made up of several layers of yellowish silk. Length: 20 mm (Plate 91, I).

Only one generation of the forest tent caterpillar occurs per year. Moths appear at the end of June and are present until August; they are active mainly at sunset and in the evening. Each female lays 150 to 350 eggs in a compact mass encircling small twigs and forming a straight-edged band. The embryo develops during the 3 weeks following the egg-laying, but the larvae leave the eggs only in the following spring, when the trembling aspen leaves begin to open. The larvae go through five instars, lasting 5 to 6 weeks in all, and are gregarious for the greater part of their development (Plate 91, D). Rather than real tents they spin a kind of veil or mattress on the surface of branches, and there they retreat, always clustered together in a group. Once they are fully developed, the larvae transform to pupae in individual, slightly transparent, yellowish cocoons which may be seen throughout the foliage (Plate 91, H).

PLATE 91

Forest tent caterpillar, *Malacosoma disstria* Hbn.

A. Forest of trembling aspen severely defoliated.
B. Severely defoliated sugar maple crowns.
C. Newly laid egg band on twig of trembling aspen.
D. Colony of young larvae on trembling aspen branch.
E. Adult of the larval parasite, *Sarcophaga aldrichi* Park.
F. Lateral view of mature larva (length: 45-55 mm).
G. Dorsal view of mature larva.
H. Larva spinning its cocoon.
I. Pupa in opened cocoon.
J. Female (wingspan: 20-45 mm).

A

B

C

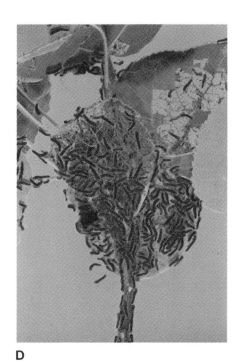

D

E

F

G

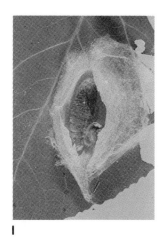

H

I

K

Damage and diagnosis

The larvae of the forest tent caterpillar are extremely voracious; it has been determined that a single larva can eat eight trembling aspen leaves, seven of them during the final instar. During a severe outbreak, all hardwoods except red maple may be completely defoliated over vast areas (Plate 91, A and B). Damage may also include the destruction of buds and flowers, and a decrease in seed production. However, even severely defoliated trees are not usually in danger of dying, because typical invasions in a given location do not last more than 3 years. Nevertheless, because the vitality of infested trees is weakened, the annual incremental growth of trembling aspen is reduced and often part of the twigs may die. In sugar maple groves, some authors have reported a decrease in the quality and quantity of sap (Batzer and Morris 1971). Also, hungry caterpillars in search of food are often a nuisance to people using parks and campgrounds.

An outbreak of this tent caterpillar is easily identified in the summer by the presence of groups of characteristically colored caterpillars on the foliage and trunks of trembling aspen. During the off-season, egg-bands, which look like brown swellings on twigs, can be seen easily. A method has even been developed for predicting the abundance of larvae in a given area for the next year by estimating the number of egg-bands per tree.

Natural control

Outbreaks of forest tent caterpillar do not usually last more than 3 or 4 years in a given location and disappear or are regulated through the action of natural factors that vary from one region to another even during an ongoing epidemic. The most common causes of mortality are related to weather conditions or parasitism.

Weather conditions, particularly frosts late in the spring, may kill larvae either directly while they are still enclosed in the egg or are newly hatched, or indirectly by destroying over vast areas the young foliage on which they depend for food. In certain cases, populations become too large for the quantity of foliage available, and larvae starve to death before they are fully grown.

Parasites and predators are also very important natural factors. About 40 species of insect parasites have been obtained from rearings of the forest tent caterpillar. The most important is a tachinid fly, *Sarcophaga aldrichi* Park., that appears early in an outbreak and that may destroy over 80 percent of the larval population. Among the predators, birds are occasionally very effective, because they consume large numbers of larvae. During prolonged outbreaks on the other hand, it is usually observed that part of the larval population dies off prematurely due to diseases caused by pathogens, viruses, microsporidia, or fungi (Bird 1971a).

Artificial control

Control of the forest tent caterpillar over vast wooded areas is out of the question, because such a program would be much too expensive. Sometimes, however, control by artificial methods becomes necessary to protect trees in recreation or camping areas. Before undertaking any treatment, an egg survey should be made during the off-season, to determine what levels of population can be expected the following spring. If only a few trees are involved, a simple method is to collect the egg-bands, which are easily seen once leaves have fallen, or else to collect colonies of young larvae when they are resting and to destroy them by dropping them in oil. When trees are too tall or too numerous, the foliage of infested trees may be sprayed, during May or June, i.e., when the larvae are still young, with a good chemical stomach insecticide or a biological insecticide, such as *Bacillus thuringiensis* Berl.

References

Abrahamson and Morris 1973; Batzer and Morris 1971; Bird 1971a; Hildahl and Campbell 1975; Pollard 1972; Raske 1975a; Retnakaran et al. 1976; Sippell 1962; Wetzell et al. 1973; Witter and Kulman 1972; and Witter et al. 1972.

Large aspen tortrix
Plate 92

The large aspen tortrix, *Choristoneura conflictana* (Wlk), is a solitary leaf roller that is considered to be one of the most serious pests of trembling aspen in Canada. This northern species was classified successively in the genera *Tortrix, Cacoecia, Archips,* and finally *Choristoneura.* In Canada, it occurs throughout the range of its preferred host, trembling aspen, and southward to the central United States. The insect has many secondary hosts, the most common being balsam poplar, white birch, various species of willow, choke cherry, and speckled alder.

History of outbreaks

Periodically, the large aspen tortrix multiplies disproportionately and causes epidemics in stands of trembling aspen in the eastern part of North America. As a rule these outbreaks, characterized by sharp upward surges in population, disappear suddenly after 2 or 3 years. In eastern Canada, this insect has been a pest mainly in Ontario, where outbreaks occurred during four distinct periods, that is, in 1912, from 1943 to 1946, from 1955 to 1960, and from 1968 to 1975. In Quebec, infestations were reported in 1938, in 1951, and from 1968 to 1975. In the Maritime provinces, the insect is common but rarely becomes abundant, although local outbreaks occurred in 1933, in 1950 and 1951, and from 1972 to 1974. Local outbreaks were reported in Newfoundland in 1973 and 1975.

Description and biology

Adult. Medium-sized moth; forewings brown gray and hindwings smoky gray; male smaller than female. Wingspan: 25-35 mm (Plate 92, H).

Egg. Oval, pale green; chorion smooth, thin, silky, and translucid. Dimensions: 0.7 mm by l mm.

Larva. Cylindrical, slightly flattened dorsoventrally; body greenish yellow initially, gradually turning dark green and sometimes black; head and legs brown. Length when full grown: 15-21 mm (Plate 92, E and F).

Pupa. Spindle-shaped; bright green, then turning brown or black.

Length: 9-17 mm (Plate 92, G).

The habits of the large aspen tortrix are fairly well known, through studies carried out in western Canada and in Alaska (Prentice 1955; Beckwith 1968, 1970, 1973).

There is only one generation of this leaf roller per year. Moths may be seen in the trees for about a month, from mid-June to mid-July. The males, whose flight is irregular, are very active, whereas the females are relatively inactive and do not move far from the pupal location. Females lay their eggs on the upper side of the leaves, in a flattened mass containing 50 to 450 eggs placed next to one another like fish scales (Plate 92, D). Incubation lasts about 10 days. The newborn larvae leave the chorion without eating it, and it thus remains stuck to the leaf until the fall. The larvae are gregarious and prefer to feed inside a shelter, which several build by attaching two leaves together with silk. In August, they leave their shelter to seek a protected place in which to pass the winter, usually at the base of the trunks of affected trees. Once settled there, each larva spins a white hibernaculum in which it overwinters after molting to the second instar. In the spring, about 10 days before the buds begin to swell, the larvae leave their winter shelter and crawl up to the buds, where sometimes they spin a second cocoon. Shortly after buds open, the larvae penetrate inside them and complete their second and third larval instars. When the surviving leaves are completely open, the larvae roll them and feed inside them during the last two larval instars (Plate 92, A). They transform to pupae in June or July, either in rolled leaves in the crown, or else in the undergrowth beneath trees that have been stripped of most of their foliage.

Damage and diagnosis

The slight damage caused by newborn larvae of the large aspen tortrix before they hibernate is negligible; on the other hand, larvae feeding on the buds in the spring may have serious consequences, because the buds are often completely destroyed and therefore no foliage is produced (Plate 92, B and C). Rolled leaves and loss of foliage detracts considerably from the appearance of ornamental trees. Massive defoliation also reduces the annual incremental growth and inhibits the growth of twigs, but only rarely does it kill the tree.

A severe attack by this leaf roller may be detected by a more-or-less pronounced delay in the opening of trembling aspen buds in the spring, and a little later in the season, by the presence either of deformed leaves or of leaves rolled into horns or attached with silk and containing larvae and excrement.

At the end of the summer, visible masses of hatched eggs on the upper side of the leaves also indicate an attack.

Natural control

The large aspen tortrix is attacked by many insect parasites, most of which also attack other common insects in Canada. Twenty-two parasitic species were obtained from rearings in Manitoba and Saskatchewan, and 13 other species were obtained in other provinces of Canada (Prentice 1955). Bradley (1974) mentions three additional species for Canada as a whole. Twenty-four species have been reported in Alaska, including eight already recorded in Canada (Torgensen and Beckwith 1974).

Predators also play a part in limiting populations, particularly two species of ants and three species of birds. Also, a disease caused by a fungus, *Beauveria bassiana* (Bals.) Vuill., caused the death of 25 percent of hibernating larvae during an outbreak in Saskatchewan in 1952. Likewise, a virus was isolated from the larval population in Ontario and appears to be quite common in that province (Cunningham et al. 1973).

Poor weather conditions, particularly frosts, may kill newborn larvae either directly while they are feeding, or indirectly by killing the foliage on which they depend for their survival (Beckwith 1968). During severe outbreaks, following destruction of the foliage on the preferred host, the larvae must feed on tree species less attractive to them. This either kills or hinders the development of a large number of larvae, and reduces the fertility of the female moths (Beckwith 1968).

Artificial control

Artificial control of this leaf roller is usually unnecessary, because natural factors are generally successful in wiping out populations after 2 or 3 years of infestation. In certain cases, however, it may be necessary to protect trees planted as ornamentals. The best method is to take advantage of the movement of the young larvae toward the buds in May, or to their hibernation niches at the base of trunks in August, periods at which they are most vulnerable. Trunks should then be painted with a sticky band at about 1 m from the ground. If too many trees are involved, a contact insecticide may be sprayed on the trunks when the larvae begin to migrate.

References

Beckwith 1968, 1970, 1973; Bradley 1974; Cunningham et al. 1973; Prentice 1955; and Torgensen and Beckwith 1974.

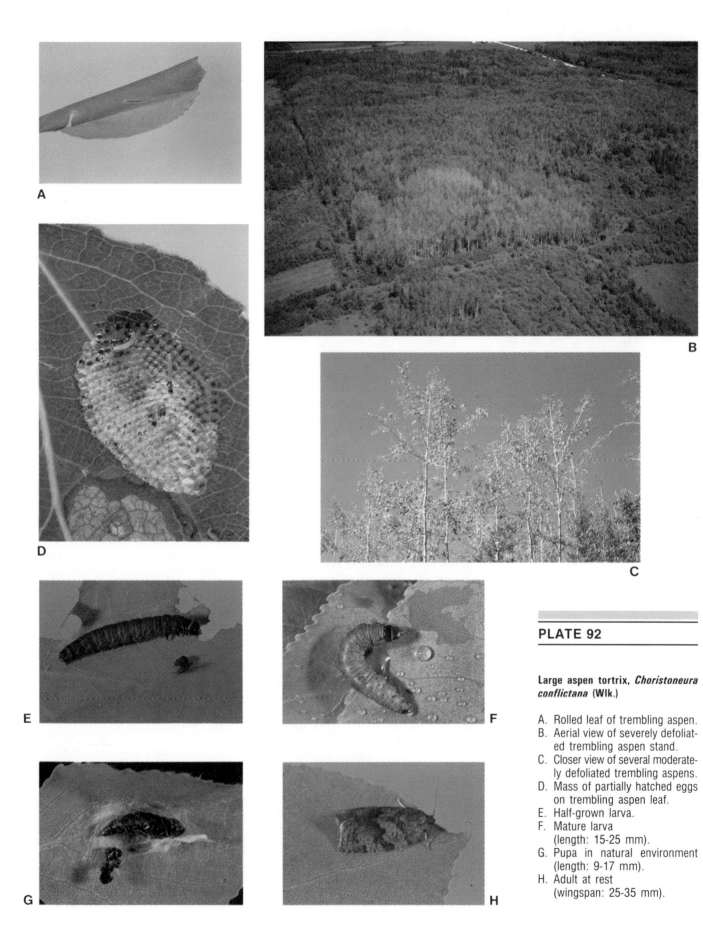

A

B

C

D

E

F

G

H

PLATE 92

Large aspen tortrix, *Choristoneura conflictana* (Wlk.)

A. Rolled leaf of trembling aspen.
B. Aerial view of severely defoliated trembling aspen stand.
C. Closer view of several moderately defoliated trembling aspens.
D. Mass of partially hatched eggs on trembling aspen leaf.
E. Half-grown larva.
F. Mature larva
(length: 15-25 mm).
G. Pupa in natural environment
(length: 9-17 mm).
H. Adult at rest
(wingspan: 25-35 mm).

214

Aspen twoleaf tier
Plate 93

The aspen twoleaf tier, *Enargia decolor* (Wlk.), is another leaf-eating lepidoptera that attacks trembling aspen, and also, occasionally, other hardwoods. In Canada, its presence has been reported from the Maritime provinces westward to British Columbia and southward in the United States to the latitudes of New York and Colorado. This leaftier often causes severe defoliation in central Canada.

History of outbreaks

In the eastern part of Canada, the province of Ontario has been the worst hit and outbreaks of the aspen twoleaf tier occurred from 1959 to 1963, and in 1970 and 1971. In Quebec, this species is generally found together with the large aspen tortrix, *Choristoneura conflictana*, which always outranks it in numbers. Populations of the aspen twoleaf tier increased considerably from 1970 on and remained above normal until 1975. The insect is fairly rare in the Maritime provinces.

Description and biology

Adult. Medium-sized moth; forewings straw yellow, shaded with dark brown and crossed with two broken brown lines; hindwings slightly paler and marked with a single brown line. Wingspan: 30-40 mm (Plate 93, E and F).

Egg. Spherical; pale yellow with reticulated chorion. Diameter: 0.67-0.73 mm.

Larva. Cylindrical, elongated; head yellow, body pale green with pronounced dorsal and subdorsal line. Length when full grown: 25-33 mm (Plate 93, B).

Pupa. Tapered, brown. Length: 16-20 mm (Plate 93, C and D).

Only one generation of the aspen twoleaf tier occurs per year. Moths are present in the field from June until the end of September, and the insect overwinters in the egg stage. The eggs, which have been observed only in laboratories, appear to be laid singly or in irregular clusters on, or near, the ground. Larvae begin to appear in the spring, and go through six larval instars. The newborn larvae feed on the mesophyll inside rolled leaves and, on reaching the second instar, they move to the outside of the leaf and feed on its surface. Older larvae chew the edges of leaves and construct flat cases made of two leaves attached one on top of the other by threads of silk. Once the larvae are fully grown, usually during the month of July, they drop to the ground and burrow underground where they pupate.

Damage and diagnosis

Damage by the aspen twoleaf tier consists mainly in the destruction of the parenchyma of leaves by larvae while feeding. During severe epidemics (Plate 93, A), trembling aspens may be entirely defoliated, but this damage is of little consequence because the insect populations are usually controlled rapidly by natural factors, and outbreaks are thus short-lived.

An attack by this species is easily identified by the presence on trembling aspen of petioles without their blade and of flat cases made by the larvae.

Natural control

The only information available on natural factors that regulate the aspen twoleaf tier is drawn from studies carried out in Alberta by Wong and Melvin (1976). They obtained 16 species of insect parasites in their rearings, the most common of which are *Aplomya caesar* (Ald.), *Winthemia fumiferanae* Toth., *Netelia* sp., and *Eulophys* sp. possibly *orgyiae*. One other species was reported by Bradley (1974); this was *Acropimpla alboricta* (Cress.).

Artificial control

Normally, no treatment is recommended against the aspen twoleaf tier; its damage is of no major economic importance, given the short-lived nature of outbreaks. In cases where control becomes necessary, its ravages could be limited by spraying foliage with a residual-action insecticide; this should be done early in the spring to destroy the larvae when they hatch and before they start rolling leaves.

References

Bradley 1974; Forbes 1954; Franclemont 1939; Prentice 1962; and Wong and Melvin 1976.

Spotted aspen leafroller

Plate 94

The spotted aspen leafroller, *Sciaphila duplex* Wlshm., is another leaf-eating insect capable of causing major defoliation on trembling aspen in eastern Canada. As the common name suggests, it is a leaf roller and its larvae roll leaves into the shape of a horn. It occurs throughout Canada and southward into the states of Pennsylvania and California. Its preferred host is trembling aspen, but it is occasionally found on 11 other hardwoods. In eastern Canada, its importance varies from region to region. It is more common in Ontario where, alone and in association with other defoliators, it causes occasional and sometimes quite severe outbreaks, over fairly large areas. In Quebec, the insect is usually found along with various other defoliators of trembling aspen, which are sometimes abundant and aggressive. In the Maritime provinces, the insect is less common and the occasional outbreaks are normally of little importance. Its presence only has been reported in Newfoundland.

Description and biology

Adult. Small moth; forewings basically gray black having the medial part and the anal tip white; hindwings pale gray. Wingspan: 18-25 mm (Plate 94, F and G).

Larva. Elongated and almost cylindrical; basically pale in color with reddish brown head; prothoracic shield, anal and piliferous plates dark brown. Length when full grown: 14-15 mm (Plate 94, B and C).

Pupa. Tapered; brown; not enclosed in a cocoon. Length: 10-12 mm (Plate 94, E).

Relatively little research has been done on the spotted aspen leafroller and little is as yet known of its biology.

Only one generation per year occurs in eastern Canada. Moths appear towards the end of May and may be seen until mid-July. The young larvae appear around mid-May and feed on the parenchyma of the leaves, which they roll into the shape of a horn and tie with a few threads of silk (Plate 94, A and D). From the end of May to the beginning of July, they pupate usually inside the rolled leaves.

Damage and diagnosis

Damage by the spotted aspen leafroller consists in the rolling and destruction of leaves by the larvae, which considerably detracts from the appearance of trees planted as ornamentals. In summer, an infestation of this insect may be recognized by the presence of leaves rolled into horns on trembling aspen. These horns contain almost white larvae with dark brown spots, or sound or empty pupal cells.

Natural control

The only information available on natural factors which may limit the spread of the spotted aspen leafroller is that collected in Canada by the FIDS. To date, eight species of insect parasites have been obtained from rearings carried out in Ontario (Raizenne 1952), and four other species have been reported for Canada as a whole by Bradley (1974).

Artificial control

Control programs for the spotted aspen leafroller are rarely justified and present difficulties because the larvae spend most of their lives safe inside a rolled leaf. The only method of control applicable against leafrollers in general consists in attempting to destroy the larvae by spraying a contact insecticide on the foliage before leaf-rolling begins in the spring.

References

Bradley 1974; Forbes 1923; MacKay 1959; Prentice 1965; Raizenne 1952; and Smirnoff and Juneau 1973.

PLATE 93

Aspen twoleaf tier, *Enargia decolor* (Wlk.), and goat sallow, *Homoglaea hircina* Morr.

A. Trembling aspen defoliated by *E. decolor*.
B. Mature *E. decolor* larva (length: 25-33 mm).
C. *E. decolor* larva spinning a pupation shelter.
D. *E. decolor* pupa (length: 16-20 mm).
E. *E. decolor* moth at rest.
F. *E. decolor* moth with wings spread (wingspan: 30-44 mm).
G. Young *H. hircina* larva.
H. Half-grown *H. hircina* larva.
I. Mature *H. hircina* larva.
J. Pinned *H. hircina* moth

A

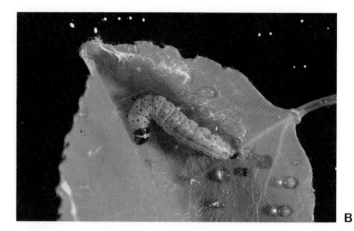

B

C

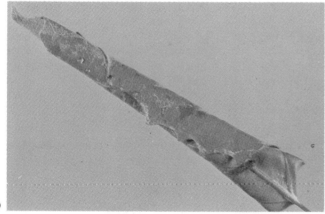

D

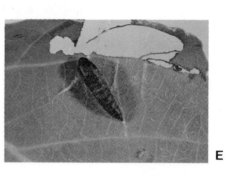

E

G

F

Other leafrollers and tiers of poplar

Three other rollers or tiers are sometimes found on trembling aspen: the birch-aspen leafroller, *Epinotia solandriana* L., and the aspen leafroller, *Pseudexentera oregonana* Wlshm., the yellowheaded aspen leaftier, *E. nisella* Clerck.

Birch-aspen leafroller
Plate 95

The birch-aspen leafroller, *Epinotia solandriana* L., has been well known in Europe since 1758, and was first reported in Canada in British Columbia during 1909. Its present range in North America covers all the Canadian provinces and the state of Washington in the United States. This solitary leafroller shows a marked preference for trembling aspen and white birch, but it is also commonly found on balsam poplar, alder, and yellow birch.

PLATE 94

Spotted aspen leafroller, *Sciaphila duplex* Wlshm.

A. Initial stages of rolling a trembling aspen leaf by the larva.
B. Trembling aspen leaf unrolled to show young larva.
C. Mature larva on leaf of large-tooth aspen (length: 14-15 mm).
D. Rolling completed on poplar leaf.
E. Pupa out of a rolled leaf (length: 10-12 mm).
F. Adult at rest.
G. Pinned adult (wingspan: 18-25 mm).

History of outbreaks

Infestations of the birch-aspen leafroller have been reported on its two main hosts in Ontario and Quebec. It is known to have been present in Ontario for quite some time, but was formerly confused with the yellowheaded aspen leaftier and its true identity was only established in 1962. That year an outbreak occurred throughout the northeastern part of Ontario and lasted until 1964. The insect became rare during the next 10 years, then a new outbreak developed north of Temagami. In Quebec, outbreaks have been reported in various regions during three separate periods, in 1964, in 1969 and 1970, and in 1973.

Description and biology

Adult. Small moth; forewings with variable basic color, marked with poorly defined striae varying from white to brown. Wingspan: 20 mm (Plate 95, E, F, G, H, I and J).
Egg. Oval with rounded surface: reddish orange initially then turning reddish brown. Length: 0.9 mm.
Larva. Elongated; first instar with dark to brownish gray head and pale cream-colored body with gray thoracic and anal plates and legs; third and fourth instars with pale to dark brown head and light-colored body.
Length: about 16 mm (Plate 95, B).
Pupa. Spindle-shaped, varying from yellow to brown. Length: 7.4-8.9 mm (Plate 95, D).

Little information was available on the life and habits of the birch-aspen leafroller in North America until Lindquist and MacLeod (1967) published their findings based on studies carried out in white birch stands of southern Ontario.

Only one generation of this species occurs per year. Moths are present throughout July and the beginning of August. Females lay their eggs singly at the base of buds, on the previous year's twigs, or on other rough parts of twigs and branches. These eggs overwinter, hatching at the end of April or the beginning of May. There are four larval instars: during the first, the larvae feed on buds; during the second, they eat unopened leaves;

and from the third instar on they feed on the parenchyma in a sort of shelter made of one or more rolled leaves. Towards the beginning of June, the larvae leave these shelters and crawl to the ground where they build fragile cocoons between the humus and the inorganic soil, and there transform first to pupae and then to adults.

Damage and diagnosis

Damage by the birch-aspen leafroller consists in the destruction of buds and leaves, which may completely defoliate the trees (Plate 95, A and C).

An attack by this leafroller may be suspected if rolled leaves containing larvae are seen on one or more of the host tree species. Identification of the larvae as to species is not easy, and it is best to refer to a specialist.

Natural control

Little information is available on natural factors that might limit the spread of the birch-aspen leafroller in its natural surroundings. However, in their rearings of this leafroller carried out in Ontario, Lindquist and MacLeod (1967) obtained eight species of entomophagous parasites, the most important of which was a braconid belonging to the genus *Apanteles*. Since that time, four other species have been reported by Bradley (1974).

Artificial control

No artificial methods have yet been developed specifically against the birch-aspen leafroller. It is likely that treatment using a residual, chemical stomach insecticide, sprayed on the foliage before the larvae begin feeding in the spring would give satisfactory results.

If only a few trees are to be protected, populations could be reduced considerably by gathering rolled leaves by hand and destroying them.

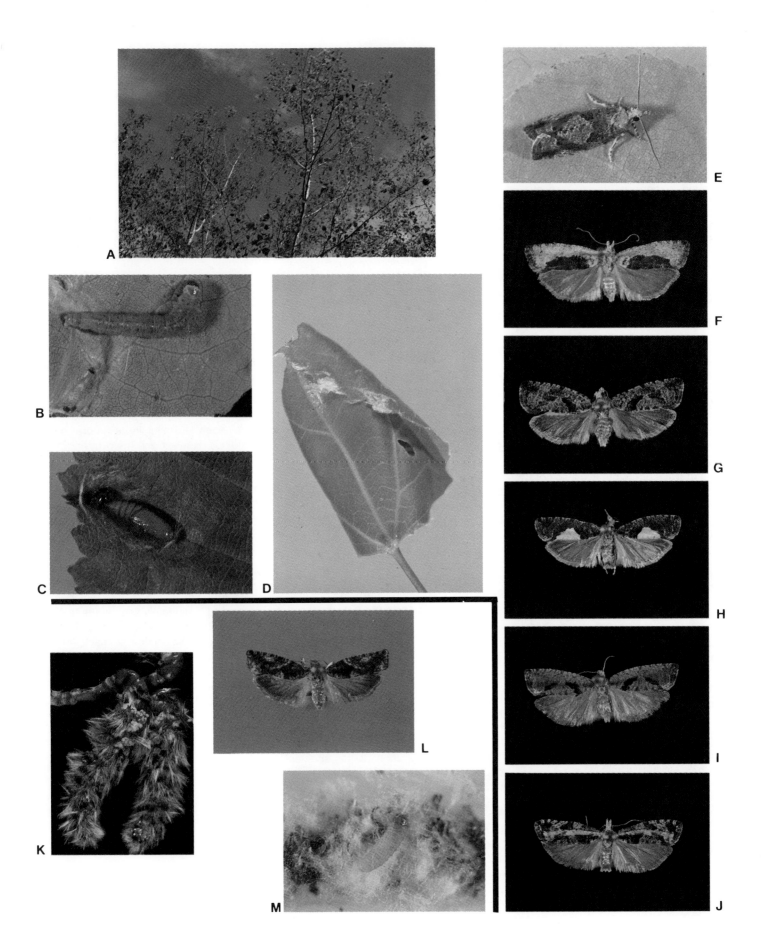

Aspen leafroller
Plate 96

The aspen leafroller, *Pseudexentera oregonana* Wlshm., is less well known than the birch-aspen leafroller, and no research has been done specifically on this insect. It is also a solitary leafroller with only one host, trembling aspen. Its known range in Canada extends from Quebec to British Columbia, and it is a particular menace in Alberta.

PLATE 95

Birch-aspen leafroller, *Epinotia solandriana* L., and yellowheaded aspen leaftier, *Epinotia nisella* Clerck

A. Trembling aspen defoliated by *E. solandriana*.
B. *E. solandriana* larva (length: 16 mm).
C. Typical damage caused by *E. solandriana*.
D. *E. solandriana* pupa.
E. *E. solandriana* adult at rest.
F to J. Variations in wing patterns of *E. solandriana* adults (wingspan: 20 mm).
K. Healthy catkin of trembling aspen.
L. *E. nisella* adult (wingspan: 12-15 mm).
M. Mature *E. nisella* larva in trembling aspen catkin (length: about 10 mm).

History of outbreaks

In eastern Canada, outbreaks of the aspen leafroller have been reported in Quebec and Ontario. In Ontario, a serious epidemic took place from 1964 to 1967, after which populations fell to very low levels. In 1974, they rose again, causing light defoliation throughout the province with a few centers of severe damage. In 1975, several pockets of severe infestation were reported. In Quebec, the insect was abundant from 1965 to 1967, after which populations declined until 1972. During the next few years they increased again reaching epidemic proportions in 1978, when a fairly large area was affected in the western part of the province.

Description and biology

Adult. Small moth; forewings dirty brown, hindwings lighter brown.
Wingspan: 16 mm (Plate 96, B).
Larva. Elongated; head ranging from brown yellow to dark brown, body pale yellow to pale green.
Length: 13-16 mm (Plate 96, E and F).
Pupa. Spindle-shaped; honey yellow.
Length: about 8 mm (Plate 96, G, H and I).

The biology of the aspen leafroller is quite similar to that of the birch-aspen leafroller, the larvae also living inside a leaf roll.

In nature, larvae are found from mid-May to the end of June, with a peak at the end of May and the beginning of June. The first pupae form towards the end of May, and moths are present from the end of May until the end of June.

Damage

Damage is identical to that of the birch-aspen leafroller, except that only trembling aspen is affected (Plate 96, A, D and J).

Artificial control

Although no specific method of treatment has yet been developed, control of the aspen leafroller is similar to that for the birch-aspen leafroller.

Yellowheaded aspen leaftier
Plate 95

The yellowheaded aspen leaftier, *Epinotia nisella* Clerck, is less well known than either the birch-aspen leafroller or the aspen leafroller. Some entomologists consider this species to be a catkin feeder (MacKay 1959), although others believe that it behaves like a solitary leaftier (Prentice 1965). It occurs in Canada from Newfoundland to Ontario, and also further west in British Columbia. This insect attacks poplar, alder, birch, and willow.

History of outbreaks

An outbreak of the yellowheaded aspen leaftier was reported in eastern Ontario in 1962, where it caused serious damage in association with other leafrollers and leaftiers. In Quebec, serious damage to catkins on trembling aspen was reported in the St. Maurice River watershed in 1973 (Plate 95, K and M).

Description and biology

Adult. Small moth; forewings grayish brown, hindwings lighter. Wingspan: 12-15 mm (Plate 95, L).
Larva. Elongated; head light brown, body cream. Length: about 10 mm.
Pupa. Spindle-shaped; honey yellow. Length: 6-8 mm.

The moth of the yellowheaded aspen leaftier is present from mid-June until the end of July, the larva comes a little later, and the pupa may be seen from the month of June on. In Quebec, larvae have only been observed on catkins, on which they dropped to the ground where they completed their development.

Diagnosis

An infestation of the yellowheaded aspen leaftier is easy to recognize by the presence of its larvae in the catkins, but all trace of the insect disappears when the catkins fall.

Artificial control

Treatment is similar to that for the birch-aspen leafroller, but in the case of the yellowheaded aspen leaftier, collecting catkins and larvae by allowing them to fall onto a sheet spread under infested trees may be used to protect a few trees.

References

Bradley 1974; Forbes 1923; Lindquist and Macleod 1967; MacKay 1959, 1962, 1965; and Prentice 1965.

PLATE 96

Aspen leafroller, *Pseudexentera oregonana* Wlshm.

A. Isolated trees showing severe defoliation.
B. Adults mating (wingspan: 16 mm).
C. Eggs on trembling aspen leaf.
D. Typical damage caused by larva.
E. Young larva in its damage.
F. Mature larva in its damage (length: 13-16 mm).
G. Pupa in its case on underside of trembling aspen leaf.
H. Appearance of upper side of leaf.
I. Pupa (length: about 8 mm).
J. Appearance of leaves following an outbreak.

Satin moth
Plate 97

The satin moth, *Leucoma salicis* (L.), was formerly classified as a member of the genus *Stilpnotia*. This very attractive moth, which gets its name from the satiny appearance of the adult's wings, is a native of Europe and western Asia and has been known in North America since 1920, when its presence was reported from opposite sides of the continent, that is, in the state of Massachusetts and in British Columbia. Since that time, it has spread easterly through the New England states, the Maritime provinces, Newfoundland, Quebec, eastern Ontario, and, in the West, into the states of Washington and Oregon. This leaf eater attacks most species of poplar and willow. When it was introduced into Canada, this insect was considered to be of secondary economic importance because only sporadic, short-term outbreaks occurred mainly on exotic species in, or nearby, towns. For the past 20 years, however, it has caused increasingly serious damage to stands of native poplar.

History of outbreaks

In eastern Canada, the satin moth was first reported in 1930 in the Maritime provinces; since that time, local and generally short-lived outbreaks have been reported almost every year. In Newfoundland, the insect first appeared in 1934, and local outbreaks have been reported almost every year from then on, with the exception of 1952 to 1957, during which a more generalized outbreak occurred over a fairly large area. In Quebec, the satin moth was first noticed in the Magdalen Islands in 1937 and a few years later in the Gaspé Peninsula; from there, it spread gradually throughout the western part of the province, causing infestations similar to those observed in the Maritime provinces. In Ontario, the insect was first reported only in 1972, in the eastern part of the province, and it is still spreading gradually towards the west.

Description and biology

Adult. Attractive moth with satiny white wings; head, thorax, and abdomen black densely clothed with white hairs. Wingspan: 30-45 mm (Plate 97, B and C).
Egg. Spherical; green; laid in clusters and covered with a foamy white secretion (Plate 97, D and E).
Larva. Elongated, practically cylindrical; head black; body black marked on the back with a line of yellow spots edged in white, and on the sides with narrow, broken white line; also, each segment has reddish brown tubercles bearing hairs. Length when full grown, 45-50 mm (Plate 97, G).
Pupa. Obtect; shiny black bearing gold and white hairs. Length: about 25 mm (Plate 97, H).

The satin moth produces only one generation per year in eastern Canada. The moths, which are found from the end of June until mid-August, are good flyers and active both day and night. Each female lays up to 1 000 eggs in one or more clusters that are more-or-less oval in shape and contain 150 to 200 eggs each. The egg clusters are laid either on the bark of trunks and branches, or on leaves, or on various nearby objects, and incubation takes about 2 weeks. On hatching, normally in August, the larvae begin by feeding on the leaf surface (Plate 97, F). With the arrival of cold weather in the fall, the larvae have reached the second instar and return to crevices in the bark of trunks and branches where they spin individual, winter cocoons called hibernacula in which they shelter for the winter. During the first warm days of spring, the larvae leave their hibernacula and feed for about a month on the new foliage, which they eat completely except for the large veins. By this time, they are fully grown and transform to pupae in individual cocoons which may be found attached to leaves, branches, fenceposts, buildings, or other solid objects. The pupal stage lasts about 10 days, and then the insect transforms to the adult stage.

Damage and diagnosis

Damage by the satin moth results from the defoliation caused by the larvae, mainly on exotic species, but also on

223

native poplars. The damage is not uniform; occasionally trees growing in the open or in groves may be completely stripped of their foliage (Plate 97, A), whereas in other cases the damage goes unnoticed. Although defoliation may cause the death of a few branches, it rarely kills trees. During epidemics, the presence of caterpillars near houses is often a nuisance to humans.

An attack by the satin moth may be suspected when isolated groups of poplars, particularly exotic species, are seen to be severely defoliated in June. The identification may be confirmed in early summer by the observation of many characteristically colored larvae and, shortly after, by the appearance of moths with satiny white wings.

Natural control

The satin moth is vulnerable to attack by many natural factors. At least 35 species of native insect parasites attack its various stages, as well as 4 species of foreign parasites which were introduced between 1927 and 1937 in an attempt to control the gypsy moth, *Lymantria dispar*, and the brown tail moth, *Euproctis chrysorrhoea* (L.), notably *Cotesia solitaria* (Ratz.) and *Compsilura concinnata* Meig. Unfortunately, the action of all these parasites is often hindered by hyperparasites, and by the fact that they attack a number of hosts.

The satin moth is also preyed upon by many predators; several species of birds, particularly sparrows, grackles and starlings, have often been observed feeding on the moths and the larvae.

In the Maritime provinces and Quebec, bacteria, fungi, and microsporidia have been isolated from diseased larvae, but their role has not yet been determined. Also, a viral polyhedrosis has been recognized in the Maritime provinces since 1950, although its true identity was only established in 1967. In New Brunswick, more than 60 percent of the larval population is believed to be infected with the same disease. The same virus was also observed in Quebec in 1968.

Climate may also play a major role in controlling this insect, particularly in the spring when late frosts may destroy huge numbers of early larvae or kill them indirectly by ruining the young foliage on which they feed.

Artificial control

It is not usually necessary to destroy the satin moth using artificial methods, because infestations are usually short-lived. However, it may occasionally be desirable to limit the damage. Populations may be reduced considerably by preventing eggs from hatching by painting them with oil or creosote. Larvae may also be destroyed by spraying a stomach insecticide onto the foliage in the spring when leaves begin to open.

In the case of small outbreaks, populations may be reduced by capturing moths with light traps and thus preventing females from laying their eggs.

References

Daviault 1951c; Forbes and Ross 1971; McGugan and Coppel 1962; and Prentice 1962.

Cherry casebearer
Plate 98

The cherry casebearer, *Coleophora pruniella* Clem.[1], occurs throughout a very large range, from Newfoundland to North Carolina on the east coast and from Alaska to California on the west coast. It is found on many hosts, most of them shrubs and fruit trees, but in certain cases it also attacks birch, alder, willow, walnut and some poplars. This species was rarely found on trees in Canada until 1975, when populations developed to the point where local infestations occurred on trembling aspen in eastern Quebec and Prince Edward Island.

Description and biology

Adult. Small, mouse brown moth; forewings speckled with darker brown scales and bearing long hairs on the distal part; hindwings edged with a peripheral fringe of long hairs. Wingspan: 13-15 mm (Plate 98, B).

Egg. Circular, bearing large concentric ridges radiating out from the top; light brown (Plate 98, C).

Larva. Usually hidden inside a yellowish brown or reddish brown case more or less of a cigar shape; short and stout-bodied; head and part of thorax shiny black. Length 7-9 mm (Plate 98, G).

Pupa. Spindle-shaped; dark brown to black, usually inside larval case. (Plate 98, H).

There is only one generation of the cherry casebearer per year, but its life cycle extends over two calendar years like that of the birch casebearer. The adult is present for about 1 month, from the end of June until the end of July. Eggs

PLATE 97

Satin moth, *Leucoma salicis* (L.)

A. Trembling aspen severely defoliated.
B. Adults mating.
C. Side view of adult at rest (wingspan: 30-45 mm).
D. Egg cluster laid on willow trunk.
E. Egg cluster on European white poplar leaf.
F. Newborn larvae on leaf of hybrid poplar.
G. Side view of larva (length: 45-50 mm).
H. Pupae attached to trembling aspen twigs (length: 25 mm).

[1]The Coleophoridae group is presently being revised by B. Wright, curator of the zoology section of the Nova Scotia Natural History Museum, who kindly provided most of the information given here on the morphology of the cherry casebearer.

are laid singly on the surface of the leaf blade, mainly along the veins. On leaving the egg, the young larva penetrates between the two leaf surfaces and feeds on the parenchyma (Plate 98, D, E and I). Then it spins a double case made up of a first one of silk inserted into a second one constructed with a section of the epidermis from a tunnelled part of the leaf. The larva continues to mine the leaves for some time settling on a part of the leaf blade and feeding on the parenchyma that it can reach without getting completely out of its case. In the fall, shortly before the leaves drop, the immature larva moves with its case to a suitable spot on the bark of a branch or twig where it settles and hibernates (Plate 98, J). The following spring, the larva moves once more with its case to the new foliage and attaches the case to the surface of a new leaf. As during the previous season, it feeds forming tunnels that radiate out from its point of attachment. The larva moves the case as necessary, so that a single larva may bore several tunnels. Once fully grown, towards the beginning of July, the larva attaches its case solidly to the leaf and transforms to a pupa and then to an adult. During severe outbreaks, all the leaves of an infested tree may be covered with little tunnelled spots and as a consequence they dry, turn brown, curl, and finally fall to the ground.

Damage and diagnosis

Damage by the cherry casebearer is caused solely by the larvae, which mine the leaves to feed. During the first larval instars, the tunnelled area is naturally small, but this surface increases as the larva grows older. With time, the damaged part of the leaf turns brown and, when there are many tunnels on a single leaf, it dries and falls to the ground (Plate 98, A). Infestations are usually confined to small wooded areas, in which completely brown crowns may be seen next to others that are almost all green. However, there are no reports of trees being killed.

Trees infested with this insect may be recognized in early summer, by the presence of small cases on the leaves of trembling aspen and balsam poplar (Plate 98, F). This diagnosis may be confirmed by the characteristic shape of the egg, which may be seen easily on the foliage during the summer with the aid of a magnifying glass. After the leaves have dropped in the fall, and even in winter when twigs are bare, small cases may be seen attached to the bark of twigs, in the crotch of two branches, or in crevices in the bark; their numbers indicate the intensity of attack likely during the following season.

Natural and artificial control

Relatively little is known about the natural factors that keep the cherry casebearer in check. To date, only two species of insect parasites have been reported (Bradley 1974). No research has yet been carried out to find an artificial means of controlling this casebearer. Satisfactory results might be obtained using the methods suggested for controlling the birch casebearer, *Coleophora serratella*, modifying the dates of the treatment to suit the particularities and biological regime of this species.

References

Bradley 1974; Braun 1927; Forbes 1923; and Prentice 1965.

PLATE 98

Cherry casebearer, *Coleophora pruniella* Clem.

A. Young trembling aspens severely defoliated.
B. Adult at rest (wingspan: 13-15 mm).
C. Sound eggs along the main vein of a trembling aspen leaf.
D. Newborn larva emerging from the egg.
E. Newborn larva before it penetrates between the two leaf surfaces.
F. Trembling aspen leaf bearing a number of cases.
G. Mature larva taken out of its case (length: 7-9 mm).
H. Pupa extracted from case.
I. Damage caused by one larva.
J. A number of cases attached to a trunk for the winter.

Poplar miners

Three microlepidoptera of eastern Canada feed by mining the foliage of trembling aspen. The aspen petiole miner, *Ectoedemia argyropeza downesi* W. and S., and the poplar petiole gall moth, *E. populella* Busck, attack the petiole, as their name indicates, whereas the third species, the poplar serpentine leafminer, *Phyllocnistis populiella* (Cham.), tunnels inside the leaf blade.

Aspen petiole miner
Plate 99

The aspen petiole miner, *Ectoedemia argyropeza downesi* W. and S., is of European origin and has recently caused major damage on trembling aspen and largetooth aspen in Canada. Its known range in Canada is limited to Ontario and Quebec.

History of outbreaks

In Quebec, the aspen petiole miner was discovered in 1966, but had no doubt been established there for some time already, as the following year it was found throughout the province. Since then, moderate-to-severe infestations have occurred in various regions. In 1967 and 1968, the insect was reported in several districts of southeastern Ontario, where it caused moderate damage.

Description and biology

Adult. Tiny gray moth: wings bearing reddish brown scales. Length of body: about 2 mm. Wingspan varies from 5.2-6.4 mm (Plate 99, C).

Egg. Almost circular, rounded on top. Length: about 0.2 mm (Plate 99, A).

Larva. Elongated, cylindrical in shape; head light brown, body greenish yellow. Length when full grown: about 5 mm (Plate 99, E and F).

In Canada, the aspen petiole miner appears to multiply by parthenogenesis, because, to date, only females have been observed. The moths appear during the month of May. The eggs are laid singly, flat on the petiole, with their number being proportional to the size of the leaf blade. Thus leaves in the lower part of the crown usually carry more eggs than those of the upper branches. On hatching, the young larva begins to tunnel in the petiole (Plate 99, B), working from its base towards the leaf blade, which it reaches by the fall. It leaves its tunnel after the leaf has fallen, around the end of October or the beginning of November, and, in the litter or in the ground, spins a round, flattened brown cocoon in which it overwinters. It transforms to a pupa the following spring.

Damage

The tunnelling in the petiole by the aspen petiole miner causes the leaf to yellow, except for a variable-shaped area at the upper end of the tunnel, which remains green even after leaf drop (Plate 99, D). This damage slightly affects the host's vitality and lowers the aesthetic value of trees planted as ornamentals.

Natural control

Natural factors that might check the spread of the aspen petiole miner in its natural surroundings have not yet been studied in detail, and to date only one parasite has been observed attacking the larva when it reaches the leaf blade.

Artificial control

Direct control of the aspen petiole miner by artificial methods is not possible over large areas, but may be organized if only a few isolated trees are to be protected by collecting the leaves with mined petioles, either by hand in the summer, or immediately after they drop in the fall and burning them. Egg-laying may also be prevented by chasing the females away in the spring by spraying the foliage with an insecticide to repulse them.

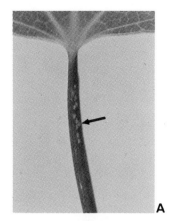

A

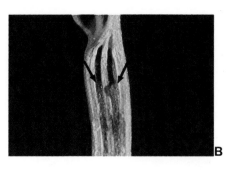

B

C

D

H

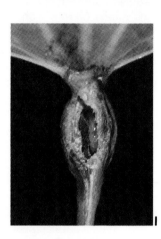

I

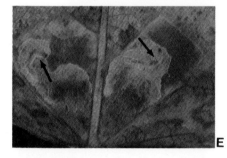

E

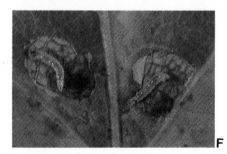

F

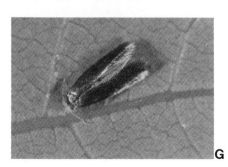

G

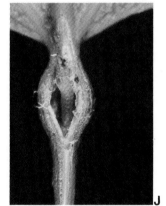

J

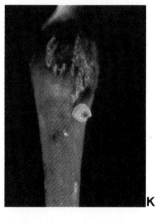

K

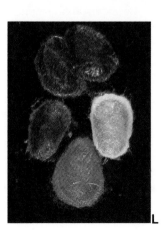

L

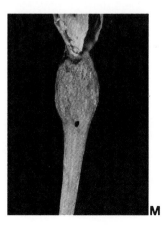

M

Poplar petiole gall moth
Plate 99

The poplar petiole gall moth, *Ectoedemia populella* Busck, attacks the same tree species as the aspen petiole miner, but it is much less common. In Canada, it is found from southern Manitoba to the Maritime provinces, whereas in the United States, it occurs in the states of New York, Massachusetts, New Hampshire, and Ohio.

Description and biology

Adult. Tiny moth. Wingspan ranges from 6.2-9.6 mm (Plate 99, G).

Larva. Elongated, oval in shape, head light brown, body yellowish green (Plate 99, I and J).

Only one generation of the poplar petiole gall moth occurs per year. The adult emerges in May, and the larvae are active from the beginning of July until completing their development in October. The activities of the larva cause the formation of a very characteristic gall about the size of a pea on the upper part of the petiole (Plate 99, H). The location, shape, and size of the gall makes it easy to identify an attack by this species.

Artificial control

The artificial methods suggested for the aspen petiole miner may also be used to control the poplar petiole gall moth.

Poplar serpentine leafminer
Plate 100

The poplar serpentine leafminer, *Phyllocnistis populiella* (Cham.), differs from the aspen petiole miner and the poplar petiole gall moth in that it attacks the leaf blade. It is also much more abundant, particularly in the western part of the continent. Only one host, trembling aspen, has been positively identified, although several other species of poplar have already been mentioned. Its distribution in Canada is transcontinental, and it is also encountered in the northern United States (Prentice 1965; Condrashoff 1964). To date, severe infestations have been reported only in the western part of the continent.

Description and biology

Adult. Small white moth. Wingspan: about 6 mm (Plate 100, C and F).

Egg. Semispherical; white. Dimensions: 0.31 mm by 0.38 mm.

Larva. Flat during first three instars, becoming cylindrical in the fourth; color ranging from white to cream. Length when full grown: 4.18-5.28 mm.

Pupa. Spindle-shaped: amber to brown. Length: 2.5-3.57 mm (Plate 100, E).

The habits of the poplar serpentine leafminer have been known since 1964 through a series of studies carried out in western Canada (Condrashoff 1964).

The moths appear in July, and live until the following spring. The eggs are laid in May on either side of the leaf near the tip of the blade; they are held in place with a substance produced by the female. Incubation lasts only a few days. On hatching, the young larva penetrates the surface of the leaf and digs the first part of its tunnel along the central rib, extending it almost to the petiole. It then heads toward the outer part of the blade by following the edge of the leaf; once it has reached the widest part of the leaf, it works back and forth between the leaf edge and the central rib. It is easy to follow the direction of the tunnel by the trail of blackish excreta left by the larva from the second instar on (Plate 100, D). The larva goes through four instars and is fully grown in June. It then transforms to a pupa and to an adult.

Damage and diagnosis

The poplar serpentine leafminer destroys the leaf parenchyma, and, during severe outbreaks when large numbers of leaves are damaged, may cause a certain reduction in annual growth (Plate 100, A and B). An attack by this microlepidoptera is easily identified simply by the appearance of the tunnelled leaves.

Natural control

Research carried out on the poplar serpentine leafminer in western Canada (Condrashoff, 1964) identified a number of factors in its natural control. When populations are large, many larvae die because of competition. Insect parasites appear to play a major role, and at least eight species, the most common of which is *Closterocerus tricinctus* Ashm., attack the larvae inside their tunnels or cocoons. Sometimes some pupae die because of drought.

Artificial control

Artificial control of the poplar serpentine leafminer is rather difficult because the larvae are constantly protected inside the leaf; however, fairly satisfactory results have been obtained by spraying the foliage, early in the spring with a systemic insecticide.

References

Cochaux 1969; Condrashoff 1958, 1962, 1964; Condrashoff and Arrand 1962; Downes 1968; Prentice 1965; and Wilkinson and Scoble 1979.

PLATE 100

Poplar serpentine leafminer, *Phyllocnistis populiella* (Cham.)

A. Trembling aspen completely infested.
B. Cluster of severely damaged trembling aspen leaves.
C. Pinned adult.
D. Trembling aspen leaf completely mined.
E. Pupa in curl of trembling aspen leaf.
F. Freshly emerged moth at rest.

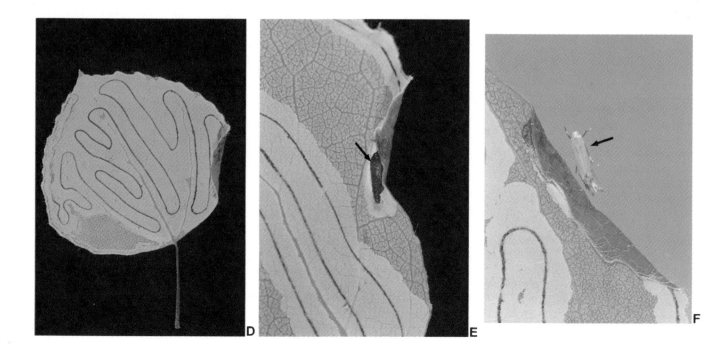

Poplar sawfly
Plate 101

The poplar sawfly, *Trichiocampus viminalis* (Fall.), is a native of Europe where it is very common. In North America, it occurs from the Atlantic to the Pacific coasts. This species shows a marked preference for Lombardy poplar, although it also adapts to trembling aspen, balsam poplar and largetooth aspen. In eastern Canada, this sawfly has caused only local and short-term infestations in Quebec and Ontario.

Description and biology

Adult. Resembles a tiny wasp; head and upper part of thorax black, lower part of thorax, abdomen, and legs orange. Length: 6-8 mm (Plate 101, A).

Egg. Ellipsoid; cream color. Dimensions: 0.46 mm by 1.36 mm (Plate 101, B and C).

Larva. Almost cylindrical; head shiny black, basic body color ranging from creamy yellow to greenish yellow; fourth instar and older larvae have body marked with orange blotches, two rows of black spots on the back and a similar row on each side; body also bears tufts of white hairs (Plate 101, E and F).

Cocoon. Cylindrical, rounded at both ends, made up of a rough outer envelope covered with plant debris and caked with earth particles. Length: 12-15 mm (Plate 101, H).

Research on the poplar sawfly has been carried out in Italy, England, and Canada.

In eastern Canada, two generations of this species may occur per year; a complete spring generation and a summer generation. Adults of the first generation appear in June and those of the second in August. The adult is a poor flier and is mainly active during the warm hours of the day. Before laying her eggs, the female explores the entire surface of the leaf blade, then begins laying eggs along one side of the petiole and then continues along the other side. Incubation of the eggs may last from 19 to 38 days depending on the weather. Male larvae go through six instars taking 17 days to complete the larval stage. The female larvae, on the other hand, go through seven instars which take 22 days. The larvae are very gregarious throughout their lives, even during their migrations which may take place six to nine times. Newborn larvae from eggs laid on the same petiole gather side by side on the underside of the leaf blade, near the apex (Plate 101, G). During the first three instars, they simply feed on the lower surface, but from the fourth instar on, they chew right through the blade. At the slightest disturbance, the larvae emit a nauseous fluid from glands located under the abdomen.

Once fully developed, the larva spins a cocoon either in bark crevices or in surface debris, or at a shallow depth in the ground. Most of the individuals from this first generation remain in diapause in the pronymphal stage in their cocoons until spring, when they transform to pupae and then to adults. However, certain individuals of the spring generation continue to develop during the summer season, transforming to pupae after about 10 days and then to adults shortly thereafter. The offspring of these adults form the summer generation, but the larvae normally do not have the time to develop fully before the onset of cold weather in the fall, and they quickly die.

Damage and diagnosis

The larvae of the poplar sawfly confine themselves at first to feeding on the lower surface of the leaf (Plate 101, I), but later on they consume the entire leaf (Plate 101, J). They are fairly voracious, and the amount of foliage consumed by a male larva and a female larva has been estimated to be 13 and 31 cm^2, respectively. During a severe outbreak, some trees may be completely stripped of their foliage, but usually defoliation is confined to the lower 4 m of the crown.

The wounds inflicted on the petioles by the females when laying their eggs cause tissues to swell; but this type of damage is usually of little importance.

An attack by this species is indicated either by the destruction of the leaves at the base of crowns, especially on Lombardy poplars, during June and July, or by the presence of young larvae feeding in very characteristically shaped colonies on the underside of the leaves (Plate 101, D). From the fourth instar on, the larvae may be easily identified by their orange color and the nauseous odor they give off when disturbed.

Natural control

Among all the natural factors that control the poplar sawfly, the first to be mentioned is a polyhedrous virus that destroys many of the larvae, as was the case in Quebec in 1957. At that time, the disease destroyed 80 percent of the larval population over a vast area, and in the following year caused the death of 90 percent of the population, reducing it to extremely low levels in subsequent years.

To date, six species of insect parasites have been mentioned in the literature, two of which are species introduced to this continent to control other harmful species of insect (Béique 1961). However, the combined action of all these parasites appears to be fairly minor. The only species which deserves any mention here is a little hymenopterous parasite of the genus *Tritneptis,* which attacks the pronymph in the cocoon.

PLATE 101

Poplar sawfly, *Trichiocampus viminalis* (Fall.)

A. Lateral view of adult (length: 6-8 mm).

B and C. Hybrid poplar leaf showing eggs on petiole and close-up of a few eggs (length: 1.36 mm).

D. Colony of young larvae on poplar leaf.

E. Side view of larva.

F. Dorsal view of larva.

G. Young and mature larvae feeding on poplar leaf.

H. Cocoons spun in corrugated cardboard in laboratory (length: 12-15 mm).

I. Damage by young larvae on poplar leaf.

J. Damage by mature larvae on poplar leaf.

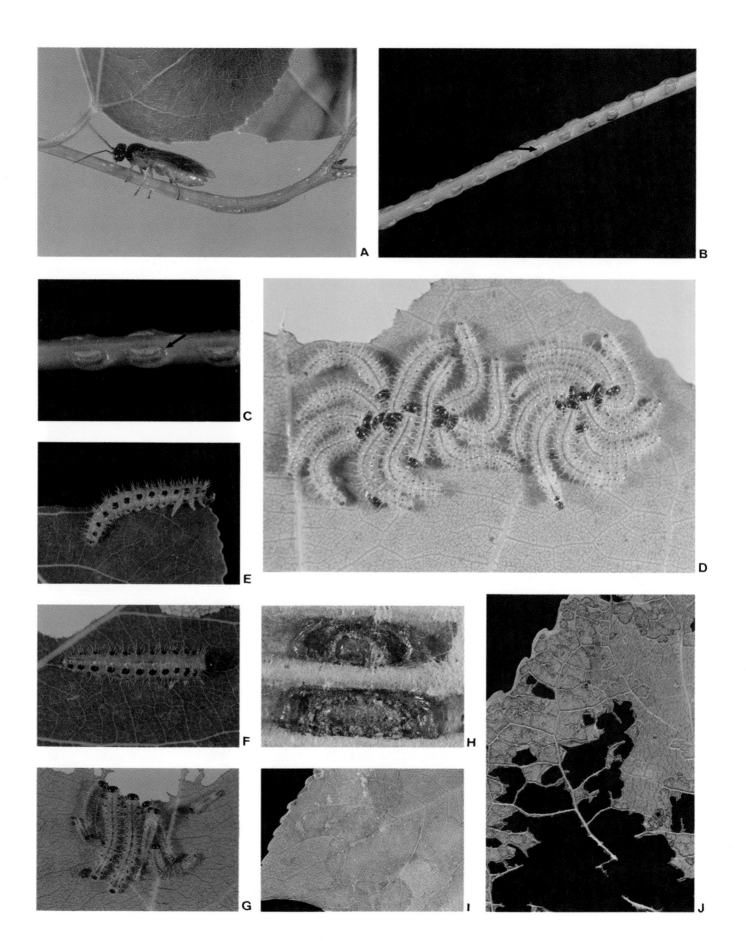

233

Predators do not appear to be attracted by the larvae because of their nauseous odor; no bird has as yet been observed feeding on them, and Downes (1925) reported that even poultry refused them as food. One species of spider and a sawfly larva have been observed attacking mature larvae, but the most common predator appears to be a pentatomid, *Apateticus cynicus* (Say), which attacks all stages of the insect.

Artificial control

It is usually unnecessary to attempt to destroy the poplar sawfly by artificial methods, because its infestations are of short duration. If necessary, the most economical way of ending an outbreak would probably be to create pockets of epizootic disease by using a concentration of the virus obtained either from a stock collected during a previous outbreak or from an area where an outbreak is retreating as a result this disease.

Trees may also be protected from excessive defoliation by spraying the crowns with a stomach insecticide when the larvae begin to develop, taking care to cover the undersides of leaves thoroughly. Where only a few small trees are involved, the most practical method is to examine carefully the lower crowns before the eggs hatch and to hand-pick and then destroy all leaves bearing eggs on the petiole.

References

Béique 1961; Connecticut Agricultural Experiment Station 1956; Downes 1925; Herrick 1935; MacGillivray 1920; Raizenne 1957; and Smirnoff and Béique 1959.

Poplar borers
Plate 102

Three long-horned beetles attack poplar in eastern Canada, the black poplar borer, *Saperda populnea moesta* Lec., the poplargall saperda, *S. concolor* Lec., and the poplar borer, *S. calcarata* Say.

The first species is often found on trembling aspen and balsam poplar in Ontario and Quebec, as well as in the eastern United States. The adult is black in color and is characterized, as are all saperdas, by a narrow and cylindrical body; it measures 9-11 mm in length (Plate 102, C). This beetle confines its activities to small-diameter branches and trunks (Plate 102, A). Little is known about the biology of this species, except that its life cycle extends over several years (Plate 102, B).

The poplargall saperda also has two preferred hosts, willow and trembling aspen, and attacks those trunks and branches at least 3 years of age. Its presence has been reported in Ontario, Quebec, and the Maritime provinces. According to the literature, this species is apparently a little better known than the black poplar borer (Wong and McLeod 1965; Craighead 1950). The adults are quite similar; the poplargall saperda is also black, but is clothed with gray hairs and measures 7-11 mm in length. The egg is spindle-shaped, creamy white in color, and it is laid in the bark of twigs in the spring. The larva develops in a tunnel inside the wood, and pupation occurs at the same place. The insect takes 2 to 3 years to complete its entire life cycle, and thus the larvae hibernate two or three times. The adults usually emerge in the spring.

The poplar borer also has two main hosts, trembling aspen and eastern cottonwood. This pest attacks the base of the trunk and the roots. Its distribution is very wide. It is particularly abundant in the western part of the North American continent, and is also found in the east, from Ontario to the Maritimes, as well as in the northeastern United States.

Its habits are better known than those of the black poplar borer and the poplargall saperda from research carried out in western Canada (Drouin and Wong 1975).

The adult is a large, sturdy beetle, basically black in color but clothed with dense gray hairs; it measures 20-30 mm in length (Plate 102, G and H). The egg is creamy white and oval in shape, measuring 4 mm at the largest point and 2.2 mm at the narrowest. When full grown, the larva measures 50 mm long. The pupa is yellowish white and measures 20-35 mm long (Plate 102, D).

Biology

The life cycles and habits of these three poplar borers on poplar and willow are very similar. The adults appear in late spring and feed on the tender bark of twigs and on the foliage of host trees. Eggs are laid in U-shaped niches cut in the bark by the female. The young larvae begin feeding in the cambium before penetrating into the wood and digging tunnels of various lengths depending on the species. The life cycle normally takes several years to be completed.

PLATE 102

Black poplar borer, *Saperda populnea moesta* Lec., and poplar borer, *Saperda calcarata* Say

A. Damage caused by *S. populnea moesta* on a trembling aspen branch.
B. *S. populnea moesta* larva in opened tunnel.
C. *S. populnea moesta* adult in trembling aspen crown.
D. *S. calcarata* pupa in pupation cell.
E. Damage caused by *S. populnea moesta* in a stand of hybrid poplar.
F. Damage by *Saperda* sp. on trembling aspen.
G. *S. calcarata* adult male.
H. *S. calcarata* adult female.

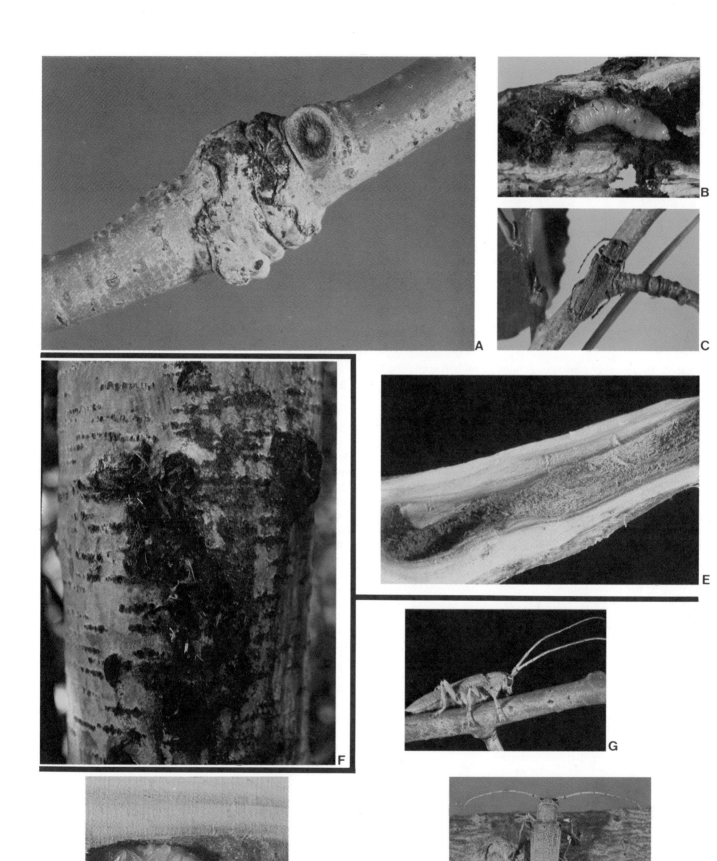

Damage and diagnosis

Damage caused by the two poplar gall makers consists of holes dug in the bark by the females when laying their eggs, swelling of twigs around the larval tunnels, and, occasionally, breakage of branches which snap off at the point of attack when blown about by wind (Plate 102, E).

Swelling of the bark due to larval activity of the poplar borer is less obvious, because this damage is concentrated at the base of the trunk and on the roots. However, because the larva cuts an opening to the outside to evacuate waste, the tunnel may easily be located by looking for piles of waste and a flow of sap.

Natural control

Little is known about factors which check the spread of these three poplar borers in nature. However, following studies in western Canada, it is known that in the case of poplargall saperda a certain number of eggs abort during their development due to unknown causes, and that a disease caused by a microorganism not yet identified kills a large number of larvae in their tunnels. Also, ten species of parasites have been obtained in rearings, and larvae are often destroyed in their tunnels by an unidentified woodpecker.

In the case of the poplar borer 13 species of parasites were obtained in rearings, and the predatory action of a woodpecker was observed (Drouin and Wong 1975).

Artificial control

Artificial methods of control prove difficult to apply against these three poplar borers because they are almost always inside a tunnel. Certain systemic insecticides have, however, given interesting results against the poplar borer in tests carried out in western Canada (Drouin and Wong 1975).

References

Baker 1972; Craighead 1950; Drouin et al. 1961; Drouin and Wong 1975; Ewan 1960; Peterson 1947; Wong and McLeod 1965; and Wong et al. 1963.

Bronze poplar borer
Plate 54

The bronze poplar borer, *Agrilus liragus* B. and B., is native to North America. Its distribution takes in all the Canadian provinces and extends southward into the states of Pennsylvania and Minnesota. This species was formerly confused with the bronze birch borer, *A. anxius,* and its true identity was recognized only in 1949. This bark and wood borer attacks several species of poplar, but only those trees that are dying or weakened because of some other cause, i.e., insects, fungi, wind, or higher animals.

Description and biology

The morphology and biology of the bronze poplar borer are similar in many respects to those of the bronze birch borer. From a morphological point of view, these two species can only be distinguished by certain characteristics of the genital organs of adult males and by other very slight differences in the larvae.

Adults are usually present in nature from mid-June to the end of August (Plate 54, H). Each female lays her eggs in several clusters of five to eight eggs each, in bark crevices, preferably on the sunny side of the trunk. Incubation of the egg lasts about 2 weeks, and, on hatching, the newborn larva tunnels through the bark and moves towards the cambium. From the second instar on, the larvae tunnel in the cambium, eating more phloem and xylem as they develop. The tunnel takes a zigzag path and its various sections or branches are usually closer together than in the case of the bronze birch borer.

Complete development of the larva extends over one or two calendar years, and usually takes in two winters. Once fully grown, the larva constructs a chamber under the cortex and, after having roughly outlined an exit hole through which the adult can leave, it overwinters in a dormant state. Pupation takes place the following spring, and the adult emerges some time later through a D-shaped exit hole.

Damage and diagnosis

The slight punctures made on leaves by feeding adults of the bronze poplar borer are of little consequence. However, galleries made by the larvae at the surface of the wood of branches or trunk may cause serious damage. These tunnels, which may be from 30 to 150 cm in length, hinder the flow of sap, causing a decrease in tree vitality, a reduction in growth, the death of some branches, and even occasionally the death of the whole tree.

An attack by this borer may be recognized by the presence on dying poplars of D-shaped holes at the surface of the bark, or of zigzag galleries which may easily be seen at the wood surface wood by lifting the bark with a knife.

Natural control

During his research in New Brunswick, Barter (1965) obtained two egg parasites and five larval parasites. He also observed that woodpeckers were major predators of mature larvae, pupae, and adults, particularly in the spring.

Artificial control

Control measures recommended against the bronze poplar borer are the same as those suggested to destroy the bronze birch borer.

References

Barter 1965; Barter and Brown 1949; and Benoit 1965.

Table 13. Other insects harmful to poplar — Other insects that are regarded as pests of poplar are listed in this table. For some insects, their characteristics are described in the chapter that applies to their primary host, and in such cases, that chapter (in Roman numerals) and the appropriate plate numbers are given. For other insects, a plate number alone is shown; and for the remaining insects, this table provides the only information.

Common and scientific names	Hosts (chap.)	Plate no.	Type of insect	Destructive stages	Period of activity	Importance*
Aspen leaf mite *Aceria dispar* (Nal.)	Poplar	55	Mite	Adult and nymph	May to Aug.	B
Fall webworm *Hyphantria cunea* (Drury)	Elm (IX)	84	—	—	—	B
Goat sallow *Homoglaea hircina* Morr.	Trembling aspen	93	—	Larva	May to Aug.	C
Gypsy moth *Lymantria dispar* (L.)	Birch (VI)	46	—	—	—	A
Leaffolding sawfly, a *Phyllocolpa popuellus* (Ross)	Trembling aspen	—	Leaffolder	Larva	May to Sept.	C
Lombardy leafminer *Paraphytomyza populicola* (Wlk.)	Trembling aspen	104	Minor	Larva	June to Oct.	C
Mourningcloak butterfly *Nymphalis antiopa* (L.)	Elm (IX)	85	—	—	—	C
Poplar-and-willow borer *Cryptorhynchus lapathi* (L.)	Trembling aspen, willow	—	Borer	Larva and adult	May to Oct.	B
Poplar flea beetle *Altica populi* Brown	Poplar	103	—	Larva and adult	June to Sept.	C
Poplar vagabond aphid *Mordwilkoja vagabunda* (Walsh)	Trembling aspen	—	Sucker	Adult and nymph	May to Nov.	C
Whitemarked tussock moth *Orgyia leucostigma intermedia* Fitch	Maple (VIII)	71	—	—	—	C

*A: Of major importance, capable of killing or severely damaging trees.
 B: Of moderate importance, capable of sporadic and localized injury to trees.
 C: Of minor importance, not known to present a threat to living trees.

A

B

C

D

E

G

F

H

J

K

I

PLATE 103

Poplar flea beetle, *Altica populi* Brown, and elm flea beetle, *Altica ulmi* Woods

A. Poplars severely damaged by *A. populi*.
B. Dorsal view of *A. populi* adult.
C. *A. populi* pupa.
D. and E. *A. populi* sound and hatched eggs.
F. Young *A. populi* larvae on trembling aspen leaf.
G. Medium-aged *A. populi* larva.
H. Leaf damage by *A. populi* larva.
I. Leaf damage by *A. populi* larva.
J. *A. ulmi* larvae.
K. *A. ulmi* adult.

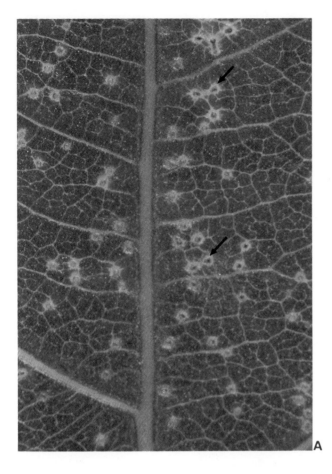

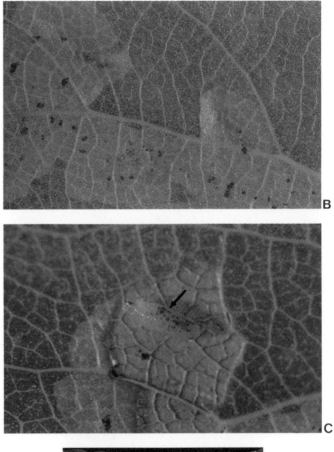

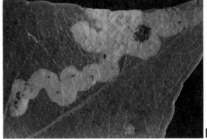

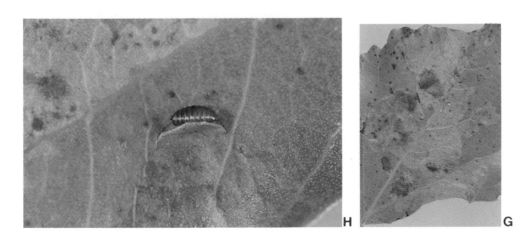

Lombardy leafminer, *Paraphytomyza populicola* (Wlk.)

A. Eggs spread on poplar leaf.
B. Poplar leaf mined by young larvae.
C. Tunnel opened to show larva.
D. Pupa.
E. Adult near the pupal cocoon.
F. Track followed by the larva inside the poplar leaf.
G. Leaf attacked by several larvae.
H. Pupal cocoon in opening bored at the end of larval mine.

BIBLIOGRAPHY

Abrahamson, L.P.; Morris, R.C. 1973. Forest tent caterpillar: Control with ULV trichlorfon in water tupilo ponds. J. Econ. Entomol. 66:574.

Agriculture Canada. 1974. Les phytoptes vésiculaires de l'érable. Publ. 1538. 4 p.

Allen, D.C. 1972. Insect parasites of the saddled prominent, Heterocampa guttivitta (Lepidoptera: Notodontidae), in the northeastern United States. Can. Entomol. 104:1609-1622.

Allen, D.C. 1973. Fecundity of the saddled prominent, Heterocampa guttivitta. Ann. Entomol. Soc. Am. 66:1181-1183.

Allen, D.C. 1976. Biology of the green-striped mapleworm, Dryocampa rubicunda (Lepidoptera: Saturniidae), in the northeastern United States. Ann. Entomol. Soc. Am. 69:857-862.

Allen, D.C.; Grimble, D.G. 1970. Identification of the larval instars of Heterocampa guttivitta with notes on their feeding behaviour. J. Econ. Entomol. 63:1201-1203.

Allen, D.C., Knight, F.B.; Foltz, J.L. 1970. Invertebrate predators of the jack pine budworm, Choristoneura pinus, in Michigan. Ann. Entomol. Soc. Am. 62:59-64.

Allen, D.C.; Knight, F.B.; Foltz, J.L.; Mattson, W.I. 1969. Influence of parasites on two populations of Choristoneura pinus (Lepidoptera: Tortricidae) in Michigan. Ann. Entomol. Soc. Am. 62:1469-1475.

Amman, G.D. 1963. A new distribution record for the balsam twig aphid. J. Econ. Entomol. 56:113.

Anderson, R.F. 1960. Forest and shade tree entomology. Duke University, School of Forestry. John Wiley and Sons Inc., New York. 428 p.

Appleby, J.E.; Randall R.; Rachesky, S. 1973. Chemical control of the bronzed birch borer. J. Econ. Entomol. 66:258-259.

Atwood, C.E.; Peck, O. 1943. Some native sawflies of the genus Neodiprion attacking pines in eastern Canada. Can. J. Res. 21:109-144.

Baker, W.L. 1972. Eastern forest insects. U.S. Dep. Agric. Misc. Publ. 1175. 642 p.

Balch, R.E. 1932. The black-headed budworm. Can. Dep. Agric., Entomol. Branch. Spec. Circ.

Balch, R.E. 1934. The balsam woolly aphid, Adelges piceae (Ratz.), in Canada. Sci. Agric. 14:374-383.

Balch, R.E. 1952. Studies of the balsam woolly aphid, Adelges piceae (Ratz.), and its effects on balsam fir, Abies balsamea (L.). Can. Dep. Agric. Publ. 867.

Balch, R.E.; Mitchell, R.G. 1973. Le puceron lanigène du sapin, Adelges (= Dreyfusia, Chermes) piceae (Ratz.). Pages 75-78 in Insectes nuisibles et maladies des arbres forestiers d'importance et d'intérêt mutuels pour le Canada, les États-Unis et le Mexique. A.G. Davidson et R.M. Prentice, compil. Environ. Can., Serv. can. forêts. Publ. 1180F.

Balch, R.E.; Underwood, G.R. 1950. The life-history of Pineus pinifoliae (Fitch) (Homoptera: Phylloxeridae) and its effect on white pine. Can. Entomol. 82:117-123.

Barger, J.H.; Hock W.K. 1971. Distribution of Dutch elm disease and the smaller European elm bark beetle in United States as of 1970. Plant Dis. Rep. 55:271-272.

Barter, G.W. 1957. Studies of the bronzed birch borer, Agrilus anxius Gory, in New Brunswick. Can. Entomol. 89:12-36.

Barter, G.W. 1965. Survival and development of the bronze poplar borer, Agrilus liragus Barter and Brown (Coleoptera: Buprestidae). Can. Entomol. 97:1063-1068.

Barter, G.W.; Brown, W.J. 1949. On the identity of Agrilus anxius Gory and some allied species (Coleoptera: Buprestidae). Can. Entomol. 81:245-249.

Batzer, H.O.; Morris, R.C. 1971. Forest tent caterpillar. U.S. Dep. Agric. For. Pest Leafl.9.

Bazinet, N.L.; Sears, M.K. 1979. Factors affecting the mortality of leaf miners Argyresthia thuiella and Pulicalvaria thujaella (Lepidoptera: Yponomeutidae and Gelechiidae) on eastern white cedar, in Ontario. Can. Entomol. 111:1299-1306.

Beal, J. 1942. Mortality of reproduction defoliated by the red-headed pine sawfly (N. lecontei Fitch). J. For. 40:562-563.

Bearns E.R., compiler and editor. 1968. Native trees of Newfoundland and Labrador. Nfld. Dep. Mines Agric. Res. 75 p.

Becker, G.C.; Wilkinson, R.C.; Benjamin, D.M. 1966. The taxonomy of N. rugifrons and N. dubiosus (Hymenoptera: Tenthredinoidea: Diprionidae). Ann. Entomol. Soc. Am. 59:173-178.

Becker, W.B. 1938. Leaf-feeding insects of shade-trees. Mass. Agric. Exp. Stn. Bull. 353. 83 p.

Beckwith, R.C. 1963. An oak leaf tier, Croesia semipurpurana (Lepidoptera: Tortricidae), in Connecticut. Ann. Entomol. Soc. Am. 56:741-744.

Beckwith, R.C. 1968. The large aspen tortrix. U.S. Dep. Agric., Forest Serv., Pacific Northwest Forest and Range Exp. Stn. PNW 81.

Beckwith, R.C. 1970. Influence of host on larval survival and adult fecundity of Choristoneura conflictana (Lepidoptera: Tortricidae). Can. Entomol. 102:1474-1480.

Beckwith, R.C. 1973. The large aspen tortrix. U.S. Dep. Agric., Forest Serv. Forest Pest Leafl. 139.

Béique, R. 1960. The importance of the European pine shoot moth, Rhyacionia buoliana (Schiff.), in Quebec city and vicinity. Can. Entomol. 92:858-862.

Béique, R. 1961. Étude sur la mouche à scie du peuplier, Trichiocampus viminalis (Fall.) (Hymenoptera: Tenthredinidae). Can. Entomol. 93:1085-1087.

Belyea, R.M.; Sullivan, C.R. 1956. The white pine weevil: a review of current knowledge. For. Chron. 32:58-67.

Benjamin, D.M. 1955. The biology and ecology of the red-headed pine sawfly. U.S. Dep. Agric., Tech. Bull. 1118. 57 p.

Benoit, P. 1965. Morphologie larvaire des Agrilus liragus Barter et Brown et Agrilus anxius Gory (Coleoptera: Buprestidae). Can. Entomol. 97:768-773.

Benoit P., complier. 1975. Noms français d'insectes au Canada. 4e éd. Agric. Qué. Publ. QA38-RA-30. 214 p.

Benoit, P. 1976. Le charançon du pin blanc. Environ. Can., Serv. can. forêts, Cent. rech. for. Laurentides, Sainte-Foy (Qc). Feuil. inf. 18.

Benoit, P.; Béique, R. 1978. Insectes et maladies des arbres, Québec 1977. Forêt-Conserv. 45(1), Suppl. 23 p.

Benoit, P.; Desaulniers, R. 1972. Épidémies passées et présentes de l'arpenteuse de la pruche au Québec. Environ. Can. Rev. bim. rech. 28:11-12.

Bird, F.T. 1971a. Malacosoma disstria Hübner, forest tent caterpillar. Pages 144-147 in Biological control programmes against insects and weeds in Canada 1959-1968. Commonw. Inst. Biol. Control, Trinidad, Commonw. Agric. Bureaux, Farnham Royal, Engl. Tech. Commun. 4.

Bird, F.T. 1971b. Neodiprion lecontei (Fitch), red-headed pine sawfly (Hymenoptera: Diprionidae). Pages 148-150 in Biological control programmes against insects and weeds in Canada 1959-1968. Commonw. Inst. Biol. Control, Trinidad, Commonw. Agric. Bureaux, Farnham Royal, Engl. Tech. Commun. 4.

Blais, J.R. 1964. History of spruce budworm outbreaks in southeastern Quebec and northern Maine. Can. Dep. For. Bi-mon. Prog. Rep. 20(5):1-2.

Blais, J.R. 1965. Spruce budworm outbreaks in the past three centuries in the Laurentides Park, Quebec. For. Sci. 11:130-138.

Blais, J.R. 1968. Regional variation in susceptibility of eastern North American forests to budworm attack based on history of outbreaks. For. Chron. 44:1-6.

Blais, J.R.; Pilon, J.G. 1968. Influence of temperature and moisture on the survival of cocoons and on adult emergence of *Bucculatrix canadensisella*. Can. Entomol. 100:742-750.

Bonnor, G.M. 1982. Canada's Forest Inventory, 1981. Environ. Can., Can. For. Serv., For. Stat. Syst. 79 p.

Brace, L.G. 1971. Effects of white pine weevil damage on tree height, volume, lumber recovery and lumber value in eastern white pine. Can. Entomol. Publ. 1303. 33 p.

Bracken, D.F. 1959. The effect of the introduction of imported parasites in the control of the larch casebearer (*Coleophora laricella* Hbn.). Can. Dep. Agric., Can. For. Biol. Lab., Quebec. Tech. Rep. 1957, 1958, 1959.

Bracken, D.F. 1960. The biology and external morphology of two eastern species of the genus *Anoplonyx* (Hymenoptera: Tenthredinidae) with special reference to *Anoplonyx luteipes* (Cresson). Master's thesis, Macdonald College, McGill Univ., Montreal.

Bracken, D.F. 1961. External morphology of two eastern species of the genus *Anoplonyx* (Hymenoptera: Tenthredinidae) with special reference to *Anoplonyx luteipes* (Cresson). Can. Entomol. 93:573-593.

Bradley, G.A. 1951. Notes on the parasites of the yellow headed spruce sawfly. Can. Entomol. 83:130-131.

Bradley, G.A., compiler. 1974. Parasites of forest Lepidoptera in Canada. Part 1. Environ. Can., Can. For. Serv. Publ. 1336. 99 p.

Braun, A.F. 1927. New lepidoptera from Ontario. Can. Entomol. 59:56.

Brewer, J.W. 1973. Control of the elm leaf beetle in Colorado. J. Econ. Entomol. 66:162-164.

Brillon, J. 1971. Contribution à l'étude du parasitisme chez les mineuses du *Thuja occidentalis* L. Thèse de maîtrise, Fac. des Sciences, Univ. Sherbrooke (Qc).

Britton, W.E. 1924. Swarms of chain-dotted geometer. Conn. Agric. Exp. Stn. Bull. 256, p. 312-313.

Britton, W.E.; Zappe, M.P. 1921. Outbreak of the arbor-vitae leaf miner. Conn. Agric. Exp. Stn. Bull. 234.

Brower, A.E. 1940. Important tree pests of the Northeast. Mass. Forest Park Assoc., Boston. 187 p.

Brown, A.W.A. 1938. Summary statement from the Forest Insect Survey. Can. Insect Pest Rev. 16(1). 23 p.

Brown, A.W.A. 1941. Foliage insects of spruce in Canada. Can. Dep. Agric. Publ. 712., Tech. Bull. 31. 29 p.

Brown, C.E. 1962. The life history and dispersal of the Bruce spanworm, *Operophtera bruceata* (Hulst) (Lepidoptera: Geometridae). Can. Entomol. 94:1103-1107.

Browne, F.G. 1968. Pests and diseases of forest plantation trees. Oxford University Press, Oxford, Engl. 1330 p.

Bryant, D.G. 1971. Balsam woolly aphid, *Adelges piceae* (Homoptera: Phylloxeridae), seasonal and spatial development in crowns of balsam fir, *Abies balsamea*. Can. Entomol. 103:1411-1420.

Bryant, D.G. 1976. Distribution, abundance, and survival of the balsam woolly aphid, *Adelges piceae* (Homoptera: Phylloxeridae), on branches of balsam fir, *Abies balsamea*. Can. Entomol. 108:1097-1111.

Bryant, D.G.; Raske, A.G. 1975. Defoliation of white birch by the birch casebearer, *Coleophora fuscedinella* (Lepidoptera: Coleophoridae). Can. Entomol. 107:217-223.

Buckner, C.H. 1953. Predation of larch sawfly by birds. Can. Dep. Agric. Bi-mon. Prog. Rep. 9(1):2.

Campbell, I.M. 1953. Morphological differences between the pupae and egg cluster of *Choristoneura fumiferana* (Clem.) and *C. pinus* Free. (Lepidoptera: Tortricidae). Can. Entomol. 15:134-135.

Campbell, R.W. 1974. Relationship between overstory composition and gypsy moth egg-mass density. U.S. Dep. Agric., Forest Serv. Res. Note 191.

Canada Department of Agriculture. 1923. Can. insect pest rev. 2.

Canada Department of Agriculture. 1940-1952. Annual report of the Forest Insect Survey.

Canada Department of Agriculture. 1953-1960. Annual report of the Forest Insect and Disease Survey 1952-1959.

Canada Department of Agriculture. 1959. Annual report of the Forest Insect Survey 1936-1937-1938.

Canada Department of Fisheries and Forestry. 1969. Annual report of the Forest Insect and Disease Survey 1968.

Canada Department of Forestry. 1961-1966. Annual report of the Forest Insect and Disease Survey

Canada Department of Forestry and Rural Development. 1967-1968. Annual report of the Forest Insect and Disease Survey.

Canadian Forestry Service. 1970-1971. Annual report of the Forest Insect and Disease Survey 1969-1970. Can. Dep. Fish. For.

Canadian Forestry Service. 1972-1981. Annual report of the Forest Insect and Disease Survey. Environ. Can.

Canadian Forestry Service. 1974a. Balsam fir sawfly. Environ. Can., Maritimes Forest Res. Cent. Fredericton, N.B. Pest Leafl.

Canadian Forestry Service. 1974b. Balsam twig aphid. Environ. Can., Maritimes Forest Res. Cent., Fredericton, N.B. Pest Leafl.

Canadian Forestry Service. 1974c. Dutch elm disease in the Maritimes. Environ. Can., Maritimes Forest Res. Cent., Fredericton, N.B. Inf. Leafl.

Canadian Forestry Service. 1974d. Balsam gall midge. Environ. Can., Maritimes Forest Res. Cent., Fredericton, N.B. Pest Control Leafl.

Canadian Forestry Service. 1974e. Spruce spider mite. Environ. Can., Maritimes Forest Res. Cent., Fredericton, N.B. Pest Leafl.

Canadian Forestry Service. 1974f. Suggested program to combat Dutch elm disease for municipalities in the Maritimes. Environ. Can., Maritimes Forest Res. Cent., Fredericton, N.B. Inf. Leafl.

Cannon, W.N.; Worsley, D.P. 1976. Dutch elm disease, elm bark beetles, *Hylurgopinus rufipes, Scolytus multistriatus*, control: performance and costs. U.S. Dep. Agric., Forest Serv., Northeast Forest Exp. Stn. Res. Pap. 345.

Carroll, W.J. 1956. History of the hemlock looper, *Lambdina fiscellaria fiscellaria* (Guen.) (Lepidoptera: Geometridae), in Newfoundland, and notes on its biology. Can. Entomol. 88:587-599.

Carroll, W.J.; Waters, W.E. 1973. L'arpenteuse de la pruche, *Lambdina fiscellaria fiscellaria* (Guen.). Pages 127-129 in Insectes nuisibles et maladies des arbres forestiers d'importance et d'intérêt mutuels pour le Canada, les États-Unis et le Mexique. A.G. Davidson et R.M. Prentice, compil. Environ. Can., Serv. can. forêts. Publ. 1180F.

Carroll, M.R.; Wooster, M.T.; Kearby, W.H.; Allen D.C. 1979. Biological observations on three oak leaftiers: *Psilocorsis quercicella, P. reflexella* and *P. cryptolechiella* in Massachusetts and Missouri. Ann. Entomol. Soc. Am. 72:441-447.

Cerezke, H.F. 1975. White-spotted sawyer beetle in logs. Environ. Can., Can. For. Serv., North. Forest Res. Cent., Edmonton, Alta. Inf. Rep. NOR-X-129. 8 p.

Cheng, H.H.; Leroux, E.J. 1965. Life history and habits of the birch leaf miner, *Fenusa pusilla* (Lepeletier) (Hymenoptera: Tenthredinidae), on blue birch, *Betula caerulea grandis* Blanchard, Morgan Arboretum, Quebec, 1964. Ann. Entomol. Soc. Que. 10:173-188.

Cheng, H.H.; Leroux, E.J. 1966. Preliminary life tables and notes on mortality factors of the birch leaf miner, *Fenusa pusilla* (Lepeletier) (Hymenoptera: Tenthredinidae), on blue birch, *Betula caerulea grandis* Blanchard, in Quebec. Ann. Entomol. Soc. Que. 11:81-104.

Cheng, H.H.; Leroux, E.J. 1968. Control of the birch leaf miner with disulfoton. Can. Entomol. 100:350-357.

Cheng, H.H.; Leroux, E.J. 1969. Parasites and predators of the birch leaf miner, *Fenusa pusilla* (Hymenoptera: Tenthredinidae), in Quebec. Can. Entomol. 101:839-846.

Cheng, H.H.; Leroux, E.J. 1970. Major factors in survival of the immature stages of *Fenusa pusilla* in southwestern Quebec. Can. Entomol. 102:995-1002.

Ciesla, W.M.; Bousfield, W.E. 1974. Forecasting potential defoliation by larch casebearer in the northern Rocky Mountains. J. Econ. Entomol. 67:47-51.

Clark, R.C.; Greenbank, D.O.; Bryant, D.G.; Harris, J.W.E. 1971. *Adelges piceae* (Ratz.), balsam woolly aphid (Homoptera: Adelgidae). Pages 113-127 *in* Biological control programmes against insects and weeds in Canada 1959-1968. Commonw. Inst. Biol. Control, Trinidad, Commonw. Agric. Bureaux, Farnham Royal, Engl. Tech. Commun. 4.

Clark, R.C.; Raske, A.G. 1974. The birch casebearer. Nfld. For. Notes 7.

Cochaux, P. 1965. Recherches sur les insectes du chêne rouge dans la région de Québec. Can., minist. Forêts, Lab. entomol. pathol. for. Qué. 44 p.

Cochaux, P. 1968. La tordeuse printanière du chêne, *Croesia semipurpurana* (Kft.) (Lepidoptera: Tortricidae). Ann. Soc. entomol. Qué. 13:98-107.

Cochaux, P. 1969. Une mineuse d'origine européenne *Stigmella (Nepticula) turbidella* H.S. sur la feuille du peuplier faux-tremble (*Populus tremuloides* Michx.) au Québec. Can., minist. Pêches Forêts. Rev. bim. rech. 25:19-20.

Cochaux, P.; Ducharme, R. 1963. Recherches sur les insectes du chêne. Can., minist. Forêts, Lab. entomol. pathol. for. Qué. 33 p.

Collingwood, G.H.; Brush, W.D. 1964. Knowing your trees. Am. For. Assoc., Washington. 349 p.

Collins, C.W. 1926. Observations on a recurring outbreak of *Heterocampa guttivitta* Walker and natural enemies controlling it. J. Agric. Res. 32:689-699.

Condrashoff, S.F. 1958. Differences in aspen phenology and survival of immature stages of *Phyllocnistis populiella* Cham. Can. Dep. Agric. Bi-mon. Prog. Rep. 14(6):3-4.

Condrashoff, S.F. 1962. A description of the immature stages of *Phyllocnistis populiella* Cham. (Lepidoptera: Gracillariidae). Can. Entomol. 94:902-909.

Condrashoff, S.F. 1964. Bionomics of the aspen leaf miner, *Phyllocnistis populiella* Cham. (Lepidoptera: Gracillariidae). Can. Entomol. 96:857-874.

Condrashoff, S.F.; Arrand, J.C. 1962. Chemical control of the aspen leaf miner, *Phyllocnistis populiella* Cham. (Lepidoptera: Gracillariidae). Proc. Entomol. Soc. B.C. 59:3-4.

Connecticut Agricultural Experiment Station. 1956. Plant pest handbook, Bull. 600. 193 p.

Coppel, H.C.; Leius, K. 1955. History of the larch sawfly with notes on origin and biology. Can. Entomol. 87:103-111.

Craighead, F.C. 1950. Insect enemies of eastern forests. U.S. Dep. Agric. Misc. Publ. 657.

Cumming, M.E.P. 1959. The biology of *Adelges cooleyi* (Gill.) (Homoptera: Phylloxeridae). Can. Entomol. 91:601-617.

Cunningham, J.C.; Burke, J.M.; Arip, B.M. 1973. An entomopoxvirus found in populations of the large aspen tortrix, *Choristoneura conflictana* (Lepidoptera: Tortricidae), in Ontario. Can. Entomol. 105:767-773.

Daviault, L. 1937. Contribution à l'étude des insectes du bouleau. Inst. Biol. Univ. Montréal. Contrib. 1. 136 p.

Daviault, L. 1947. La chenille à houppes jaunes. La Forêt québécoise 12:28-31.

Daviault, L. 1946a. L'agrile du bouleau. La Forêt québécoise 11:573-575.

Daviault, L. 1946b. Les insectes forestiers du Québec. *In* Rapport annuel sur les insectes forestiers 1946. Can., minist. Agric.

Daviault, L. 1948a. Le scieur longicorne noir. La Forêt québécoise 13:592-596.

Daviault, L. 1948b. Notes pour servir à l'histoire de la tenthrède du mélèze. Ann. Assoc. can. fr. av. sci. 14:85.

Daviault, L. 1949a. Charançon de l'épinette. Forêt-Conserv. 1:96-97.

Daviault, L. 1949b. Épidémies d'insectes dans le Québec. Qué., minist. Terres Forêts., bur. entomol. Circ. 18.

Daviault, L. 1949c. Notes sur la biologie et les parasites du porte-case du mélèze (*Coleophora laricella* Hbn.) dans la province de Québec. Ann. Assoc. can. fr. av. sci. 15:90-93.

Daviault, L. 1950a. La chenille à tente d'automne. Forêt-Conserv. 2:991-994.

Daviault, L. 1950b. Puceron à galle de l'épinette. La Forêt québécoise. 16:874-878.

Daviault, L. 1951a. La tenthrède de LeConte, *Neodiprion lecontei* (Fitch), dans la province de Québec. 33e rapp. de la Soc. prot. plantes Qué., p. 165-184.

Daviault, L. 1951b. Le papillon satiné. Forêt-Conserv. 3:6.

Daviault, L. 1951c. Les ravageurs des cônes. Forêt-Conserv. 3:69-72; 132-134.

Daviault, L.; Ducharme, R. 1966. Life history and habits of the green spruce leaf-miner, *Epinotia nanana* (Treitschke) (Lepidoptera: Tortricidae). Can. Entomol. 98:693-699.

Deboo, R.F.; Dimond, J.B.; Lowe, J.H. 1964. Impact of pine leaf aphid, *Pineus pinifoliae* (Chermidae), on its secondary host, eastern white pine. Can. Entomol. 96:765-772.

Deboo, R.F.; Hildahl, V. 1971. Chemical control of the jack pine and spruce budworms with ground application equipment in Manitoba. Man. Entomol. 5:57-67.

Deboo, R.F.; Laplante, J.P. 1975. *Contarinia baeri*, a pest of Scots pine. Environ. Can. Bi-mon. Res. Notes 31:1.

Dimond, J.B.; Allen, D.E. 1974. Sampling populations of pine leaf chermid, *Pineus pinifoliae* (Homoptera: Chermidae). Can. Entomol. 106:509-518.

Dimond, J.B.; Osgood, E.A. 1970. Control of the balsam gall midge in Maine. Am. Christmas Tree J. 14:33-34.

Dorais, L. 1977. Rapport préliminaire des inventaires entomologiques effectués au Québec en 1977 et reliés au programme de lutte contre la tordeuse des bourgeons de l'épinette. Qué., minist. Terres Forêts. 75 p.

Dowden, P.B.; Blaisdell, H.L. 1959. Gypsy moth. U.S. Dep. Agric. Forest Pest Leafl. 41.

Dowden, P.D. 1941. Parasites of the birch leaf mining sawfly, *Phyllotoma nemorata*. U.S. Dep. Agric. Tech. Bull. 757. 55 p.

Downes, J.A. 1968. A nepticulid moth feeding at the leaf-nectaries of poplar. Can. Entomol. 100:1078-1079.

Downes, W. 1925. The poplar sawfly, *Trichiocampus viminalis* (Fall.). Proc. Entomol. Soc. B.C. 22:26-32.

Drooz, A.T. 1956. The larch sawfly. U.S. Dep. Agric., Forest Serv., Lake States For. Exp. Stn. Forest Pest Leafl. 8.

Drooz, A.T. 1960. The larch sawfly; its biology and control. U.S. Dep. Agric. Tech. Bull. 1212. 52 p.

Drouin, J.A.; McLeod, B.B.; Wong, H.R. 1961. A roundheaded borer in the root collar of poplars. Can. Dep. For. Bi-mon. Prog. Rep. 17(2):2-3.

Drouin, J.A.; Wong, H.R. 1975. Biology, damage, and chemical control of the poplar borer (*Saperda calcarata*) in the junction of the root and stem of balsam poplar in western Canada. Can. J. For. Res. 5:433-439.

Durkin, J.J. 1972. Fall webworms and how to control them, *Hyphantria cunea*. N.M. State Univ. Ext. Circ. 439.

Eikenbary, R.D.; Raney, H.G. 1968. Population trends of insect predators of the elm leaf beetle. J. Econ. Entomol. 61:1336-1339.

Ewan, H.G. 1957. Jack pine sawfly. U.S. Dep. Agric., Forest Serv. Forest Pest Leafl. 17.

Ewan, H.G. 1960. The poplar borer in relation to aspen stocking. U.S. Dep. Agric., Lake States Forest Exp. Stn. Tech. Note 580.

Ferguson, D.C. 1971. The moths of America north of Mexico. Fasc. 20. 2A, Bombycoidea: Saturniidae (Part). E.W. Classey Ltd., and R.B.D. Publ. Inc., London. 153 p.

Ferguson, D.C. 1978. The moths of America north of Mexico. Fasc. 22.2, Noctuoidea: Lymantriidae. E.W. Classey Ltd., London. 110 p.

Finnegan, R. 1957. Elm bark beetles in southwestern Ontario. Can. Entomol. 89:275-280.

Fisher, G.T. 1970. Parasites and predators of the species of saddled prominent complex at Groton, Vermont. J. Econ. Entomol. 63:1613-1614.

Fletcher, J. 1885. The larch sawfly *Nematus ericksonii* Htg. 15th Rep. of the Entomol. Soc. Ont., p. 72-77.

Foltz, J.L.; Knight, F.B.; Allen, D.C. 1972. Numerical analysis of population fluctuations of the jack pine budworm. Ann. Entomol. Soc. Am. 65:82-89.

Forbes, R.S. 1949. The yellow-headed spruce sawfly. Can. Dep. Agric. Bi-mon. Prog. Rep. 5(3):1.

Forbes, R.S.; Ross, D.A. 1971. *Stilpnotia salicis* (L.), satin moth (Lepidoptera: Liparidae). Pages 205-212 in Biological control programmes against insects and weeds in Canada 1959-1968. Commonw. Inst. Biol. Control, Trinidad, Commonw. Agric. Bureaux, Farnham Royal, Engl. Tech. Commun. 4.

Forbes, W.T.M. 1923. Lepidoptera of New York and neighboring states. Cornell Univ., Agric. Exp. Stn. Mem. 68. 729 p.

Forbes, W.T.M. 1954. Lepidoptera of New York and neighboring states. Part III. Noctuidae. Cornell Univ., Agric. Exp. Stn. Mem. 329. 433 p.

Ford, R.P.; Dimond, J.B. 1973. Sampling populations of pine leaf chermid *Pineus pinifoliae* (Homoptera: Chermidae). II. Adult Gallicolae on the secondary host. Can. Entomol. 105:1265-1274.

Franclemont, J.G. 1939. Revision of the American species of the genus *Enargia* Hübner (Lepidoptera: Phalaenidae, Amphipyrinae). Can. Entomol. 71:113-116.

Franclemont, J.G. 1946. A revision of the species of *Symmerista* Hübner known to occur north of the Mexican border (Lepidoptera: Notodontidae). Can. Entomol. 78:97-98.

Freeman, T.N. 1953. The spruce budworm, *Choristoneura fumiferana* (Clem.), and an allied new species on pine (Lepidoptera: Tortricidae). Can. Entomol. 85:121-127.

Freeman, T.N. 1967. Annotated keys to some nearctic leaf mining Lepidoptera on conifers. Can. Entomol. 99:419-435.

Freeman, T.N. 1972. The coniferous feeding species of *Argyresthia* in Canada (Lepidoptera: Yponomeutidae). Can. Entomol. 104:687-697.

Friend, R.B. 1927. The biology of the birch skeletonizer, *Bucculatrix canadensisella* Chambers. Conn. Agric. Exp. Stn. Bull. 288, p. 396-496.

Friend, R.B. 1933. The birch leaf mining sawfly, *Fenusa pusilla* Klug. Conn. Agric. Exp. Stn. Bull. 348.

Friend, R.B. 1936. The eastern spruce gall aphid, *Adelges abietis* L. Mass. For. Pest Assoc. Tree Pest Leafl.

Friend, R.B.; Wilford, B.H. 1933. The spruce gall aphid as a forest pest. J. For. 31:816-826.

Gardiner, L.M. 1957. Deterioration of fire-killed pine in Ontario and the causal wood-boring beetles. Can. Entomol. 89:241-263.

Gibbons, C.F.; Butcher, J.W. 1961. The oak skeletonizer, *Bucculatrix ainsliella*, in a Michigan woodlot. J. Econ. Entomol. 54:681-684.

Giese, R.L. 1964. Studies on the maple blight. Part II. The insect complex associated with maple blight. Univ. Wis. Res. Bull. 250, p. 21-58.

Giese, R.L.; Benjamin, D.M. 1959. The biology and ecology of the balsam gall midge in Wisconsin. For. Sci. 5:193-208.

Gillespie, A. 1932. The birch casebearer in Maine. Maine For. Serv. Bull. 7. 23 p.

Gobeil, A.R. 1937. Notes sur *Phyllotoma nemorata* Fall. Qué., minist. Terres Forêts, Serv. entomol. Bull. 1. 7 p.

Gobeil, A.R. 1938a. Dommages causés aux forêts de la Gaspésie par les insectes. Qué., minist. Terres Forêts, Serv. entomol. Bull. 2. 23 p.

Gobeil, A.R. 1938b. Les insectes forestiers du Québec en 1939. Qué., minist. Terres Forêts, Serv. entomol. Bull. 3. 48 p.

Graham, S.A. 1931. The effect of defoliation on tamarack. J. For. 29:199-206.

Graham, S.A. 1952. Forest entomology. McGraw-Hill Book Co. Inc., N.Y. 351 p.

Gray, D.E.; Mol, W.H.A. 1969. Water-sprinkling to control woodborers. Can. Dep. Fish. For. Bi-mon. Res. Notes 25(2):12.

Green, G.W. 1962. Low winter temperatures and the European pine shoot moth, *Rhyacionia buoliana* (Schiff.), in Ontario. Can. Entomol. 94:314-336.

Greenbank, D.O. 1970. Climate and the ecology of the balsam woolly aphid. Can. Entomol. 102:546-578.

Guèvremont, H.; Juillet, J. 1974. Recherches sur la dynamique des populations naturelles de *Coleophora fuscedinella* Zeller (Lepidoptera: Coleophoridae) dans la région de Sherbrooke, Québec. Phytoprotection 55:121-134.

Guèvremont, H.; Juillet, J. 1975. Parasites du porte-case du bouleau, *Coleophora fuscedinella* Zeller (Lepidoptera: Coleophoridae), dans la région de Sherbrooke, Québec. Phytoprotection 56:1-17.

Harman, D.M. 1971. White pine weevil attack in large white pines in Maryland. Ann. Entomol. Soc. Am. 64:1460-1462.

Harman, D.M.; Kulman, H.M. 1968. Biology and natural control of the white pine weevil in Virginia. Ann. Entomol. Soc. Am. 61:280-285.

Harman, D.M.; Wallace, J.B. 1971. Description of immature stages of *Lonchea corticis*, with notes on its role as a predator of the white pine weevil, *Pissodes strobi*. Ann. Entomol. Soc. Am. 64:1221-1226.

Herrick, G.W. 1935. Insect enemies of shade trees. Comstock Publishing Co. Inc., Ithaca, N.Y. 417 p.

Hesterberg, G.A.; Wright, C.J.; Frederick, D.J. 1976. Decay risk for sugar maple borer scars. J. For. 74:443-445.

Hildahl, V.; Campbell, A.E. 1975. Forest tent caterpillar in the Prairie provinces. Environ. Can., Can. For. Serv., North. Forest Res. Cent., Edmonton, Alta. Inf. Rep. NOR-X-35. 11 p.

Hodgkiss, H.E. 1930. The Eriophyidae of N.Y. II. The maple mites. N.Y. Agric. Exp. Stn. Tech. Bull. 163. 45 p.

Hodson, A.C.; Zehngraff, P.J. 1946. Budworm control in jack pine by forest management. J. For. 44:198-200.

Hopping, R. 1938. Forest insect conditions for 1937 in British Columbia. Can. Dep. Agric. Can. Insect Pest Rev. 16:74-76.

Hosie, R.C. 1972. Native trees of Canada. 8th ed. Environ. Can., Can. For. Serv. 389 p.

Houseweart, M.W.; Kulman, H.M. 1976. Lifetables of the yellow-headed spruce sawfly, *Pikonema alaskensis* (Hymenoptera: tenthredinidae), in Minnesota. Environ. Entomol. 5:859-867.

Howard, L.O. 1897. A study of insect parasitism: A consideration of the white-marked tussock moth, with description of new species. U.S. Dep. Agric., Entomol. Div. Bull. 5. 57 p.

Howse, G.M.; Dimond, J.B. 1965. Sampling populations of pine leaf adelgid, *Pineus pinifoliae* (Fitch). I. The gall and associated insects. Can. Entomol. 97:952-961.

Huard, V.A. 1929. Faune entomologique de la province de Québec. Nat. Can. (Qué.) 55:241-264

Hughes, K.M. 1976. Notes on nuclear polyhedrosis viruses of tussock moths of the genus *Orgyia* (Lepidoptera). Can. Entomol. 108:479-484.

Hutchings, C.B. 1923. Some biological observations on the bronze birch borer. 15th Ann. Rep. of Soc. prot. plantes Qué., p. 89-92.

Hutchings, C.B. 1925. Two important enemies of maple. 17th Ann. Rep. of Soc. prot. plantes Qué., p. 45.

Jobin, L. 1973. L'arpenteuse de la pruche. Environ. Can., Cent. rech. for. Laurentides, Sainte-Foy (Qc). Feuil. Inf. 4.

Johnson, W.T.; Lyon, H.H. 1976. Insects that feed on trees and shrubs. Comstock Publishing Associates, Cornell Univ. Press, Ithaca, N.Y. 464 p.

Johnson, W.T.; Zepp, D.B. 1978. Insect control on trees and shrubs. *In* Cornell recommendations for pest control for commercial production and maintenance of trees and shrubs. N.Y. State Coll. Agric. Life Sci., Ithaca, N.Y.

Johnson, W.T.; Zepp, D.B. 1978. Insect control on trees and shrubs. *In* Cornell recommendations for pest control for commercial production and maintenance of trees and shrubs. N.Y. State Coll. Agric. Life Sci., Ithaca, N.Y.

Jones, J.M.; Raske, A.G. 1976. Notes on the biology of the birch leafminer, *Fenusa pusilla* (Lep.), in Newfoundland (Hymenoptera: Tenthredinidae). Phytoprotection 57:69-76.

Jones, T.H.; Schaffner, J.V. 1939. Cankerworms. U.S. Dep. Agric. Leafl. 183.

Jones, T.H.; Schaffner, J.V. 1953. Cankerworms. Revised. U.S. Dep. Agric. Leafl. 183.

Kaston, B.J. 1936. The morphology of the native elm bark beetle, *Hylurgopinus rufipes* (Eichhoff). Conn. Agric. Exp. Stn. Bull. 387. 37 p.

Kaston, B.J. 1939. The native elm bark beetle, *Hylurgopinus rufipes* (Eichhoff) in Connecticut. Conn. Agric. Exp. Stn. Bull. 420. 39 p.

Kaya, H.K. 1977. Transmission of a nuclear polyhedrosis virus isolated from *Autographa californica* to *Alsophila pometaria, Hyphantria cunea* and other defoliators. J. Econ. Entomol. 70:9-12.

Kecber, H.H. 1946. A review of North American eriophyid mites. J. Econ. Entomol. 39:563-570.

Keen, F.P. 1952. Insect enemies of western forests. U.S. Dep. Agric. Misc. Publ. 273. 280 p.

Kegg, J.D. 1966. Leaf roller control on oaks with carbaryl. J. Econ. Entomol. 59:1298-1299.

Kerr, T.W. Jr. 1952. Further investigations of insecticides for control of insects attacking ornamental trees and shrubs. J. Econ. Entomol. 45:209-212.

Kotinsky, J. 1921. Bronze birch borer. U.S. Dep. Agric. Farmer's Bull. 1169. 97 p.

Kulman, H.M.; Hodson, A.C. 1961. Parasites of the jack pine budworm, *Choristoneura pinus*, with special reference to parasitism at particular stand locations. J. Econ. Entomol. 54:221-224.

Labonté, G.A.; Stark, D.A.; Nash, R.W., editors. 1968. Forest trees of Maine. 9th ed. Maine For. Dep. Bull. 24.

Lambert, R. 1941a. Les insectes forestiers du Québec en 1940. Qué. minist. Terres Forêts Chasse Pêche, Serv. entomol. Contrib. 10. 38 p.

Lambert, R. 1941b. Les insectes forestiers du Québec en 1941. Qué., minist. Terres Forêts Chasse Pêche, Serv. entomol. Contrib. 15. 46 p.

Lambert, R. 1942. Les insectes forestiers du Québec en 1941. Nat. Can. (Qué.) 69:173-205.

Lambert, R.; Genest, M.E. 1940. Les insectes forestiers du Québec en 1939. Qué., minist. Terres Forêts Chasse Pêche, Serv. entomol. Bull 4. 38 p.

Larson, L.V.; Ignoffo, C.M. 1971. Activity of *Bacillus thuringiensis*, varieties *thuringiensis* and *galleriae*, against fall cankerworm. J. Econ. Entomol. 64:1567-1568.

Laviolette, R.; Juillet, J. 1976. Identification des mineuses du *Thuya occidentalis* L. par la position et l'apparence de leurs infestations. Phytoprotection 57:86-95.

Lejeune, J.J. 1955. Population ecology of the larch sawfly. Can. Entomol. 87:111-117.

Lewis, F.B.; Daviault, L. 1973. La spongieuse, *Porthetria dispar* (L.). Pages 161-165 *in* Insectes nuisibles et maladies des arbres forestiers d'importance et d'intérêt mutuels pour le Canada, les États-Unis et le Mexique. A.G. Davidson et R.M. Prentice, compil. Environ. Can., Serv. can. forêts. Publ. 1180F.

Lindquist, O.H. 1955. La mouche à scie mineuse des feuilles du bouleau en Ontario. Can. Minist. Agric., Bull. inf. bim. 11(5):1.

Lindquist, O.H. 1959. A key to the larvae of leaf-mining sawflies on birch in Ontario with notes on their biology. Can. Entomol. 91:625-627.

Lindquist, O.H. 1964. Keys to the immature stages of insect pests of spruce and balsam fir in Ontario. Environ. Can., Forest Res. Lab., Sault Ste. Marie, Ont. Interim Res. Rep. 33 p.

Lindquist, O.H. 1973. Notes on the biology of the larch needleworm, *Zeiraphera improbana* (Lepidoptera: Olethreutidae), in Ontario. Can. Entomol. 105:1129-1131.

Lindquist, O.H.; Harnden, A.A. 1966. Notes on *Epinotia nanana* Treitschke (Lepidoptera: Olethreutidae), and keys to the immature stages of four needle miners of spruce in Ontario. Can. Entomol. 98:1312-1315.

Lindquist, O.H.; Macleod, L.S. 1967. A biological study of *Epinotia solandriana* (Lepidoptera: Olethreutidae), a leaf roller on birch in Ontario. Can. Entomol. 99:1110-1114.

Lindquist, O.H.; Thomson, M.J. 1970. The biology of a birch leaf miner, *Messa nana* (Hymenoptera: Tenthredinidae), new to Canada. Can. Entomol. 102:108-111.

Lyon, R.L.; Brown, S.J. 1970. Contact toxicity of insecticides applied to fall cankerworm reared on artificial diet. J. Econ. Entomol. 63:1970-1971.

Lyons, L.A. 1957. Insects affecting seed production in red pine; II — *Dioryctria disclusa* Heinrich, *D. abietella* (D. and S.), and *D. cambiicola* (Dyar) (Lepidoptera: Phycitidae). Can. Entomol. 89:70-79.

MacAloney, H.J. 1957. The red-headed pine sawfly. U.S. Dep. Agric. Forest Pest Leafl. 14.

MacAloney, H.J. 1968. The bronze birch borer. U.S. Dep. Agric. Forest Pest Leafl. 111.

MacAloney, H.J. 1971. Sugar maple borer. U.S. Forest Serv. Forest Pest Leafl. 108.

MacAndrews, A.H. 1927. Biological notes on *Zeiraphera fortunana* Kft. and *Z. ratzeburgiana* Ratz. (Eucosmidae, Lepid.). Can. Entomol. 59:27-30.

MacGillivray, A.D. 1920. Two new species of *Platycampus* (Hymenoptera: Tenthredinidae). Can. Entomol. 52:61.

MacGillivray, A.D. 1923. A century of Tenthredinoidea. Univ. Ill. Bull. 20. 50 p.

MacGown, M.W.; Osgood, E.A. Jr. 1972. Taxonomy and biology of Chalcidoid and Proctotrupoid Hymenoptera associated with *Dasineura balsamicola* (Diptera: Cecidomyiidae) in Maine. Can. Entomol. 104:1259-1269.

MacKay, M.R. 1943. The spruce foliage worm and the spruce coneworm (*Dioryctria* spp.) (Lepidoptera: Pyralidae). Can. Entomol. 75:91-98.

MacKay, M.R. 1952. A new species of *Sparganothis* allied to *S. pettitana* (Rob.) with descriptions of larvae and adults of both species (Lepidoptera: Tortricidae). Can. Entomol. 84:233-242.

MacKay, M.R. 1959. Larvae of the North American Olethreutidae (Lepidoptera). Can. Entomol. Suppl. 10. 338 p.

MacKay, M.R. 1962. Additional larvae of the North American Olethreutinae (1) (Lepidoptera: Tortricidae). Can. Entomol. 94:626-643.

MacKay, M.R. 1965. The larva of *Epinotia criddleana* Kft. and a note on *Pseudexentera oregonana* Wlshm. (Lepidoptera: Tortricidae). Can. Entomol. 97:666-668.

Maine Forest Service. 1968. A summary of forest and shade trees insect disease conditions for Maine 1967. Maine For. Dep., Entomol. Div. Forest Pest Notes 6.

Martin, J.L. 1960. The bionomics of *Profenusa thomsoni* (Konow) (Hymenoptera: Tenthredinidae), a leaf-mining sawfly on *Betula* spp. Can. Entomol. 92:376-384.

Martineau, R. 1943. Population studies of the European spruce sawfly (*Gilpinia hercyniae* Htg.) in Quebec. For. Chron. 19:87-107.

Martineau, R. 1959. Sur une infestation de la mouche à scie à tête rouge du pin gris, *Neodiprion virginianus* complexe, dans le Québec. Can., minist. Agric. Bull. inf. bim. 15(5):1.

Martineau, R. 1961. Nouvelle invasion d'arpenteuses dans les érablières du Québec. Can., minist. Forêts. Bull. inf. bim. 17(5):1.

Martineau, R. 1963. Facteurs naturels de régulation des populations de la tenthrède européenne de l'épinette, *Diprion hercyniae* (Htg.), dans le sud du Québec. Can. Entomol. 95:317-326.

Martineau, R. 1973. Arpenteuse de Bruce. Environ. Can., Serv. can. forêts, Cent. rech. for. Laurentides, Sainte-Foy (Qc). Feuillet infor. 7.

Martineau, R. 1974. Porte-case du bouleau. Environ. Can., Serv. can. forêts, Cent. rech. for. Laurentides, Sainte-Foy (Qc). Feuillet infor. 11.

Martineau, R.; Monnier, C. 1967. L'invasion récente de l'arpenteuse de Bruce au Québec. Can., minist. Forêts Dév. rur. Rev. Bim. Rech. 23(1):3.

Massey, C.L.; Wygant, N.D. 1954. Biology and control of the Engelmann spruce beetle in Colorado. U.S. Dep. Agric., For. Serv. Circ. 944. 35 p.

McClanahan, R.J. 1970. Cottony maple scale and its natural control. Entomophaga 15:287-289.

McGuffin, W.C. 1958. Larvae of the nearctic Larentiinae (Lepidoptera: Geometridae). Can. Entomol., Suppl. 8. 104 p.

McGugan, B.M., coordinator. 1958. Forest Lepidoptera of Canada recorded by the Forest Insect Survey. Vol. I. Papilionidae to Arctiidae. Can. Dep. Agric., For. Biol. Div. Publ. 1034. 76 p.

McGugan, B.M.; Coppel, H.C. 1962. Biological control of forest insects, 1910-1958. Pages 35-216 *in* A review of the biological control attempts against insects and weeds in Canada. Commonw. Inst. Biol. Control, Trinidad, Commonw. Agric. Bureaux, Farnham Royal, Engl. Tech. Commun. 2.

McLeod, J.M. 1962. The adults and immature stages of four species of *Eucordylea* Dietz (Lepidoptera: Gelechiidae) on spruce in Quebec. Can. Entomol. 94:1198-1227.

McLeod, J.M. 1966. Notes on the biology of a spruce needle miner, *Pulicalvaria piceaella* (Kearfott) (Lepidoptera: Gelechiidae). Can. Entomol. 98:225-236.

McLeod, J.M. 1970. The epidemiology of the Swaine jack pine sawfly *Neodiprion swainei* Midd. For. Chron. 46:126-133.

McLeod, J.M.; Blais, J.R. 1961a. Defoliating insects on field spruce in Quebec. Can. Dep. For. Bi-mon. Prog. Rep. 17(1):2.

McLeod, J.M.; Blais, J.R. 1961b. Présence d'insectes défoliateurs sur l'épinette des champs dans le Québec. Can., minist. Forêts. Bull inf. bim. 17(1):1.

McLeod, J.M.; Daviault, L. 1963. Notes on the life history and habits of the spruce cone worm, *Dioryctria reniculella* (Grt.) (Lepidoptera: Pyralidae). Can. Entomol. 95:309-317.

McLeod, J.M.; Tostowaryk, W. 1971. Outbreaks of pitch nodule makers (*Petrova* spp.) in Quebec jack pine forests. Can. For. Serv., Laurentian For. Res. Cent., Ste. Foy, Que. Inf. Rep. Q-X-24.

McLintock, T.L. 1955. How damage to balsam fir develops after a spruce budworm epidemic. U.S. Dep. Agric., Forest Serv., Northeast Forest Exp. Stn. Res. pap. 75. 18 p.

Middleton, W. 1921. Leconte's sawfly, an enemy of young pines. J. Agric. Res. 20:741-760.

Middleton, W. 1933. Five new sawflies of the genus *Neodiprion* Rohwer. Can. Entomol. 65:77-84.

Miller, C.A. 1950. A key to some lepidopterous larvae associated with the spruce budworm. Can. Dep. Agric. Bi-mon. Prog. Rep. 6(1):1.

Miller, C.A. 1963. *In* The dynamics of epidemic spruce budworm populations. Mem. Entomol. Soc. Can.

Morris, R.F. 1963. *In* The dynamics of epidemic spruce budworm populations. Mem. Entomol. Soc. Can.

Morris, R.F. 1964. The value of historical data in population research, with particular reference to *Hyphantria cunea* Drury. Can. Entomol. 96:356-368.

Morris, R.F. 1971. The influence of land use and vegetation on the population density of *Hyphantria cunea*. Can. Entomol. 103:1525-1536.

Morris, R.F. 1972a. Predation by insects and spiders inhabiting colonial webs of *Hyphantria cunea*. Can. Entomol. 104:1197-1207.

Morris, R.F. 1972b. Predation by wasps, birds and mammals on *Hyphantria cunea*. Can. Entomol. 104:1581-1591.

Morris, R.F. 1976a. Hyperparasitism in populations of *Hyphantria cunea*. Can. Entomol. 108:685-687.

Morris, R.F. 1976b. Relation of mortality caused by parasites to the population density of *Hyphantria cunea* on deciduous trees and shrubs. Can. Entomol. 108:1291-1294.

Morris, R.F.; Bennett, C.W. 1967. Seasonal population trends and extensive census methods for *Hyphantria cunea*. Can. Entomol. 99:9-17.

Mosher, E. 1914. The classification of the pupae of the Ceratocampidae and Hemilencidae. Ann. Entomol. Soc. Am. 7:277-300.

Mosher, F.H. 1915. Food plants of the gypsy moth in America. U.S. Dep. Agric. Bull. 250. 39 p.

Mutuura, A.; Freeman, T.N. 1966. The North American species of the genus *Zeiraphera*. J. Res. Lepid. 5:153-176.

Nash, R. 1939. The yellow headed spruce sawfly in Maine. J. Econ. Entomol. 32:330-334.

Neilson, M.M.; Martineau, R.; Rose, A.H. 1971. *Diprion hercyniae* (Hartig.), European spruce sawfly (Hymenoptera: Diprionidae). Pages 136-143 *in* Biological control programmes against insects and weeds in Canada 1959-1968. Commonw. Inst. Biol. Control, Trinidad, Commonw. Agric. Bureaux, Farnham Royal, Engl. Tech. Commun. 4.

New York State College of Agriculture and Life Science. 1976. Cornell recommendations for pest control for commercial production and maintenance of trees and shrubs. Ithaca, N.Y. 63 p.

New York State College of Agriculture and Life Science. 1978. Cornell recommendations for pest control for commercial production and maintenance of trees and shrubs. Ithaca, N.Y. 63 p.

Nichols, J.O. 1968. Oak mortality in Pennsylvania. J. For. 66:681-684.

Nigam, P.C. 1970. Toxicity of insecticides to six instar jack pine budworm larvae under laboratory conditions. Can. Dep. Fish. For. Bi-mon. Res. Notes 26:2-3.

Nilmczyk, E.; Olszak, R. 1978. The effectiveness of *Trichogramma cacoesiae* March in parasitization of overwintering eggs of the vapourer moth (*Orgyia antiqua* L.). Fruit. Sci. Rep. 5(2):33-38.

Nordin, G.L.; Rennels, R.; Maddox, J.V. 1972. Parasites and pathogenes of the fall webworm in Illinois. Environ. Entomol. 1:351-354.

Novak, V. 1976. Atlas of insects harmful to forest trees. Vol. 1. Elsevier Sci. Publ. Co., Amsterdam. 123 p.

O'Dell, W.V. 1959. The gypsy moth control program. J. For. 57:271-273.

Osgood, E.A.; Dimond, J.B. 1970. Parasites of the balsam gall midge, *Dasineura balsamicola* (Diptera: Cecidomyiidae). Can. Entomol. 102:182-184.

Osgood, E.A.; Gagné, R.J. 1978. Biology and taxonomy of two gall midges (Diptera: Cecidomyiidae) found in galls on balsam fir needles with description of a new species of *Paradiplosis*. Ann. Entomol. Soc. Am. 71:85-91.

Ostrander, M.D. 1957. Weevil attacks apparently unrelated to height of eastern white pine. U.S. Dep. Agric., Forest Serv., Northeast Forest Exp. Stn. Forest Res. Note 67.

Otvos, I.S. 1973. Biological control agents and their role in the population fluctuations of the eastern hemlock looper in Newfoundland. Environ, Can., Can. For. Serv., Nfld. For. Res. Cent., St. John's, Nfld. Inf. Rep. N-X-102. 34 p.

Otvos, I.S.; Bryant, D.G. 1972. An extraction method for rapid sampling of eastern hemlock looper eggs, *Lambdina fiscellaria fiscellaria* (Lepidoptera: Geometridae). Can. Entomol. 104:1511-1514.

Packard. 1905. Memoirs of the National Academy of Sciences. Vol. IX. 270 p.

Page, M.; Lyon, R.L.; Greene, L.E. 1974. Contact toxicity of eleven insecticides applied to the spring cankerworm. J. Econ. Entomol. 67:460-461.

Patch, E.M. 1909. Chermes of Maine conifers. Univ. Maine, Agric. Exp. Stn. Bull. 173.

Peirson, H.B. 1947. Yellow-headed spruce sawfly. Can. Dep. Agric. Bi-mon. Prog. Rep. 3(6):7.

Peirson, H.B.; Brower, A.E. 1936. Biology and control of the birch leaf-mining sawfly. Maine For. Serv. Bull. 11. 37 p.

Peterson, L.O.T. 1945. The yellow-headed spruce sawfly. Can. Dep. Agric. Bi-mon. Prog. Rep. 1(3):3.

Peterson, L.O.T. 1947. Some aspects of the poplar borer *Saperda calcarata* Say (Cerambycidae) in infestations under park-belt conditions. 78th rep. of the Entomol. Soc. Ont., p. 56-61.

Philip, H.G. 1978. Insect pests of Alberta. Alberta Agric. Agdex 612-1. 77 p.

Phillips, H.H. 1962. Description of the immature stages of *Pulvinaria vitis* (L.) and *P. innumerabilis* (Rathvon) (Homoptera: Coccidae), with notes on the habits of these species in Ontario, Canada. Can. Entomol. 94:497-502.

Phipps, C.R. 1928. The chain-dotted measuring worm: a blueberry pest. Maine Agric. Exp. Stn. Bull. 345. 48 p.

Phipps, C.R. 1930. Blueberry and huckleberry insects. Maine Agric. Exp. Stn. Bull. 356.

Pilon, J.G. 1965. Bionomics of the spruce budmoth, *Zeiraphera ratzeburgiana* Ratz. (Lepidoptera: Olethreutidae). Phytoprotection 46:5-13

Plumb, G.H. 1953. The formation and development of the Norway sprucegall caused by *Adelges abietis* L. Conn. Agric. Exp. Stn. Bull. 566. 77 p.

Pointing P.J.; Miller, W.E. 1973. La tordeuse européenne des pousses du pin, *Rhyacionia buoliana* (Schiff.). Pages 171-175 *in* Insectes nuisibles et maladies des arbres forestiers d'importance et d'intérêt mutuels pour le Canada, les États-Unis et le Mexique. A.G. Davidson et R.M. Prentice, compil. Environ. Can., Serv. can. forêts. Publ. 1180F.

Pollard, D.F.W. 1972. Estimating woody dry matter loss resulting from defoliation. For. Sci. 18:135-138.

Prebble, M.L. 1975. Traitements aériens pour combattre les insectes forestiers au Canada. Can., minist. Pêches Environ. 373 p.

Prentice, R.M. 1955. The life history and some aspects of the ecology of the large aspen tortrix, *Choristoneura conflictana* (Wlkr.) (N. Comb.) (Lepidoptera: Tortricidae). Can. Entomol. 87:461-473.

Prentice, R.M., coordinator. 1962. Forest lepidoptera of Canada. Vol. 2. Can. Dep. For. Bull. 128(2). 281 p.

Prentice, R.M., coordinator. 1963. Forest lepidoptera of Canada. Vol. 3. Can. Dep. For. Publ. 1013. 543 p.

Prentice, R.M., coordinator. 1965. Forest lepidoptera of Canada recorded by the Forest Insect Survey. Vol. 4. Can. Dep. For. Publ. 1142. 840 p.

Price, P.W.; Tripp, H.A. 1972. Activity pattern of parasitoids on the Swaine jack pine sawfly, *Neodiprion swainei* (Hymenoptera: Diprionidae), and parasitoid impact on the host. Can. Entomol. 104:1003-1016.

Provancher, L. 1886. Le némate d'Erichson (*Nematus ericksonii* Htg.). Nat. Can. 1885(15):45-53.

Québec, ministère de l'Industrie, du Commerce et du Tourisme. 1973. Annuaire statistique du Québec 1972-1973.

Quednau, F.W. 1966. A list of aphids from Quebec with description of two species (Homoptera: Aphididae). Can. Entomol. 98:415-430.

Quednau, F.W. 1970. Competition and cooperation between *Chrysocharis laricinellae* and *Agathis pumila* on larch case-bearer in Quebec. Can. Entomol. 102:602-612.

Raizenne, H. 1952. Forest lepidoptera of southern Ontario and their parasites received and reared at the Ottawa Forest Insect Survey laboratory from 1937 to 1948. Can. Dep. Agric., Sci. Serv. 277 p.

Raizenne, H. 1957. Forest sawflies of southern Ontario and their parasites. Can. Dep. Agric., Biol. Div. Publ. 1009. 45 p.

Raske, A.G. 1973a. Differences between two species of birch in attack and susceptibility to defoliation by the birch casebearer. Environ. Can. Bi-mon. Res. Notes 29(3):17-18.

Raske, A.G. 1973b. Relationship between felling date and larval density of *Monochamus scutellatus*. Environ. Can. Bi-mon. Res. Notes 29(4):23-24.

Raske, A.G. 1974a. Introduction of the parasites *Campoplex* spp. into Newfoundland for the biological control of the birch casebearer. Environ. Can., Can. For. Serv., Nfld. Forest Res. Cent., St. John's, Nfld. Inf. Rep. N-X-108. 22 p.

Raske, A.G. 1974b. Mortality of birch casebearer eggs. Environ. Can. Bi-mon. Res. Notes 30(1):1-2.

Raske, A.G. 1975a. Cold hardiness of first instar larvae of the forest tent caterpillar, *Malacosoma disstria* (Lepidoptera: Lasiocampidae). Can. Entomol. 107:75-80.

Raske, A.G. 1975b. Foliage consumption by late-instar birch casebearer larvae. Environ. Can. Bi-mon. Res. Notes 31(2):9.

Raske, A.G. 1975c. Mortality of overwintering birch casebearer larvae. Environ. Can. Bi-mon. Res. Notes 31(2):9-10.

Raske, A.G. 1976. Complexities in the number of larval instars of the birch casebearer in Newfoundland, Canada (Lepidoptera: Coleophoridae). Can. Entomol. 108:401-405.

Raske, A.G.; Jones, J.M. 1975. Introduction of parasitoids of the birch leaf miner into Newfoundland. Environ. Can. Bi-mon. Res. Notes 31(3):20-21.

Reeks, W.A. 1951. The birch casebearer, *Coleophora salmani* Heinr. Can. Dep. Agric. Bi-mon. Prog. Rep. 7(4):1.

Reeks, W.A. 1954a. An outbreak of the larch sawfly (*Pristiphora erichsonii*) (Htg.) in the Maritime provinces (Hymenoptera: Tenthredinidae) and the role of parasites in its control. Can. Entomol. 86:471-480.

Reeks, W.A. 1954b. Damage to red pine by a midge. Can. Dep. Agric. Bi-mon. Prog. Rep. 10(3):1.

Retnakaran, A.; Smith, L.; Tomkins, B. 1976. Application of Dimilin effectively controls forest tent caterpillar populations and affords foliage protection. Environ. Can. Bi-mon. Res. Notes 32(5): 26-27.

Robert, A. 1948. Recherches sur les insectes de l'orme. Rapp. pour l'année 1947-1948. Qué., minist. Terres Forêts, p. 131-137.

Robert, A. 1949a. Notes sur deux kermès de l'épinette: *Adelges abietis* L. et *Physokermes piceae* Schr. 15e rapp. ann., Qué. minist. Terres Forêts, p. 86-87.

Robert, A. 1949b. Recherches sur les insectes de l'orme. Rapp. pour l'année 1948-1949. Qué., minist. Terres Forêts, p. 142-145.

Robert, A. 1952a. Les insectes de l'orme aux niveaux de l'écorce et du bois et leur rôle avec la maladie hollandaise de l'orme. Thèse de doctorat, Inst. Biol., Univ. Montréal. 364 p.

Robert, A. 1952b. Recherches sur les insectes de l'orme. Rapp. pour l'année 1951-1952. Qué., minist. Terres Forêts, p. 143-147.

Rose, A.H. 1957. Notes on the biology of *Monochamus scutellatus* (Say) (Coleoptera: Cerambycidae). Can. Entomol. 89:547-553.

Rose, A.H.; Lindquist, O.H. 1973. Insects of eastern pines. Environ. Can., Can. For. Serv. Publ. 1313. 127 p.

Rose, A.H.; Lindquist, O.H. 1977. Insects of eastern spruces, fir and hemlock. Environ. Can., Can. For. Serv. For. Tech. Rep. 23. 159 p.

Ross, D.A. 1958. The maple leaf cutter, *Paraclemensia acerifoliella* Fitch (Lepidoptera: Incurvariidae). Description of stages. Can. Entomol. 90:541-555.

Ross, D.A. 1962. Bionomics of the maple leaf cutter, *Paraclemensia acerifoliella* (Fitch) (Lepidoptera: Incurvariidae). Can. Entomol. 94:1053-1063.

Ross, H.H. 1951. Superfamily Tenthredinoidea. Pages 12-82 *in* C.F. Muesebeck et al., Hymenoptera of America north of Mexico, Synoptic catalog. U.S. Dep. Agric. Agric. Monograph 2.

Ross, H.H. 1955. Taxonomy and evolution of the sawfly genus *Neodiprion*. For. Sci. 1:196-209.

Roy, R. 1948. Qué. minist. Terres Forêts, Serv. entomol. Rapp. inédit.

Royer, R. 1958. Pertes causées par la tordeuse des bourgeons de l'épinette au cours de la présente épidémie. Rapport de la 38e ass. gén. ann. Corp. ing. for. Qué.

Safranyik, L.; Raske, A.G. 1970. Sequential sampling plan for *Monochamus* larvae in decked lodgepole pine logs (Coleoptera: Cerambycidae). J. Econ. Entomol. 63:1903-1906.

Salman, K.A. 1929. Notes on the immature stages and biology of a birch casebearer. Ann. Entomol. Soc. Am. 22:480-488.

Saunders, J.L. 1971. Trunk drenches and infections for elm leaf beetle control. J. Econ. Entomol. 64:1287-1288.

Schaffner, J.V. 1959. Microlepidoptera and their parasites reared from field collections in the northeastern United States. U.S. Dep. Agric., Forest Serv. Misc. Publ. 767. 97 p.

Schaffner, J.V.; Griswold, C.L. 1934. Macrolepidoptera and their parasites reared from field collections in the northeastern part of the United States. U.S. Dep. Agric. Misc. Publ. 188.

Schedl, K. 1930. Notes on the jack pine sawflies in northern Ontario. 61st Ann. Rep. of the Entomol. Soc. Ont., p 75-79.

Schedl, K. 1935. Zwei neue Blattwespen aus Kanada (Hym. Tenthr.) Mittel. Deut. Entomol. Ges. 6:39-44.

Scheer, C.F.; Johnson, G.V. 1970. Systemic insecticides against the spirea aphid, birch leafminer and Nantucket pine tip moth. J. Econ. Entomol. 63:1205-1207.

Schierbeck, O. 1923. Treatise on the spruce budworm. F.J.D. Barnjum, Montreal.

Schmid, J.M.; Beckwith, R.C. 1975. The spruce beetle. U.S. Dep. Agric., Forest Serv. Forest Pest Leafl. 127.

Schmiege, D.C. 1966. The relation of weather to two population declines of the black-headed budworm, *Acleris variana* (Fern.) (Lepidoptera: Tortricidae), in coastal Alaska. Can. Entomol. 98:1045-1050.

Schread, J.C. 1960. Systemic insecticides for control of scales, leafminers and lacebugs. J. Econ. Entomol. 53:406-408.

Schread, J.C. 1964. Control of birch leafminer with systemics. J. Econ. Entomol. 57:761.

Séguy E. 1967. Dictionnaire des termes techniques d'entomologie élémentaire. Éditions Paul Lechevalier, Paris Ve. 465 p.

Shigo, A.L.; Leak, W.B.; Filep, S.M. 1973. Sugar maple borer injury in four hardwood stands in New Hampshire. Can. J. For. Res. 3:512-515.

Silver, G.T. 1957a. A method for sampling eggs of the black-headed budworm. J. For. 57:203-205.

Silver, G.T. 1957b. Separation of the species of arborvitae leaf miners in New Brunswick (Lepidoptera: Yponomeutidae and Gelechiidae). Can. Entomol. 89:97-107.

Silver, G.T. 1957c. Studies on the arborvitae leaf miners in New Brunswick (Lepidoptera: Yponomeutidae and Gelechiidae). Can. Entomol. 89:171-182.

Silver, G.T. 1960. The relation of weather to population trends of the black-headed budworm, *Acleris variana* (Fern.) (Lepidoptera: Tortricidae). Can. Entomol. 92:401-410.

Silver, G.T. 1963. A further note on the relation of weather to population trends of the black-headed budworm, *Acleris variana* (Fern.) (Lepidoptera: Tortricidae). Can. Entomol. 95:58-61.

Simmons, G.; Wilson, L. 1977. How to control the pine root collar weevil. Mich. Trees J. Spring, p. 10.

Simmons, G.A. 1973. The oblique-banded leafroller and *Cenopis pettitana* infesting maple buds in Michigan. Ann. Entomol. Soc. Am. 66:1166-1167.

Sippell, W.L. 1962. Outbreaks of the forest tent caterpillar, *Malacosoma disstria* Hbn., a periodic defoliator or broad-leaved trees in Ontario. Can. Entomol. 94:408-416.

Smirnoff, W.A. 1961. A virus disease of *Neodiprion swainei* Midd. (Hymenoptera: Tenthredinidae). J. Insect Pathol. 3:29-47.

Smirnoff, W.A. 1962. A nuclear polyhedrosis of *Erannis tiliaria* (Harr.) (Lepidoptera: Geometridae). J. Insect Pathol. 4:393-400.

Smirnoff, W.A. 1964. A nucleopolyhedrosis of *Operophtera bruceata* (Hulst) (Lepidoptera: Geometridae). J. Insect Pathol. 6:384-386.

Smirnoff, W.A. 1970. Fungus diseases affecting *Adelges piceae* in the fir forest of the Gaspe Peninsula, Quebec. Can. Entomol. 102:799-805.

Smirnoff, W.A. 1973. Polyédroses nucléaires (baculovirus) chez *Actebia fenica*, *Orgyia leucostigma* et *Cingilia catenaria*. Ann. Assoc. can. fr. av. sci. 3(1):135.

Smirnoff, W.A. 1974. Sensibilité de *Lambdina fiscellaria fiscellaria* (Lepidoptera: Geometridae) à l'infection de *Bacillus thuringiensis* Berliner seul ou en présence de chitinase. Can. Entomol. 106:429-433.

Smirnoff, W.A. 1976. Sensibilité de la noctuelle d'automne *(Hyphantria cunea)* à l'infection par la polyédrose nucléaire de *thymelicuslioneola* (Lepidoptera: Hesperiidae). Can. Entomol. 108:327-330.

Smirnoff, W.A.; Béique, R. 1959. On a polyhedral disease of *Trichiocampus viminalis* (Fall.) larvae (Hymenoptera: Tenthredinidae). Can. Entomol. 91:379-381.

Smirnoff, W.A.; Jobin, L.J. 1973. Étude de certains facteurs affectant les populations de *Lambdina fiscellaria fiscellaria* dans le bassin de la rivière Vauréal, île d'Anticosti. Can. Entomol. 105:1039-1040.

Smirnoff, W.A.; Juneau, A. 1973. Quinze années de recherches sur les micro-organismes des insectes forestiers de la province de Québec (1957-1972). Ann. Soc. Entomol. Qué. 18(3):147-181.

Smith, C.C. 1974a. A leaf roller of maple. Environ. Can., Can. For. Serv., Maritimes Forest Res. Cent., Fredericton, N.B. Inf. Leafl.

Smith, C.C. 1974b. Fall cankerworm. Environ. Can., Can. For. Serv., Maritimes Forest Res. Cent., Fredericton, N.B. Inf. Leafl.

Smith, C.C. 1974c. Galls of hardwoods. Environ. Can., Can. For. Serv., Maritimes Forest Res. Cent., Fredericton, N.B. Inf. Leafl.

Smith, C.C. 1974d. White marked tussock moth. Environ. Can., Can. For. Serv., Maritimes Forest Res. Cent., Fredericton, N.B. Inf. Leafl.

Smith, C.C. 1979. Bruce spanworm. Environ. Can., Can. For. Serv. Maritimes Forest Res. Cent., Fredericton, N.B. Inf. Leafl.

Smith, D.R. 1964. A review of the subfamily Heterarthrinae in North America (Hymenoptera: Tenthredinidae). Proc. Entomol. Soc. Wash. 69:277-284.

Stein, J.D. 1974. Spring cankerworm, *Paleacrita vernata* (Lepidoptera: Geometridae), feeding on flax as a secondary host. Can. Entomol. 106:783-784.

Stein, J.D.; Kennedy, P.C. 1972. Key to shelterbelt insects in the northern great plains. U.S. Dep. Agric., Forest Serv. Res. Pap. RM-85. 153 p.

Strubble, D.B.: Osgood, E.A. 1976. Predation on larvae of the balsam gall midge, *Dasineura balsamicola* (Diptera: Cecidomyiidae), within galls in Maine. Can. Entomol. 108:1443-1444.

Strubble, G.R. 1957. Biology and control of the white fir sawfly. For. Sci. 3:306-313.

Sullivan, C.R. 1960. The effect of physical factors on the activity and development of adults and larvae of the white pine weevil, *Pissodes strobi* (Peck). Can. Entomol. 92:732-745.

Sullivan, C.R. 1961. The effect of weather and physical attributes of white pine leaders on the behaviour and survival of the white pine weevil, *Pissodes strobi* (Peck), in mixed stands. Can. Entomol. 93:721-741.

Swaine, J.M. 1924. Le grand rongeur de l'épinette et les moyens de le combattre dans l'est du Canada. Can., minist. Agric. Feuil. inf. 48.

Swaine, J.M.; Craighead, F.C. 1924. Studies on the spruce budworm (*Cacoecia fumiferana* Clem.). Can. Dep. Agric. Tech. Bull. 37. New series. 91 p.

Syme, P.D. 1971. *Rhyacionia buoliana* (Schiff.), European pine shoot moth (Lepidoptera: Olethreutidae). Pages 194-205 *in* Biological control programmes against insects and weeds in Canada 1959-1968. Commonw. Inst. Biol. Control, Trinidad, Commonw. Agric. Bureaux, Farnham Royal, Engl. Tech. Commun. 4.

Talerico, R.L. 1962. A study of damage caused by the sugar maple borer. J. For. 60:178-180.

Taylor, R.L. 1929. The biology of the white pine weevil, *Pissodes strobi* (Peck), and a study of its insect parasites from an economic viewpoint. Entomol. Am. 9:166-246.

Ticehurst N.; Allen, D.C. 1973. Notes on the biology of *Telenomus coelodasidis* (Hymenoptera: Scelionidae) and its relationship to the saddled prominent, *Heterocampa guttivitta* (Lepidoptera: Notodontidae). Can. Entomol. 105:1133-1143.

Torgensen, T.R.; Beckwith, R.C. 1974. Parasitoids associated with the large aspen tortrix, *Choristoneura conflictana* (Lepidoptera: Tortricidae), in interior Alaska. Can. Entomol. 106:1247-1265.

Tostowaryk, W. 1972. Coleopterous predators of the Swaine jack pine sawfly, *Neodiprion swainei* Middleton (Hymenoptera: Diprionidae). Can. J. Zool. 50:1139-1146.

Tripp, H.A. 1962. The relationship of *Spathimeigenia spinigera* (Townsend) (Diptera: Tachinidae) to its host, *Neodiprion swainei* Midd. (Hymenoptera: Diprionidae). Can. Entomol. 94:809-818.

Tripp, H.A. 1965. The development of *Neodiprion swainei* Middleton (Hymenoptera: Diprionidae) in the province of Quebec. Can. Entomol. 97:92-107.

Turner, K.B.; Kirby, C.S.; Dance, B.W. 1975. Common pests of ornamental trees and shrubs. Ont. Minist. Nat. Res., Pest Control Sect. Publ. PC. 3. 64 p.

Turnock, W.J. 1953. Some aspects of the life history and ecology of the pitch nodule maker, *Petrova albicapitana* (Busck.) (Lepidoptera: Olethreutidae). Can. Entomol. 85:233-243.

Turnock, W.J.; Muldrew, J.A. 1971. *Pristiphora erichsonii* (Hartig), larch sawfly (Hymenoptera: Tenthredinidae). Pages 175-194 *in* Biological control programmes against insects and weeds in Canada 1959-1968. Commonw. Inst. Biol. Control. Trinidad, Commonw. Agric. Bureaux, Farnham Royal, Engl. Tech. Commun. 4.

Twinn, C.R. 1934. Can. Dep. Agric. Can. Insect Pest Rev. 13(1). 20 p.

U.S. Department of Agriculture. 1960. The elm leaf beetle. Leafl. 184.

Van Sickle, G.A.; Sterner, T.E. 1976. Sanitation: a practical protection against Dutch elm disease in Fredericton, New-Brunswick. Plant. Dis. Rep. 60:336-338.

Volney, J. 1975. The role of defoliators in the arthropod community of red maple crowns. J. N.Y. Entomol. Soc. 83:283.

Walley, G.S. 1953. Hymenopterous parasites of *Choristoneura pinus* Free. (Lepidoptera: Tortricidae) in Canada. Can. Entomol. 85:152.

Wallner, W.E. 1971. Suppression of four hardwood defoliators by helicopter application of concentrate and dilute chemical and biological sprays. J. Econ. Entomol. 64:1487-1490.

Warren, G.L. 1953. A study of *Hypomolyx piceus* (DeG.) (Coleoptera: Curculionidae) and its relationship to white spruce, *Picea glauca* (Moench) Voss. Master's thesis, McGill Univ., Montreal.

Warren, G.L. 1956a. The effects of some site factors on the abundance of *Hypomolyx piceus* (Coleoptera: Curculionidae). Ecology 37:132-139.

Warren, G.L. 1956b. Root injury to conifers in Canada by species of *Hylobius* and *Hypomolyx* (Coleoptera: Curculionidae). For. Chron. 32:7-10.

Warren, G.L.; Whitney, R.D. 1951. Spruce root borer (*Hypomolyx* sp.), root wounds, and root diseases of white spruce. Can. Dep. Agric. Bi-mon. Prog. Rep. 7(4):2-3.

Watson, E.B. 1934. An account of the eastern hemlock looper, *Ellopia fiscellaria* Gn., on balsam fir. Sci. Agric. 14:669-678.

Watson, W.Y. 1959. The larva of *Profenusa alumna* (MacG.) (Hymenoptera: Tenthredinidae). Can. Entomol. 91:618-625.

Webb, F.E. 1952. The larch casebearer in the Maritime provinces and Great Lakes Region. Can. Dep. Agric. Bi-mon. Prog. Rep. 8(1):1.

Webb, F.E. 1957. Sampling techniques for the overwintering stage of the larch casebearer. Can. Dep. Agric. Bi-mon. Prog. Rep. 13(4):1-2.

Webb, F.E.; Denton, R.E. 1973. Le porte-case du mélèze, *Coleophora laricella* (Hbn.). Pages 89-92 *in* Insectes nuisibles et maladies des arbres forestiers d'importance et d'intérêt mutuels pour le Canada, les États-Unis et le Mexique. A.G. Davidson et R.M. Prencice, compil. Environ. Can., Serv. can. forêts. Publ. 1180F.

Webb, F.E.; Drooz, A.T. 1973. La tenthrède du mélèze, *Pristiphora erichsonii* (Htg.). Pages 166-170 *in* Insectes nuisibles et maladies des arbres forestiers d'importance et d'intérêt mutuels pour le Canada, les États-Unis et le Mexique. A.G. Davidson et R.M. Prentice, compil. Environ. Can., Serv. can. forêts. Publ. 1180F.

Webb, F.E.; Quednau, F.W. 1971. *Coldophora laricella* (Hübner), larch casebearer (Lepidoptera: Coleophoridae). Pages 131-136 *in* Biological control programmes against insects and weeds in Canada, 1959-1968. Commonw. Inst. Biol. Control, Trinidad, Commonw. Agric. Bureaux, Farnham Royal, Engl. Tech. Commun. 4.

Webster, F.M. 1892. Insects affecting the blackberry and raspberry. Ohio Agric. Exp. Stn. Bull. 45, p. 179-180.

Wene, G.P. 1968. Biology of the elm leaf beetle in southern Arizona. J. Econ. Entomol. 61:1178-1180.

Wene, G.P. 1970. Evaluation of systemic drenches and trunk infections as controls for the elm leaf beetle in Arizona. J. Econ. Entomol. 63:1326-1328.

Werner, F.G. 1982. Common names of insects and related organisms. Committee on Common Names of Insects, Entomol Soc. Am. 132 p.

Wetzell, B.W.; Kulman, H.M.; Witter, J.A. 1973. Effects of cold temperatures on hatching of the forest tent caterpillar, *Malacosoma disstria* (Lepidoptera: Lasiocampidae). Can. Entomol. 1973:1145-1149.

Wheeler, A.G.; Colburn, R.B.; Lehman, R.D. 1973. *Stethorus punctillume* associated with spruce spider mite on ornamentals. Environ. Entomol. 2:718-720.

Whitten, L.R. 1958. The Dutch elm disease and its control. U.S. Dep. Agric. Inf. Bull. 193. 15 p.

Whitten, L.R.: Reeks, W.A. 1973. La tenthrède du pin d'Écosse, *Neodiprion sertifer* (Geoff.). Pages 142-145 *in* Insectes nuisibles et maladies des arbres forestiers d'importance et d'intérêt mutuels pour le Canada, les États-Unis et le Mexique. A.G. Davidson et R.M. Prentice compil. Environ. Can., Serv. can. forêts. Publ. 1180F.

Wilford, B.H. 1937. The spruce gall aphid *(Adelges abietis)* (L.) in southern Michigan. Univ. Mich. Sch. For. Conserv. Circ. 2. 34 p.

Wilkinson, C.; Scoble, M.J. 1979. The nepticulidae (Lepidoptera of Canada). Mem. Entomol. Soc. Can. 107, p. 129.

Wilkinson, R.C.; Becker, G.C.; Benjamin, D.M. 1966. The biology of *Neodiprion rugifrons* (Hymenoptera: Diprionidae), a sawfly infesting jack pine in Wisconsin. Ann Entomol. Soc. Am. 59:768-792.

Wilson, L.F. 1962a. Yellow-headed spruce sawfly 1962. U.S. Dep. Agric., Forest Serv. Pest Leafl. 69.

Wilson, L.F. 1962b. White-spotted sawyer. U.S. Dep. Agric., Forest Serv. Pest Leafl. 74.

Wilson, L.F. 1971. The green striped mapleworm. U.S. Dep. Agric. Forest Serv. Forest. Pest Leafl. 77.

Wilson, L.F. 1977. A guide to insect injury of conifers in the Lake States. U.S. Dep. Agric., Forest Serv. Agric. Handbook 501. 218 p.

Wilson, L.F.; Reeks, W.A. 1973. La tenthrède de LeConte, *Neodiprion lecontei* (Fitch). Pages 139-141 *in* Insectes nuisibles et maladies des arbres forestiers d'importance et d'intérêt mutuels pour le Canada, les États-Unis et le Mexique. A.G. Davidson et R.M. Prentice, compil. Environ. Can., Serv. can. forêts, Publ. 1180F.

Winn, A.F. 1912. Liste préliminaire des insectes de la province de Québec. Tome I. Les lépidoptères. Suppl. Rapp. ann., Soc. prot. plantes Qué.

Witter, J.A.; Kulman, H.M. 1972. Mortality factors affecting eggs of the forest tent caterpillar, *Malacosoma disstria* (Lepidoptera: Lasiocampidae). Can. Entomol. 104:705-710.

Witter, J.A., Kulman, H.M.; Hodson, A.C. 1972. Lifetables for the forest tent caterpillar, *Malacosoma disstria* (Lepidoptera: Lasiocampidae). Can. Entomol. 104:705-710.

Wong, H.R. 1951. Cocoons of some sawflies that defoliate forest trees in Manitoba and Saskatchewan. 82nd Ann. Rep. of the Entomol. Soc. Ont., p. 61-67.

Wong, H.R. 1955. Larvae of the nearctic species of *Anoplonyx* (Tenthredinidae: Hymenoptera). Can. Entomol. 87:224-227.

Wong, H.R.; McLeod, B.B. 1965. Two species of gall producing *Saperda* in Manitoba and Saskatchewan. Can. Dep. For. Bi-mon. Prog. Rep. 21(5):3.

Wong, H.R.; McLeod, B.B.; Drouin, J.A. 1963. *Saperda calcarata* Say in the root collar of poplars. Can. Dep. For. Bi-mon. Prog. Rep. 19(5):2.

Wong, H.R.; Melvin, J.C.E. 1976. Biological observations and larval descriptions of *Enargia decolor* (Lepidoptera: Noctuidae) on trembling aspen in northern Alberta. Can. Entomol. 108:1213-1220.

Wood, S.L. 1957. The North American allies of *Hylobius piceus* (DeG.) (Coleoptera: Curculionidae). Can. Entomol. 89'37-43.

Wood, S.L. 1969. New synonymy and records of Platypotidae and Scolytidae. Great Basin Nat. 29:113-128.

Zon, R. 1903. Balsam fir. U.S. Dep. Agric. Tech. Bull. 55.

CREDITS FOR PHOTOGRAPHY

This text is illustrated with more than 800 color photographs, most of which were provided by the Laurentian Forest Research Centre. The names of those providing photographs are in the following list with the plate number and letters to identify the photographs.

Arcand, T.:
1 A to G; 2 B to K; 3 A to H; 4 A to C, E to I; 5 A to C, E to K; 6 A to F, H, I; 7 B to F; 8 B, E, F; 9 B to F; 10 A, B, E to G, I; 11 B to G; 12 B to D, F, G; 13 A to G; 14 E, F; 15 C to H; 16 A to G; 17 B, C, E to H; 18 A to D; 19 C to J; 20 C to I; 21 D to G; 22 D to L; 23 D to K; 24 B to J, L; 25 E to J; 26 B to F; 27 A to E; 28 B to E; 29 A to C, F; 30 B to F, H, I; 31 B to H; 32 B to J; 33 A to E; 34 B; 35 C to H; 36 C to G; 37 B to F; 38 A to E; 39 A to H; 40 F, H; 41 A to E, G, H; 42 A to F; 43 B to E, G to J; 44 A to I; 45 C to J; 46 D to K; 47 B to F, H to J; 48 B, D to H; 49 A to F; 50 C to H; 51 A to E; 52 A to D, F; 53 A to E; 54 B to E, G, H; 55 B to E; 56 B, D, E; 57 A to I; 58 A to D, F to H; 59 B to E, G to K; 60 B, D to K; 61 A to J; 62 A to J, L; 63 A to E; 64 A to I, K; 65 A to I; 66 B, D to H; 67 A to D, F; 68 C to F; 69 B to J; 70 B to H; 71 B to H; 72 B, D to H; 73 C to I; 74 A to I; 75 C to H; 76 B, E, F; 77 A, B, C to G; 78 A to D, E; 79 A to I; 80 A to J; 81 A; 82 A to F; 83 A to I; 84 A to E; 85 A to G; 86 B to F; 87 A to H; 88 B, C, E to K; 89 A to F; 90 A to D; 91 C to J; 92 A, D to H; 93 B to F, I, J; 94 A to C, E to G; 95 B to L; 96 B to J; 97 B to H; 98 B to H, I to J; 99 B to M; 100 B to F; 101 A to C, E to J; 102 A to E, G, H; 103 B to K; 104 B to H.

Béique, R.:
104 A.

Benoit, P.:
7 G; 10 C; 54 A; 55 A; 76 A, C.

Bérubé, J.-P.:
28 A; 35 A, B; 36 H; 38 G; 45 A, B; 85 H; 96 A.

Blais, R.:
5 D; 11 A; 15 B; 19 A; 24 K; 30 A; 40 A; 43 A; 62 K; 66 A; 72 A; 73 A; 97 A; 98 A.

Bolduc, M.:
15 A; 24 A; 30 G; 61 K; 86 A.

Boutin, J.C.:
46 B; 84 G; 92 B.

Cochaux, P.:
25 A to D; 60 A, C; 66 C; 99 A.

Connecticut Agricultural
Experiment Station (USA):
6 G; 45 F.

Côté, L.:
88 A; 91 A.

Deboo, R.:
21 H, I.*

Dimond, J.:
22 A, C.**

Gagnon, R.:
16 H; 40 H; 48 C, I.

Jobin, L.:
12 A, E; 37 A, G to I.

Laplante, J.-P.:
10 D; 14 A to D, G, H; 17 D, I; 22 B; 47 G; 50 B; 58 E; 64 J; 67 E; 68 G, H; 72 C; 75 B; 76 D; 93 G, H; 94 D; 95 M; 101 D.

Martineau, R.:
1 H, I; 8 A, C, D; 16 J; 18 E, F; 38 F, G; 40 B, E; 69 A.

Monnier, C.:
4 D; 7 A; 9 A; 16 I; 21 A, C; 23 A to C; 26 A; 29 D, E; 31 A; 32 A; 36 A, B, I; 40 C, D, G; 41 F; 43 F; 46 A; 47 A; 48 A; 52 E; 54 F; 63 F, G; 67 G; 68 A, B; 71 A; 73 B; 75 A; 81 B to D; 84 F; 91 B; 93 A; 95 A; 102 F.

Paquet, R.:
21 B; 56 A, C; 59 A, F; 103 A.

Roy, R.:
20 B; 81 E; 92 C.

St-Hilaire, A.:
2 A.

Therrien, P.:
10 H; 17 A; 19 B; 20 A; 34 A, C, D; 46 C; 50 A; 70 A; 87 I; 88 D; 100 A.

*Great Lakes Forest Research Centre.
**Maine Forest Service, USA.

TREES

254

INSECTS AND NATURAL CONTROL AGENTS

258